Communications
in Computer and Information Science   122

Tai-hoon Kim   Wai-chi Fang
Muhammad Khurram Khan   Kirk P. Arnett
Heau-jo Kang   Dominik Ślęzak (Eds.)

Security Technology, Disaster Recovery and Business Continuity

International Conferences, SecTech and DRBC 2010
Held as Part of the Future Generation
Information Technology Conference, FGIT 2010
Jeju Island, Korea, December 13-15, 2010
Proceedings

 Springer

Volume Editors

Tai-hoon Kim
Hannam University, Daejeon, South Korea
E-mail: taihoonn@hnu.kr

Wai-chi Fang
National Chiao Tung University, Hsinchu, Taiwan
E-mail: wfang@mail.nctu.edu.tw

Muhammad Khurram Khan
King Saud University, Riyadh, Saudi Arabia
E-mail: mkhurram@ksu.edu.sa

Kirk P. Arnett
Mississippi State University, Mississippi State, MS, USA
E-mail: kpa1@msstate.edu

Heau-jo Kang
Mokwon University, Daejeon, South Korea
E-mail: hjkang@mokwon.ac.kr

Dominik Ślęzak
University of Warsaw & Infobright, Poland
E-mail: dominik.slezak@infobright.com

Library of Congress Control Number: 2010940174

CR Subject Classification (1998): C.2, K.6.5, D.4.6, E.3, H.4, J.1

ISSN	1865-0929
ISBN-10	3-642-17609-7 Springer Berlin Heidelberg New York
ISBN-13	978-3-642-17609-8 Springer Berlin Heidelberg New York

springer.com

© Springer-Verlag Berlin Heidelberg 2010
Printed in Germany

Typesetting: Camera-ready by author, data conversion by Scientific Publishing Services, Chennai, India
Printed on acid-free paper   06/3180

Preface

Welcome to the proceedings of the 2010 International Conferences on Security Technology (SecTech 2010), and Disaster Recovery and Business Continuity (DRBC 2010) – two of the partnering events of the Second International Mega-Conference on Future Generation Information Technology (FGIT 2010).

SecTech and DRBC bring together researchers from academia and industry as well as practitioners to share ideas, problems and solutions relating to the multifaceted aspects of security and disaster recovery methodologies, including their links to computational sciences, mathematics and information technology.

In total, 1,630 papers were submitted to FGIT 2010 from 30 countries, which includes 250 papers submitted to SecTech/DRBC 2010. The submitted papers went through a rigorous reviewing process: 395 of the 1,630 papers were accepted for FGIT 2010, while 57 papers were accepted for SecTech/DRBC 2010. Of the 250 papers 10 were selected for the special FGIT 2010 volume published by Springer in the LNCS series. 34 papers are published in this volume, and 13 papers were withdrawn due to technical reasons.

We would like to acknowledge the great effort of the SecTech/DRBC 2010 International Advisory Boards and members of the International Program Committees, as well as all the organizations and individuals who supported the idea of publishing this volume of proceedings, including SERSC and Springer. Also, the success of these two conferences would not have been possible without the huge support from our sponsors and the work of the Chairs and Organizing Committee.

We are grateful to the following keynote speakers who kindly accepted our invitation: Hojjat Adeli (Ohio State University), Ruay-Shiung Chang (National Dong Hwa University), and Andrzej Skowron (University of Warsaw). We would also like to thank all plenary and tutorial speakers for their valuable contributions.

We would like to express our greatest gratitude to the authors and reviewers of all paper submissions, as well as to all attendees, for their input and participation.

Last but not least, we give special thanks to Rosslin John Robles and Maricel Balitanas. These graduate school students of Hannam University contributed to the editing process of this volume with great passion.

December 2010

Tai-hoon Kim
Wai-chi Fang
Muhammad Khurram Khan
Kirk P. Arnett
Heau-jo Kang
Dominik Ślęzak

SecTech 2010 Organization

Organizing Committee

General Chair   Wai-chi Fang (National Chiao Tung University, Taiwan)

Program Co-chairs   Muhammad Khurram Khan (King Saud University,
Saudi Arabia)
Tai-hoon Kim (Hannam University, Korea)
Kirk P. Arnett (Mississippi State University, USA)

Publicity Co-chairs   Antonio Coronato (ICAR-CNR, Italy)
Damien Sauveron (Université de Limoges, France)
Hua Liu (Xerox Corporation, USA)
Kevin R.B. Butler (Pennsylvania State University, USA)
Guojun Wang (Central South University, China)
Tao Jiang (Huazhong University of Science and Technology,
China)
Gang Wu (UESTC, China)
Yoshiaki Hori (Kyushu University, Japan)

Publication Chair   Yong-ik Yoon (Sookmyung Women's University, Korea)

International Advisory Board
Edwin H-M. Sha (University of Texas at Dallas, USA)
Justin Zhan (CMU, USA)
Kouichi Sakurai (Kyushu University, Japan)
Laurence T. Yang (St. Francis Xavier University, Canada)
Byeong-Ho Kang (University of Tasmania, Australia)
Aboul Ella Hassanien (Cairo University, Egypt)

Program Committee

A. Hamou-Lhadj
Ahmet Koltuksuz
Albert Levi
A.L. Sandoval-Orozco
ByungRae Cha
Ch. Chantrapornchai
Costas Lambrinoudakis
Dieter Gollmann
E. Konstantinou
Eduardo B. Fernandez
Fangguo Zhang
Filip Orsag
Gerald Schaefer
Han-Chieh Chao
Hiroaki Kikuchi
Hironori Washizaki
Hongji Yang
Hsiang-Cheh Huang
Hyun-Sung Kim
J.H. Abbawajy
Jan deMeer

Javier Garcia Villalba
Jongmoon Baik
Jordi Forne
Jungsook Kim
Larbi Esmahi
Lejla Batina
Luigi Buglione
MalRey Lee
Mario Marques Freire
Martin Drahansky
Masahiro Mambo
N. Jaisankar
Nobukazu Yoshioka
Paolo D'Arco
Paolo Falcarin
Petr Hanacek
Pierre-François Bonnefoi
Qi Shi
Raphael C.-W. Phan
Reinhard Schwarz
Rhee Kyung-Hyune

Robert Seacord
Rodrigo Mello
Rolf Oppliger
Rui Zhang
S.K. Barai
Serge Chaumette
Sheng-Wei Chen
Silvia Abrahao
Stan Kurkovsky
Stefanos Gritzalis
Swee-Huay Heng
Tony Shan
Wen-Shenq Juang
Willy Susilo
Yannis Stamatiou
Yi Mu
Yijun Yu
Yingjiu Li
Yong Man Ro
Yoshiaki Hori
Young Ik Eom

DRBC 2010 Organization

Organizing Committee

General Chair   Heau-jo Kang (Mokwon University, Korea)

Program Co-chairs
> Tai-hoon Kim (Hannam University, Korea)
> Byeong-Ho Kang (University of Tasmania, Australia)

Publicity Co-chairs
> Martin Drahansky (Brno University of Technology, Czech Republic)
> Aboul Ella Hassanien (Cairo University, Egypt)

Publication Co-chair
> Rosslin John Robles (Hannam University, Korea)
> Maricel Balitanas (Hannam University, Korea)

International Advisory Board
> Wai-chi Fang (National Chiao Tung University, Taiwan)
> Young-whan Jeong (Korea Business Continuity Planning Society, Korea)
> Adrian Stoica (NASA Jet Propulsion Laboratory, USA)
> Samir Kumar Bandyopadhyay (University of Calcutta, India)

Program Committee

Fabrizio Baiardi	Simin Nadjm-Tehrani	Snjezana Knezic
Erol Gelenbe	Sokratis Katsikas	Emiliano Casalicchio
Rüdiger Klein	Teodora Ivanusa	Stefan Brem
Simin Nadjm-Tehrani	Sandro Bologna	Stefan Wrobel

Table of Contents

Impact of Finger Type in Fingerprint Authentication

Davrondzhon Gafurov, Patrick Bours, Bian Yang, and Christoph Busch

Norwegian Information Security Lab
Gjøvik University College
P.O. Box 191, 2802 Gjøvik, Norway
{Firstname.Lastname}@hig.no

Abstract. Nowadays fingerprint verification system is the most widespread and accepted biometric technology that explores various features of the human fingers for this purpose. In general, every normal person has 10 fingers with different size. Although it is claimed that recognition performance with little fingers can be less accurate compared to other finger types, to our best knowledge, this has not been investigated yet. This paper presents our study on the topic of influence of the finger type into fingerprint recognition performance. For analysis we employ two fingerprint verification software packages (one public and one commercial). We conduct test on GUC100 multi sensor fingerprint database which contains fingerprint images of all 10 fingers from 100 subjects. Our analysis indeed confirms that performance with small fingers is less accurate than performance with the others fingers of the hand. It also appears that best performance is being obtained with thumb or index fingers. For example, performance deterioration from the best finger (i.e. index or thumb) to the worst fingers (i.e. small ones) can be in the range of 184%-1352%.

Keywords: biometric authentication, fingerprint recognition, finger type, performance evaluation, GUC100 data set.

1 Introduction

Nowadays fingerprint verification system is the most widespread and accepted biometric technology. Furthermore, its market share is expected to grow even further [1]. Fingerprint recognition technology explores various features of the human fingers for this purpose. Many fingerprint verification algorithms are based on a ridge feature called minutiae which is ridge termination and ridge bifurcation [2]. In general, a number of minutiae points in a finger can be correlated with a size of the finger. Every normal person has 5 fingers with different size on each of his two hands. Although using all ten fingers (at the same time) for verification can improve performance and robustness, most of the current systems do not employ all ten fingers because of usability aspects, if only a single-finger scanner is available, or the distracting higher cost of multi-finger scanners. Indeed, the process of presenting all ten fingers separately for authentication can be inconvenient. Thus, one needs to decide which fingers to use or not to use. It is claimed that recognition performance with little fingers can be less accurate compared to other finger types. However, to our best knowledge, this fact has not been confirmed by research yet.

T.-h. Kim et al. (Eds.): SecTech/DRBC 2010, CCIS 122, pp. 1–7, 2010.

This paper presents our investigation on the topic of influence of the finger type into fingerprint recognition performance. We evaluate performance using ten fingers separately and then compare individual performances. For analysis we used two publicly available fingerprint verification software packages (one is free and the other is for purchase). We conducted test on GUC100 multi sensor fingerprint database which contains fingerprint images of all 10 fingers from 100 subjects. The rest of the paper is structured as follow. Section 2 provides an overview of the fingerprint database and verification software packages. Section 3 presents performance evaluation with respect to finger types, and section 4 concludes the paper.

2   Data Set

In order to investigate the impact of the finger type into fingerprint verification system we have chosen two different verification algorithms which are publicly available. The free publicly available fingerprint verification program is NIST's mindtct and bozorth3 [3]. The second one is Neurotechnology's VeriFinger which is commercially available at [4].

As a test database we used GUC100 fingerprint data set which consists of over 70000 fingerprint images from 100 subjects. For our study main advantages of this database are following:

- It has equal number of images from all 1000 fingers (except very few) which minimizes a bias. The number of images per finger per scanner is 12;
- Each fingerprint image of the finger was collected on separate days (usually one week in between) during several months which accounts for natural variability of the fingers condition;
- The used database was composed using five different fingerprint sensors, namely L-1 DFR2100, Cross Match LSCAN100, Precise 250MC, Lumidigm V100 and Sagem MorphoSmart.

More information on GUC100 fingerprint database and its availability to other researchers for testing can be found at [5].

3   Results and Discussion

Since the aim of this study is not on comparing performance between different scanner technologies but rather on comparing performance between different finger types, in figures and tables scanner names are anonymized (i.e. are not given). Performance metric curves are reported in terms of false match rate (FMR on x-axis) versus false non-match rate (FNMR on y-axis) plots. Figures 1 and 2 present performance evaluations for all ten fingers on five scanners using Neurotechnology and NIST software packages, respectively. The EERs of the curves (in percentage %) are also shown in the legends of the plots. The finger ID in the figures are numbered according to ISO standard [6] and are following:

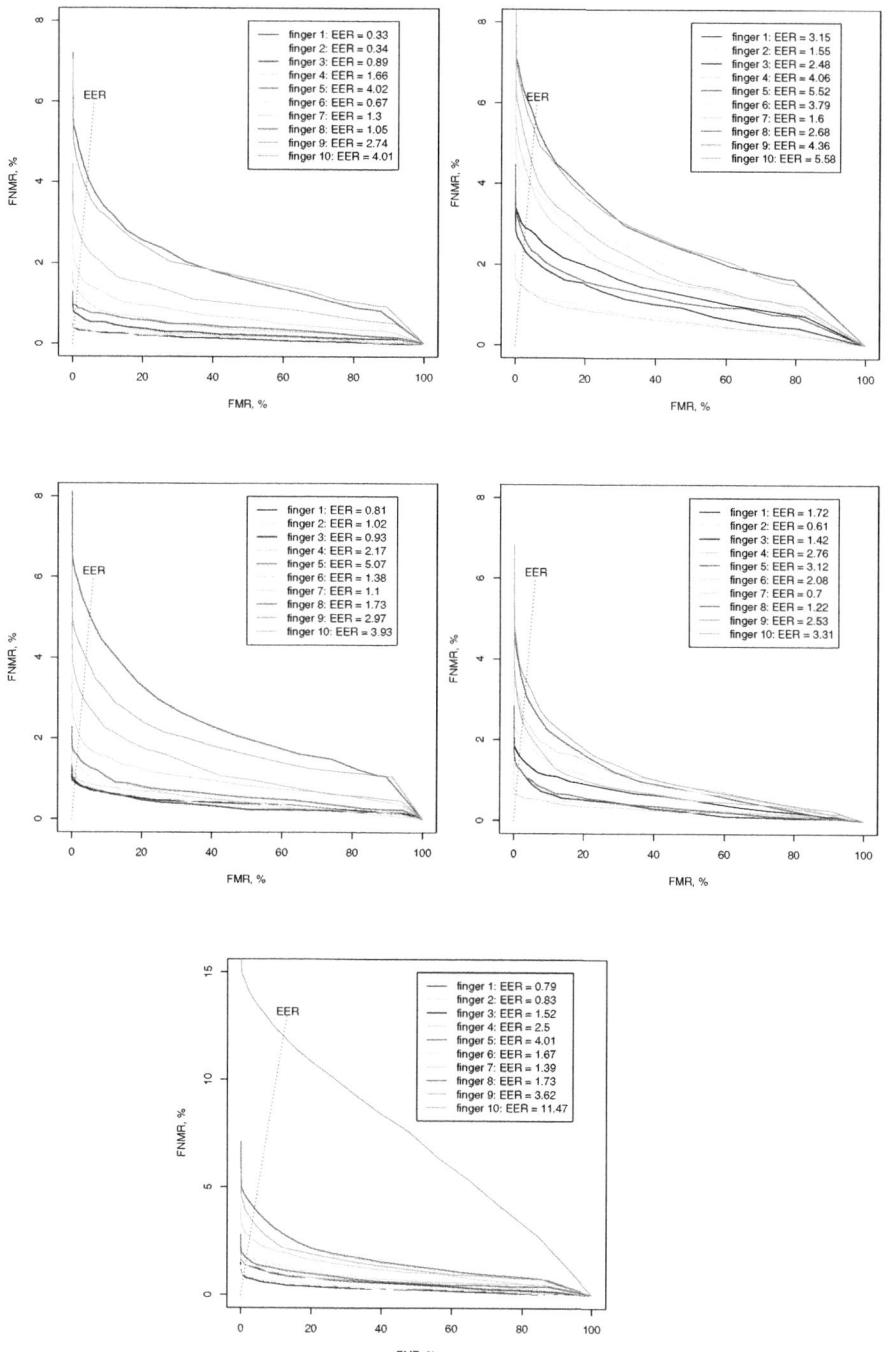

Fig. 1. Performance using Neurotechnology's software for each scanner

4   D. Gafurov et al.

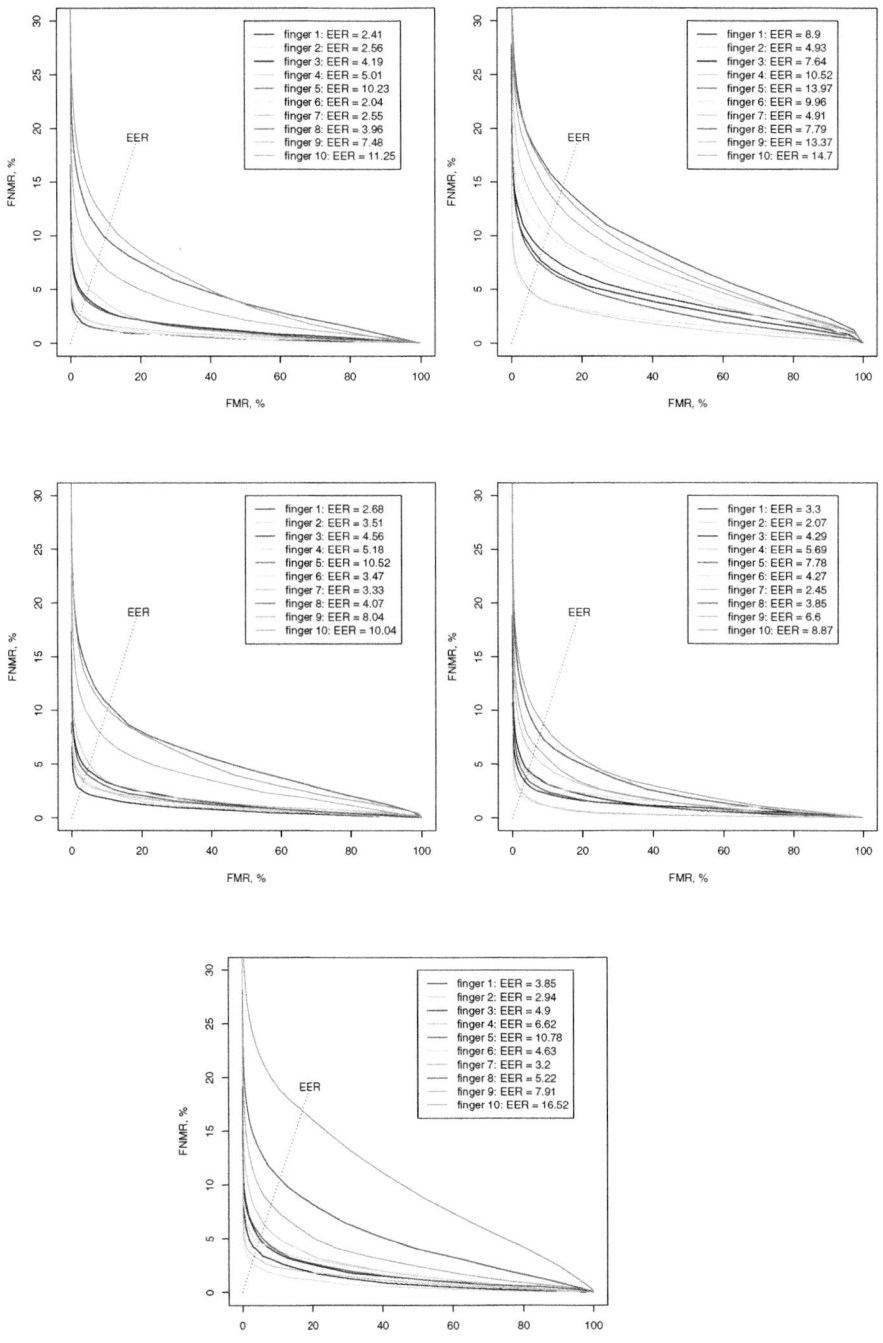

Fig. 2. Performance using NIST's software for each scanner

- Finger 1 - right thumb
- Finger 2 - right index
- Finger 3 - right middle
- Finger 4 - right ring
- Finger 5 - right small
- Finger 6 - left thumb
- Finger 7 - left index
- Finger 8 - left middle
- Finger 9 - left ring
- Finger 10 - left small

From all figures it can be observed that two small fingers (5 and 10) have the highest EER values. Likewise, in all of these plots it appears that best performance (i.e. smallest EER) is with either thumb finger (1 or 6) or index finger (2 or 7) mostly of the right hand. We define performance deterioration (in terms of EER) between fingers F_i and F_j $((i, j) = \{1, ..., 10\})$ according to formula below:

$$\Delta_{ij} = \frac{(EER_{F_i} - EER_{F_j})}{EER_{F_j}} \cdot 100\%$$

where EER_{F_i} and EER_{F_j} are EERs of fingers F_i and F_j, respectively. Tables 1 and 2 show such decrease of the performances of small fingers (i.e. F_5 and F_{10}) with respect to other fingers with Neurotechnology and NIST, respectively. As can be seen from Tables 1 and 2 deterioration performances of small fingers with respect to the best finger performance can be in the range of 260%-1351.9% with Neurotechnology (minimum and maximum of bolded numbers in Table 1), and 184.5%-461.9% with NIST (minimum and maximum of bolded numbers in Table 2).

Table 1. Relation of the small fingers to other fingers (Neurotechnology). Numbers are given in %. Bold is with respect to the best finger.

Finger type	Scanner 1		Scanner 2		Scanner 3		Scanner 4		Scanner 5	
	F_5	F_{10}	F_5	F_{10}	F_5	F_{10}	F_5	F_{10}	F_5	F_{10}
Finger 1	**1118.2**	**1115.2**	75.2	77.1	525.9	**385.2**	81.4	92.4	**407.6**	**1351.9**
Finger 2	1082.4	1079.4	**256.1**	**260**	397.1	285.3	**411.5**	**442.6**	383.1	1281.9
Finger 3	351.7	350.6	122.6	125	445.2	322.6	119.7	133.1	163.8	654.6
Finger 4	142.2	141.6	36	37.4	133.6	81.1	13	19.9	60.4	358.8
Finger 6	500	498.5	45.6	47.2	267.4	184.8	50	59.1	140.1	586.8
Finger 7	209.2	208.5	245	248.8	360.9	257.3	345.7	372.9	188.5	725.2
Finger 8	282.9	281.9	106	108.2	193.1	127.2	155.7	171.3	131.8	563
Finger 9	46.7	46.4	26.6	28	70.7	32.3	23.3	30.8	10.8	216.9

It is worth mentioning that the influence of finger type into performance was noted previously as well [7]. The significant difference of our work is that we focus on all 10 fingers while in [7] 8 fingers (small fingers are omitted) were considered. Furthermore, we carried out our analysis using fingerprint images from various scanner technologies.

Table 2. Relation of the small fingers to other fingers (NIST). Numbers are given in %. Bold is with respect to the best finger.

Finger type	Scanner 1		Scanner 2		Scanner 3		Scanner 4		Scanner 5	
	F_5	F_{10}	F_5	F_{10}	F_5	F_{10}	F_5	F_{10}	F_5	F_{10}
Finger 1	**324.5**	**366.8**	57	65.2	**292.5**	**274.6**	135.8	168.8	180	329.1
Finger 2	299.6	339.5	183.4	198.2	199.7	186	**275.8**	**328.5**	266.7	**461.9**
Finger 3	144.2	168.5	82.9	92.4	130.7	120.2	81.4	106.8	120	237.1
Finger 4	104.2	124.6	32.8	39.7	103.1	93.8	36.7	55.9	62.8	149.5
Finger 6	401.5	451.5	40.3	47.6	203.2	189.3	82.2	107.7	132.8	256.8
Finger 7	301.2	341.2	**184.5**	**199.4**	215.9	201.5	217.6	262	236.9	416.2
Finger 8	158.3	184.1	79.3	88.7	158.5	146.7	102.1	130.4	106.5	216.5
Finger 9	36.8	50.4	4.5	9.9	30.8	24.9	17.9	34.4	36.3	108.8

The two factors that can influence finger performance are the finger size and ergonomics associated to its presentation. Low performance with little fingers can be attributed to their relatively small sizes, and thumb finger's good performance can be related to its larger surface area. Good performance accuracy with index fingers can be related to its ergonomics. In other words we believe among finger types the index fingers are easiest (least effort) to present to the sensor. This observation can be due to the fact that index finger has commonly a well established muscular structure such that presentation to a fingerprint sensor would provide a suitable pressure that is needed especially on optical fingerprint sensors. Furthermore this finger has the greatest range of extension/flexion [8]. The other factor that has been shown to influence performance is a finger force applied on the sensor [9]. It is also worth noting that all scanners in GUC100 database was single finger, and consequently performances of individual fingers can be different with multi-finger scanners.

Another thing to note from these plots is that performances using Neurotechnology' software are better compared to the performances using NIST's software.

4   Conclusion

In this paper we presented our analysis on the topic of influence of finger type into fingerprint verification performance. The two publicly available fingerprint verification software packages, one from NIST (available for free) and one from Neurotechnology (available for purchase), were applied on a fingerprint database consisting of over 70000 fingerprint images from 100 individuals. These database contains images from all 10 fingers of the person obtained on separate days during several months using five different fingerprint scanners. Our study indicates that performance with the little fingers is less accurate compared to the performances with the other finger types. In addition the best performance is being observed with either the thumb or index fingers. On average performance deterioration from the worst fingers (i.e. little) to the best fingers (i.e. thumb/index) in terms of EER was in the range of 184%-1352% using two different fingerprint verification software packages. Knowing such information can be useful for decision-makers in order to select a relevant finger for their system.

Acknowledgment

This work is supported by funding under the Seventh Research Framework Programme of the European Union, Project TURBINE (ICT-2007-216339). This document has been created in the context of the TURBINE project. All information is provided *as is* and no guarantee or warranty is given that the information is fit for any particular purpose. The user thereof uses the information at its sole risk and liability. The European Commission has no liability in respect of this document, which is merely representing the authors' view.

References

1. International Biometric Group. Biometrics market and industry report 2009-2014 (2008), http://www.biometricgroup.com/reports/public/market_report.php (Last visit: 17.11.2008)
2. Maltoni, D., Maio, D., Jain, A.K., Prabhakar, S.: Handbook of Fingerprint Recognition. Springer, Heidelberg (2009)
3. NIST's Fingerprint verification software, http://fingerprint.nist.gov/NBIS/nbis_non_export_control.pdf (Last visit: 14.10.2009)
4. Neurotechnology's VeriFinger 6.0., http://www.neurotechnology.com/ (Last visit: 14.10.2009)
5. Gafurov, D., Bours, P., Yang, B., Busch, C.: GUC100 multi-scanner fingerprint database for in-house (semi-public) performance and interoperability evaluation. In: International Conference on Computational Science and Its Applications (ICCSA) (2010), http://www.nislab.no/guc100
6. ISO/IEC 19794-2:2005, Information technology - Biometric data interchange formats – part 2: Finger minutiae data (2005)
7. Wayman, J.L.: Multi-finger penetration rate and ROC variability for automatic fingerprint identification systems. In: National Biometric Test Center (Collected Works 1997-2000), pp. 177–188 (2000)
8. Bundhoo, V., Park, E.J.: Design of an artificial muscle actuated finger towards biomimetic prosthetic hands. In: 12th International Conference on Advanced Robotics (2005)
9. Kukula, E.P., Blomeke, C.R., Modi, S.K., Elliott, S.J.: Effect of human-biometric sensor interaction on fingerprint matching performance, image quality and minutiae count. International Journal of Computer Applications in Technology (2009)

Using Arabic CAPTCHA for Cyber Security

Bilal Khan[1], Khaled S. Alghathbar[1,2], Muhammad Khurram Khan[1],
Abdullah M. AlKelabi[2], and Abdulaziz AlAjaji[2]

[1] Center of Excellence in Information Assurance (CoEIA), King Saud University, Saudi Arabia
[2] Department of Information Systems, College of Computer and Information Sciences,
King Saud University, Saudi Arabia
bilalkhan@ksu.edu.sa, kalghathbar@ksu.edu.sa,
mkhurram@ksu.edu.sa, amk.sa@me.com, azajaji@gmail.com

Abstract. Bots are automated programs designed to make auto registrations in online services, resulting in wastage of resources and breach of web security. English based CAPTCHAs are used to prevent bots from abusing these online services. However, English based CAPTCHAs have some inherent flaws and have been broken by bots. In this paper, an Arabic text based CAPTCHA is proposed. The CAPTCHA text image is distorted with background noise. Background noise and dots in the Arabic text makes CAPTCHA hard to be broken by Arabic OCRs. The proposed scheme is useful in Arabic speaking countries and in protecting internet resources. The proposed CAPTCHA scheme is both secure and robust. Experimental results show that background noise is a good defense mechanism against OCR recognizing Arabic text.

Keywords: CAPTCHA; Arabic; automated-bots; security; spam.

1 Introduction

Bots are automated programs that crawl through the web sites and make auto registrations. Automated bots target free email services, blogs and other online membership websites. They cause various problems by signing in to multiple accounts, sending junk emails and causing denial of service etc. CAPTCHA stands for Completely Automated Public Turing test to tell Computer and Humans Apart, is used to prevent automated bots from abusing online services.

Gimpy and EZ-Gimpy [7] are two well-known text based CAPTCHAs. Gimpy uses an image of seven words from the dictionary and generates a distorted image of the words to make it hard for the OCR to recognize (see figure 1a) [11]. The image is then presented to the user. In order to be successful, the user has to read three words from the image and enter them.

In contrast to Gimpy, EZ-Gimpy CAPTCHA is an image consisting of a single word [11]. The image is distorted with different techniques (Figure 1b) to confuse OCR.

In this paper, Arabic CAPTCHA is proposed which uses Arabic text image for securing online services from automated bots. Arabic text is more resistant to optical character recognition due to its natural complexity [10].

T.-h. Kim et al. (Eds.): SecTech/DRBC 2010, CCIS 122, pp. 8–17, 2010.
© Springer-Verlag Berlin Heidelberg 2010

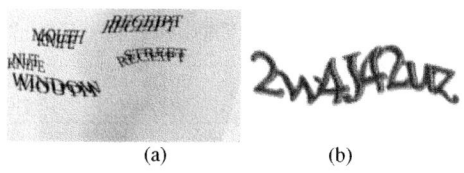

(a)   (b)

Fig. 1. An example of (a) Gimpy CAPTCHA. (b) EZ-Gimpy CAPTCHA.

It is expected that the proposed CAPTCHA will be useful in protecting internet resources, being wasted by spam, in Arabic speaking countries where the trend of using internet is growing fast. There are almost two dozen countries where Arabic is spoken as a first language. These countries are listed in Table 1, including Iran where Persian is spoken, a language that uses Arabic script. The table shows the usage of internet in these countries in 2003 and 2010 [9]. It is evident that there is an increase in the number of internet users from 2003 to 2010. As shown in Figure 2, Iran is on the top where the number of internet users exceeds 32.20 million in 2010, followed by Egypt and Morocco where these figures are reaching to 12.50 million and 10.30 million, respectively.

Apart from Arabic speaking regions, Arabic script is used in other languages, spoken by people in different parts of the world. These languages are Persian, Urdu, Pashto, Sindhi, Punjabi, which are spoken in different parts of Asia. A majority of these people are the users of internet.

In addition to Yahoo, Google, MSN and Instant Messengers, there are thousands of websites that provides services in Arabic language to the Arabic speaking users. These include websites from educational institutions, government organizations, online shopping, non/semi government organizations and social networking websites. In many of these websites, the user has to register itself before she uses services provided by these websites.

Many online service providers will take interest in providing services with our proposed security mechanism, hence optimizing the potential of internet in these countries. The proposed scheme not only prevents automated-bots but also facilitate the user while interacting the authentication process.

The rest of the paper is organized as follows: section 2 is previous work. Section 3 explains Arabic script and weaknesses of Arabic OCR and section 4 is the proposed Arabic CAPTCHA scheme. Section 5 concludes the paper.

2 Previous Work

Alta vista first practically implemented the idea of CAPTCHA to prevent automated-bots from automatically registering the web sites [1]. The mechanism behind the idea was to generate slightly distorted letters and to present it to the user.

Thomas et al. proved that OCR is unable to recognize text that is handwritten or closer to human handwriting [4] [3]. Therefore they proposed synthetic handwritten CAPTCHAs.

Table 1. Internet usage in Arabic speaking countries

Serial #	Country	Internet Usage, in Dec/2000	Internet Usage, Latest Data (2009)
1	Iran	250,000	32,200,000
2	Egypt	450,000	12,568,900
3	Morocco	100,000	10,300,000
4	Saudi Arabia	200,000	7,761,800
5	Sudan	30,000	4,200,000
6	Algeria	50,000	4,100,000
7	Syria	30,000	3,565,000
8	United Arab Emirates	735,000	3,558,000
9	Tunisia	100,000	2,800,000
10	Jordan	127,300	1,595,200
11	Kuwait	150,000	1,000,000
12	Lebanon	300,000	945,000
13	Oman	90,000	557,000
14	Qatar	30,000	436,000
15	Bahrain	40,000	402,900
16	Yemen	15,000	370,000
17	Palestine (West Bank)	35,000	355,500
18	Libya	10,000	323,000
19	Iraq	12,500	300,000
20	Eritrea	5,000	200,000
21	Mauritania	5,000	60,000

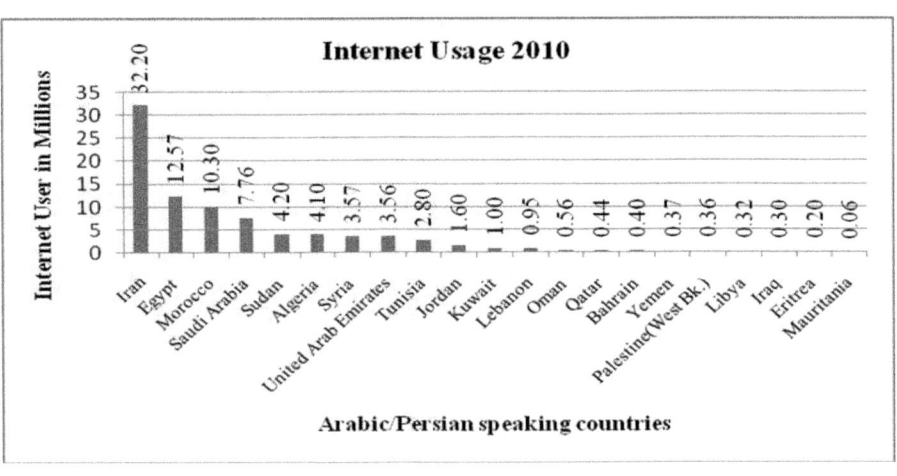

Fig. 2. Graph showing the internet usage in 2010 in Arabic/Persian speaking countries

Datta et al. used image recognition test to distinguish human from machine [6]. They proved that image based CAPTCHA is better than text based CAPTCHA. Their work is based on hard AI problem of automated image matching and recognition [6].

Gupta et al. proposed the method of embedding numbers in text CAPTCHAs [5]. They state that the tagged numbers in the text confuses the OCR and make it unable to segment characters. Jain et al. did comparative analysis of different types of CAPTCHAs proposed by Gupta et al [5] with respect to security and readability [16].

Ahn gave the idea of automated Turing test that is not based on the difficulty of the optical character recognition, rather on hard artificial intelligence problems [2]. Their proposed method uses hard AI problems to construct CAPTCHAs in order to differentiate humans from computers.

Although, CAPTCHA has been used for long for securing web from automated-bots, however, emphasis is mostly on the CAPTCHAs using Latin script. On the other hand, little work has been done on the CAPTCHAs using Persian language [8]. Therefore, we consider our work a good progress in the field of cyber security using CAPTCHAs based on Arabic script.

This paper presents a CAPTCHA scheme based on the Arabic text. The Arabic text is presented as image and distorted with different techniques so that it is unbreakable by OCRs, but still easily readable by humans.

3   Arabic Script and Weaknesses of Arabic OCR

Arabic script has some special characteristics which do not exist in others, e.g., Latin, Chinese, and Japanese. Arabic writing is someway like handwritten Latin [10] and it has 28 letters. It is written from right to left (see figure 3), whereas Arabic numbers are written from left to right. A word consists of different number of letters. Some letters are not connectable from the left with the succeeding letter. For example, 'ر'in figure 3 is not connectable.

جدّي يعمل في التجارة

Fig. 3. A sample of Arabic text

Arabic letters have different shapes depending on its position in the word, i.e., initial, middle, final or isolated. In contrast to Latin, Arabic letters have different sizes [12]. Moreover, several characters have different number of dots as well as different positions of dots, i.e., above, below and in the middle of the character (see figure 4). In addition, diacritics, e.g., shadda, maddah, hamza etc, are used in Arabic text [10].

ق ج ب غ ض

Fig. 4. Characters having different positions and number of dots

In contrast to Latin script, the recognition of Arabic characters is relatively more difficult due to its inherent characteristics. The crucial step in recognizing Arabic characters is the segmentation of word into separate characters [10]. Varying sizes of characters is one of the reasons that make the segmentation and recognition hard.

Baseline detection is also a problem that makes the segmentation step difficult in machine printed as well as handwritten Arabic text [13].

Arabic OCRs are font dependent. They are developed for a few font types and unable to recognize text that is written in a different font type. Especially, the font types in which the characters or sub words are overlapped, poses a serious problem in the segmentation stage.

There are many Arabic characters that have similar shapes, e.g., ج , ع غ,ص ض,ت ب خ ظ,ح خ ,ط ,و ز ر ذ د ,ق ف . The differences between these pairs of letters are the number and position of dots. These similar characters and dots confuse OCR to recognize characters correctly [15].

Keeping in view the weaknesses of the Arabic OCR, the following CAPTCHA scheme is proposed.

4   Proposed Arabic CAPTCHA Scheme

This section explains the features of our proposed and developed CAPTCHA scheme. It shows how the CAPTCHA scheme has been designed with different techniques before it is presented to the user.

The proposed CAPTCHA is designed in such a way that it makes the different stages of CAPTCHA solving hard, namely preprocessing, segmentation and character recognition. Figure 5 shows the sample of an image generated by our program. The salt and pepper noise is added in the image. Such background clutter increases problems for the OCR in the preprocessing, as diacritics, e.g., 'ء', dots etc., will be removed in the noise removal process.

Fig. 5. A sample CAPTCHA with diacritics

The background and foreground colors have been selected that are indistinguishable. Such color combination looks good and is hard for the OCR to separate the foreground from the background.

The program picks the number of letters randomly that ranges from 4 to 9. In addition to the number of letters, the type of font is selected randomly from out 52 different font types. And finally the font size is selected before the CAPTCHA image is displayed to the user. So each time the generated CAPTCHA varies in features with respect to number of characters, characters selected, and font type and font size. As Arabic OCRs are font dependent, so recognizing different font types will be a problem. The word in figures 5 has six letters, whereas the images in figures 6 and 8 have four and five letters respectively.

Fig. 6. A sample CAPTCHA with four letters

The font type shown in images in figure 7 complicates the job for the OCR. Because figures show that the original text in the image has its duplicate copy in the form of shadow. As opposed to human user, the OCR will detect two words in the image instead of one. Such feature confuses OCR in recognizing the characters of the word.

Fig. 7. A sample CAPTCHA

Character overlapping in text is a good feature which makes the segmentation step hard for the OCR. The program generates words with overlapping features. For example, in figure 8 letter Ra 'ر' is overlapped with Teh 'ة' and Ghen 'غ'. In such situation, OCR is unable to separate overlapped words and hence is unable to recognize the character in the image.

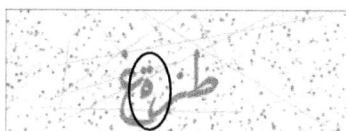

Fig. 8. Overlapping encircled in our generated CAPTCHA

Baseline detection helps OCR to solve CAPTCHA. Some techniques have been used in our CAPTCHA generation scheme to make the baseline detection difficult. In figure 9, the letter Ra 'ر' is below and 'ط' is above the baseline.

The program generates a unique CAPTCHA each time, which avoids the possibility of making database of the images by spammers.

Fig. 9. A sample CAPTCHA with baseline detection problem

In addition to font type, size and noise, another parameter that varies from image to image is the position of image. The program changes the coordinates of the image while displaying it as shown in figure 5,6,7,8 and 9. Such randomly placed words in CAPTCHAs make the segmentation and recognition hard [14].

4.1 CAPTCHA Generation and Verification

Implementation of Arabic CAPTCHA makes it secure from various types of attacks. There are two types of CAPTCHAs. In first type of CAPTCHA, text is selected randomly from a dictionary of 271000 Arabic words. In the second type, a word is randomly generated with different number of Arabic characters and font type.

Three levels of CAPTCHA complexity are employed to prevent automated-bots from reading CAPTCHA. These levels are easy, medium and hard.

Easy level CAPTCHA use easy font types with the number of characters ranging from 4 to 5 and less background distortion that is easily read by human. Whereas medium level CAPTCHA has 5 to 6 numbers of Arabic characters with more background noise in the form of dots and lines.

In contrast to easy and medium level, hard level CAPTCHA has the number of characters ranging from 7 to 9, with more complex Arabic characters and font types and high intensity of distortion in the form of arcs, lines and dots.

The user is initially presented with easy level CAPTCHA. If the requests are originated from bots, the CAPTCHA complexity level is gradually increased to medium and then to hard level. Algorithm 1 and 2 illustrate the implementation of different levels of CAPTCHA complexity.

Algorithm 1. Text generation	
Input: level of CAPTCHA complexity, Type of CAPTCHA	
Output: text generation for CAPTCHA (String)	
1.	**Procedure**
2.	text_length = select a number randomly in the range of 4 to 9.
3.	**If** text_length = 4 or 5 **then**
4.	**Select** captcha level as easy
5.	**Else if** text_length = 6 or 7 **then**
6.	**Select** captcha level as medium
7.	**Else if** text_length = 8 or 9 **then**
8.	**Select** captcha level has hard
9.	**End if**
10.	if captcha level=easy **then**
11.	**For** a=1 to text_length **do**
12.	**Select** letters from a collection of already specified easy letters.
13.	**End for**
14.	**Else If** captcha level=medium **then**
15.	**For** a=1 to text_length **do**
16.	**Select** letters from the collection of already specified letters
17.	**End for**
18.	**Else If** captcha level=hard **then**
19.	**For** a=1 to text_length **do**
20.	**Select** letters from 28 Arabic alphabets in addition to hard letters like ء, ى, ژ, ! and ~ etc.
21.	**End for**
22.	**End if**
23.	**End procedure**

Algorithm 2. Image generation with white background and blue foreground text.

Input: text string
Output: image generation

1.	**Procedure**
2.	A fixed size rectangle is selected.
3.	An image is generated within the rectangle
4.	Drawobject.backgroundcolor = white
5.	Randomly generate four points (P1, P2, P3, P4) with random horizontal and vertical coordinates in the image.
6.	**Select** one font type out of 50 Arabic font types depending on the CAPTCHA complexity level.
7.	Draw the input text within four selected points (coordinates).
8.	**If** CAPTCHA complexity level = easy **then**
9.	Size of text image = 60-70% of the whole image **else if** CAPTCHA complexity level = medium **then** size of text image = 50-59% of the whole image **else if** CAPTCHA complexity level = hard **then** size of text image =40-49% of the whole image size
10.	**End if**
11.	drawobject.foregoudcolor = blue
12.	**end procedure**

4.2 Robustness of Arabic CAPTCHA

Security of the Arabic CAPTCHA is evaluated by finding whether the OCR is able to recognize the image text. In order for the OCR to recognize text correctly, the image has to be preprocessed. Figure 10 shows the images after preprocessing in MATLAB. It shows that noise was removed in addition to original dots.

          (a)   (b)

Fig. 10. Image (a) before preprocessing (b) after preprocessing

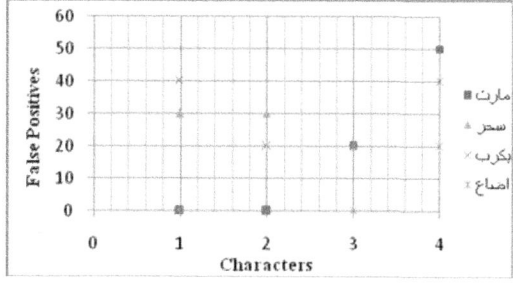

Fig. 11. False positives for characters in each of four words

After preprocessing, OCR places dots on each character for correct recognition. There is the probability that the OCR places dot in the incorrect position or on the incorrect character. We call this false positive.

False positive means OCR considers the placement of dots is in correct position when in reality it is wrong. Suppose that the false positive rate for any character that could have a dot is 10 then the false positive for each character in 'مارث' are 0,0,20 and 50. The graph in figure 11 shows the false positive rates for each character in four words.

4.3 Readability of Arabic CAPTCHA

To find out how readable is our proposed CAPTCHA, a survey was conducted. Over one hundred and fifty individuals participated in the survey, both male and female, and their ages ranging from 17 to over 50 years. Each participant was presented with fifty five different CAPTCHA images. From the analysis of the result of the survey, it was found that it was very easy for the users to read all the images in 50 out of 52 font types. For some font types the readability rate was 100%. In addition to font types, all Arabic alphabetic letters were also very easy to read. There were only few letters which were hard to read and were replaced by readers with similar looking letters. Table 2 shows the letters that were replaced with similar looking letters. Despite the fact that the images were distorted, the overall readability rate was 96.6%.

Table 2. List of characters difficult to read

Original letter	Replaced by
أ	ا
ك	خ
د	ر
غ	ف
د	ر
ش	ن
ص	م
ض	ح
ح	ج
ي	ب
ؤ	و
ق	ت
ن	ز
ض	ح
ظ	ط

5 Conclusion and Future Work

This paper presented a novel CAPTCHA scheme. The proposed scheme uses Arabic script to generate a text image. The image is distorted with different techniques. Various types of noises are added in the background in the form of dots, lines and arcs. The varying number of letters, font types and font sizes make it extremely hard for bots to break our CAPTCHA. The algorithm is efficient and the user does not have any problem while interacting with the system. The proposed program is developed in VB.Net, ASP.Net and JavaScript. It is comparatively useful and robust than Persian CAPTCHA.

References

[1] Lillibridge, M.D., Abadi M., Bharat K., and Broder A. Z.: Method for selectively restricting access to computer systems. Us patenet 6195698. Applied April 1998 and approved February 2001

[2] Ahn, L.V., Blum, M., Hopper, N.J., Langford, J.: CAPTCHA: using hard AI problems for security. In: Proceedings of the 22nd International Conference on Theory and Applications of Cryptographic Techniques 2003, Warsaw, Poland (2003)

[3] Rusu, A., Thomas, A., Govindaraju, V.: Generation and use of handwritten CAPTCHAs. International Journal on Document Analysis and Recognition 13(1), 49–64 (2010)

[4] Thomas, A.O., Rusu, A., Govindaraju, V.: Synthetic handwritten CAPTCHAs. Journal of New Frontiers on Handwriting Recognition 42(12), 3365–3373 (2009)

[5] Gupta, A., Jain, A., Raj, A., Jain, A.: Sequenced tagged CAPTCHA: generation and its analysis. In: International Advance Computing Conference, India (March 2009)

[6] Datta, R., Li, J., Wang, J.Z.: Exploiting the human-machine gap in image recognition for designing CAPTCHAs. IEEE Transactions on Information Forensics and Security 4(3) (2009)

[7] Ahn, L.V.: Telling humans and computers apart or how lazy cryptographers do AI. Communications of the ACM 47(2), 57–60 (2004)

[8] Shirali-shahreza, M.H., Shirali-Shahreza, M.: Persian/Arabic Baffle text CAPTCHA. Journal of Universal Computer Science 12(12), 1783–1796 (2006)

[9] Internet usage in the Middle East, source online
     http://internetworldstats.com/stats5.htm (accessed on June 10, 2010)

[10] Zheng, L., Hassin, A.H., Tang, X.: A new algorithm for machine printed Arabic character segmentation. Journal of Pattern Recognition Letter 25(15), 1723–1729 (2004)

[11] Mori, G., Malik, J.: Recognizing objects in adversarial clutter: breaking visual CAPTCHA. In: Conference on Computer Vision and Pattern Recognition 2003, pp. 134–141 (2003)

[12] Moussaa, S.B., Zahourb, A., Benabdelhafidb, A., Alimia, A.M.: New features using fractal multi-dimensions for generalized Arabic font recognition. Journal of Pattern recognition letters 31(5), 361–371 (2010)

[13] Al-Shatnavi, A., Omar, K.: A comparative study between methods of Arabic baseline detection. In: International Conference on Electrical Engineering and Informatics 2009, Malaysia, pp. 73–77 (2009)

[14] Hindle, A., Godfrey, M.W., Holt, R.C.: Reverse Engineering CAPTCHAs. In: Proceedings of the 15th Working Conference on Reverse Engineering 2008, Washington, USA, pp. 59–68 (2008)

[15] Sattar, S.A., Haque, S., Pathan, M.K., Gee, Q.: Implementation Challenges for Nastaliq Character Recognition. In: International Multi Topic Conference, IMTIC 2008, Pakistan, pp. 279–285 (2008)

[16] Jain, A., Raj, A., Pahwa, T., Jain, A., Gupta, A.: Overlapping variants of sequenced tagged CAPTCHA (STC): generation and their comparative analysis. In: NDT 2009, Ostrava (2009)

Information Assurance in Saudi Organizations – An Empirical Study

Syed Irfan Nabi[1,3], Abdulrahman A. Mirza[1,2], and Khaled Alghathbar[1,2]

[1] Center of Excellence in Information Assurance (CoEIA),
King Saud University, Saudi Arabia
[2] Department of Information Systems, College of Computer and Information Science,
King Saud University, Saudi Arabia
[3] Faculty of Computer Sciences, Institute of Business Administration, Karachi, Pakistan
{syedirfan,amirza,kalghathbar}@ksu.edu.sa

Abstract. This paper presents selective results of a survey conducted to find out the much needed insight into the status of information security in Saudi Arabian organizations. The purpose of this research is to give the state of information assurance in the Kingdom and to better understand the prevalent ground realities. The survey covered technical aspects of information security, risk management and information assurance management. The results provide deep insights in to the existing level of information assurance in various sectors that can be helpful in better understanding the intricate details of the prevalent information security in the Kingdom. Also, the results can be very useful for information assurance policy makers in the government as well as private sector organizations. There are few empirical studies on information assurance governance available in literature, especially about the Middle East and Saudi Arabia, therefore, the results are invaluable for information security researchers in improving the understanding of information assurance in this region and the Kingdom.

Keywords: Information Assurance, governance, empirical study, policy.

1 Introduction

Information is the life blood of the modern day organization [1] and thus life blood of economy. It is the gelling agent that keeps an organization together as one whole and all other resources are control due to it [2]. To make the best use of information it has to be shared and there is a need to keep up with the ever increasing demand for sharing information even outside an organization, with the partners, customer, suppliers and other stake holders. With the importance of information and its sharing comes the necessity of securing it. The increase in connectivity has increased the exposure of an organization, which is both good and bad. Good because grater market access is available and bad because the increased risk of detrimental loss due to failure of information security. Since the connectivity is not going to be curtailed this increased

T.-h. Kim et al. (Eds.): SecTech/DRBC 2010, CCIS 122, pp. 18–28, 2010.

risk has made information security into a global concern both for public as well as private sectors and even for governments [3]. With the prevalence of information security incidents it is very important for organizations to work diligently towards securing their information assets.

Information security breaches do happen and organization need to be aware of the risks to their information and take proactive measures to secure them. It is vital to proactively control such incidents. The awareness in an organization about severity of the outcome of an information security breach along with the probability of it happening can keep an organization focused on assuring that its information is secure [4]. This is also supported by Hagen [5]. To provide true information security a comprehensive framework/theory is required that takes a holistic approach towards information security [6, 7] so as to built information security in the system from the start and not as an afterthought. In this regards various frameworks have been proposed and in vogue but this is a dynamic world and information assurance is a moving target [8]. Thus, continuous research is required to find out new models and new paradigms of information assurance.

Reviewing the relevant literature it may be seen that information security researchers either focus on technology aspects (most of the time) or less commonly adopt theories and frameworks from other fields - sociology, philosophy, psychology, management etc. – modified with reference to information security to explain the human aspect of security [9]. Some of the pertinent ones are [10-14]. To get to the desired level of information security it is important to know the current existing status of information security. For this reason survey and studies are conducted. There has been a dearth of studies on the status of information security in the developing world but the problem is compounded in case of Middle East. There have not been many studies with reference to Saudi Arabia. Abu Musa has explored the information technology governance [15] and implementation of CoBIT [16] while Alnather [17] has provided a framework for understanding information security culture in Saudi Arabia.

The studies discussed above are either focused on IT governance or on behavioral aspect alone. The methodology used by them was to send the questionnaire to randomly selected respondents. Thus there was a need to combine the two aspects. Further, in order to get a better overall picture of information assurance in the Kingdom, it was deemed necessary to get responses from various segments. Thus, it was decided to take a stratified sample of the organizations in KSA. To improve the response rate, instead of sending out the questionnaires, the participants were invited from selected representative sample of organizations to attend a daylong workshop of which the survey was an important component.

The rest of the paper is organized such that the section 2) describes the research methodology and the sampling while section 3) gives details of some of the selected results along with discussion on them to reflect the status of information assurance in Saudi Arabia. It is followed by section 4) that includes conclusions as well as the future research direction.

2   Research Methodology

The research method used was surveying. A total of 120 Saudi organizations representing the major stake holder in four key sectors were preselected and their CIOs/IT
Managers were invited to participate in a daylong workshop to discuss information
security and assurance. More than 70 people participated in the workshop. At the end
of the workshop participants were asked to fill-in the questionnaire. From the organization with more than one participant only one representative response was solicited.
Thus, a total of 53 valid responses were collected. Majority of the questions in it were
close-ended. Some open-ended questions elicited additional information based on
answer to previous questions. The respondents' demographics are that 23(43.40%)
were from information security (IS) departments and 22 (41.51%) were from IT departments while 8 (15%) were from other departments. Further, 34 (64.15%) respondents were IT or IS Managers while 11 (20.75%) were non-managerial IT/IS staff.

2.1   Sample Distribution

The sampling technique used was stratified sampling where the population was divided into 4 groups based on the number of employees in the organizations. They
ranged from less than 100 to more than 1000 with two intermediate groups of 101 to
500 and 501 to 1000 employees. The sample distribution is given in Fig.1. Further,
because of the uniqueness of the requirements and needs of different organizations
the population was divided into 4 sectors. This grouping was based on the homogeneity of information security requirements within the groups (i.e. minimizing the
intra-class variation) along with unique differentiating needs of each group compared
to other groups (i.e. maximizing inter-class variation). The composition of the groups
was such that the Government sector included the ministries and other public sector
organizations that run a government but excluding defense related organizations. The
Defense sector included all military, non-military, and law enforcement organizations that are primarily tasked with safeguarding the country. The Bank sector comprised of the financial institutions while the rest of the organizations were clubbed
together as Private/Commercial sector. The sector-wise sample distribution is given
in Fig. 2. Since larger organization would have more profound impact on the information assurance status because of the number of employees as well as the amount
of budget that they can spend on information assurance, therefore, a larger share of
sample distribution was given to the larger organizations. Similarly, government
organizations have more financial resources to put in so their share in the sample was
also kept high.

   The distribution of respondents as given in Fig. 1 and Fig. 2 clearly shows that the
objective of sampling as described above was achieved. About 2/3rd of the respondents were from large organizations with more than 1000 employees and a similar
ratio was for governmental organizations (both defense related and non-defense
related) in the sample.

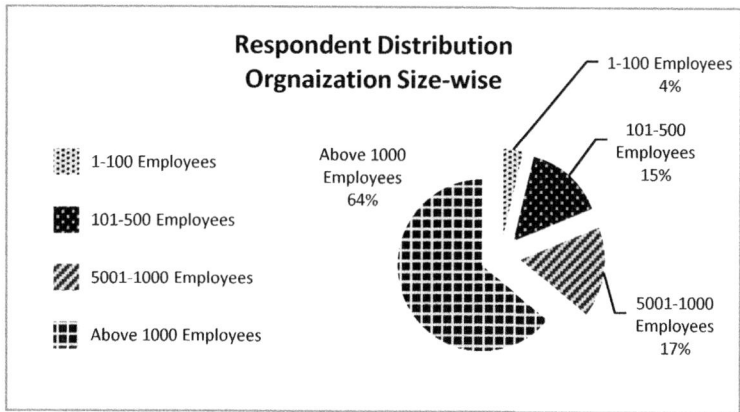

Fig. 1. Respondents' distribution based on the size of the organization that they represented

Further, the sampling was designed in this way because larger organizations are more likely to have information security as a priority, likewise government organizations are keen to have greater information security and have the will and the resources to invest in information security.

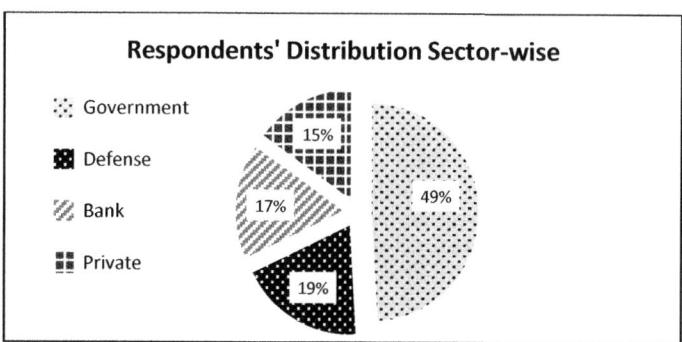

Fig. 2. Respondents' distribution based on the uniqueness of the information security requirements

Although the survey was quite comprehensive, yet for the sake of brevity not all the results can be mentioned here. Selected results in the relevant areas are given that would give a thorough picture of the whole situation. To that end the results from the areas of information security policies, information security standards and risk management are included.

3 Results and Discussion

In this section the results are given along with discussion on these results.

3.1 Information Security Policies

Information security (IS) policies are very important to ensure that appropriate controls are put in place. Without policies the consistency and assurance of results may not be ensured. The survey results in Fig. 3 show that a little more than half (53%) of the organizations had an information security policy. Defense and bank categories are the best since almost 2/3rd of them had an IS policy compared to about 2/5th of the government organizations.

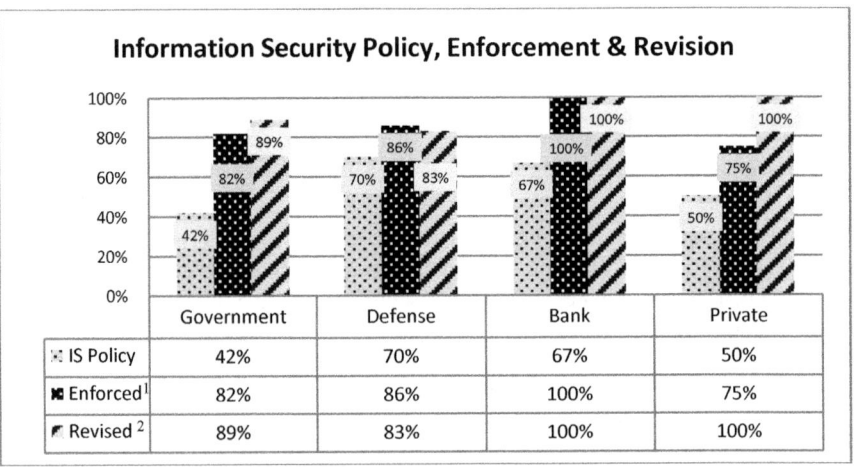

Fig. 3. The percentages are not absolute rather relative based on the previous question, i.e. the percentages of "Enforced" (1) are for organizations that have "IS policies" and similarly the percentages of "Revised" (2) are for the organizations that have IS policies "Enforced" not of the total sample size e.g. in case of Government organizations 42% of the Government organizations in the sample had IS Policies, out of these 82% (1) enforced them out of which 89% (2) revise them.

It is interesting to note that all the banks and 86% of the organizations that had an IS policy were enforcing it as well. It means that the organizations that have an IS policy are highly likely to enforce it as well. Thus, the presence of IS policy is a good indicator of its implementation as well as the fact that these organizations are serious about their security.

It might be worthy of note that over all among the organizations that enforce IS policies, almost 9 out of 10 (92%) regularly revise it. Further, all the banks and private organizations that have an IS policy not only implement it but also revise it as well. While some of the Government and Defense organization neither enforce IS policies not revise them. Possible explanation for this might be that Government and Defense organizations have developed IS policies and are enforcing them due to some directive or regulation without being convinced of their necessity. While the banks and private organizations only go for it only if they see it as a necessary part of remaining in the business and likely to be more serious about it. Thus, those among them that have an IS policies not only enforce it but also revise it.

3.2 Information Security Certification and Standards

Information security management certifications are important for an organization to establish the confidence of their customer, partners and stakeholders in them that the required processes to ensure information security are in place in the organization. One of the important information security standard is ISO 27000 series that incorporates ISO 17799 in it as well.

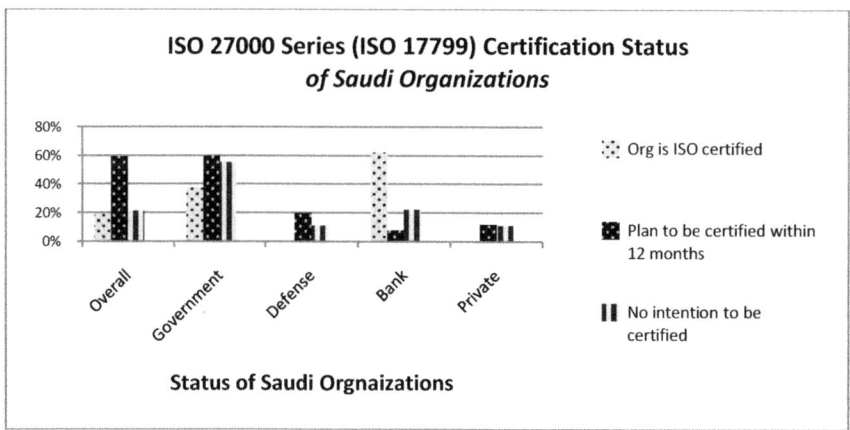

Fig. 4. Status of ISO 27000 certification of Saudi organizations

The survey results (excluding those organizations that responded in 'Not Sure') given in Fig. 4 show that 1 in 5 Saudi organizations (predominantly from large & government sector) have ISO 27000 series (or ISO 17799) certification and an equal number do not plan to have such certification while about 3 out of 5 are seriously thinking about getting themselves certified perhaps may be as soon as within next 1 year.

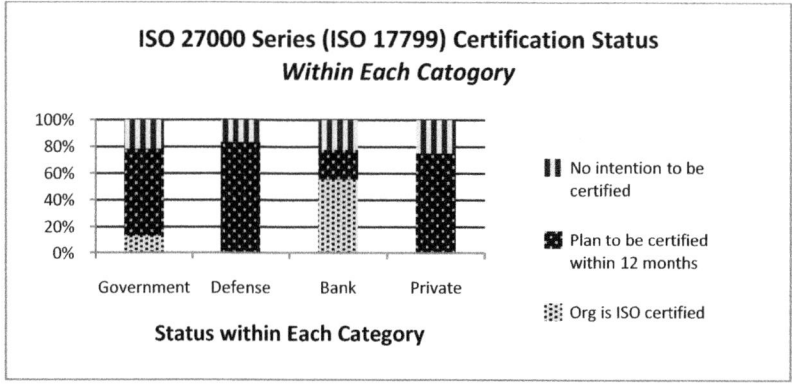

Fig. 5. Status of ISO 27000 certification of Saudi organizations within each category

Further, the results given in Fig. 5 show that Banks have the largest share of the ISO 27000 series (ISO 17799) certified companies while in Defense sector a few organizations are thinking of getting certified but none of them among the sample is ISO 27000 series (ISO 17799) certified.

A probable reason might be that the primary purpose of ISO 27000 series (ISO 17799) is to establish trust in an organization's processes with respect to information security for the partners, stakeholders and customers. Since defense organizations, unlike other organizations, have predetermined fixed interaction, they cannot select who to take as partners, customers, and stakeholders and trust is not an issue per se due to the this fixed nature of relationship, therefore, defense sector does not seem to be much concerned about ISO 27000 series (ISO 17799) certification.

3.3 Risk Management

Risk assessment and management is an important aspect of IS. The important charac-teristics of having effective risk management are risk assessment policy and updating of asset inventory and operations procedures. The results given in Fig. 6 show that about 50% of the Saudi organizations have a risk assessment process in place and a little less than 80% have an updated assets inventory while operations and procedures seems to be the most important aspect to them thus more than 90% of them keep these updated. Overall the banks have a better risk management with all of them keeping their assets inventory updated while defense organizations are more concerned with updated operations and procedures and all of the defense organizations in the sample keep it up to date.

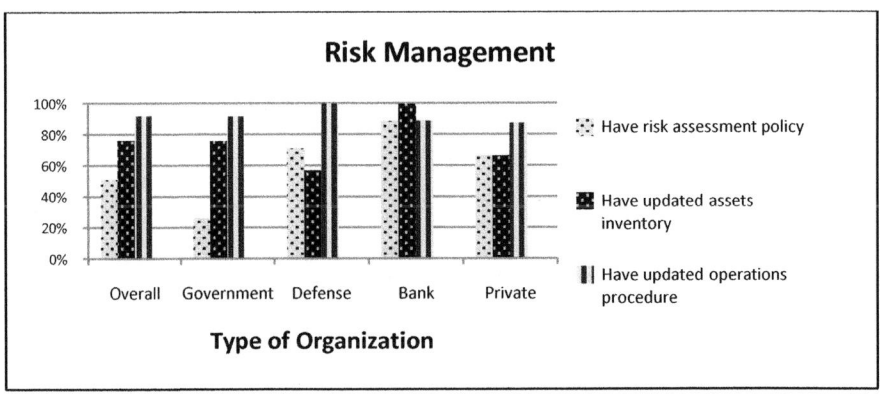

Fig. 6. Risk management status of Saudi organization based on risk assessment policy and updated assets inventory and operations procedure

To manage risk it is essential to start with risk assessment. In this regard one the important criteria is to see how strong is the actual security of an organization by attempting to circumvent it i.e. running a penetration test. It is very important tool to find out the effectiveness of information security controls. The survey results in Fig. 7 show that representatives from about 1 in five organization were not sure if penetra-tion testing is done in their organizations or not. Excluding these the results show that a little less than a third of the organizations did not do any penetration testing while a third did it once a year and the rest; a little more than the third did it more than once per year.

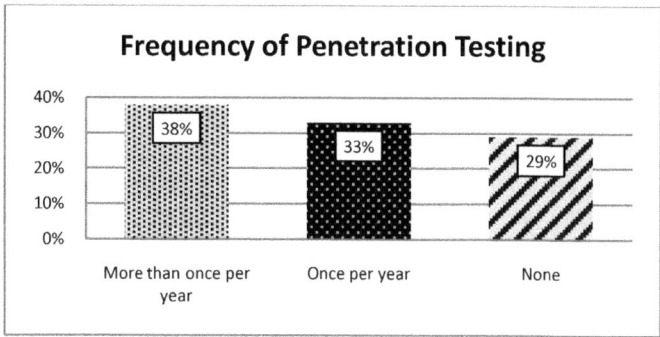

Fig. 7. Frequency of penetration testing in Saudi organizations

Among the private sector 25% organizations were not sure if they did penetration testing of their organization while in the banking sector not only that all the banks in the sample were doing penetration testing at least once a year but also all of them knew about it.

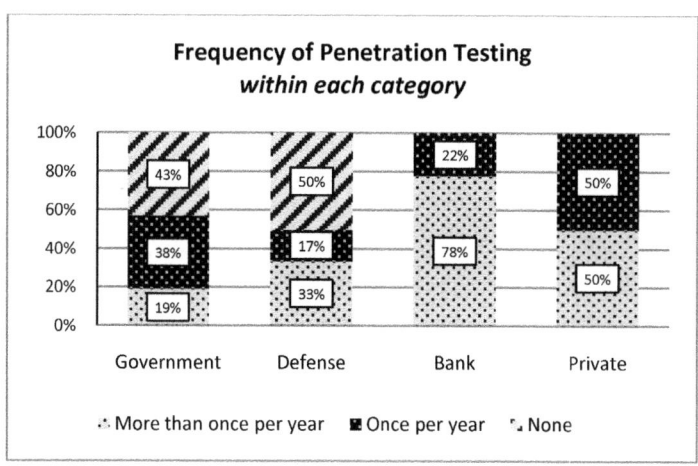

Fig. 8. Frequency of penetration testing within each category

The results in Fig. 8 show that Banks are the most serious of all the categories in terms of finding out the effectiveness of their information security controls as all of them were performing penetration testing at least once a year as compared to only half of the Defense organizations. This could be attributed to the fact that probably Defense is such a critical sector that it cannot allow an outsider/third party to conduct a penetration testing lest any secret information is leaked due to some security hole thus found. Also, it seems to be against its interest that any other organization (the penetration tester) to find out about security hole in its information security.

3.4 Information Security Concerns and Issues

Information security issues exist in all organizations but criticality of the information dictates how much effort and resources are going to be put in by the organization to secure it. Not all the information is equally critical. Similarly not all the vulnerabilities are treated equally. Rather the treatment is based on the threats that can exploit a vulnerability and the likelihood of those threats to be realized. Based on this analysis security measures are prioritized. The survey results show that having an antivirus is the top most security priority while lack of well-trained information security personnel is the top most security concern for the Saudi organizations. Table 1 lists the top five information security priorities and Table 2 lists the top five information security concerns.

Table 1. List of top five information security priority of the Saudi organizations

Information Security Priorities	Rank
Antivirus	1st
Data Loss Prevention	2nd
Firewall	3rd
Intrusion Detection and Prevention	4th
Network Access Control	5th

Table 2. List of top five information security concerns of the Saudi organizations

Information Security Concerns	Rank
lack of well-trained information security personnel	1st
lack of sufficient security policy with the organization	2nd
lack of sufficient practices for data protection	3rd
lack of good practices in password choices/updates/protection	4th
lack of adherence to information security standards	5th

3.5 Security Awareness

Security awareness has been recommended as one of the most important aspect of information security management and compliance within an organization [18] [19].

Table 3. Specialized information security training provided to its employees by Saudi organizations

		For IT Staff	
		"No"	"Yes"
For Non-IT Staff	"No"	**16%**	21%
	"Yes"	11%	**52%**

The survey results show that Saudi organizations are very serious in creating awareness and providing information security since more than half of the sampled organizations had specialized information security training for its employees; both IT as well as non-IT staff as shown in Table 3, while about 16 % had no specialized information security training either for IT staff or for non-IT staff.

4 Conclusion

This study has tried to meet the need for finding the present situation vis-à-vis Information Assurance in Saudi Arabian organizations. This is a pioneer study as not much information is available in the literature about information assurance in the Kingdom. The results provide an insight into the information security policies, risk management, network access and security standards adopted by the organizations in the Kingdom. The results presented seem to be very helpful for researcher and practitioners in getting to know the organizations' information security requirements. The next step in this research is to compare the findings with similar studies from other developed as well as developing countries to ascertain the comparative level of information assurance in the Kingdom. Further, the researchers intend to develop a model to provide conceptual explanation of the results to enhance the understanding information security, culture and organizational behavior in Saudi Arabian context. Also, the researchers intend to use the results to do a gap analysis between the desired level of information assurance and the existing situation so that remedial actions may be suggested to bridge this gap.

References

1. Halliday, S., Badenhorst, K., Solms, R.V.: A business approach to effective information technology risk analysis and management. Information Management & Computer Security 4, 19–31 (1996)
2. Eloff, J.H.P., Labuschagne, L., Badenhorst, K.P.: A comparative framework for risk analysis methods. Comput. Secur. 12, 597–603 (1993)
3. Corporate Governance Task Force: Information security governance: a call to action (2004),
   http://www.cyber.st.dhs.gov/docs/
   Information_Security_Governance-A_Call_to_Action.pdf
4. Whitman, M.E.: Enemy at the gate: threats to information security. Communications of the ACM 46, 91–95 (2003)
5. Hagen, J.M., Albrechtsen, E., Hovden, J.: Implementation and effectiveness of organizational information security measures. Information Management & Computer Security 16, 377–397 (2008)
6. Freeman, E.H.: Holistic Information Security: ISO 27001 and Due Care. Information Systems Security 16, 291–294 (2007)
7. Hong, K., Chi, Y., Chao, L.R., Tang, J.: An integrated system theory of information security management. Information Management & Computer Security 11, 243–248 (2003)
8. Dlamini, M., Eloff, J., Eloff, M.: Information security: The moving target. Computers & Security 28, 189–198 (2009)

9. Siponen, M.T., Oinas-Kukkonen, H.: A review of information security issues and respective research contributions. SIGMIS Database 38, 60–80 (2007)
10. Summerfield, M.: Evolution of Deterrence Crime Theory (2006),
    http://mobile.associatedcontent.com/article/32600/
    evolution_of_deterrence_crime_theory.html
11. Straub, D.W.: Effective IS Security: An Empirical Study. Information Systems Research 1, 255–276 (1990)
12. Stanfford, M.C., Warr, M.: A Reconceptualization of General and Specific Deterrence. Journal of Research in Crime and Delinquency 30, 123–135 (1993)
13. Siponen, M.: A conceptual foundation for organizational information security awareness. Information Management & Computer Security 8, 31–41 (2000)
14. Leonard, L.N.K., Cronan, T.P., Kreie, J.: What influences IT ethical behavior intentions: planned behavior, reasoned action, perceived importance, or individual characteristics? Information and Management 42, 143–158 (2004)
15. Abu-Musa, A.A.: Exploring Information Technology Governance (ITG) in Developing Countries: An Empirical Study. International Journal of Digital Accounting Research 7, 71–120 (2007)
16. Abu-Musa, A.A.: Exploring the importance and implementation of COBIT processes in Saudi organizations: An empirical study. Information Management & Computer Security 17, 73–95 (2009)
17. Alnatheer, M., Nelson, K.: A proposed framework for understanding information security culture and practices in the Saudi context. In: Proceedings of the 7th Australian Information Security Management Conference, pp. 6–17. SECAU - Edith Cowan University, Australia, Perth, Australia (2009)
18. Siponen, M., Pahnila, S., Mahmood, M.: Compliance with Information Security Policies: An Empirical Investigation. Computer 43, 64–71 (2010)
19. Puhakainen, P., Siponen, M.T.: Improving employees' compliance through information systems security training: An action research study. MIS Quarterly 34 (2010)

Emerging Biometric Modalities: Challenges and Opportunities

Davrondzhon Gafurov

Norwegian Information Security Lab (NISLab)
Gjøvik University College,
P.O. Box 191, 2802 Gjøvik, Norway
davrondzhon.gafurov@hig.no

Abstract. Recent advances in sensor technology and wide spread use of various electronics (computers, PDA, mobile phones etc.) provide new opportunities for capturing and analyses of novel physiological and behavioural traits of human beings for biometric authentication. This paper presents an overview of several such types of human characteristics that have been proposed as alternatives to traditional types of biometrics. We refer to these characteristics as emerging biometrics. We survey various types of emerging modalities and techniques, and discuss their pros and cons. Emerging biometrics faces several limitations and challenges which include subject population coverage (focusing mostly on adults); unavailability of benchmark databases; little research with respect to vulnerability/robustness against attacks; and some privacy concerns they may arise. In addition, recognition performance of emerging modalities are generally less accurate compared to the traditional biometrics. Despite all of these emerging biometrics posses their own benefits and advantages compared to traditional biometrics which makes them still attractive for research. First of all, emerging biometrics can always serve as a complementary source for identity information; they can be suitable in applications where traditional biometrics are difficult or impossible to adapt such as continuous or periodic re-verification of the user's identity etc.

Keywords: biometrics, emerging biometrics, novel biometrics, biometric challenges, biometric systems.

1 Introduction

In todays society the demand for reliable verification of user identity is increasing. Conventional knowledge-based authentications such as passwords and PIN codes can be easy and cheap in implementation but they possess usability limitations. For instance, it is difficult to remember long and random passwords/PIN codes, and manage multiple password. Moreover, knowledge based authentication merely verifies that the claimed person knows the secret and it does not verify identity per se. In the contrary, biometric authentication, which is based on measurable physiological or behavioural signals of human being, establishes

T.-h. Kim et al. (Eds.): SecTech/DRBC 2010, CCIS 122, pp. 29–38, 2010.

an explicit link to the identity. Thus, it can provide more reliable user authentication compared to the password-based mechanisms as well as lacking aforementioned usability limitations associated with passwords. Various characteristics of human beings have been proposed for biometrics. Traditional examples of such characteristics include fingerprint, iris, retina, face, speaker recognition, writer recognition, hand geometry, video based gait and so on.

Recent technological advances and widespread use of personal electronics enabled to explore a new physiological and behavioural characteristics of human beings for biometric authentication. In the rest of paper we will refer to such type of biometrics as *emerging biometrics*. In this paper we identify and discuss the challenges and opportunities related to emerging biometrics. We do not focus on algorithmic specifics of each proposed methods but rather aim to outline main limitations and advantages of emerging biometrics. The rest of the paper is organized as follow. After an overview of biometric system and its performance evaluation metrics in section 2, we provide introduction to emerging biometric modalities that have been proposed so far in section 3. Section 4 outlines the challenges and opportunities related to emerging biometrics. Section 5 concludes paper with a summary.

2   Biometric System and Its Performance Evaluation

A general architecture of biometric system is depicted in Figure 1. If a user is new to the system then he or she passes enrollment phase where his biometric template is created and stored in the database. Afterwards, in subsequent uses of the system user follows verification phases. Any biometric system essentially goes through the following steps: data capture by a sensor, pre-processing of captured biometric sample (e.g. noise reduction, quality improvement), feature extraction (e.g. minutiae points from fingerprint image), comparison and decision. Decision of the system (e.g. accept or reject) is essentially based on similarity of biometric feature (captured in verification phase) and template from the database with respect to a threshold value. The threshold value is usually selected based on a typical application scenario by system managers.

Biometric system can operate in two modes namely authentication (also called verification) or identification. In authentication mode the system conducts one to one comparison and aims to answer the question "Am I who I claim I am?". In identification mode the system performs one to many comparisons and aims to answer the question "Who am I?". In general DET (Decision Error Tradeoff) and CMC (Cumulative Match Characteristics) curves can be used to show performance evaluation results in authentication and identification modes, respectively. The DET curve is a plot of FAR (False Accept Rate) versus FRR (False Reject Rate) and shows performance of biometric system in authentication mode under various decision thresholds [1]. The CMC curve is a plot of identification probabilities versus rank and indicates the probability of the

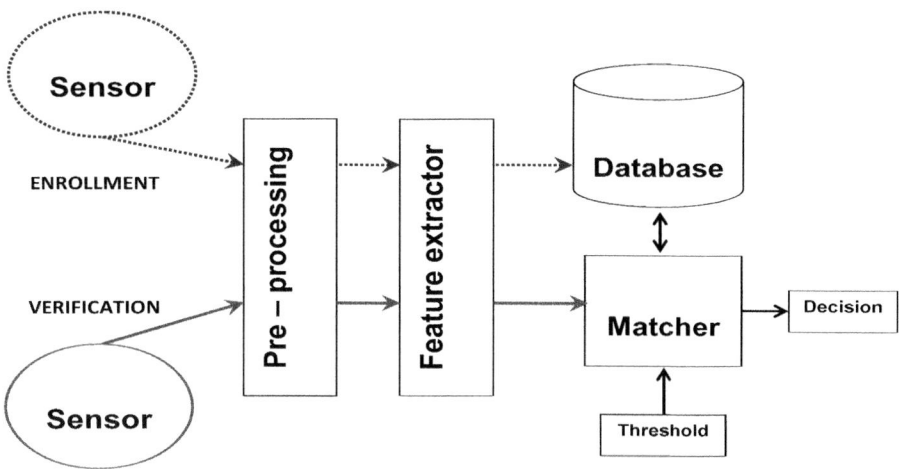

Fig. 1. A general architecture of biometric system

target being in top n-closest matches [1]. There are also several performance metrics that are used to indicate biometric's performance by a single value such as:

- Equal Error Rate (EER). The EER is a point in the DET curve where FAR=FRR;
- FRR at specific FAR;
- GAR (Genuine Accept Rate) at specific FAR;
- identification probability at rank 1 (or recognition rate).

In addition to them, there are also two other error types exists which are also important (especially for real applications). These are FTE (Failure To Enroll) and FTC (Failure To Capture).

3   Emerging Biometric Modalities

Human biometrics can be classified into two groups (not necessarily disjoint sets), physiological and behavioral. The first group is based on stable physical characteristics, while the second group uses learned, alterable behavioral characteristics. Most of emerging biometrics can be classified to the behavioural group. Below list includes several examples of emerging characteristics that have been proposed for considering as biometric modality.

- *Wearable Sensor (WS) based gait.* Gait information is collected using sensors (e.g. accelerometer) attached to the body or clothes of the person. The recorded motion signals is then analyzed for recognition purposes. Motions from following body location were analyzed:

- foot [2, 3]
- hip [4, 5]
- waist [6, 7]
- pocket [8]
- wrist [9]

– *Floor Sensor (FS) based gait*. Gait information is captured using sensors installed on the floor when person walks on them [10].
– *Ballprint/Footprint*. Verification is based on the shape and local ridge characteristics of the foot [11].
– *Typing style*. This refers to the user's typing style on computer's or mobile phone's keyboard [12, 13, 14].
– *Mouse usage*. This refers to the how user uses and interacts with a mouse device when working with computer [15, 16, 17].
– *Brain signals*. Electroencephalogram (EEG) is an electrical activity signal along the scalp produced by neurons within the brain which is captured by placing sensors around the head [18].
– *Heart signals*. Electrocardiogram (ECG or EKG) is an electrical activity of the heart over time externally recorded by sensors on the skin [19, 20, 21, 22, 23, 24].
– *Acoustic ear*. Acoustic properties of the pinnar (outer flap of the ear) and ear canal appears to provide some identity information [25].
– *Hipprint*. Verification is based on pressure distribution captured by sensors attached on the chair when person sits on them [26].
– *Fingerback*. Unlike fingerprint, in this biometrics features (e.g. finger knuckle) are extracted from back surface of the finger [27].
– *Lip*. Verification is based on lips shape and color features [28].
– *Tounge*. Verification is based on geometric shape and texture information of the tongue [29, 30].

Lately emerging biometrics have attracted research attention. It is interesting to point out that there are even companies which started to provide security/authentication services based on emerging biometrics such as keystroke [31, 32], foot motion [33], etc.

4 Challenges and Opportunities of Emerging Biometrics

Table 1 shows performance accuracies of the emerging biometric modalities. Performances are given in terms of recognition rate, EER and FRR at specific FAR. In this table the column #S represents the number of subjects in experiment of the study. It is should be noted that direct comparison of performance (even for the same modality) may not be adequate because of difference in the collected data sets.

Table 1. Performance summary of the current emerging biometrics

Study	Modality	Performance, %	#S	Subject population
Riera et al. [18]	EEG signal	$EER = 3.4$	51, 36	
Yamakawa et al. [3]	WS-based (shoe)	$FRR = 6.9$ at $FAR = 0.02$	10	
Gafurov et al [2]	WS-based (foot)	$EER = \{ 5\text{-}18.3 \}$	30	
Ailisto et al. [6]	WS-based (waist)	$EER = 6.4$	36	
Rong et al. [7]	WS-based (waist)	$EER = \{5.6, 21.1 \}$	21	
Sprager and Zazula [5]	WS-based (hip)	$Rr = 93.1$	6	
Gafurov et al [4]	WS-based (hip)	$EER = 13$	100	
Gafurov and Snekkenes [9]	WS-based (wrist)	$EER = \{ 10\text{-}15 \}$	30	
Gafurov et al [8]	WS-based (pocket)	$EER = \{ 7.3\text{-}20 \}$	50	
Everitt and McOwan [15]	mouse and keystroke	$FAR=4.4, GAR=99$	41	age range 20-30
Schulz [16]	mouse	$EER = \{11.2\text{-}24.3\}$	72	-
Ahmed and Traore [17]	mouse	$EER = 2.46$	22	
Hocquet et al. [12]	keystroke	$EER = 1.8$	15	
Clarke and Furnell [13]	keystroke (on phone)	$EER = 12.8$	32	
Hosseinzadeh and Krishnan [14]	keystroke	$EER = 4.4$	41 (30+11)	age range 18-65 (average 30.1)
Campisi et al. [34]	keystroke	$EER = 13$	30	age range 25-40
Uhl and Wild [11]	Ballprint/Footprint	$FRR=1.56$ at $FAR=0$	32	
Yamada et al. [26]	hipprint	$FRR=9.2$ at $FAR=1.9$	20	?
Akkermans et al. [25]	acoustic ear	$EER = \{ 1.5 \text{ - } 7 \}$	31	-
Zhang et al. [29]	tongue	$GAR=93.3$ at $FAR=2.9$	134 (89+45)	age range 20-49
Zhang et al. [30]	tongue	$EER = 4.1, P_1=95$	174 (115+59)	age range 20-49 (young and middle-aged)
Choras [28]	lip	$P_1=82$	38	
Kumar and Ravikanth [27]	fingerback surface	$EER = \{ 1.39 \text{ - } 5.81 \}$	105	age range 18-60 (mostly 20-25)

4.1 Challenges and Open Issues

There are several issues that needs to be addressed before emerging biometrics can really find their way into real applications. These include:

Subject population coverage:
In most of the current studies, in experiments subjects are mainly involved from adult population. This limits performance generalization only to this group of population. There is not much research of emerging biometrics with small/young children and old people. It is evident that most of the aforementioned emerging biometrics change significantly when individual grows from small/young age to adultness and from adultness to old ages. Some of them are not even applicable to young/old populations. For example, small children are not accustomed to use keyboard or mouse while muscles get weak in old ages. Furthermore, no FTE or FTC is reported in the studies. Thus, emerging biometrics needs to be studied with these two populations and then probably approximate age borders of their applicabilities needs to be identified. It is worth to note that population coverage of biometrics is not restricted only to emerging biometrics, it is related to the

traditional biometrics (e.g. face) as well. This can be one of the big challenges for biometrics in years ahead due to aging population of the earth (especially in the developed countries) [35].

Benchmark database:
Unlike conventional biometric modalities where well established benchmark databases are available (e.g. FVC200x databases for fingerprint, USF data set for video based gait [36] etc.), there is not much benchmark database for emerging biometrics (to our best knowledge only [37] dataset for keystroke biometrics). Although various studies of emerging biometrics reported encouraging performance results, most of them are based on restricted "home" collected databases. In other words, data collections are not conducted in similar conditions/environment which limits direct comparison of algorithms, and most of collected data sets are not public due to privacy regulations. Therefore, in order to advance in the area of emerging biometrics the availability of publicly accessible database is essential.

Hardware/Sensor:
Some types of emerging biometrics require special kind of sensors for capturing biometric data. Such sensors can be expensive or inconvenient in daily usage. For instance, for collecting EEG signals of the brain one needs sensor to place around head. Unless such sensors are integrated with clothing (e.g. caps) it is considered as an inconvenient and obtrusive data collection which likely to result in low acceptance by user.

Security:
Many reported papers on emerging biometrics model impostor as being passive. In other words an impostor score is generated by comparing a "normal" biometric of one subject to a "normal" biometric of another subject. Such type of performance evaluation is referred as "friendly scenario" [4]. However, in real life scenarios assumption of impostor being passive is not adequate. Impostor needs to be modeled as active and performance evaluation need to be conducted in "hostile scenario" [4]. In hostile scenario attackers can perform some actions to increase their acceptance chances (e.g. by observing and training of typing behaviour or walking style) or even can posses some vulnerability knowledge about authentication techniques. For instance, in gait biometrics it appears that knowing the gender of users in the database can be helpful for attackers to increase their acceptance chances [38]. Thus, it is important to study emerging biometrics robustness against active and motivated attackers in order to be able to answer questions like "whether it is possible to learn someone else's typing rhythm or mouse usage by learning and training", "how much effort is required to achieve this", etc.

In addition to the above, another widely discussed topic with conventional biometrics in general and emerging biometrics in particular is the privacy issue. Since the technology is based on human biology it is claimed that various types of sickness can be identified from biometric sample. To address privacy aspects in biometrics some approaches have been proposed [39, 40].

4.2   Opportunities

Once the identified challenges and open issues of emerging biometrics are addressed properly they can bring advantages and benefits over traditional biometrics. Although emerging biometrics cannot replace the conventional biometrics, it does not prevent them to serve as complimentary source for identity information. In addition, emerging biometrics can have following advantages and benefits.

Hardware/Sensor:
In previous subsection we pointed out that special sensor requirement can be a limitation for few types of emerging biometrics. However, several other types of emerging biometrics do not require an additional hardware for capturing biometric characteristics, since such hardware is already part of the system per se. For instance in case of keystroke and mouse dynamics, the keyboard and mouse device are already standard input devices of any computer, and most of the mobile phones (except touch one) have keyboard. Likewise, various motion detecting and recording sensors have been integrated into some models of mobile phones, e.g. Apple's iPhone [41] has an accelerometer sensor for detecting orientation of the phone.

Liveness: One of the challenges of traditional biometrics is assuring biometric sample is coming from live person i.e. "liveness" detection. For example, some fingerprint scanner cannot distinguish whether presented finger is fake or real one. Many of the mentioned emerging types implicitly assume that signals are coming from live person, e.g. no heart/brain signals can be generated by dead person.

Application scenarios: One of the main motivation of emerging biometrics are being to be better suitable in some application scenarios or environments like ubiquitous and pervasive. Some of them can be suitable for continuous authentication. For instance, when motion recording sensors are integrated in the mobile phone the identity of the phone's owner can be verified periodically to ensure its identity throughtout phone usage.

5   Conclusion

In this paper we gave an overview of emerging biometric modalities and techniques. We identified and discussed several limitations, challenges or open issues associated with emerging biometrics which can include population coverage (i.e. only adults), lacking benchmark databases, security with respect to active impostors and privacy concerns. In order for emerging biometrics to advance, these challenges need to be addressed. In addition, short survey of performances indicate that recognition accuracies of such biometrics are not as accurate as to be used alone. Despite of all of these, emerging biometrics can always serve as a complementary source of information for providing identity information. In addition, some of such biometrics do not require extra sensor and can be very suitable for continuous or periodic re-verification.

References

1. ISO/IEC IS 19795-1: Information technology, biometric performance testing and reporting, part 1: Principles and framework (2006)
2. Gafurov, D., Snekkenes, E.: Towards understanding the uniqueness of gait biometric. In: IEEE International Conference Automatic Face and Gesture Recognition (2008)
3. Yamakawa, T., Taniguchi, K., Asari, K., Kobashi, S., Hata, Y.: Biometric personal identification based on gait pattern using both feet pressure change. In: World Automation Congress (2008)
4. Gafurov, D., Snekkenes, E., Bours, P.: Spoof attacks on gait authentication system. IEEE Transactions on Information Forensics and Security 2(3) (2007) (Special Issue on Human Detection and Recognition)
5. Sprager, S., Zazula, D.: Gait identification using cumulants of accelerometer data. In: 2nd WSEAS International Conference on Sensors, and Signals and Visualization, Imaging and Simulation and Materials Science (2009)
6. Ailisto, H.J., Lindholm, M., Mäntyjärvi, J., Vildjiounaite, E., Mäkelä, S.-M.: Identifying people from gait pattern with accelerometers. In: Proceedings of SPIE. Biometric Technology for Human Identification II, vol. 5779, pp. 7–14 (2005)
7. Rong, L., Jianzhong, Z., Ming, L., Xiangfeng, H.: A wearable acceleration sensor system for gait recognition. In: 2nd IEEE Conference on Industrial Electronics and Applications (ICIEA) (2007)
8. Gafurov, D., Snekkenes, E., Bours, P.: Gait authentication and identification using wearable accelerometer sensor. In: 5th IEEE Workshop on Automatic Identification Advanced Technologies (AutoID), Alghero, Italy, June 7-8, pp. 220–225 (2007)
9. Gafurov, D., Snekkenes, E.: Arm swing as a weak biometric for unobtrusive user authentication. In: IEEE International Conference on Intelligent Information Hiding and Multimedia Signal Processing (2008)
10. Jenkins, J., Ellis, C.S.: Using ground reaction forces from gait analysis: Body mass as a weak biometric. In: International Conference on Pervasive Computing (2007)
11. Uhl, A., Wild, P.: Personal identification using eigenfeet, ballprint and foot geometry biometrics. In: IEEE International Conference on Biometrics: Theory, Applications and Systems (BTAS) (2007)
12. Hocquet, S., Ramel, J.-Y., Cardot, H.: Fusion of methods for keystroke dynamic authentication. In: Fourth IEEE Workshop on Automatic Identification Advanced Technologies (2005)
13. Clarke, N.L., Furnell, S.M.: Authenticating mobile phone users using keystroke analysis. International Journal of Information Security, 1-14 (2006) ISSN:1615-5262
14. Hosseinzadeh, D., Krishnan, S.: Gaussian mixture modeling of keystroke patterns for biometric applications. IEEE Transactions on Systems, Man, and Cybernetics, Part C: Applications and Reviews (2008)
15. Everitt, R.A.J., McOwan, P.W.: Java-based internet biometric authentication system. IEEE Transactions on Pattern Analysis and Machine Intelligence (2003)
16. Schulz, D.A.: Mouse curve biometrics. In: Biometric Consortium Conference (2006)
17. Ahmed, A.A.E., Traore, I.: A new biometric technology based on mouse dynamics. IEEE Transactions on Dependable and Secure Computing (2007)

18. Riera, A., Soria-Frisch, A., Caparrini, M., Grau, C., Ruffini, G.: Unobtrusive biometric system based on electroencephalogram analysis. EURASIP Journal on Advances in Signal Processing (2008)
19. Biel, L., Pettersson, O., Philipson, L., Wide, P.: ECG analysis: a new approach in human identification. In: 16th IEEE Instrumentation and Measurement Technology Conference (1999)
20. Biel, L., Pettersson, O., Philipson, L., Wide, P.: ECG analysis: a new approach in human identification. IEEE Transactions on Instrumentation and Measurement (2001)
21. Irvine, J.M., Israel, S.A.: A sequential procedure for individual identity verification using ECG. EURASIP Journal on Advances in Signal Processing (2009)
22. Boumbarov, O., Velchev, Y., Sokolov, S.: ECG personal identification in subspaces using radial basis neural networks. In: IEEE International Workshop on Intelligent Data Acquisition and Advanced Computing Systems: Technology and Applications (2009)
23. Fatemian, S.Z., Hatzinakos, D.: A new ECG feature extractor for biometric recognition. In: 16th International Conference on Digital Signal Processing (2009)
24. Micheli-Tzanakou, E., Plataniotis, K., Boulgouris, N.: Electrocardiogram (ECG) biometric for robust identification and secure communication. Biometrics: Theory, Methods, and Applications (2009)
25. Akkermans, A.H.M., Kevenaar, T.A.M., Schobben, D.W.E.: Acoustic ear recognition for person identification. In: Fourth IEEE Workshop on Automatic Identification Advanced Technologies (2005)
26. Yamada, M., Kamiya, K., Kudo, M., Nonaka, H., Toyama, J.: Soft authentication and behavior analysis using a chair with sensors attached: hipprint authentication. Pattern Analysis & Applications (2009)
27. Kumar, A., Ravikanth, C.: Personal authentication using finger knuckle surface. IEEE Transactions on Information Forensics and Security (2009)
28. Choras, M.: The lip as a biometric. Pattern Analysis & Applications (2010)
29. Zhang, D., Liu, Z., Yan, J.q., Shi, P.f.: Tongue-print: A novel biometrics pattern. In: 2nd International Conference on Biometrics (2007)
30. Zhang, D., Liu, Z., Yan, J.q.: Dynamic tongueprint: A novel biometric identifier. Pattern Recognition (2010)
31. bioChec, http://www.biochec.com/ (Online accessed: 13.04.2010)
32. Authenware Corp., http://www.authenware.com/ (Online accessed: 13.04.2010)
33. Plantiga Technologies Inc., http://www.plantiga.com/ (Online accessed: 13.04.2010)
34. Campisi, P., Maiorana, E., Lo Bosco, M., Neri, A.: User authentication using keystroke dynamics for cellular phones. IET Signal Processing (2009)
35. Mann, W.C.: The aging population and its needs. IEEE Pervasive Computing (2004)
36. Nixon, M.S., Tan, T.N., Chellappa, R.: Human Identification Based on Gait. Springer, Heidelberg (2006)
37. Giot, R., El-Abed, M., Rosenberger, C.: GREYC keystroke: A benchmark for keystroke dynamics biometric systems. In: IEEE 3rd International Conference on Biometrics: Theory, Applications, and Systems (2009)
38. Gafurov, D.: Security analysis of impostor attempts with respect to gender in gait biometrics. In: IEEE International Conference on Biometrics: Theory, Applications and Systems (BTAS), Washington, D.C., USA, September 27-29 (2007)

39. Yang, B., Busch, C., Gafurov, D., Bours, P.: Renewable minutiae templates with tunable size and security. In: 20th International Conference on Pattern Recognition (ICPR) (2010)
40. Bringer, J., Chabanne, H., Kindarji, B.: Anonymous identification with cancelable biometrics. In: International Symposium on Image and Signal Processing and Analysis (2009)
41. Apple's iphone with integrated accelerometer, http://www.apple.com/iphone/features/index.html (Last visit: 09.04.2008)

On Distinguished Points Method to Implement a Parallel Collision Search Attack on ECDLP

Ju-Sung Kang and Ok-Yeon Yi

Department of Mathematics, Kookmin University, Korea
{jskang,oyyi}@kookmin.ac.kr

Abstract. To perform a distributed version of Pollard's rho-method by Oorschot and Wiener [5], each processor repeatedly finds a distinguished point and adds it to a single common list. Thus θ, the proportion of the distinguished points, must be determined cautiously by considering performance and communication overload. We propose a practical method to determine an optimal θ by taking account of both communication overload and computational efficiency under a given implementation environment to solve the ECDLP.

Keywords: Parallel collision search attack, Pollard's rho-method, Distinguished points, Elliptic curve discrete logarithm problem, Cryptography.

1 Introduction

Elliptic curve cryptosystems (ECC) were proposed independently by Koblitz [3] and Miller [4]. The security of ECC depends on how difficult it is to determine d given dP. This is referred to as the elliptic curve discrete logarithm problem (ECDLP). The best algorithm known to date for the ECDLP in general is the Pollard rho-method [6] which, with the speed up proposed by Gallant, Lambert and Vanstone [2], and Wiener and Zuccherato [10], takes about $\sqrt{\pi n/2}$ steps, where a step here is an elliptic curve addition and n is the order of a point P.

Oorschot and Wiener [5] showed how the Pollard rho-method can be parallelized so that if m processors are used, then the expected number of steps by each processor before a single discrete logarithm obtained is about $\sqrt{\pi n/2}/m + 1/\theta$, where θ is the proportion of points which satisfy the distinguishing property. That is, using m processors results in nearly an m-fold speed-up. This distributed version of Pollard rho-method is the fastest general-purpose algorithm known for the ECDLP [1]. To perform a distributed version of Pollard rho-method, each processor repeatedly finds a distinguished point and adds it to a single common list. Thus θ must be determined cautiously by considering practical running time and communication overload. Theoretically, the larger we choose θ, the more we obtain efficient algorithm. However we have to determine an appropriate θ which maintain optimal efficiency under a given implementation environment. In this paper we propose a practical method to determine an optimal θ by taking account of both communication overload and computational efficiency under a

T.-h. Kim et al. (Eds.): SecTech/DRBC 2010, CCIS 122, pp. 39–46, 2010.

given implementation environment. As far as we know, there was no previous result which specifically mentioned about an optimal θ on the view point of practical implementation.

2   The Distinguished Points Method

The ECDLP is defined as follows:

- Given an elliptic curve E defined over a finite field F_q which we denote as $E(F_q)$, a point $P \in E(F_q)$ with order n, and another point $Q \in E(F_q)$, find the smallest non-negative integer d between 1 and n such that $Q = dP$, assuming such an integer exists.

The basic idea behind the Pollard's rho-method is to find a collision which equivalent to solving the ECDLP. If we find a collision pair (X_i, a_i, b_i) and (X_j, a_j, b_j) such that

$$X_i = a_i P + b_i Q , \quad X_j = a_j P + b_j Q ,$$

$$X_i = X_j , \quad a_i \neq a_j , \quad b_i \neq b_j ,$$

then we can solve the ECDLP by obtaining d that

$$a_i P + b_i Q = a_j P + b_j Q$$
$$\Leftrightarrow d = (a_i - a_j)(b_j - b_i)^{-1} \pmod{n} .$$

In the Pollard's rho-method, an iterating function $f : E(F_q) \rightarrow E(F_q)$ is used to define a sequence $\{X_i\}$ by $X_{i+1} = f(X_i)$ for $i = 0, 1, 2, \cdots$, with some starting point X_0. The sequence $\{X_i\}$ represents a walk in the group $E(F_q)$. The basic assumption for the expected run time analysis of the rho-method is that the walk $\{X_i\}$ behaves as a random walk. $E(F_q)$ is partitioned into 3 subsets S_1, S_2, and S_3 of roughly equal size in the Pollard's original walk, and two numbers a_0 and b_0 are randomly generated such that $1 \leq a_0, b_0 \leq n - 1$. Starting with $X_0 = a_0 P + b_0 Q$, a sequence $\{X_i\}$ is calculated using the relation, for all $i \geq 1$,

$$X_i = \begin{cases} P + X_{i-1} & \text{if } X_{i-1} \in S_1, \\ 2X_{i-1} & \text{if } X_{i-1} \in S_2, \\ Q + X_{i-1} & \text{if } X_{i-1} \in S_3. \end{cases}$$

Since it is known that the Pollard's original walk does not achieve the performance of a random walk in fact, Teske [7] [8] [9] studied some better random walks such as modified walks, linear walks with r-adding, and combined walks. Throughout this paper we assume that $X_{i+1} = f(X_i)$ is a random walk.

Oorschot and Wiener [5] showed how the Pollard's rho method can be parallelized with linear speed up. In their method, a set of distinguished points D of $E(F_q)$ is selected. Each client calculates a sequence $\{X_i\}$ by a specified random walk until it finds an $X_i \in D$. This X_i and its associated (a_i, b_i) are submitted to central server and the client starts again from a new starting point. The central server stores all the submitted points until a point X_i is received twice and the private key d is calculated. Oorschot and Wiener [5] proved that assuming each processor is the same speed, the overall running time T of the algorithm satisfies

$$E[T] = \left(\frac{\sqrt{\pi n/2}}{m} + \frac{1}{\theta} \right) t \, , \tag{1}$$

where m is the number of processors used, θ is the proportion of points in D and t is the time taken to calculate the next X_i.

3 Optimal Proportion of Distinguished Points

In this section we take into consideration a reasonable method to determine an optimal proportion θ of distinguished points. We propose an appropriate θ to a given practical implementation environment by adding communication overload to the parameter set that determine the overall efficiency of the algorithm. Note that, from the equation (1), the larger we choose θ, the more we obtain efficient algorithm. However, by some simulations, we can be comprehended this is not always true, since there will be a communication overload between clients and the server in real implementation environment.

For fixed θ and m, the number of clients (processors), let $\{N_{\theta,m}(\tau), \ \tau \geq 0\}$ be the counting process that $N_{\theta,m}(\tau)$ denotes the number of distinguished points stored in the server during time τ. Then

$$E\left[N_{\theta,m}(\tau)\right] = \frac{\theta}{t} \cdot m \cdot \tau \, ,$$

where t is the time required in a client side to calculate the next point X_i from X_{i-1}, since the required numbers of iterations to obtain a distinguished point are geometrically distributed with mean $1/\theta$. That is, $N_{\theta,m}(\tau)$ has the Poisson distribution with parameter $\lambda\tau$, where $\lambda = \theta m/t$.

Let $\tau_0, \tau_1, \cdots$ be given by

$$\tau_0 = 0, \quad \tau_j = \inf\{\tau \ : \ N_{\theta,m}(\tau) = j\} \, .$$

Then τ_j is the time of the j-th arrival. The interarrival times are the random variables $I_1, I_2, \cdots$ given by $I_j = \tau_j - \tau_{j-1}$. It is well known that $I_1, I_2, \cdots$ are independent and each having the exponential distribution with parameter λ. Let $S(N)$ be the run-time of the search algorithm for N elements in the central server, then the communication overload is defined as follows:

– We say that a communication overload is occurred, if $I_j < S(j-1)$ for some positive integer j.

If the binary search algorithm is used in the central server, note that $S(N^\alpha) \approx \alpha \cdot S(N)$, since the time complexity of binary search algorithm is $O(\log_2 N)$.

Now we can drive a reasonable method to determine an optimal proportion θ from the results of a simulation attack on an elliptic curve with smaller order than the given $E(F_q)$. Under a given communication and computation environment, assume that by an appropriate simulation, we obtain the optimal θ' for the ECDLP of l'-bit long order with m' processors. In fact, we choose θ' as the maximum value that doesn't cause a communication overload, that is,

$$\theta' = \max\{\theta \; : \; E\left[S(N_{\theta,m'}(T'))\right] \le E[I']\} \; ,$$

where I' is a random variable having the same distribution as any interarrival time I'_j and T' is the time taken to detect the first collision for the ECDLP of l'-bit long order with m' processors.

In the central server, for fixed θ' and m', we can independently select the maximum number $N^*(\theta', m')$ of distinguished points which doesn't occur a communication overload as follows:

$$N^*(\theta', m') = \max\left\{N \; : \; E\left[S(N)\right] \le E[I'] = \frac{t'}{\theta'm'}\right\} \; ,$$

where t' is the time taken to calculate one iteration of the random walk function for the ECDLP of l'-bit long order. Note that we can obtain $N^*(\theta', m')$ by a simulation only for the search algorithm used in the server side.

Now it is possible that we determine the optimal θ for the original given ECDLP of l-bit long order with m processors.

Theorem 1. Assume that the binary search algorithm is used for finding a collision in the central server, then the optimal proportion θ^* of the distinguished points set which doesn't cause a communication overload is given by

$$\theta^* = \max\left\{\theta \; : \; \theta \le \sqrt{\frac{2}{\pi n}}\,(N^*(\theta', m'))^{\frac{\theta'm't}{\theta mt'}}\right\} \; .$$

Proof. If the binary search algorithm is used for finding a collision in the server, by the definition of $N^*(\theta', m')$, we can drive the following formula:

$$E[S(N^*(\theta', m'))] = \frac{t'}{\theta'm'}$$

$$\Leftrightarrow E\left[S\left((N^*(\theta', m'))^{\frac{\theta'm'}{t'}}\right)\right] = 1 \; ,$$

$$\Leftrightarrow \frac{\theta m}{t}E\left[S\left((N^*(\theta', m'))^{\frac{\theta'm't}{\theta mt'}}\right)\right] = 1 \; ,$$

$$\Leftrightarrow E\left[S\left((N^*(\theta', m'))^{\frac{\theta'm't}{\theta mt'}}\right)\right] = \frac{t}{\theta m} \; . \tag{2}$$

We have to keep the inequality

$$E\left[S\left(\theta\sqrt{\pi n/2}\right)\right] \le E[I] = \frac{t}{\theta m} \tag{3}$$

in order to don't cause a communication overload, since

$$E[N_{\theta,m}(T)] = \theta\sqrt{\pi n/2}\ .$$

By the equation (2) and the fact that $S(\cdot)$ is an increasing function, the inequality (3) is equivalent to

$$\theta\sqrt{\frac{\pi n}{2}} \le (N^*(\theta', m'))^{\frac{\theta' m' t}{\theta m t'}}\ .$$

Therefore it is reasonable that we choose the optimal θ^* as follows:

$$\theta^* = \max\left\{\theta\ :\ \theta \le \sqrt{\frac{2}{\pi n}}\ (N^*(\theta', m'))^{\frac{\theta' m' t}{\theta m t'}}\right\}$$

$\square$

For any fixed positive integer k, let D_k be a distinguished subset of $E(F_q)$ such that $X \in D_k$ if the k most significant bits in the representation of X as a binary string are zero. If the order n of the point $P \in E(F_q)$ is l-bit long, the proportion of D_k is $\theta \approx 2^{l-k}/2^l = 1/2^k$. If we select the set of all distinguished points as D_k, then by Theorem 1, we get the following fact.

Corollary 1. If we consider the form of D_k as the set of all distinguished points, then k^* corresponding to θ^* is given by

$$k^* = \min\left\{k \in Z^+\ :\ k \ge \frac{1}{2}(l - 1 + \log_2 \pi)\right.$$

$$\left. - 2^{k-k'}\frac{m't}{mt'}\log_2 N^*(\theta', m')\right\},$$

where k' is the positive integer corresponding to θ' and $D_{k'}$.

Proof. It is straightforward that k^* is determined by the above formula, since $\theta = 1/2^k$ and $\theta' = 1/2^{k'}$ in Theorem 1. $\square$

On the other hand, the efficiency of the search algorithm can be improved, if we divide the storage space of the central server into some partitions. Let $S_r(N)$ be the run-time of the search algorithm for N elements where the storage space is divided into r partitions of equal size. Then we know that $S_r(rN) \approx S_1(N) = S(N)$. This relation produces the following fact.

Corollary 2. If the storage space of the central server is divided into r partitions of equal size, then k^* corresponding to θ^* is given by

$$k^* = \min\left\{k \in Z^+\ :\ k \ge \frac{1}{2}(l - 1 + \log_2 \pi)\right.$$

$$\left. - 2^{k-k'}\frac{m't}{mt'}\log_2 rN^*(\theta', m') - \log_2 r\right\}.$$

Proof. If we divide the storage space into r partitions of equal size, $N^*(\theta', m')$ is increased to $rN^*(\theta', m')$. Thus, by the same argument as the proof of Theorem 1, we obtain that

$$\theta^* = \max\left\{ \theta \ : \ \theta \leq \sqrt{\frac{2}{\pi n}} \left(N^*(\theta', m')\right)^{\frac{\theta' m' t}{\theta m t'}} r^{\frac{\theta' m' t}{\theta m t'} - 1} \right\}.$$

This is equivalent to the above formula for k^*. □

We summarize our method as an algorithm to determine the optimal k^* under the assumption that the binary search algorithm is used for finding a collision in the central server and the form of D_k is used for the set of all distinguished points by Corollary 1.

Algorithm 1

1. Under a given communication and computation environment, obtain the optimal k' for the ECDLP of l'-bit long order with m' processors such that k' is the minimum value which $D_{k'}$ doesn't cause a communication overload. This can be accomplished by choosing an ECDLP of l'-bit long order appropriate for the simulation.

2. For fixed k' and m' of the first step, in the central server, select the maximum number $N^*(k', m')$ of distinguished points which doesn't occur a communication overload as follows:

$$N^*(k', m') = \max\left\{ N \ : \ E\left[S(N)\right] \leq E[I'] \approx \frac{t' 2^{k'}}{m'} \right\},$$

where t' is the time taken to calculate one iteration of the random walk function for the ECDLP of l'-bit long order.

3. Determine the optimal k^* as follows:

$$k^* = \min\left\{ k \in Z^+ \ : \ k \geq \frac{1}{2}(l - 1 + \log_2 \pi) \right.$$
$$\left. - 2^{k-k'} \frac{m't}{mt'} \log_2 N^*(\theta', m') \right\}.$$

4   Experimental Results

To validate our algorithm, we conducted experiments in a computer cluster system with 50 processors of 3.2GHz Xeon CPUs and 2.0GB RAM connected by Cisco-Linksys 24p SRW2024 networks. The messaging API was MPI. We fixed an ECDLP of 50-bit ($l' = 50$) long order and $m' = 25$ in order to find k' in the first step of Algorithm 1. We obtained $k' = 10$ from the average value of 100 independent running time results as Figure 1, where $t' = 0.018$ $msec$. In the second step of Algorithm 1, we got $N^*(k', m') = 10,000$ by testing the search algorithm used in the server side. Then by the third step of algorithm, we can obtain the result that $k^* = 12$ ($\theta^* = 1/2^{12}$) is the optimal value for an ECDLP

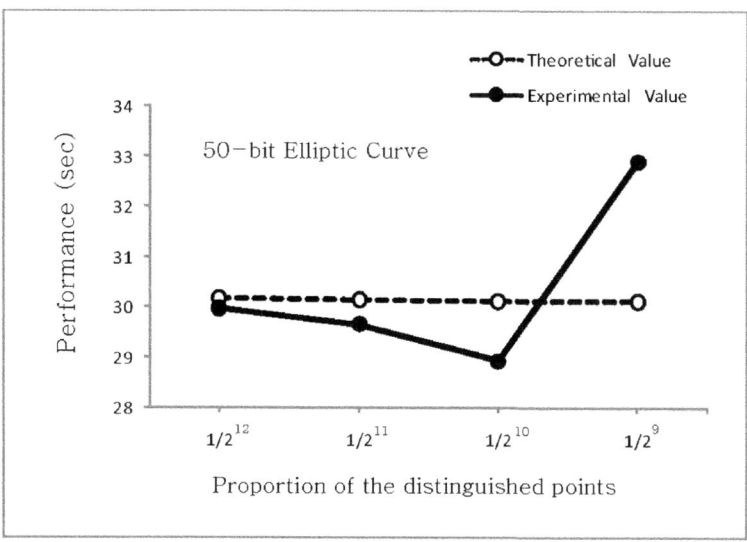

Fig. 1. Performance of parallel collision search attacks on ECDLP of 50-bit long order according to proportions of distinguished points

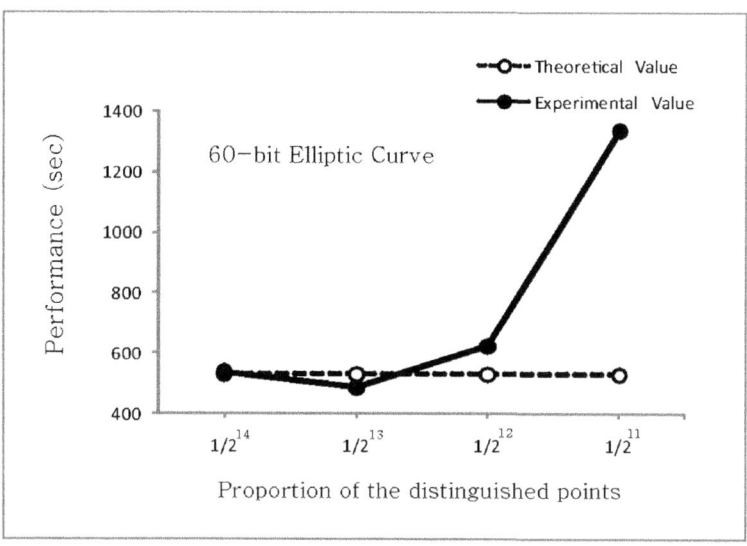

Fig. 2. Performance of parallel collision search attacks on ECDLP of 60-bit long order according to proportions of distinguished points

of 60-bit long order, where $t = 0.020\ msec$. Figure 1 and 2, respectively, show the average performance of 30 independent trials for the parallel Pollard-rho attack for ECDLPs of 50-bit and 60-bit long order with respect to proportions of distinguished points. It can be seen that $\theta^* = 1/2^{10}$ and $\theta^* = 1/2^{12}$ are the critical point to determine the performance of a parallel Pollard attack on ECDLP of 50-bit and 60-bit long order, respectively.

For example, if we want to attack an ECDLP of 160-bit long order with $m = 2,500$ processors under the same implementation environment as the above experiment, then we obtain that $k^* = 18$, since $t = 0.057\ msec$ in this case.

5   Conclusion

We have dealt with a practical issue for an implementation of the parallel collision search attack on ECDLP. To perform this attack, each processor repeatedly finds a distinguished point and adds it to a single common list. Thus the proportion of the distinguished points must be determined cautiously by considering both practical running time and communication overload. In this paper we proposed a practical method to determine an optimal proportion of the distinguished points by taking account of both communication overload and computational efficiency under a given implementation environment. Our result is different from the previous theoretical fact.

References

1. Certicom ECC Challenge, www.certicom.com
2. Gallant, R., Lambert, R., Vanstone, S.: Improving the parallelized Pollard lambda search on binary anomalous curves. Mathematics of Computation 69, 1699–1705 (1999)
3. Koblitz, N.: Elliptic curve cryptosystems. Mathematics of Computation 48, 203–209 (1987)
4. Miller, V.: Uses of elliptic curves in cryptography. In: Williams, H.C. (ed.) CRYPTO 1985. LNCS, vol. 218, pp. 417–426. Springer, Heidelberg (1986)
5. van Oorschot, P., Wiener, M.: Parallel collision search with cryptanalytic applications. Journal of Cryptology 12, 1–28 (1999)
6. Pollard, J.: Monte Carlo methods for index computation mod p. Mathematics of Computation 32, 918–924 (1978)
7. Teske, E.: Better random walks for Pollard's rho method, Research Report CORR 98-52, Department of Combinatorics and Optimization, University of Waterloo, Canada (1998)
8. Teske, E.: Speeding up Pollard's rho method for computing discrete logarithms. In: Buhler, J.P. (ed.) ANTS 1998. LNCS, vol. 1423, pp. 541–554. Springer, Heidelberg (1998)
9. Teske, E.: On random walks for Pollard's rho method. Mathematics of Computation 70, 809–825 (2000)
10. Wiener, M., Zuccherato, R.: Faster attacks on elliptic curve cryptosystems. In: Tavares, S., Meijer, H. (eds.) SAC 1998. LNCS, vol. 1556, pp. 190–200. Springer, Heidelberg (1999)

Data Confidentiality and Integrity Issues and Role of Information Security Management Standard, Policies and Practices – An Empirical Study of Telecommunication Industry in Pakistan

Syed Irfan Nabi[1,2], Syed Waqar Nabi[3], Syed Awais Ahmed Tipu[4], Bushra Haqqi[2], Zahra Abid[2], and Khaled Alghathbar[1,5]

[1] Center of Excellence in Information Assurance (CoEIA), King Saud University, Saudi Arabia
[2] Faculty of Computer Sciences, Institute of Business Administration, Karachi, Pakistan
[3] Namal College, Mianwali, Pakistan
[4] Department of Management, School of Business, University of Sharjah
[5] Department of Information Systems, College of Computer and Information Science, King Saud University, Saudi Arabia
syedirfan@ksu.edu.sa

Abstract. The amount of data communications is increasing each day and with it comes the issues of assuring its security. This research paper explores the information security management issues with respect to confidentiality and integrity and the impact of Information Security Management Standards, Policies and Practices (ISMSPP) on information security. This research has been conducted on the telecommunication industry of Pakistan that was ranked 9th globally in 2009 in terms of subscription. The research methodology was case study based in which perceptions were gathered as well as thematic analysis of the interviews was done. The research focus is on breach of data integrity and confidentiality by the internal users in the industry and the perception of improvement, if any, of the data security due to implementation of security management policies and controls. The results show that information security measure are perceived to have a positive impact on reducing data confidentiality and integrity breaches but still falls short of what is required. It concludes that security policies might improve the situation provided, firstly, that the top managements takes information security seriously, and secondly, the non-technical human aspects of the issues are taken into consideration.

Keywords: Information security, confidentiality, integrity, telecommunications, policies and practices, human.

1 Introduction

Telecommunications industry has grown tremendously in the last couple of decades. With this rapid expansion, the issues of securing the communications have grown as well. Three major characteristics of information that have remained as the basis of all information security are *confidentiality*, *integrity* and *availability*. Information security

T.-h. Kim et al. (Eds.): SecTech/DRBC 2010, CCIS 122, pp. 47–56, 2010.

is defined as maintenance of these three qualities [1]. Consumers are immediately effected by loss of *availability* (both of the service as well as the billing and other consumer data); therefore, telecom operators are mostly concerned with ensuring the availability of their services. Confidentiality and integrity, although not less important, are typically ignored. For this research the focus is on the confidentiality and integrity of the consumer data and the risks to these information security aspects due to insiders.

The rest of the paper is organized such that the section 2) has background information about confidentiality, integrity, and role of information security policies, practices and standards, information security in telecommunications industry globally and telecommunications sector in Pakistan. Section 3) discusses research question and section 4) research methodology. Section 5) has the results and discussion along with limitations and finally section 6) has conclusion and future research directions.

2 Background

2.1 Information Security

Information security is concerned with preserving the important characteristics of information and among them the three basic ones are confidentiality, integrity and availability.

2.1.1 Data Confidentiality, Integrity and Availability

Data confidentiality is making data available only to those that are approved to have it while data integrity is defined as ensuring that the data is complete and accurate [2]. It is also defined as "ensuring that data cannot be corrupted or modified and transactions cannot be altered" [3]. Data availability may be defined as data and information systems being always ready when you need them and perform as required [4]. Leaving out the important human aspect just the technical controls alone may not provide effective and complete security [5].

2.2 Information Security and Telecommunications Industry

Telecommunication enables easy access to and dissemination of information. However, no telecommunication system or technology has yet been able to guarantee that the information available or provided is complete and has not been tampered with either intentionally or accidentally [6].

2.3 Information Security Problems and Issues in Telecommunications

The telecommunication systems have evolved into very complex structures within themselves. These systems interconnect with various other such systems to provide wider telecommunications coverage to the users. Thus, the augmented complexity has given rise to newer categories of data integrity risks [7]. Also, while expanding telecommunication, the companies usually focus on introducing new technologies and systems. The haste in implementing these upgraded and improved technologies and systems often leads to neglecting information security concerns. The companies are usually so concerned about "time-to-market" and "capturing new opportunities" that they disregard the data integrity issues which can potentially arise [6].

2.4 Information Security Management Standards, Policies and Practices (ISMSPP)

Information security management standards, policies and practices provide basis for and details of going about establishing uniformity of actions to managing information security. Standards are a "common ground where uniform actions will lead to predictable results" and serve as benchmarks against which a company measures its policies and practices [8]. Policies are the guiding principles of running a business developed by the management of an organization for its internal use [9]. It provides a set framework for the employees to perform accordingly [8]. A [best] practice is defined as a "technique or methodology that, through experience and research, has been proven to reliably lead to a desired result"[10].

The ISMSPP have a vital role in ensuring information security in an organization. However, information security standards are concerned only with making certain the existence of security procedures and not the effectiveness of them [11], which needs to be assessed separately if required. The policies, practices and standards do provide help but they have their shortcomings. The stringent policies may restrict the exchange of information whereas the relaxed ones may expose information to information security risks [12].

2.4.1 Limitation of ISMSPP

The promulgation of information security policies is no guarantee that the employees would be fully aware of information security concerns. Neither does it ensure that the employees would be motivated to follow them [13]. Maintaining over-ambitious policies in black and white usually have no impact on the employees unless they are encouraged to abide by them by the senior management throughout the organization via their personal examples of religiously following these ISMSPP [14, 15]. The information security policies and practices should ideally be imbibed well into the organizational values [9]. Telecommunication companies often neglect the role which the employees play in ensuring information security. They tend to believe that data integrity can only be protected by having robust systems and state-of-the-art technologies. The policies, practices and standards implemented are focused on the technology aspects rather than on the human emotive facets. These have to be made part of the organizational values and instilled into the employees. Collaboration with the Human Resource department is essential in promulgating and instilling these as organizational values [5]. Also, the current information security management (ISM) guidelines need to be empirically validated not only for their technical contents but also for the value of these as perceived by the end users and manager [16]. This research is therefore aimed at addressing this gap about perceived value.

2.5 Telecommunication Industry of Pakistan

The telecommunications industry (primarily mobile communications) in Pakistan has seen tremendous growth in last decade since deregulation and it has sustained an average growth rate of over 100% during 2003-2008 with substantial growth during 2007 [17]. This flourishing industry that is booming because of fast growing and sophisticated telecommunications systems [18] offers both fixed line and cellular communication services. It has evolved from a state-owned-fixed-line-only monopoly to a deregulated industry in last 20 years with vast and sophisticated infrastructure both in rural as well as urban areas. The number of mobile subscribers have increased from less than 2 million in 2002 to more than 94 million in 2009 [19] and now it is ranked 9th by subscriptions in the global mobile market [20]. Thus the telecommunications industry in Pakistan is of interest to many.

For the purpose of this research only voice services providers, both fixed line and cellular, are considered as the population. The Wireless Local Loop (WLL), Long Distance and International (LDI) etc. service providers have not been considered as part of the population of interest. Also very small players have been ignored e.g. out of 6 companies the 2 major players in fixed line account for 98.8%. The population of interest thus consists of the major 08 players listed in Table - 1.

Table 1. List the competitors (population of interest) in telecommunications industry in Pakistan with their service brands and market share [21, 22]

S No.	Company Name	Brand(s)	Operating Since	Fixed line or cellular	Market Share* as of May 2010
1	M/s Pakistan Mobile Company Limited	Mobilink	1994	Cellular	32.64%
2	M/s CMPak Limited	Zong (formerly Paktel)	1991	Cellular	6.69%
3	M/s Telenor Pakistan Limited	Telenor	2006	Cellular	24.14%
4	M/s Warid Telecom Limited	Warid	2006	Cellular	16.98%
5	M/s Pakistan Telecom Mobile Limited	Ufone	2001	Cellular	19.55%
6	M/s Pakcom Limited	Instaphone	1991	Cellular	~0.001%**
7	PTCL (Previously government owned)	PTCL	1947	Fixed line	95.82% as of March 2009
8	NTC (Government owned)	NTC	1995	Fixed line	2.96% as of March 2009

* - Subscriber base - mobile 98,0001,002 and for fixed line 3,525,824.

** - Instaphone is under suspension after being practically dormant but Aarfeen Group, the owner of Instaphone, is still in the market with it s WLL service GoCDMA and so has not been dropped out of the population of interest.

Pakistan Telecommunications Authority (PTA) has issued policies and regulations with regard to licensing, interconnection, tariff, etc. but nothing about information security except one clause; **Part –IV, (16)** "Confidentiality of information" of consumer usage of service in the Telecommunication Rules, 2000 [23]. In the absence of any meaningful regulations from PTA, information security in telecommunications industry is mostly managed by internal company policies that are in line with globally accepted norms of voluntarily accepting ethical, societal and environmental responsibilities for their operations and practices. For example Telenor Pakistan has following personal data protection policy [24],

Protection of personal data

Telenor Pakistan's processing of Personal Data shall be subject to the care and awareness which is required according to law and regulations and relevant for information that might be sensitive, regardless whether the data refer *to customers, employees or others. Processing of personal data should be limited to what is needed for operational purposes, efficient customer care, relevant commercial activities and proper administration of human resources.*

It may be seen that majority of the ISMSPP in vogue in different companies as given in Table – 2 are primarily based on ISO 17799 or ISO 27001. Although none of the companies are certified (as of first quarter of 2009 when the research was conducted), yet, they know the importance of these standards and are using them as guidelines.

Table 2. Information security standards and policies followed by some of the leading telecommunications companies in Pakistan based on the data collected through interviews

S. No.	Company	Standard Followed	Other Guidelines	IS* Awareness	Remarks
1	PTCL	ISO 17799	In-house developed by Security Unit	In house training	Has a complete separate IS* department
2	Ufone	ISO 17799	In-house developed by security group		It is a wholly owned subsidiary of PTCL
3	Warid	ISO 27001	IS employees trained on ISO 27001		Reported to have a full fledged IS* department which doesn't exist now
4	Arfeen	PTA guidelines	In-house developed policies		No dedicated IS* setup
5	Telenor	ISO 27001	ISO27006	Regular training	Has an ISO 27001 certified 100% owned subsidiary.
6	NTC	ISO 17799			IS* in initial stages and has a long way to go.

* - Information Security.

The authors do not know of any related study about the telecommunications industry of Pakistan and thus it is very important to find out the confidentiality and integrity issues of this industry in Pakistan and to assess the role of standards, policies and practices in it.

3   Research Question

The problems this research has tried to address are, firstly, the information security issues in two areas; 1) confidentiality and 2) integrity; and secondly, the role of ISMSPP in solving these issues. More specifically the researchers were interested to find what are the data confidentiality and integrity issues in the telecommunications industry of Pakistan and how effective the implementation of self-imposed ISMSPP have been in ensuring security. This was to empirically verify the role of ISMSPP, as suggested by Siponen [16].

4   Research Methodology

Since the population was very small - only eight companies - therefore a case study approach was used to find value perception and to do thematic analysis based on interviews. The major issues as found in the literature were used to develop interview questions. These were further enhanced by discussing them with telecom experts. All the eight companies in the target group were approached and two persons from each organization were interviewed one for the perception of value (total of 08) and the other for thematic analysis (total of 08). The interviews consisted of both open as well as close ended questions and were about 30 minutes long. It was decided not to record the interviews because the respondents felt that they would not be able to give candid and straight answers to the questions or to discuss issues in depth with particular examples if the interviews were recorded. Certain comments and discussion were termed 'off-line' to be used only for better understanding by the researchers and not to be quoted. Since it is a very small industry with only a handful of senior executive and technical staff, therefore, in order to maintain the confidentiality of the respondents not only their names, but also their designations are kept undisclosed. The interviews were done face-to-face except for the companies that are not based in Karachi – the largest city of Pakistan and where the research was primarily conducted. For companies outside Karachi telephonic interviews were done. The research was conducted in the 1st quarter of 2009.

5   Results and Discussion

In this section first the perception of problems, issues and effect of solutions are discussed and are followed by the insights revealed by thematic analysis of the interviews. Before moving to the results it may be of interest to mention that one of the noteworthy insights revealed during the research was that in majority of the cases the information security policies have been implemented at these organizations as a response to some security breach.

5.1   Value Perceptions

Most of the respondents (5 out of 8) perceived accidental disclosure as the major cause of confidentiality breach followed by deliberate disclosure by disgruntled employees as the major cause. Thus human aspect of security, as emphasized in the literature, cannot be ignored. To err is human and thus information security awareness along with user education and training are very important.

The perception about internal threats to confidentiality was that exchange of passwords (deliberate, perhaps to help colleagues) and gossip about the work where certain confidential information is leaked (unintentional disclosure of confidential data during loose talk) were considered as the major threats to confidentiality by most (7 out of 8). Once again the human element and the "helpful" attitude of employees seem to be at the heart of the problem.

As far as the perception about the effectiveness of a particular practice in reducing the confidentiality breach was concerned, auditing was perceived as the most valuable and important practice by most (6 out of 8 with 1 respondent disagreeing), while biometric access control along with Employee Exit policy and Non-Disclosure Agreement were also considered important by most (5 out of 8 with 2 respondents disagreeing). It is interesting to note that although audits are not proactive measures to stop any information security breach, yet, these were considered as very effective. Perhaps it is the risk of being caught even after the incident that is seen as a potent deterrent preventing the employees from getting involved in any unacceptable behavior. Based on deterrence theory this is an indication that the policies may assist in behavior modifications if there is certainty and severity of punishment associated with it. Also, Biometric access control is considered as effective in controlling threats but at the same time few (2 out of 8) did not agree with it. It may be because biometric technology is relatively new in Pakistan and people are still not comfortable with it. Technology adoption model might be used to further research this issue.

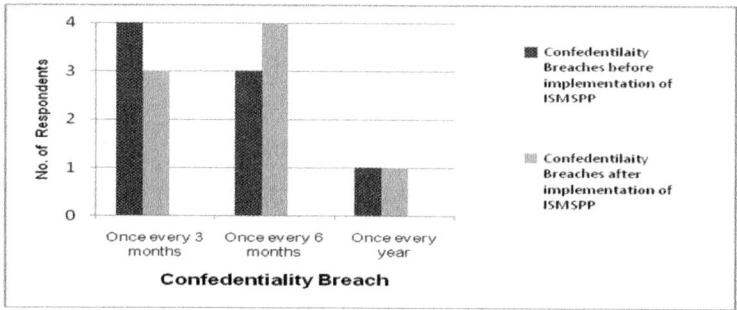

Fig. 1. Perception of Confidentiality Breaches Before and After Implementation of ISMSPP

Implementation of ISMSPP had a perception of positive effect on information security but their effect was perceived as more pronounced in improving integrity as compared to confidentiality of information. As given in Figure 1, it was perceived that the confidentiality breaches have not decreased considerably after the implementation ISMSPP but nevertheless have lessened for some companies.

Table 3. Perception of data integrity breaches before & after the implementation of information security policies, practices & standards

Information Security Management System, Policies, Practices	Perception of Breaches of Data Integrity					
	Always	Very Often	Sometimes	Rarely	Never	Total
Before Implementation	0	5	3	0	0	8
After Implementation	0	0	3	5	0	8

While Table 3 clearly illustrates the perception of decrease in data integrity breaches after the implementation of ISMSPP as compared the situation before the implementation. Similarly the perception of enhancement of data integrity due to implementation of ISMSPP was found to be close to 40% as given in Table 4. Thus, it may be suggested that ISMSPP are helpful in ensure data integrity.

Table 4. Perception of degree of data integrity enhancement after implementation of ISMSPP

	Degree of Data Integrity Enhancement after implementation of ISMSPP					Total
	50%	40%	30%	20%	10%	
No. of Respondents	0	5	3	0	0	8

5.2 Thematic Analysis of Interviews

The interviews were analyzed qualitatively using thematic analysis techniques to find the repeating ideas expressed during the interview and from these ideas themes were extracted. These were then consolidated into major themes and based on them recommendations were made. The major themes extracted are given in Table 5 while the recommendations are given in Table 6.

Table 5. Major Themes

Major Themes
1. Top management support and technical measures are a prerequisite to establishing effective information security.
2. Policies, practices and standards can help to a great extent in developing an environment conducive to information security
3. Humans are detrimental in providing information security in an organization but must be delicately handled.

Table 6. Recommendation

Recommendations
1. In order to establish effective information security it is imperative that the top management provides all out support in the form of budget, finances, resources so as to send a clear message that they mean to establish information security in the organization.
2. Technical measures represent the seriousness of top management in establishing information security.
3. ISMS, policies, practices are very important in getting the whole organization onboard regarding the criticality of information security.
4. The most sophisticated, state-of-the-art technical measures and most stringent and comprehensive policies written in black and white cannot ensure effectiveness of the information security unless the humans are taken on board and treated humanely.

5.3 Limitations

The authors could not find any relevant previous research to compare their results with but future research can benefit from these results as a comparative analysis can then be made. The WLL and LDI segment of the telecommunications industry was not considered since these were nascent then but future research might include them as well.

6 Conclusion with Future Research Direction

The ISMSPP have problems because they are generic and have not be validated [16], thus Siponen is in favor of empirical testing of these to validate them and to find the perception of their value of effectiveness. This gap is addressed in this research. In the absence of any meaningful information security regulations from the regulator (PTA), the companies are adopting certain ISMSPP derived mostly from ISO 17799/ISO27001 on their own and trying to fill in the gap probably as part of corporate social responsibility. The managers as well as the end-users perceive that ISMSPP do enhance integrity and to some extent the confidentiality of information but then much neglected human aspect is also very important. The major issues identified are 1) Top management support and technical measures are a prerequisite to establishing effective information security, 2) Policies, practices and standards can help to a great extent in developing an environment conducive to information security, 3) Humans are detrimental in providing information security in an organization but must be handled tactfully. It is recommended that in order to establish effective information security; 1) it is imperative that the top management provides all out support in the form of budget, finances, resources and sends a clear message that they mean to establish information security in the organization, 2) technical measures are a very important evidence of the top management's seriousness in providing the necessary resources to ensure information security, 3) The ISMS, policies, practices are very important in getting the whole organization onboard regarding the criticality of information security as it ensures that the information security performance of all employees are recorded 4) the most sophisticated, state-of-the-art technical measures and most stringent and comprehensive policies written in black and white cannot ensure effectiveness of the information security unless the humans are taken on board and treated perceptively.

Further research is required to develop and test information security frameworks that take into account the human influence both as a threat as well as a resource. Also, comparing the results with other similar researches in the developing countries can give insights into the security issues prevalent in the developing countries.

References

1. United Nations: Glossary of Recordkeeping Terms
2. ISO: ISO 17799
3. Weise, J.: Public Key Infrastructure Overview (2001),
   http://www.sun.com/blueprints/0801/publickey.pd
4. The ShockwaveWriter's Reply To Donn Parker. Computer Fraud & Security 2001, 19–20 (2001)
5. Myler, E.E., Broadbent, G.: ISO 17799: Standard for Security. The Information Management Journal (2006)
6. Richman, S.H., Pant, H.: Reliability Concerns for Next-Generation Networks. Bell Labs Technical Journal 12, 103–108 (2008)
7. Prnjat, O., Sacks, L.E.: Integrity methodology for interoperable environments. Communications Magazine, IEEE 37, 126–132 (1999)
8. Kramer, J.: The CISA prep guide: mastering the certified information systems auditor exam. John Wiley and Sons, New Jersey (2003)
9. Höne, K., Elof, J.H.P.: Information security policy — what do international information security standards say? Computers & Security 21, 402–409 (2002)

10. Visser, W., Matten, D., Pohl, M., Tolhurst, N.: The A to Z of corporate social responsibility. John Wiley and Sons, New Jersey (2008)
11. Siponen, M.: Information Security Standards Focus on the Existence of Process, Not Its Content. Communications of the ACM 49, 97–100 (2006)
12. Bodin, L.D., Gordon, L.A., Loeb, M.P.: Information security and risk management. Commun. ACM 51, 64–68 (2008)
13. Albrechtsen, E.: A qualitative study of user's view on information security. Computers & Security 26, 276–289 (2006)
14. Solms, B.V.: Information Security — A Multidimensional Discipline. Computers & Security 20, 504–508 (2001)
15. von Solms, B., von Solms, R.: The 10 deadly sins of information security management. Computers & Security 23, 371–376 (2004)
16. Siponen, M., Willison, R.: Information security management standards: Problems and solutions. Information & Management 46, 267–270 (2009)
17. Kenneth, R.: Telecom industry: mobile firms getting 2 million subscribers every month (2008), http://www.dailytimes.com.pk/default.asp?page=2008\03\07\story_7-3-2008_pg5_9
18. Londesborough, R., Feroze, J.: Pakistan telecommunications report. Business Monitor International, London (2008)
19. Pakistan - Key Statistics, Telecom Market and Regulatory Overviews. Totel Pty Ltd. (2010)
20. Global Wireless Data Market _- 2009 Update. Chetan Sharma Consulting (2010)
21. Moblie Cellular Services. Pakistan Telecommunications Authority (2010)
22. Fixed Line Services. Pakistan Telecommunications Authority (2010)
23. Telecommunication Rules 2000 (2000)
24. Codes of Conduct, Group Governance Document (2010), http://www.telenor.com.pk/cr/pdf/newCOC.pdf

Evaluation of Performance of Secure OS Using Performance Evaluation Mechanism of LSM-Based LSMPMON

Kenji Yamamoto and Toshihiro Yamauchi

Graduate School of Natural Science and Technology, Okayama University,
3-1-1 Tsushima-naka, Kita-ku, Okayama, 700-8530 Japan
yamamoto-k@swlab.cs.okayama-u.ac.jp, yamauchi@cs.okayama-u.ac.jp

Abstract. Security focused OS (Secure OS) is attracting attention as a method for minimizing damage caused by various intrusions. Secure OSes can restrict the damage due to an attack by using Mandatory Access Control (MAC). In some projects, secure OSes for Linux have been developed. In these OSes, different implementation methods have been adopted. However, there is no method for easily evaluating the performance of the secure OS in detail, and the relationship between the implementation method and the performance is not clear. The secure OS in Linux after version 2.6 has often been implemented by Linux Security Modules (LSM). Therefore, we determine the effect of introducing the secure OS on the performance of the OS, and a characteristic by the difference of the implementation method by using the overhead measurement tool, the LSM Performance Monitor (LSMPMON); the LSMPMON can be used to evaluate three different secure OSes.

Keywords: Performance Evaluation, Secure OS, Linux, LSM.

1 Introduction

It is very difficult to prevent all the attacks that occur when the weakness of a system is exploited. In addition, applying patches to compensate for vulnerabilities is not sufficient for preventing attackers from attacking computers. Therefore, secure OSes have attracted attention as a solution to these problems. A secure OS provides forced access control (Mandatory Access Control, MAC) and the minimum special privileges so that minimal damage occurs even if the root privilege is obtained by an attacker. The secure OS is based on the label system or path name system or others. There are several methods for implementing the secure OS, and the functions in these methods are different. Therefore, it is not easy to select a secure OS that is appropriate for use in the user's environment. In addition, the consequences of introducing a secure OS are not clear, and the change in the specifications and performance with the change of the version is difficult to determine.

After Linux 2.6, the function of the secure OS is implemented by a hooking system that calls a function group named Linux Security Modules (LSM) [1].

T.-h. Kim et al. (Eds.): SecTech/DRBC 2010, CCIS 122, pp. 57–67, 2010.

We paid attention to LSM, and we implement the performance evaluation mechanism of the LSM-based secure OS; this mechanism is named the LSM Performance Monitor (LSMPMON)[2]. The LSMPMON records the processing time at the each hook point of LSM and the calling count. Therefore, we can evaluate the processing time for each hook and the point at which bottlenecks exist in the secure OS. The monitor enables us to easily compare the performances achieved by using secure OSes.

LSMPMON has been developed for evaluating LSM-based secure OSes. In this paper, a new version of LSMPMON developed for 2.6.30 is described and results of the evaluation of Security-Enhanced Linux (SELinux)[3][4], TOMOYO Linux [5][6], and LIDS [7], which are representative secure OSes in Linux, are presented. The unit of access control for resources in SELinux is label-based MAC, that in TOMOYO Linux is path-name-based MAC, and that in LIDS is i-node-based MAC. LSMPMON can be used to evaluate the influence of different methods of resource identification on performance. We evaluate the performance using a benchmark software and report an analysis of the overhead incurred when a secure OS and each LSM hook are used. We perform the same evaluation for different versions of the kernel, namely, for the current kernel (2.6.30) and the old kernel (2.6.19), in order to verify the changes in performance. As a result, we clarify influence on performance by using the secure OS, and a characteristic by the difference of the identification method of resources and a change of the performance at the version interval.

The contributions of this paper are as follows:

(1) In this paper, a new version of the LSMPMON is described. All evaluation methods for LSM-based secure OSes require the use of the LSMPMON. The LSMPMON can record the processing time and the calling count of each LSM hook. The results are useful for analyzing the performance of secure OSes.

(2) In this paper, first, the difference between different secure OSes is reported. The reports are based on the evaluation results obtained by using LSMPMON. The reports clarify the relation between the access control method and the performance of secure OSes.

(3) The difference between different kernel versions of Linux is described. These results reveal that the performance of the secure OS strongly depends on the kernel version.

2   Security Focused OS

2.1   Evaluation of Secure OS

Secure OS indicates OS that has the function to achieve MAC and the minimum privilege. In the secure OS, a security policy is enforced, according to which operations are limited to permitted operations that consume permitted resources; further, access control is implemented in the root privilege. Therefore, a secure OS can limit its operation, even if an attacker obtains root privileges via an unauthorized access.

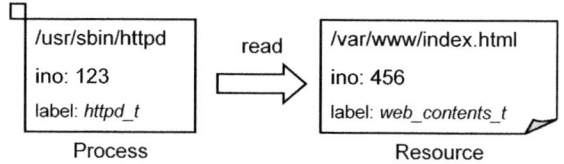

Fig. 1. Process by which the Web server reads a Web page

In addition, by the secure OS, it can authorize every user and process to the minimum privilege. We evaluated the secure OS developed by using LSM that is implemented on Linux. In particular, we used SELinux, TOMOYO Linux, and LIDS. These secure OSes (refer to Figure 1) are used to explain the difference between the features and resource identification schemes. The resource identification methods used in the secure OS involve the use of a label, a path name, and an i-node number for management. In this example, the Web server is the target to be accessed, the path name is /usr/sbin/httpd, and the i-node number is 123, and the Web server is attached to the label called httpd_t. The resource is accessed as an object, the path name is /var/www/index.html, the i-node number is 456, and it is attached to the label called web_contents_t.

SELinux is included in the Linux kernel standard as a secure OS. In SELinux, offers increased safety since it is based on TE (Type Enforcement), MAC, and RBAC (Role-Based Access Control). In SELinux, the label base method is used for resource identification and control by assigning a label, which is called a domain, and attaching a type to a process or a file. In the example shown in Figure 1, it can be seen that the process in which a domain called httpd_t was added reads the file that was assigned a type called web_contents_t.

TOMOYO Linux is included in a Linux kernel standard as a secure OS. In TOMOYO Linux, the path name base method is used for resource identification. In the example shown in Figure 1, it is understood that /usr/sbin/httpd reads /var/www/index.html. In addition, the identification process is based on knowledge of the path name and the execution history of the process.

LIDS uses the path name for setting the access control. On the other hand, it uses an i-node number internally in order to manage resources.

2.2   LSM

LSM is a function that defines the hook system calls for function group to the security check mechanism in the Linux kernel. A user can initially expand the security check function of the kernel by using this function. After Linux2.6, the LSM is incorporated in a kernel, and the function of the secure OS is often implemented by the LSM. When LSM is valid, this is checking of the safety before accessing an object of the kernel inside by the callback function of LSM which is registered by user. The structure of the LSM is described below. When an AP invokes a system call, the DAC performs a security check. Next, a hook

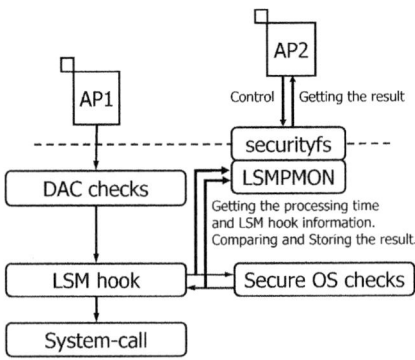

Fig. 2. Structure of the LSMPMON

function of the registered LSM is called at a security checkpoint (Linux 2.6.30, 186 points) in the kernel, and a security check is performed by each secure OS. When the operation is approved by these checks, system call processing is performed, and access to resources is enabled. In addition, the security check is performed not only before system call processing but also during the system call processing.

3   LSMPMON

3.1   Function

The main functions of LSMPMON are described below.

(1) Performance measurement of each LSM hook

Figure 2 shows the structure of the LSMPMON. The LSMPMON records the time before and after all the LSM hooks are called, in order to measure the processing time and calling count of the LSM hooks.

(2) Detection of the context switch

We prepare the flags that are used to detect context switches during the processing of the LSM hooks. The value of the flag can be checked in order to determine whether a context switch has occurred.

(3) Control using a simple interface We use "securityfs" to simplify the user interface. Securityfs is a special virtual file system for security modules available in Linux 2.6.14. Securityfs is mounted on /sys/kernel/security, and it is used as an interface for controlling the secure OS and confirming the policy mainly. The module in which securityfs is used along with the LSM can easily perform data exchange in the user space and the kernel space without making original file system.

Figure 3 shows an example LSMPMON behavior. Transferring data between kernel space and user space such that data is transmitted to an existing AP and performed, by using securityfs.

```
   Enable LSMPMON
%  echo 1 > /sys/kernel/security/lsmpmon/control

   Disable LSMPMON
%  echo 0 > /sys/kernel/security/lsmpmon/control

   Show the result
%  cat /sys/kernel/security/lsmpmon/result
hook              min   max  ave   count  cs_count
--------------------------------------------------------
         :
inode_create   97  67103  105  2725605   0
inode_link
inode_unlink   97  72728  114  2725600   0
         :
```

Fig. 3. A behavior example of the LSMPMON

(4) Limited function of the measurement target

The manner in which a measurement target can be limited by using securityfs has been illustrated in (3). If the character string "s foo" is written for a specific file in securityfs, the LSMPMON stores a measurement result only when the subject name is "foo." Similarly, If the character string "o bar" is written for a specific file in securityfs, the LSMPMON stores a measurement result only when the object name is "bar."

(5) Function using the information of the system call

When an audit is effective, in the system call interface, the system call numbers are saved in the audit context structure, which is a member of the task structure of the process (AP1) that published the system call. When the LSMPMON monitor determines the processing time of the LSM hooks, it refers to audit context that is the member of the task structure of AP1 in order to acquire the system call number. For this reason, the system calls for each LSM will be able to measure the processing time, and thus, processing time can be saved.

3.2 Processing Flow of the LSMPMON

Processing performed by the LSMPMON is described below. First of all, AP invokes a system call. This time, if LSM hooks are called, rdtscll() function loads current Time Stamp Counter before LSM hooks is processed. Then actual processing of the LSM hook is done, Time Stamp Counter read again after the results came back. Then get the subject name and object name which performed access control and make a decision whether it is a measurement save object.

If it is a measurement object, confirmed the presence of context switches. If no context switch occurs, compare the processing time and the registered data of the processing time of same LSM hooks that same result in the access control. In that case, the shortest or longest processing time is saved the value. Furthermore, this processing time is added to the total processing time of the LSM hook that called in this time. Next, one adds the caling count that no context switch, and return to the original process. Finally, if a context switch occurs, one adds the calling count context switch. It will come back to the original process.

In the behavior example in Figure 3, min is the shortest processing time, max is the longest processing time, ave is the average processing time for no context switch, count is the calling count without a context swich, cs count is the calling count of the no context switch.

4   Evaluation of Secure OS Using LSMPMON

4.1   Criteria in the Evaluation

We evaluated the secure OS on the basis of the following three criteria in order to determine the performance of the secure OS and effects of using different Linux kernels.

(A) Effect of introducing the secure OS on performance
(B) A characteristic by the difference from the access control unit for resources in the secure OS
(C) Changes in the performance and specifications across different versions

4.2   Evaluation Methods

We evaluated the file operation that the secure OS frequently performed access control processing. Contents of Evaluations are described below.

(A) Effect of performance by the secure OS
(Evaluation 1) By using the benchmark software LMbench[8], we measured the performance of each secure OS and evaluated the results in terms of the file operation. We show the effect of introducing the OS on performance.

(B) A characteristic by the difference from the access control unit for resources in the secure OS
Evaluation 1 does not indicate the time consumed by each LSM hook and the location of the bottleneck point. Therefore, we implemented the following steps:
(Evaluation 2) We measured the processing time corresponding to every LSM hook by using the LSMPMON in order to compare and evaluate these values. Thus, we clarify the effect of differences in the access control unit for resources on performance and show the characteristics of this effect.

(C) Changes in performance and specifications across versions
(Evaluation 3) We perform similar evaluation in the Linux kernel of the version that is different from that in Evaluation 1; then, we compare the results and consider the change in the performance of each secure OS. However, by evaluation in LMbench alone, we cannot understand the factors that cause the change in the performance and determine the bottleneck point. Therefore, in order to determine the point at which the performance changed in this evaluation, we implemented the following steps:
(Evaluation 4) We compared every system call with the LSMPMON in detail. We measured the overhead of the LSM hooks in each system call by the LSMPMON, and we compared the results for different versions and evaluated

Table 1. Compare to each secure OS in the new kernel

	SELinux	TOMOYO Linux	LIDS
Use of LSM hooks	154	14	46
Identification method of the resource	label	path-name + execution history	inode
Version	3.6.12-39.fc11	2.2.0	2.2.3rc8

Table 2. Compare to each secure OS in the old kernel

	SELinux	TOMOYO Linux	LIDS
Use of LSM hooks	149	17	38
Identification method of the resource	label	path-name + execution history	inode
Version	2.4.6-80.fc6	2.0	2.2.3rc1

the results. Therefore, we compare the overhead in detail and show the change in the performance and specifications across versions. The evaluation environment was as follows: CPU, Pentium 4 (3.0 GHz); Memory, 1 GB; OS, Linux 2.6.30.4 (new kernel) and Linux 2.6.19.7 (old kernel) is. In addition, all the measurements were obtained while running LMbench five times, and the results show the average processing time. The identification method for each secure OS and the object that performs access control, the calling count of LSM hooks, and the Secure OS version are shown in Table 1 and Table 2.

4.3 Evaluation of the Effect on Performance by the Introduction of the Secure OS

Table 3 shows the results of Evaluation 1. In SELinux, the rates of increase in the processing time of stat, read/write, and 0K file creation are the highest among the rates for the three secure OSes. In addition, in the other items of Table 3, the rate of increase in the processing time is comparatively high. Thus, it is thought that file processing involves a large overhead.

The processing time for the stat operation in TOMOYO Linux is the shortest among that in the three secure OSes. On the other hand, the file creation and deletion in this are much slower in this kernel than in the old kernel. Further, a large overhead is incurred in open/close. Thus, the overhead in particular may become large as the email server repeats the creation of a file.

The processing time of file generation and deletion in LIDS is shorter than in the two other secure OSes. Thus, the rate of increase in the processing time is small in the other items of Table 3. Therefore, it is thought that LIDS is the most suitable OS for file processing.

4.4 Features of Differences of Implementation

Table 4 shows the results of Evaluation 2. In addition, "N/A" in Table 4 indicates that the LSM hooks are not implemented. LSM hooks based on i-node are used in SELinux and LIDS, while LSM hooks based on the path name are used in TOMOYO Linux.

In SELinux, the processing time of inode_create and inode_init_security is particularly long. This is because it is necessary to perform the recomputation

Table 3. Processing time of file operations and its increase rate in Linux kernel 2.6.30 measured by LMbench (unit:μs)

	Normal	SELinux	TOMOYO	LIDS
stat	1.79	2.67 (48%)	1.83 (2%)	2.20 (22%)
open/close	2.74	3.94 (44%)	4.78 (75%)	3.28 (20%)
read/write	0.37	0.47 (29%)	0.37 (0%)	0.37 (0%)
0Kfile Create	15.16	58.18 (283%)	53.58 (253%)	16.84 (11%)
0Kfile Delete	8.20	9.26 (12%)	33.10 (303%)	9.91 (21%)
10Kfile Create	47.84	89.38 (87%)	83.32 (74%)	48.42 (1%)
10Kfile Delete	20.06	20.18 (0.6%)	42.68 (112%)	21.16 (5%)

Table 4. Processing time of LSM hooks called in each file operation (unit:μs)

hookname	No_secure	SELinux	TOMOYO	LIDS
path_mknod	0.045	N/A	13.609	N/A
path_unlink	0.035	N/A	23.164	N/A
path_truncate	0.060	N/A	13.426	N/A
inode_init_security	0.036	20.658	N/A	N/A
inode_create	0.035	19.037	N/A	N/A
inode_unlink	0.036	0.216	N/A	0.127
inode_permission	0.035	0.159	N/A	0.192
dentry_open	0.041	0.222	17.381	N/A

of the label and to initialize each i-node that is newly created. In TOMOYO Linux, the processing time increases because of the function based on path name, such as path_mknod and path_unlink. It is thought that in order to check access permissions, it is necessary to compare of the character string and to obtain the path name.

In LIDS, there is no need to obtain the path name and to determine the label on LSM hooks. Thus, the total processing time consumed by the LSM hooks is short. It is thought that this is the factor because of which the overhead of the whole secure OS is small.

From the above evaluations, the following results were obtained:

(1) In SELinux, the overhead of creating files is large. This is because labeling is necessary. Further, other items have a relatively large overhead.

(2) In the case of for TOMOYO Linux, where the path name is distinguished, the overhead is particularly large when the path name is obtained and deleted. In addition, the open/close operation is slow because it is necessary to reference the path name (compare the character string).

(3) LIDS has a small overhead in file processing because in LIDS, it is not necessary to perform labeling and to obtain the path name.

4.5   Differences between Performance and Specifications of Different Kernel Versions

Comparison of performance of different kernel versions

Table 5 lists the results of the Evaluation 3. In SELinux, the performance of current kernel is considerably better than that of the old kernel in almost all aspects. In particular, the rate of increase in the processing time for read/write reduced from 157% to 29%. Similarly, the rate of increase in the processing time for 0K file delete reduced from 80% to 12%. However, the rate of increase in the

Table 5. Processing time of file operations and its increase rate in Linux kernel 2.6.19 measured by LMbench (unit:μs)

	Normal	SELinux	TOMOYO	LIDS
stat	2.64	4.34 (64%)	2.63 (0%)	2.79 (6%)
open/close	3.98	6.45 (62%)	9.33 (134%)	3.96 (0%)
read/write	0.58	1.49 (157%)	0.58 (-1%)	0.58 (-1%)
0Kfile Create	11.76	42.80 (264%)	16.36 (39%)	14.00 (19%)
0Kfile Delete	6.25	11.22 (80%)	9.61 (54%)	6.67 (7%)
10Kfile Create	34.34	69.26 (102%)	37.78 (10%)	35.48 (3%)
10Kfile Delete	16.14	19.28 (19%)	19.02 (18%)	16.90 (5%)

processing time for stat, read/write, and 0K file create are still highest among the three secure OSes.

In TOMOYO Linux, the performance of file creation and deletion of current kernel has greatly deteriorated compared to that of the old kernel. On the other hand, the rate of increase in the processing time for open/close has reduced.

Compared to the previous LIDS kernel, the processing time has increased for many items. However, there is not the item where processing time extremely increases. In addition, the processing time for file creation and deletion is considerably shorter than the corresponding time required for the other two secure OS's.

Detailed evaluation of the overhead in each system call
On the basis of the results of Evaluation 3, we compared old and new kernel to measure its performance in detail, especially in the case of items with respect to which the performance of the old and new kernel differ greatly. Details of Evaluation 4 and evaluations are provided below.
(Evaluation 4-1) File deletion in SELinux (close system call)
(Evaluation 4-2) File creation in TOMOYO Linux (creat system call)
By using the system call information of LSMPMON, we evaluated the processing time required by LSM hooks (μs) for a system call. As in the past evaluation, we performed the evaluation by running LMbench five times.

Table 6 lists the results of Evaluation 4-1 A comparison of the new kernel with the old kernel shows that the processing time of LSM hooks has increased in the latter for many items. However, the processing time for sock_rcv_skb hook has significantly reduced. In the old kernel, this LSM hook has an especially large overhead. In the new kernel, the processing time of LSM hooks has decreased, resulting in the reduction of the overall processing time.

Table 7 lists the results of the Evaluation 4-2. The main overheads in the old kernel are path_mknod and dentry_open, and the main overheads in the new kernel is inode_create. Both inode_create and path_mknod are LSM hooks for acquiring path name. In the case of the old kernel, inode_create can also acquire a relative path, which had used its own implementation of TOMOYO Linux, to acquire the absolute path. In the new kernel, the absolute pathname is obtained from the root directory by path_mknod. Therefore, the overhead of the LSM hook function increases. In addition, dentry_open is an LSM hook that is used to reduce the number of times policy search has to be carried out; however, this function in itself results in a large overhead. The change in the performance of the LSM hooks results in a large overhead in the case of creat system call. We

Table 6. Close system call in defferent version of SELinux kernel (unit:μs)

2.6.30				2.6.19			
hookname	sum	count	ave	hookname	sum	count	ave
file_free	183043.630	1370941	0.133	file_free	166246.612	1591046	0.104
inode_free	2105.578	10458	0.201	inode_free	2380.437	14669	0.162
inode_delete	97.809	973	0.100	inode_delete	62.058	1074	0.058
sock_rcv_skb	989.218	8253	0.120	sock_rcv_skb	11027.765	14583	0.756
sk_free	1617.659	5821	0.278	task_free	3.907	31	0.126
cred_free	10.074	92	0.109				
		average sum	0.942			average sum	1.206

Table 7. Creat system call in different version of TOMOYO Linux kernel (unit:μs)

2.6.30				2.6.19			
hookname	sum	count	ave	hookname	sum	count	ave
inode_permission	127585.395	3588000	0.035	inode_permission	366962.831	8124000	0.045
file_alloc	31367.404	897000	0.035	file_alloc	77799.981	2031000	0.038
inode_create	31240.724	897000	0.035	inode_create	5971299.965	2031000	2.940
inode_alloc	31425.973	897000	0.035	inode_alloc	72487.431	2031000	0.036
inode_init_security	33046.422	897000	0.035	inode_init_security	74019.938	2031000	0.036
d_instantiate	32385.181	898000	0.036	d_instantiate	72418.537	2031000	0.035
path_mknod	12207508.304	897000	13.609	task_free	2.593	8	0.324
dentry_open	22372903.197	897000	24.942	task_kill	0.402	2	0.201
cred_free	0.138	2	0.069				
		average sum	38.830			average sum	3.655

arrive at the following conclusions on the basis of the above-mentioned evaluation results.

(1) In SELinux, there is a decrease in the overhead for file deletion because of a decrease in the rate of increase in the processing time of specific LSM hooks. In addition, it may be said that rate of increase in the processing time for all items except file creation decreased, and the performance improved.

(2) In TOMOYO Linux, the rate of increase in the processing time for the generation and deletion of a file is very large. This is because the function of obtaining the path name that is a unit of access control, from its own implementation for changes the implementation that using LSM hooks. In addition, the rate of increase in the processing time for open/close decreased.

(3) In LIDS, the rate of increase in processing time has increased in general; however, in the case of file generation and the deletion, rate of increase in processing time is the still smallest among the three OS's.

5   Conclusion

The secure OS in Linux is often implemented using an LSM. In this paper, a new version of LSMPMON developed for 2.6.30 is described, and the results of evaluation of three secure OSes is presented. We evaluated the LSM hooks function that is frequently used, especially during file operations. Below, we present the conclusion on the effect of introducing the secure OS introduction on performance, the features of the identification method of resources, and the change in the performance across different versions of each secure OS.

In SELinux, the performance improves in many items. However, the overhead is large in many file operations that involve file creation, etc. The main factor affecting the overhead of file creation is the determination and initialization of the label because it using a label-based method.

The overhead of the file creation and file deletion, for which it is necessary to obtain and delete of the path name, is large because TOMOYO Linux controls it by a path-name-based method. In addition, the overhead of the open/close operation is comparatively large because it is necessary to reference the path name (compare the character string).

The overhead of file creation and file deletion in LIDS is small compared to that in the two other methods because LIDS is an i-node-based method, and it is not necessary to determine a label and obtain of the pass-name. In addition, the overhead in the other file operations is comparatively small.

The following features are known as characteristics of the function of each secure OS: strict and strong security can be realized in SELinux, and a function for automatic learning of the policy is available in TOMOYO Linux.

On the other hand, the performance of these OSes has not been widely discusses. In embedded applications, the focus is on the secure OS, and it is important to evaluate the performance. Further, the effective environments vary because of differences in the resource identification methods.

In this article, we presented the above evaluation for an index in the introduction. In addition, we showed that the LSMPMON could perform an accurate evaluation of the LSM hooks in every system call, analyze the performance of the secure OS, and determine the bottleneck points. Thus, we showed the utility of the LSMPMON.

The source code of the LSMPMON has been published on the LSMPMON project page[9].

Acknowledgments. This research was partially supported by a grant from the Telecommunications Advancement Foundation (TAF).

References

1. Wright, C., Cowan, C., Smalley, S., Morris, J., Kroah-Hartman, G.: Linux Security Modules: General Security Support for the Linux Kernel. In: Proceedings of 11th Annual USENIX Security Symposium, pp. 17–31 (2002)
2. Matsuda, N., Satou, K., Tabata, T., Munetou, S.: Design and Implementation of Performance Evaluation Function of Secure OS Based on LSM. The Institute of Electronics,Information and Communication Engineers Trans. J92-D(7), 963–974 (2009)
3. NSA: Security-Enhanced Linux, http://www.nsa.gov/selinux/
4. Loscocco, P., Smalley, S.: Integrating Flexible Support for Security Policies into the Linux Operating System. In: Proceedings of the FREENIX Track: 2001 USENIX Annual Technical Conference, pp. 29–42 (2001)
5. TOMOYO Linux, http://tomoyo.sourceforge.jp/
6. Harada, T., Handa, T., Itakura, Y.: Design and Implementation of TOMOYO Linux. IPSJ Symposium Series, vol. 2009(13), pp. 101–110 (2009)
7. LIDS, http://www.lids.org/
8. LMbench, http://www.bitmover.com/lmbench/
9. LSM Performance Monitor,
   http://www.swlab.cs.okayama-u.ac.jp/lab/yamauchi/lsmpmon/

Sample Bytes to Protect Important Data from Unintentional Transmission in Advanced Embedded Device

Bo-heung Chung and Jung-nye Kim

Electonics and Telecommunications Research Institute, 138 Gajeongno,
Yuseong-gu, Daejeon, Korea
{bhjung,jnkim}@etri.re.kr

Abstract. Illegal or unintentional file transmission of important data is a sensitive and main security issue in embedded and mobile devices. Within restricted resources such as small memory size and low battery capacity, simple and efficient method is needed to lessen much effort for preventing this illegal activity. Therefore, we discuss a protection technique taking into account these considerations. In our method, sample bytes are extracted from an important file and then it is used to prohibit illegal file transfer and modification. To avoid attacker's easy prediction about the selection position of the sample bytes, it is selected within whole extent of the file by equal distribution and at the random location. To avoid huge increase of the number of the sample bytes, candidate sampling area size of the file is chosen carefully after the analysis of the length and number of files. Also, considering computational overhead to calculate the number and position of the sample bytes to be selected, we propose three types of sampling methods. And we will show the evaluation result of these methods and recommend proper sampling approach to embedded device with low computational power. With the help of this technique, it has advantages that data leakage can be protected and prohibited effectively and the device can be managed securely within low overhead.

Keywords: sample bytes selection, illegal leakage prevention, embedded device security.

1 Introduction

As embedded devices are getting more popular and widely used, they have had more powerful functionalities than before. These advanced embedded devices which are usually called as mobile devices, as the capabilities are being increased, they are not a simple and additional device anymore; they provide more strong computing power to deal with various services together: E-mail, business document processing, banking, and entertainment. And then a user who is using the mobile device often keeps some important information(ex. user's data of contact list and certifications, and so on.) on its internal storage. If the user didn't pay attention to them, these data might have leaked by malicious programs such as virus and worm. Usually the leakage is done through file copying operation from internal to external storage. To solve this problem, many kinds of researches have been done in various areas such as DRM and

T.-h. Kim et al. (Eds.): SecTech/DRBC 2010, CCIS 122, pp. 68–73, 2010.
© Springer-Verlag Berlin Heidelberg 2010

water-marking. But these techniques need not only much computational capabilities but also additional applications to read or write a modified document containing such high-valued information. Therefore, it is required a new approach to handle unintentional leakage without additional application and with a minimum cost.

This paper introduces an effective approach to prohibit illegal outflow and shows how to select a SB(sample bytes) needed to do this job correctly. Our main idea is to detect un-authorized file copy without pre-modification which is done in the DRM or water-marking case. The selected and extracted SB is used for distinguishing itself from other files in the middle of the file copy process. We suggest three kinds of sampling approaches according to how to select the SB and how many they are selected. And we evaluated those methods to find out what is the best way.

In Section 2 we explain other researches to protect or hide important information. In Section 3 we describe the strategies of the proposed methods about considerations to select and the mechanisms. In Section 4 we explain how to evaluate these methods and show the results. Finally, in Section 5 contains some concluding remarks.

2 Backgrounds

Nowadays, the rapid proliferation of mobile devices and mobile networks has prompted the need to offer security for them[7,8]. Such as Personal Digital Assistants(PDAs), mobile phones(Smart Phone), laptops, and tablet personal computers(PCs) are classified as mobile devices. To compare non-mobile devices, it has several special properties include small size memory capability, using battery as a power, and etc[2,3]. In this environment, it must be considered above limitations to develop security functions of mobile device.

There have been studies concerned specifically with security enhancement approaches of mobile device as using information hiding techniques[8,9,10]. These hiding approaches have a pre-modification work doing cryptographic action or inserting hidden markers. The one is well-known for DRM[14] and others are steganography, watermarking and fingerprinting[8,11,12]. But, these methods are required some modifications on original messages to hide and to insert secrete message in it, and needed more computational overheads to do this work. Due to this, additional application is needed to access a file from converted message to original message before using it. Therefore, without the hardware support like special-purpose co-processor chip, these overheads will be a big burden to a mobile device because it is needed an intensive mathematical calculations.

There are also other approaches focused on making and using special bytes stream called a signature or a hash value[2,4,5]. The hash value such as CRC or MD5 is calculated and generated byte stream after scanning whole message or file. With a bit or bytes change of original data, the value must be changed and re-generated and then it has an advantage on detecting update or modification at small amount of variation. But it is not suitable for detection of copy or transfer operation to external device but for catching internal file operation such as re-naming. The signature, sometimes called a detection signature or virus pattern, is subset bytes stream extracted from some part of whole message or file. In this case, after analyzing network packets or virus program, the signature is selected and extracted in some region to uniquely distinguish it from other files or packets in the form of original bytes stream. Without the overheads of crypto-graphical converting or hidden mark creation, we can easily detect illegal copy through bytes comparing between the signature and the bytes stream transferred. With the help of this advantage, it is more suitable way than that of others. As this signature generation is possible for a well-known virus or pattern, it is difficult to use at the case of not knowing any kinds of information about the file in advance. Therefore, a new protection method is required to overcome these issues described above.

3 Protection Method Using SB Selection

In this section, we shall see how these issues are being unveiled. This section covers that how the SBs are extracted and also it will be described that the considerations to get them and the mechanisms to sampling in more detail.

3.1 Main Strategies

Before looking more closely at our approach, it is necessary to consider that we use signature method as a protection technique. But, there are some difficulties using this method as a main idea. The one difficulty is that it is required pre-acquired knowledge on a file. In other words, identifying a file as a virus or worm, the signature can be taken as smaller as possible with many efforts to catch it. Another difficulty is that it is needed content recognition process which identifies important bytes patterns on a file. In more detail, the signature selection can be possible after finding out an important data on a file with computational intensive inspections and much time. Therefore, we take into account a new approach to identify an important file with these overheads. The aim of the new approach is to select a signature as simple as possible without pre-acquired knowledge or content recognition and to correctly identify an important file as much as this signature-based method does. In our approach, we search for candidate SBs and then extract some of them as SBs according to three kinds sampling method.

3.2 Considerations

To select SBs from a file, two considerations must be taken into account in this job. The one is making it difficult about easy prediction of SB's extraction position(EP) in the file. The other is keeping a burden to determine SBs as small as possible. For the first, to avoid simple and easy prediction, the location has to be determined by random sampling. And it should be selected in multiple positions, but the number of the SBs must be minimized as small as possible. In extracting the SB, the length of it carefully be chosen to find it easily among files and to detect through minimum byte comparison. But, the lesser the length of it, the SB's uniqueness tends to be dwindled down. Therefore, as considering this, we decide 24 bytes as the length of the SB and choose the number of SBs from 1 to maximum limit. As this limit depending on our proposed methods, we will discuss at next section.

In the view of another consideration, it is difficult to determine the positions and the numbers of SBs with minimum overhead. Therefore, basically, we divided a file into several SB sampling regions - called window at each region – and select the SB at each window. In this selection method which we call it as a full sampling(FS), it is high possibility that there are too many SBs because they are extracted in every window. To prevent this situation, we select the SB not in the whole window but in some windows. These widows are decided by binomial sampling(BS) and dynamic sampling(DS). As the BS is based on binomial distribution theory[13], there is a run-time mathematical computational overhead. In the DS, SBs are sampled at the peak positions of the binomial distribution curves generated by mathematical function with static sampling table(SST) holding pre-computed values of this function.

3.3 Mechanism for SB Selection

As described before, we use three kinds of SB sampling. Although these three methods are similar as a whole, there is difference in selecting windows where SBs are sampled or extracted. In short, the FS takes SBs in every window and others take them in a few windows of all. Describing overall process of SB selection, it consists of setting window size, choosing the window sampled and random sampling in the window. The size of the window is determined according to the size distributions of files. After the size determined, SBs are taken at random positions in the selected windows. In this process, if duplicated SB is taken, the SB has to be re-extracted at another random position until there is no collision. For this purpose, all extracted SBs are stored on a SB table(SBT). To describe window choosing process more easily, assuming that there are 10 windows in a certain file and we are trying to extract SBs on that file, we describe how to select windows at each methods. To begin with, FS takes all 10 windows. In the case of the BS, as selected windows are determined by calculating mathematical function of binomial distribution, from one to 10 windows are maybe taken. Because many optional parameters affect to the BS, it is very hard to correctly predict the number of windows. Last, DS selects just only one window which has maximum SBs among selected windows in the BS methods. For example, assuming 4 out of 10 windows are selected and there are 2, 5, 4 and 3 SBs at each selected windows, the DS methods takes second window and extracts five SBs. Although the DS is similar to the BS, it is different that only one SB is extracted from one out of selected windows and SST is used for the window selection instead of mathematical computations.

4 Evaluations

We shall show the results of the evaluation of our methods in this section. We evaluated our solution in quantifying the overhead of sampling time at each method described before. After analysis based on security policy, 43 Files which contain important information were selected among many files in mobile devices. During the evaluation, we measure the computational overhead changing the window size from 4K bytes to 4M bytes. All of our measurements were made on a 2.67 GHz Intel PC with 3GB RAM, running Windows XP.

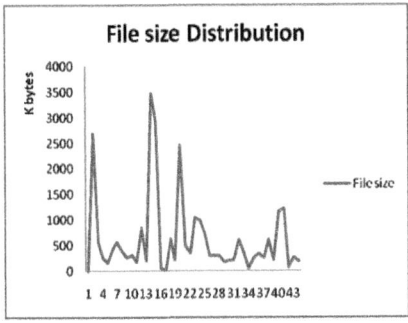 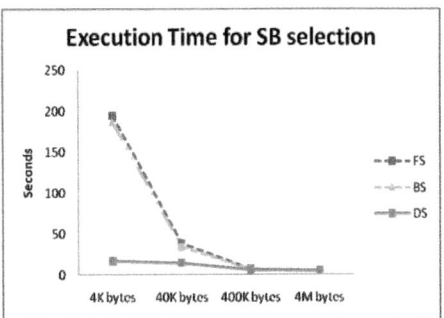

Fig. 1. File size distributions and execution times for SB selection

For evaluation, size distribution value of the files must be gathered in advance and then do tests about overheads at each method. There are two results of file size distributions and execution times in the Fig. 1. According to these distributions, four values of the window size are chosen from 4K bytes to 4M bytes. The gap of those values is set to be as 10 times bigger than the previous one start from 4K bytes. As shown in Fig. 1., FS and BS take much time to get SBs that that of the DS at small window size but they take similar time as the DS does at the large window size. The smaller case we choose, the correctness will be higher to identify important file during the file transfer to external but the number of SBs will be increased. And, FS or BS is efficient in the small case and DS is done well at the large case. As the cost sharply being increased at 40K, the determination of appropriate window size is recommended selecting it from 40K to 400K.

5 Conclusions

The SB sampling was proposed to prevent unintentional data leakage in this paper. To get SBs from important files, three types of methods were introduced according to their selection strategies, and we showed the mechanisms how they extract the SBs as changes of the window size and the evaluation results. According to this work, we found that getting proper SBs is tightly influenced to the window size and the size must be fixed after analysis of file length distributions. Also, we found that recommended window size is one of the values which are in between average file length and one tenth of it. After the window size had been decided in this range, the mechanism to choose the SB was determined one of FS, BS and DS according to computational power of the device. Through these mechanisms and simple bytes comparing using SB, the transferring block which has sensitive information will be efficiently blocked. With the help the simplicity of the method and minimized computational overhead for SB selection, it is more suitable prevention method for embedded device than others. Therefore, we are planning on further research about minimum SB sampling method, dynamic change method of the window size in run-time. And it will be also studied to ensure high correctness with very small SBs.

Acknowledgment

This work was supported by the IT R&D program of MKE/KEIT [10035708, The development of CPS (Cyber-Physical Systems) core technologies for high confidential autonomic control software].

References

1. Smith, T.F., Waterman, M.S.: Identification of Common Molecular Subsequences. J. Mol. Biol. 147, 195–197 (1981)
2. Shi, Z., Ji, Z., Hu, M.: A Novel Distributed Intrusion Detection Model Based on Mobile Agent. In: ACM InfoSecu04, pp. 155–159 (2006)
3. Yong-guang, Z., Wenke, L., Yi-an, H.: Intrusion Detection Technique for Mobile Wireless Networks. In: ACM MONET, pp. 545–556 (2003)
4. Deepak, V.: An Efficient Signature Representation and Matching Method for Mobile Devices. In: Proceedings of the 2nd Annual International Workshop on Wireless Internet, vol. 220 (2006)
5. Geetha, R., Delbert, H.: A P2P Intrusion Detection System based on Mobile Agents. In: ACM ACME 2004, pp. 185–195 (2004)
6. National Center for Biotechnology Information, http://www.ncbi.nlm.nih.gov
7. Yogesh Prem, S., Hannes, T.: Protecting Mobile Devices from TCP Flooding Attacks. In: ACM mobiArch 2006, pp. 63–68 (2006)
8. Benjamin, H.: Mobile Device Security. In: ACM InfoSecCD Conference 2004, pp. 99–101 (2004)
9. Ingemar, J., Ton, K., Georg, P., Mathias, S.: Information Transmission and Steganography. In: Barni, M., Cox, I., Kalker, T., Kim, H.-J. (eds.) IWDW 2005. LNCS, vol. 3710, pp. 15–29. Springer, Heidelberg (2005)
10. David, C., Sebastian, H., Pasquale, M.: Quantitative Analysis of the Leakage of Confidential Data. Electronic Notes in Theoretical Computer Science 59(3) (2003)
11. Christian, C.: An Information-Theoretic Model for Steganography. In: Aucsmith, D. (ed.) IH 1998. LNCS, vol. 1525, pp. 306–318. Springer, Heidelberg (1998)
12. Dan, B., James, S.: Collusion-Secure Fingerprinting for Digital Data. IEEE Transactions on Information Theory 44(5) (September 1998)
13. Binomial Distribution, http://en.wikipedia.org/wiki/Binomial_distribution
14. Digital Rights Management, http://en.wikipedia.org/wiki/Digital_rights_management

Secure OSGi Platform against Service Injection

Intae Kim[1], Keewook Rim[2], and Junghyun Lee[1]

[1] Department of Computer Science and Information Technology, Inha University, 253
Yonghyun-dong, Nam-gu, Incheon 402-751, Republic of Korea
[2] Department of Computer and Information Science, Sunmoon University,
Asan-si, Chungnam, 336-708, Republic of Korea
inking007@gmail.com, rim@sunmoon.ac.kr, jhlee@inha.ac.kr

Abstract. OSGi platform provides Java-based open standard programming interface that enables communication and control among devices at home. Service-oriented, component based software systems built using OSGi are extensible and adaptable but they entail new types of security concerns. Security concerns in OSGi platforms can be divided into two basic categories: vulnerabilities in Java cross-platform (or multi-platform) technology and vulnerabilities in the OSGi framework. This paper identifies a new OSGi platform-specific security vulnerability called a service injection attack and proposes two mechanisms of protection against this newly identified security risk in the OSGi framework.

Keywords: Service injection, OSGi, Security.

1 Introduction

In today's dynamic service deployment environment, distributing large, fully-integrated software packages is diminishing. Applications or components provided by third parties are dynamically and remotely loaded to be deployed into a system [1]. The OSGi [2] framework that resolves code dependencies at run time in addition to installing and updating components without requiring a reboot plays an important role in such a runtime extensible component distribution and management environment.

Service-oriented, component based software systems built using OSGi are extensible and adaptable but they entail new types of security concerns. Several research efforts have been devoted security in service-oriented programming environment [3-5]. Security concerns in OSGi platforms can be divided into two basic categories: vulnerabilities in Java cross-platform (or multi-platform) technology and vulnerabilities in the OSGi framework. Examples of security vulnerabilities in Java's cross-platform execution environments are a denial-of-service attack that attempts to make a computer resource (CPU and memory) unavailable to its intended users and a data modification attack that involves reordering of static variables as well as padding between them. To defend against such attacks, a mechanism that isolates and manages Java resources per process is used [6-9].

A recent work in [10] identified 25 security vulnerabilities by analyzing existing open source OSGi platforms and suggested safeguards against 17 OSGi-specific security

T.-h. Kim et al. (Eds.): SecTech/DRBC 2010, CCIS 122, pp. 74–83, 2010.
© Springer-Verlag Berlin Heidelberg 2010

vulnerabilities. In [11], the use of digital signatures (i.e., digitally signing the bundles and verifying the signature) was proposed to provide the integrity of vulnerable components. This paper identifies a new OSGi platform-specific security vulnerability called a "service injection attack" that was not addressed in [10]. The service injection attack can arise in the course of component updates. The paper proposes two mechanisms of protection against this newly identified security risk in the OSGi framework.

The rest of this paper is organized as follows. Section 2 describes the principal structure of OSGi platforms and their security vulnerabilities. Section 3 identifies new security vulnerability in OSGi that has not been discussed so far and proposes mechanisms for preventing this attack. In Section 4, the proposed mechanisms are implemented using Knopflerfish that is an open source OSGi service platform [12], and they are compared with other open source OSGi implementations. Finally, conclusions are given in Section 5.

2 Security Vulnerabilities in OSGi Platforms

This section describes the principles of modularity and service-orientation in the OSGi framework and presents security vulnerabilities in OSGi platforms that have previously been identified.

2.1 OSGi Service Platform

The OSGi platform is conceptually divided into module layer, lifecycle layer and service layer. The module layer defines the component called bundle, which enable to share and restrict among components. The lifecycle layer defines how bundles are dynamically installed and managed. The service layer registers service through a java interface and allows searching by LDAP [15]. The service in OSGi platform is composed of interface and service implementation. OSGi Bundles are Java Archive files [16] including meta-data, and resources such as Java classes, data files and native libraries. Modularity and dependency among bundles is represented using the meta-file, following headers information can be set up for sharing of bundles and access restriction.

- `Export-Package`: Defined to share their packages with other bundles.
- `Import-Package`: Defined to use the packages shared from other bundles.

A bundle activator is a Java class that implements the org.osgi.framework.Bundle Activator interface and is instantiated when the bundle is started. The activator class is the bundle's hook to the lifecycle layer for management. The bundle activator is specified in the metadata in the bundle's manifest file. In a bundle's lifecycle, the bundle state is transferred from RESOLVED to STARTING when the BundleActivator.start method is called. The bundle state is changed to ACTIVE if the bundle is activated according to its activation policy (i.e., the Bundle Activator start method has been called and returned). The bundle is stopped (i.e., it goes to the STOP state) when the BundleActivator.stop method is called.

2.2 Security in OSGi Platform

In [10], various security vulnerabilities that can occur in existing open source OSGi platforms were identified and their countermeasures were suggested. Table 1 shows attacks that can be performed through malicious OSGi bundles.

Table 1. Vunerabilites and countermeasueres in OSGi

Layer	Security Attacks	Countermeasures
1	Disrupting normal bundle installation by redundantly importing packages	Prohibit redundant imports
2	Making disk space full by installing a large-sized bundle.	Limit the size of a bundle to be downloaded
3	Making the bundle management utilities inoperable by placing an infinite loop (the repetition statement that never terminates) in the start method of the activator class when the bundle is started	Apply a threads implementation to bundle management utility executions.
4	Disrupting normal service registration by registering too many services	Limit the possible number of service registrations per bundle

3 Service Injection Attack and Proposed Protection Mechanisms

3.1 Service Injection

The OSGi platform supports bundle updates without service interruptions. This is one of the main advantages of OSGi but malicious services can be injected in such an environment. This work assumes that attackers do not have bundle management authority to perform privileged administrative operations — i.e., they cannot meddle with the lifecycle of other bundles. Attacks made by manipulating the lifecycle of other bundles can be prevented through Java permissions. The service injection attack addressed in this paper occurs even if malicious bundles do not have bundle management authority.

Fig. 1 illustrates how a service injection attack occurs. In Fig 1-a, a normal service call sequence before bundle updates is shown. Bundle A that is a normal bundle registers A-S, a normal service, in the service registry, and another bundle C calls the A-S service for use. Bundle M that is a malicious bundle registers M-S, a malicious service, to replace the normal A-S service.

In Fig. 1-b, a normal service has been substituted by a malicious service after bundle updates. An update request was made to install a new version of bundle A. For bundle updates, the A-S service is stopped. The A-S service is re-registered after replacing the JAR file of the previous version of bundle A with the JAR file of a new version. Service requesters that called the A-S service before updates adapt to changes in the service registry resulting from updates of bundle A by retrieving again `Ser-viceReference` objects from the service registry. Here, the service that is eventually bound to service requesters is M-S registered by bundle M, not A-S.

As shown in Fig. 1, an attack that replaces a normal service by a malicious service can occur during bundle updates. This attack is called a "service injection attack." This paper proposes two mechanisms to defend against this attack.

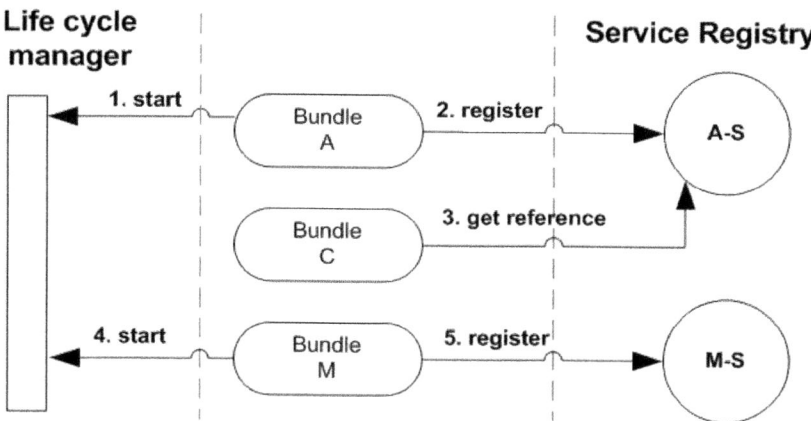

(a)   Call sequence before updating bundle

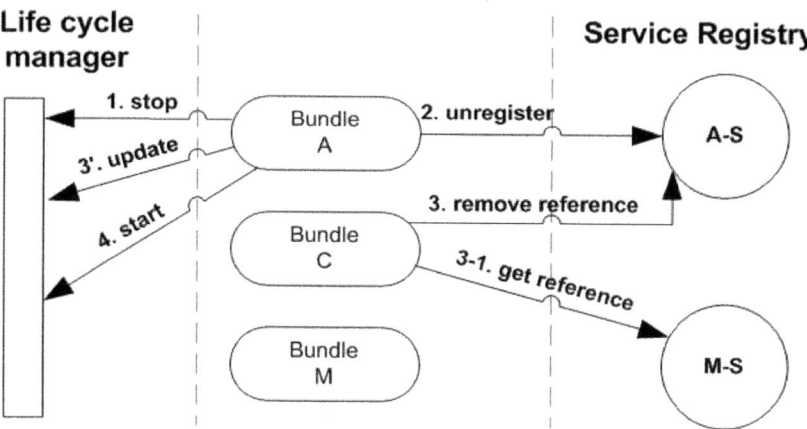

(b)   Call sequence after updating bundle

Fig. 1. Service injection in OSGi

3.2 Protection of Signed Bundles

The previous work in [11] enforces bundle integrity by signing bundles and checking the validity of the signature. This section proposes an enhanced service registration and retrieval mechanism that can protect signed bundles against the service injection attack.

In OSGi, the following API is defined in the bundle context (`BundleContext` class) to register services in the service registry.

```
registerService(Service Name, Service Object, Filter);
```

In the service registration process, the class type of the specified service object that is the second parameter of the `registerService` method (represented as `java.lang.Object` service) is examined. If the examined class type is already in the service registry (i.e., there are previously registered services of that type), the service is added under that class type. Otherwise, the service is registered under a newly created class type.

To defend against the service injection attack, the service registration process is modified as follows:

1) When installing digitally signed bundles, the validity of the signature of bundles is checked to provide bundle integrity.
2) If the validity check is ok, the bundle manager adds the signature information to the bundle context (the signature of a bundle and related resources are stored).
3) When the bundle requests for a service registration, the bundle's signature information is also registered (i.e., the signature information becomes service properties that are used by the filter to select the registered services).

In order to distinguish normal services from services provided by malicious bundles, the proposed mechanism includes the bundle's signature information in service registrations. The existing API is extended to exploit the added signature information. In OSGi, the following APIs are currently used to get a ServiceReference object (or an array of `ServiceReference` objects).

```
public ServiceReference getServiceReference( String
clazz )

public ServiceReference[] getServiceReferences( String
clazz, String filter)
```

- `getServiceReference` method: Among `ServiceReference` objects that implement and are registered under the specified class, return the reference (service) with the highest priority.
- `getServiceReferences` method: Among `ServiceReference` objects that implement and are registered under the specified class, return an array of `ServiceReference` objects that match the filter (the filter is placed in the second parameter of this method).

The first API method presented above is extended to contain a new parameter for a filter that is used to select services registered by signed bundles, as shown below. This filter is different from the filter in the `getServiceReferences` method, the second API method shown above. Service properties that are filtered out by the filter newly added in the proposed mechanism are only those associated with digital signatures.

3.3   Protection of Unsigned Bundles

As presented in the previous section, signed bundles are protected against service injection attacks by exploiting bundle signature information in service registrations and retrievals. In the real world, not all OSGi bundles are digitally signed, and thus a protection mechanism for bundles that are not signed is also needed. This section presents an enhanced bundle update mechanism that protects unsigned bundles against service injection attacks.

The existing bundle update mechanism operates as follows:

1) If the current bundle state is ACTIVE, the bundle should be stopped.
2) Download a new version of the bundle by referring to the Bundle-UpdateLocation (an URL) specified in the metadata.
3) Verify the metadata of the downloaded bundle. Replace the existing bundle's JAR file with the JAR file of a new version.
4) Remove the classes loaded by the previous version of the bundle.
5) The updated bundle is being started if the bundle state before updates was ACTIVE

In the existing bundle update process, a malicious service is injected when the bundle stops. The bundle is stopped when the `BundleActivator.stop` method is called. In general, the implemented `BundleActivator.stop` method invokes the unregister method of the `ServiceRegistration` class to remove a registered service from the service registry. A malicious service with the next highest priority waits for the moment when a normal service is removed from the registry. If a caller (service requester) that uses a normal service invokes the `getServiceReference` method under these circumstances, it binds with the service provider of the malicious service. To defend against such malicious service injections, the proposed mechanism adds a new bundle state that is UPDATING to the bundle lifecycle. In Fig. 2, proposed state transition of bundle is depicted comparing the existing mechanism.

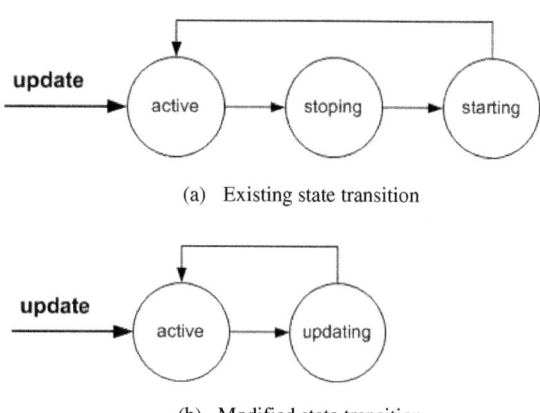

(a)   Existing state transition

(b)   Modified state transition

Fig. 2. State transition when updating bundle

While updating the bundle, the state of the bundle is UPDATING. In the UPDAT-
ING state, services are normally provided so there is no change from the perspective of
service requesters. When the JAR file of a new bundle version is downloaded and
installed, the information about the previous version of the bundle along with the priority information of the services registered by the previous version of the bundle is added
to the bundle context. When the state of the newly installed bundle is changed to AC-
TIVE, services are registered based on the stored service priority information. Once the
state of the updated bundle becomes ACTIVE, the state of the previous version of the
bundle is changed to STOP. That is, the previous version of the bundle continues to
provide its services until the update for a new version is entirely completed. In this
way, the proposed mechanism can prevent malicious services from being injected
during bundle updates. The modified bundle lifecycle is depicted in Fig. 3.

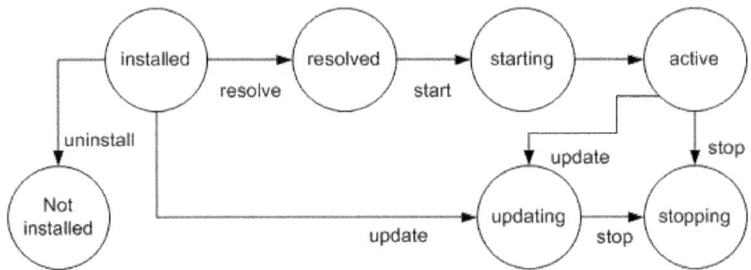

Fig. 3. Lifecycle of bundle included UPDATING state

4   Experiments

The proposed protection mechanisms against the service injection attack were implemented by modifying Knopflerfish, an open source OSGi implementation. The implementation of the protection mechanism for signed bundles utilizes SF-Jarsigner
that supports the publication of signed bundles: signature and loading onto a public
repository [11].

SF-Jarsinger checks the validity of the signature of bundles according to the steps
presented below:

1) Verify the order of resources in the signed JAR file.
2) Verify the validity of the signature block file.
3) Verify the validity of the signature file.
4) Verify the validity of the meta-data content

If the signature block file, a digest value in the manifest file and a digest value in the
signature file that are examined in the validation of bundle signatures change whenever the bundle is updated, it is not worth checking their validity. This paper assumes
that the authentication information of the signer who signs the bundle is issued by a
certification authority (CA) and it remains unique and identical after bundle updates.
Based on this assumption, the digital signature is used to authenticate the signer —
i.e., it is possible to verify that a service is registered by a bundle that is signed by the
original bundle publisher.

For implementation of the proposed mechanisms, the `BundleImpl` class that implements the `Bundle` interface in Knopflerfish is modified to add the UPDATING state to the bundle lifecycle. In the conventional bundle update process, the current version of the bundle is sopped, the bundle is updated, and the updated version is restarted. In the enhanced update mechanism proposed in this paper, the updated bundle is re-started and then the previous version of the bundle is stopped. To give service priorities to the service registry in which `ArrayList` and `HashMap` are used to assemble various OSGi services, new "priority" property is added to the `ServiceRegistrationImpl` class. The `Collection.sort` function is used to sort the assembled services.

To compare with the implemented mechanisms, existing open source OSGi implementations, Equinox [13], Felix [14] and Knopflerfish, are evaluated in terms of their resilience against service injection attacks during bundle updates. For experiments, the following 4 bundles are implemented.

— Normal Bundle: A bundle that provides only the service interface.
— NormalImpl Bundle: This bundle has service implementations and registers normal services in the service registry. It returns the "good" message when its services are called.
— MaliciousImpl Bundle: This bundle has service implementations and registers malicious services. It returns the "malicious" message when its services are invoked.
— Target Bundle: This bundle calls services for use. It creates threads in the start method of the Activator class to call services periodically.

The order of bundle installation is Normal, NormalImpl, MaliciousImpl, and Target. The execution order is NormalImpl, MaliciousImpl, and Target. When all bundles are in the ACTIVE state, a request for the NormalImpl bundle update is made. Messages outputted by services that the Target bundle calls after bundle updates are examined to determine whether or not existing open source OSGi implementations can defend against the service injection attack. In Table 2, the proposed mechanisms for preventing the service injection attack are compared with existing open source OSGi implementations.

Table 2. Evaluation againt existing open source OSGi implementations

Platform type	Result
Equinox 3.6	Target bundle calls malicious service
Felix 2.05	Target bundle calls malicious service
Knoflerfish 3.0	Target bundle calls malicious service
Proposed mechanism	Target bundle calls normal service

As shown in Table 2, malicious service injections occur during bundle updates in existing open source OSGi platforms. This security vulnerability was not studied in previous works. Table 3 lists the characteristics of this newly identified security threat.

Table 3. Characterization of vunlerability

item	value
Subject	Service Injection
Entity	Malicious Bundle
Location	Management on Bundle's Life cycle
Target	Service of updating bundle
Temporal point	Updating bundle

5 Conclusion

This paper identifies a security threat in the OSGi framework associated with malicious service injections during bundle updates and proposes two mechanisms to defend against this threat. The first protection mechanism distinguishes normal services from malicious services using the bundle signature information added in service registrations. The other mechanism enhances the conventional bundle update process by adding the UPDATING state to the bundle lifecycle. The proposed mechanisms are evaluated in comparison with existing open source OSGi platforms. The experiment results show that the proposed mechanisms are more resilient against service injection attacks.

Acknowledgments

This research was supported by the MKE (The Ministry of Knowledge Economy), Korea, under the ITRC(Information Technology Research Center) Support program supervised by the NIPA(National IT industry Promotion Agency) (NIPA-2010-C1090-1031-0004).

References

1. Royon, Y., Frénot, S.: Multiservice home gateways: business model, execution environment, management infrastructure. IEEE Communications Magazine 45(10), 122–128 (2007)
2. OSGi Alliance. OSGi service platform, core specification release 4.2. release 03 (2010)
3. Binder, W.: Secure and Reliable Java-Based Middleware Challenges and Solutions. In: 1st International Conference on Availability, Reliability and Security. ARES, pp. 662–669. IEEE Computer Society, Washington (2006)
4. Parrend, P., Frenot, S.: Classification of component vulnerabilities in Java service oriented programming platforms. In: Chaudron, M.R.V., Ren, X.-M., Reussner, R. (eds.) CBSE 2008. LNCS, vol. 5282, pp. 80–96. Springer, Heidelberg (2008)
5. Lowis, L., Accorsi, R.: On a classification approach for SOA vulnerabilities. In: Proc. IEEE Workshop on Security Aspects of Process and Services Eng (SAPSE). IEEE Computer Press, Los Alamitos (2009)

6. Czajkowski, G., Daynès, L.: Multitasking without compromise: a virtual machine evolution. In: Proceedings of the Object Oriented Programming, Systems, Languages, and Applications Conference, Tampa Bay, USA, pp. 125–138. ACM, New York (2001)
7. Geoffray, N., Thomas, G., Folliot, B., Clement, C.: Towards a new Isolation Abstraction for OSGi. In: Engeland, M., Spinczyk, O. (eds.) The 1st Workshop on Isolation and Integration in Embedded Systems, IIES 2008, pp. 41–45. ACM, New York (2008)
8. Gama, K., Donsez, D.: Towards Dynamic Component Isolation in a Service Oriented Platform. In: Lewis, G.A., Poernomo, I., Hofmeister, C. (eds.) CBSE 2009. LNCS, vol. 5582, pp. 104–120. Springer, Heidelberg (2009)
9. Geoffray, N., Thomas, G., Muller, G., Parrend, P., Frenot, S., Folliot, B.: I-JVM: a Java Virtual Machine for Component Isolation in OSGi. Research Report RR-6801, INRIA (2009)
10. Parrend, P., Frénot, S.: Security benchmarks of OSGi platforms: toward hardened OSGi. Software: Practice and Experience 39(5), 471–499 (2009)
11. Parrend, P., Frenot, S.: Supporting the secure deployment of OSGi Bundles. In: First IEEE WoWMoM Workshop on Adaptive and Dependable Mission and Business Critical Mobile Systems, Helsinki, Finland (2007)
12. Knopflerfish OSGi - Open Source OSGi service platform, http://knopflerfish.org/
13. Equinox, http://www.eclipse.org/equinox
14. Apache felix, http://felix.apache.org/site/index.html
15. Howes, T.: The String Representation of LDAP Search Filters. IETF RFC, Network Working Group, Request for Comments: 2254 (1997)
16. Sun Microsystems Inc., JAR file specification. Sun Java Specifications (2003), http://java.sun.com/j2se/1.5.0/docs/guide/jar/jar.html

A Mechanism That Bounds Execution Performance for Process Group for Mitigating CPU Abuse

Toshihiro Yamauchi, Takayuki Hara, and Hideo Taniguchi

Graduate School of Natural Science and Technology, Okayama University,
3-1-1 Tsushima-naka, Kita-ku, Okayama, 700-8530 Japan
{yamauchi,tani}@cs.okayama-u.ac.jp, hara@swlab.cs.okayama-u.ac.jp

Abstract. Secure OS has been the focus of several studies. However, CPU resources, which are important resources for executing a program, are not the object of access control. For preventing the abuse of CPU resources, we had earlier proposed a new type of execution resource that controls the maximum CPU usage [5,6]. The previously proposed mechanism can control only one process at a time. Because most services involve multiple processes, the mechanism should control all the processes in each service. In this paper, we propose an improved mechanism that helps to achieve a bound on the execution performance of a process group, in order to limit unnecessary processor usage. We report the results of an evaluation of our proposed mechanism.

Keywords: Process scheduling, operating system, anti-DoS technique, execution resource.

1 Introduction

The number of computers connected to network has increased with the widespread use of the Internet. In addition, the number of reports of software vulnerabilities has been increasing every year. This increase in the number of incidents of software vulnerability can be attributed to the widespread use of automated attack tools and the increasing number of attacks against systems connected to the Internet [1]. Therefore, various defense mechanisms against such attacks have been studied extensively, and these studies have gained a lot of attention.

Various defense mechanisms include firewalls, an Intrusion Detection System (IDS) [2]; buffer overflow protection and access control mechanisms such as Mandatory Access Control (MAC) and Role Based Access Control (RBAC) [3]; and secure OS are examples of such defense mechanisms.

The secure OS [4] has been the focus of several studies. In particular, Security-Enhanced Linux (SELinux) has become of major interest. Even if the authority is taken, secure OS makes the range of the influence a minimum. However, the CPU resource, which is an important resource for executing a program, is not the object of the access control. As a result, such OSes cannot control the CPU

T.-h. Kim et al. (Eds.): SecTech/DRBC 2010, CCIS 122, pp. 84–93, 2010.

usage ratio. For example, a secure OS cannot prevent attackers from carrying out DoS attacks, which affect the CPU resources. In general, the OSes can only limit the maximum CPU time for each process and not the proportion of CPU time allocated to the processes.

In an earlier study, we proposed a new type of execution resource that controls the maximum CPU usage such that the abuse of CPU resources can be prevented [5,6]. In order to prevent the abuse of the CPU resources, we propose an execution resource that can limit the upper bound of CPU usage. The previously proposed mechanism can control only one process at a time. Because, most of services involve multiple processes, the mechanism should control all the processes involved in each service. In this paper, we propose an improved mechanism for achieving a bound on execution performance of a process group, in order to limit unnecessary processor use. The proposed mechanism is based on a previously proposed mechanism. The proposed mechanism introduces execution tree which deploy the upper bound of execution resource for the nodes of execution tree.

2   Execution Resource

In this section, we explain the concept of execution resource on the basis of the presentation in previous papers [5,6].

2.1   Overview

A process may be described as a unit of program execution in an existing OS, and it has a degree of CPU usage. For example, a priority is associated with each process in UNIX. We have separated the degree of CPU usage from a process. The degree of CPU usage has been named execution resource. Therefore, only the execution resource involves the degree of CPU usage, and a process does not have a degree of CPU usage. Prior to the introduction of the execution resources, processes are listed on a linked list on the basis of their priority. After the introduction of the execution resources, it is these execution resources that are maintained on the linked list on the basis of their priority. Processes are then linked to executions. A process can be executed by linking it to an execution.

The execution manager points to an execution with the highest degree of CPU usage. All processes need to be linked to executions to be assigned a CPU time. The execution manager selects a process from the scheduling queues. When the state of a process is READY, it is linked to the execution with the highest priority. The amount of CPU time that is assigned to a process is proportional to the total amount of CPU usage time required for the executions linked to the process.

2.2   Types of Execution Resources

There are two types of execution resources. One is execution with performance and the other is execution with priority.

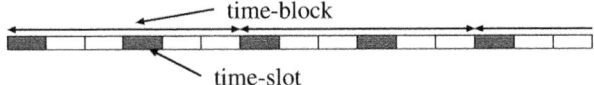

Fig. 1. Time slots and a time block

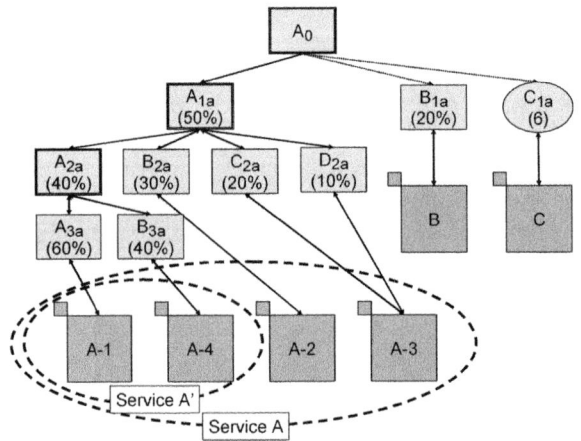

Fig. 2. Relationships between a process group and executions

Execution with performance. Execution with performance includes a degree of CPU usage that indicates the proportion of bare processor performance. The bare processor performance can be defined as 100%. When a process is linked to an execution with n% performance, the assigned CPU time is n% of the bare processor performance. We named a unit of CPU usage as a "time slot." We termed a group of time slots as a "time block." Fig. 1 shows the relation between time slots and a time block. An execution in which the degree of CPU usage is n% is assigned n% of the time slots in a time block.

Execution with priority. Execution with priority includes the degree of performance that indicates the priority. The execution manager assigns the execution with priority that has the highest priority to the processor. However, execution with performance takes precedence over execution with priority because the former is guaranteed an assigned CPU time.

2.3   Hierarchical Execution Tree

The structure of a process group is represented as a tree structure of executions because the relation between a process group and its processes is represented as a parent and a child. Fig. 2 shows the relationships between a process group and executions. The node of an execution tree is called "directory execution" and it

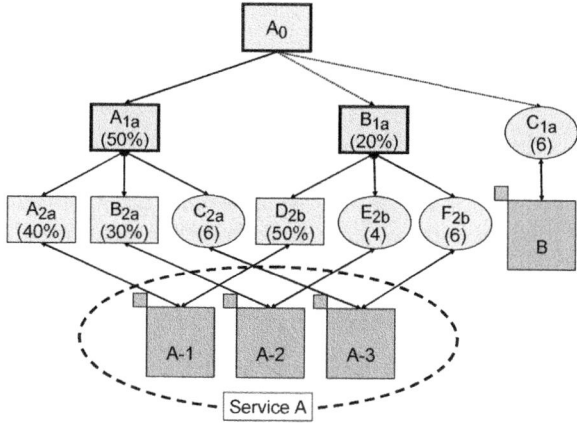

Fig. 3. Two process group executions

represents the degree of CPU usage for a process group. A leaf is called "leaf execution"; every leaf execution is linked to a process.

The total assigned CPU time for leaf executions equals the assigned CPU time for the parent directory execution. The degree of CPU usage for leaf executions indicates the priority or a ratio (%) to assigned CPU time of parent directory execution. In the leaf execution, the ratio corresponds to the point where the parent directory execution is defined as 100%. The depth of an execution tree is greater than one. As a result, it is possible to create a process group within another process group.

Fig. 3 shows a case where more than one execution is linked to a process group. When the second execution (B_{1a}) is linked to a process group, leaf executions (D_{2b}, E_{2b}, F_{2b}) have to be created and linked to each process (A, B, C) in the process group. As a result, each process within the process group is linked to two leaf executions.

2.4   Operation Interface of Execution Resource

We designed 8 operation interfaces for the execution resource for constructing an execution tree and controlling a program execution. Table 1 shows the interfaces.

3   Execution Resource with Upper Bound

3.1   Rate-Limiting Mechanism Based on the Use of Execution Resources

In existing OSes, whose operation is based on the time-sharing technique, the CPU time used by a process according to its priority does not have an upper bound. Therefore, the allocation of CPU time to other services is affected when

Table 1. Operation Interfaces of the execution resource

Form	Contents of operation
creat_execution (mips)	Create the execution specified by mips and return the execution identifier execid. When mips is between 1 and 100 it signifies the performance regulation execution degree (as a percentage with the performance of the processor itself taken to be 100 percent), when it is 0 or negative is signifies the priority of the execution degree (the absolute value is the process priority).
delete_execution (execid)	Delete the execution execid.
attach_execution (execid, pid)	Associate the execution execid and the process pid.
detach_execution (execid, pid)	Remove the association between execution execid and process pid.
wait_execution (pid, chan)	Forbid the assignment of processor [time] to process pid and its associated execution[s]; this puts the process in the WAIT state.
wakeup_execution (pid, chan)	Make it possible to assign CPU time to the process pid and its associated executions; this puts the process in the READY state.
dispatch(pid)	Run process pid.
control_execution (execid, mips)	Change the execution degree of execid to mips. mips is interpreted as in creat_execution.

two or more programs that demand infinite CPU time run simultaneously. In this case, the performance of the service deteriorates significantly.

To prevent the abuse of the CPU resources, we propose an execution resource that helps to achieve an upper bound for the CPU usage ratio. In this execution resource, the CPU time is allocated according to the priority until the usage reaches a specified ratio in a time slice. When it reaches the specified ratio, the state of the currently running process is changed to a WAIT state until the current time slice expires. Even if a process that is linked to an execution for which the CPU usage is limited by an upper bound suffers a malicious attack, the execution system can prevent the program from using excessive CPU time. Moreover, the execution resource can be grouped with a user or a service. Therefore, the CPU usage ratio of a user or a service can be specified. As a result, the impact of a DoS attack can be controlled within the process group even if a new child execution is created, because the execution belongs to the same group.

As described in a previous paper [5,6], we can guarantee that the important processes will be carried out effectively by using the execution resources with a good performance.

3.2   Execution Resource with Upper Bound for Process Group

In the previous mechanism, the execution resource with an upper bound was a leaf execution. Thus, the previous mechanism could be used only to control a process. We introduce directory execution as an execution resource with an

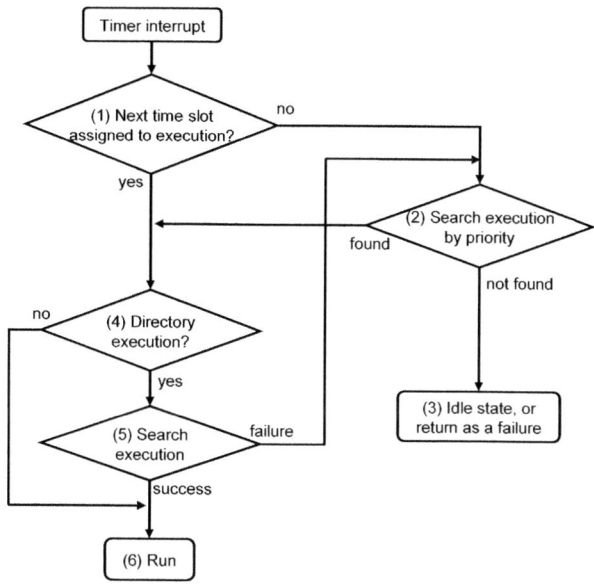

Fig. 4. Process flow of the process scheduler

upper bound. In order to do so, the process scheduler was changed for the control of an execution resource with upper bound of directory execution.

The process flow of the new process scheduler is depicted in Fig. 4 and Fig. 5. Fig. 4 shows the process flow of the process scheduler. The search performed by the process scheduler for the execution resource has the highest priority. If directory execution is selected in step (4) of the process, (Fig. 4), the process scheduler searches the leaf executions of the directory execution. Fig. 5 shows the process flow of the process scheduler when the directory execution is the execution resource with an upper bound. If a leaf execution resource is assigned a CPU time slot, the process illustrated in Fig. 5 is successfully completed.

4   Evaluation

We investigated whether the proposed method can control upper bound of the CPU resources for the services. We performed a basic evaluation and an evaluation for a case involving an attack.

4.1   Basic Evaluation

An execution tree was constructed before the evaluation. This execution tree included three process groups (services A, B, and C). Each process group involved three processes. Table 2 shows the performance and priority of execution resource of each process group in the execution tree. The execution resource

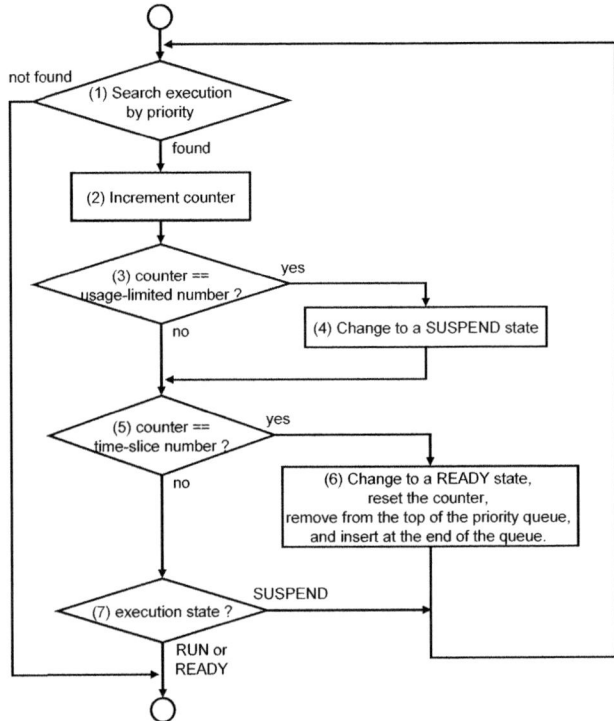

Fig. 5. Process flow when the directory execution with an upper bound is found

(directory execution) of service A was given priority. The execution resources (directory executions) of service B and C were limited by an upper bound. The upper bounds of these execution resources were varied in this evaluation.

Fig. 6 shows the results of the basic evaluation. These results indicate that our proposed mechanism can control each process group according to the upper bound and that our proposed mechanism effectively limits the upper bound for process groups.

4.2 Evaluation for a Case Involving an Attack

We evaluated the processing time of a normal service A (SA) and an attack service B (SB). SB tries to obtain as much CPU time as possible. In this evaluation, SB was attached to the directory execution with an upper bound. Fig. 7 shows the behavior of the processing time as the number of processes in SB changes. The processing time of each service is plotted on the y-axis, and the number of processes in SB is plotted on the x-axis. The processing time of SA is constant because the upper bound of SB is restricted by the directory execution with an upper bound.

Table 2. Degree of execution resource in the basic evaluation

	Service A	Service B	Service C
case	exec 1	exec 2	exec 3
1	6	6, MAX 100%	6, MAX 100%
2	6	6, MAX 100%	6, MAX 75%
3	6	6, MAX 100%	6, MAX 50%
4	6	6, MAX 100%	6, MAX 25%
5	6	6, MAX 50%	6, MAX 50%
6	6	6, MAX 50%	6, MAX 25%

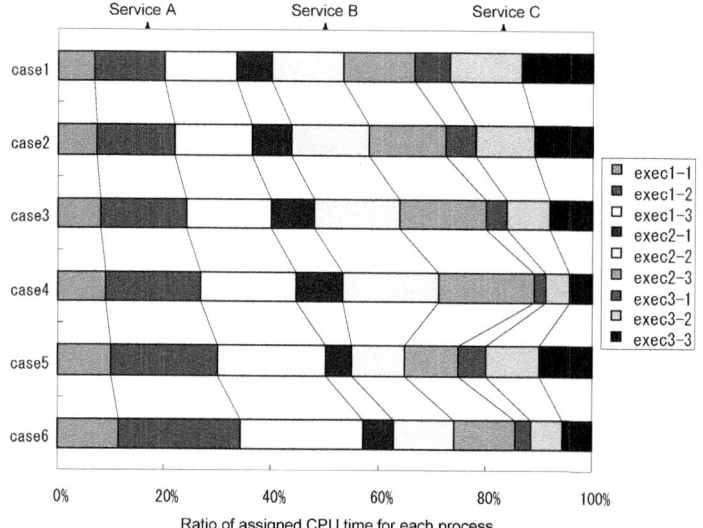

Fig. 6. Results of the basic evaluation

Fig. 8 shows the processing time of each service when the upper bound of the execution resource attached to SB is changed. The upper bound was increased from 25% to 100%. As the proposed mechanism restricted the deterioration in the performance of SB, the processing time of SA decreased. These results show that the proposed mechanism can restrict CPU abuse caused by a malicious service.

5 Related Work

Most defense techniques against Internet-originated DoS attacks have targeted the transport and network layers of the TCP/IP protocol stack [7]. Our research focuses on the access control mechanism of and the rate limiting technique for CPU resources.

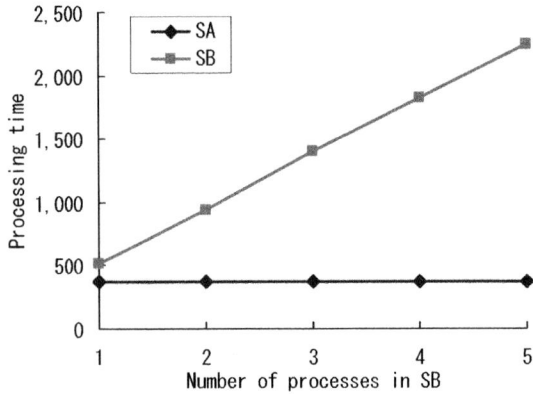

Fig. 7. Behavior of processing time as the number of processes in SB changes

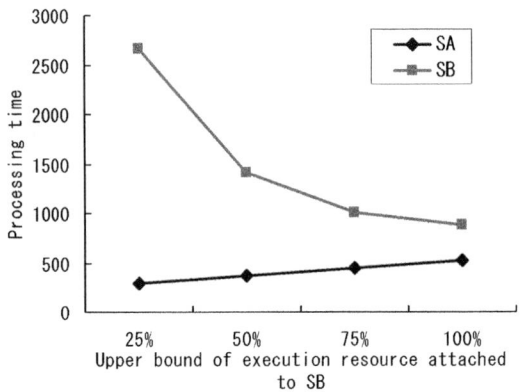

Fig. 8. Processing time when the upper bound of the execution resource attached to SB is changed

In the past decade, resource accounting techniques and resource protection techniques for defending against DoS attacks have been proposed, and these techniques have been successfully utilized to counter DoS attacks. The Scout operating system has an accounting mechanism for all the resources employed by each I/O path [8]. Scout also has a separate protection domain for each path. The present research focuses on the I/O paths and not on the access control of CPU resources.

Resource containers [9] have been proposed, and they can be used to account for and limit the usage of kernel memory. This container mechanism supports a multilevel scheduling policy; however, it only supports fixed-share scheduling and regular time-shared scheduling.

Execution resources with upper bounds are classified under resource accounting techniques [10]. The execution resource can control the maximum extent of CPU usage of programs for preventing abuse of CPU resources. The policy of rate limiting can be enforced for a CPU resource by using an access control mechanism for the execution resource. In addition, the proposed access control model can be applied to general OSes and secure OSes.

6   Conclusion

We proposed an improved mechanism for achieving a bound on the execution performance of process groups, in order to limit unnecessary processor use. We improved the previously proposed mechanism used for controlling the upper bound for a process. We introduced directory execution as an execution resource with an upper bound. In order to do so, the process scheduler was changed for the control of an execution resource with upper bound of directory execution.

The results of evaluations show that our proposed mechanism can control each process group according to the upper bound. These results also show that our proposed mechanism is effective in limiting the upper bound for the process groups.

References

1. CERT/CC Statistics (1988-2005), http://www.cert.org/stats/
2. Sekar, R., Bendre, M., Bollineni, P., Dhurjati, D.: A Fast Automaton-Based Method for Detecting Anomalous Program Behaviors. In: Proc. of IEEE Symposium on Security and Privacy, pp. 144–155 (2001)
3. Sandhu, R.S., Coyne, E.J., Feinstein, H.L., Youman, C.E.: Role-Based Access Control Models. IEEE Computer 29(2), 38–47 (1996)
4. Security-Enhanced Linux, http://www.nsa.gov/selinux/
5. Tabata, T., Hakomori, S., Yokoyama, K., Taniguchi, H.: Controlling CPU Usage for Processes with Execution Resource for Mitigating CPU DoS Attack. In: 2007 International Conference on Multimedia and Ubiquitous Engineering (MUE 2007), pp. 141–146 (2007)
6. Tabata, T., Hakomori, S., Yokoyama, K., Taniguchi, H.: A CPU Usage Control Mechanism for Processes with Execution Resource for Mitigating CPU DoS Attack. International Journal of Smart Home 1(2), 109–128 (2007)
7. Garg, A., Reddy, A.: Mitigation of DoS attacks through QoS regulation. In: IEEE International Workshop on Quality of Service (IWQoS), pp.45–53 (2002)
8. Spatscheck, O., Petersen, L.L.: Defending Against Denial of Service Attacks in Scout. In: 3rd Symp. on Operating Systems Design and Implementation, pp. 59–72 (1999)
9. Banga, G., Druschel, P., Mogul, J.C.: Resource containers: A new facility for resource management in server systems. In: The Third Symposium on Operating Systems Design and Implementation (OSDI 1999), pp. 45–58 (1999)
10. Mirkovic, J., Reiher, P.: A taxonomy of DDoS attack and DDoS defense mechanisms. ACM SIGCOMM Comput. Commun. Rev. 34(2), 39–53 (2004)

Probabilistic Route Selection Algorithm for IP Traceback

Hong-bin Yim and Jae-il Jung

Department of Electronics and Computer Engineering, Hanyang University,
17, Haengdang-dong, Sungdong-gu, Seoul, 133-791, Korea
hbyim@mnlab.hanyang.ac.kr, jijung@hanyang.ac.kr

Abstract. DoS(Denial of Service) or DDoS(Distributed DoS) attack is a major
threaten and the most difficult problem to solve among many attacks. Moreover, it is very difficult to find a real origin of attackers because DoS/DDoS
attacker uses spoofed IP addresses. To solve this problem, we propose a probabilistic route selection traceback algorithm, namely PRST, to trace the attacker's real origin. This algorithm uses two types of packets such as an agent
packet and a reply agent packet. The agent packet is in use to find the attacker's
real origin and the reply agent packet is in use to notify to a victim that the
agent packet is reached the edge router of the attacker. After attacks occur, the
victim generates the agent packet and sends it to a victim's edge router. The attacker's edge router received the agent packet generates the reply agent packet
and send it to the victim. The agent packet and the reply agent packet is forwarded refer to probabilistic packet forwarding table (PPFT) by routers. The
PRST algorithm runs on the distributed routers and PPFT is stored and managed by routers. We validate PRST algorithm by using mathematical approach
based on Poisson distribution.

Keywords: IP Traceback, DDoS attack, Network Security, PRST.

1 Introduction

Nowadays, Internet which can connect the whole world is the ocean of information as
well as an important communication media that makes human life convenient. However, Internet protocol has implemented simple so it has many vulnerabilities about
defending several attacks because of its characteristic. In these days, there are many
attacks such as attacking an anonymous server or an arbitrary node to decrease network resources or system performance using vulnerabilities of Internet protocol. Especially, DoS or DDoS attack is a major threaten and the most difficult problem to
solve among many attacks. The purpose of DoS/DDoS attack is to shutdown an arbitrary node or specific server such as DNS (Domain Name Server) to interrupt normal
services. In this case, attackers send enormous packets to a victim to exhaust the network resources or shutdown the target system.

As mentioned above, the targets of DoS/DDoS attack are a network bandwidth and
system resources. In case of system attack, there are three kinds of attacks such as TCP
SYN attack, UDP flood attack and ICMP flood attack[1]. TCP SYN attack makes half-
open TCP connection to make the victim wait a certain time after sending SYN/ACK to

T.-h. Kim et al. (Eds.): SecTech/DRBC 2010, CCIS 122, pp. 94–103, 2010.

the attacker. In case of UDP flood attack, an attacker sends UDP packets to random ports of a victim and then a victim makes a decision that there are no specific applications. After this procedure, a victim sends an ICMP destination unreachable message to the attacker. In case of ICMP flood attack, an attacker uses ICMP echo packets which are in use to check whether it is alive and then a victim sends an ICMP_ECHO_REPLY to the attacker. All these cases, the victim sends the message such as SYN/ACK, ICMP destination unreachable and ICMP_ECHO_REPLY to the attacker, which has a spoofed IP address, so that a victim cannot find the real origin of the attacker.

The purpose of network attack is to make the communication channel of ISP network congest to interrupt normal services through generating packet loss. In this case, the attacker sends a large stream of data to ISP network. ISP cannot distinguish attack packets from normal packets so ISP drops these two kinds of packets with same probability. If the amount of attack packets increases, packet loss of normal packets also increases then ISP lose its service availability.

In the case of DDoS attack, it is more difficult to prevent than DoS attack because there are several distributed attackers. Moreover, it is very difficult to find a real origin of attackers because DoS/DDoS attacker uses spoofed IP addresses.

DoS/DDoS attacks classify into 5 categories according to attack types such as network device level attack, OS level attack, application level attack, data flooding attack and protocol features based attack. There are various defense mechanisms according to attack types. However, we focus on IP traceback after attacking to find a real origin of attacker in this paper.

This paper explains in detail a new algorithm to find a real origin of attacker in case of DoS/DDoS attack environment. The rest of this paper is organized as follows. Chap 2 describes related work and background. Chap 3 describes the probabilistic route selection traceback algorithm we propose. Chap 4 shows the validation of the PRST algorithm, and Chap 5 presents the conclusions.

2   Related Works

IP traceback belongs to intrusion response among attack defense mechanisms [1]. Once detecting attack, next step is to find the attack origin and block the attack traffic. In present, manual control is in use to block attack traffic. IP traceback is a method to trace attack origin and up to now many traceback algorithms have been proposed.

IP traceback algorithms classify into 6 categories [1].

Bellovin [2] proposed an ICMP traceback technique. In this scheme, when a router receives a packet to a destination, the router generates an ICMP traceback message, called an iTrace packet, with low probability. The iTrace packet contains the address of the router, and is sent to the destination. The destination can reconstruct the route that was taken by the packets in the flow. In the ICMP traceback, the router has capability to process iTrace message and the performance is varied with sampling probability.

Burch and Cheswick [3] proposed a link testing traceback technique. In this scheme, it makes a route map of every network from victim and generates burst traffic each link using UDP chargen service. If the loaded link is located on the attack path, packet loss probability increases. This makes perturb the attack traffic so we find the real source. This scheme requires considerable knowledge of network topology and the ability to generate huge traffic in any network link. Moreover, generating bursty traffic can degrade the network performance itself.

Stone [7] proposed an overlay network architecture, called a CenterTrack, to overcome limitation of link testing traceback. As a CenterTrack method is an overlay network based traceback algorithm, tracking router module is installed in the network additionally. When an attack occurs, a CenterTrack method forwards traffic information which is received from network edge router to tracking router using tunneling mechanism. Tracking router can reconstruct an attack path using packet information which is collected by a CenterTrack. In this scheme, tracking router cannot manage a whole network so it suits a small size network and has disadvantage that cannot apply to heterogeneous network environment.

Savage et al. [4] proposed probability packet marking technique, called a PPM. In this scheme, the router samples packet that traverse the router with an arbitrary probability p and marks its IP address into the incoming packet and sends this packet to a destination. When an attack occurs, this scheme reconstructs a real attack path using router IP address information that is recorded in the packet. This scheme has a problem that many packets are required to reconstruct an attack path.

Snoeren et al. [5] proposed hash based IP traceback technique. Hash based IP traceback divides the whole network into several groups and each group has SCAR agent that can manage the sub network and traceback an attack path. In this case, each sub group has to have a SPIE, SCAR and DGA system additionally and a SCAR needs a memory to store and manage hash value of packets periodically.

Wang et al. [6] proposed an active network based intrusion response framework which is called Sleepy watermark trace. Sleepy Watermark Tracing (SWT) performs traceback as to insert a watermark into response packet corresponding with an attack. The SWT architecture consists of two components, the SWT guardian gateway and the SWT guarded host. Each SWT guarded host has a unique SWT guardian gateway, and it maintains a pointer to its SWT guardian gateway. Each SWT guardian gateway may guard one or more SWT guarded hosts. SWT method operates as follows. When an attack occurs, intrusion detection system in the guarded host detects an attack. When an attack is detected, the sleepy intrusion response module of SWT subsystem in guarded host is operated and then SWT marks in response packet corresponding with incoming packet at host by watermark enabled application. SWT sends response packet with watermark. Once starting traceback, SWT finds a watermark inserted packet cooperated with active tracing module in the guardian gateway. In this scheme, it is possible to traceback faster because of using response packet corresponding with an attack packet to find a real origin of attacker. However, it has a big problem to apply real Internet environment because this scheme requires a watermark enabled application. Moreover, there is a disadvantage that cannot trace a real origin of attacker if an attacker uses an encrypted communication link.

3 Problem Solution

In this paper, we propose a probabilistic route selection traceback algorithm to trace the real origin of the attacker. In this scheme, we need three kinds of requirements as below.

1. The link status on attack paths will be changed when attacks occur.
2. The intermediate router records the number of the incoming packets and out-going packets traverses each network interface card and calculates the Poisson packet forwarding probability all the time during running router.
3. Probabilistic packet forwarding table has to be stored in the router.

3.1 Probabilistic Route Selection Traceback Algorithm

It is impossible to find an attacker's real origin in case of DoS/DDoS attack because attackers usually use spoofed IP address to hide their real origin. As we mentioned in chap 2, most traceback methods have some restrictions to find a real origin of the attackers.

In this paper, we propose an algorithm to trace a real origin of attackers, called probabilistic route selection traceback algorithm (PRST), when attacks occur. The PRST is an algorithm to find a real origin of the spoofed IP addresses based on prob-abilistic route selection method. The probabilistic route selection method is to choose a route one hop by one hop to find attacker's real origin using an agent packet and a reply agent packet.

The agent packet is the packet to find attackers' real origin and the reply agent packet is the packet to notify to the victim that the agent packet is reached the edge router of the attacker.

Before a router forwards packet, the router stores a probability in a probabilistic packet forwarding table (PPFT) based on Poisson distribution that forwards packets from incoming interface to outgoing interface and then the router can decide the backward route from a victim to an attacker using PPFT. Using this procedure at all router, an agent packet can reach an edge router of the spoofed source IP address' real origin. We will mention about the operation of the agent packet and the reply agent packet next section in details.

The router calculates the packet forwarding probability based on Poisson distribu-tion between incoming interface and outgoing interface. The router counts the number of packets forwarded from incoming interface to outgoing interface in normal net-work condition and then the router decides an average traffic volume(λ_{io}) of Poisson distribution that is calculated using equation 1.

$$\lambda_{io} = (1-\alpha)\lambda_{old} + \alpha\lambda_{new} \, (0 < \alpha < 1) \dots\dots\dots\dots\dots(1)$$

When the network condition is normal, a Poisson packet forwarding probability has range between certain values. However, when attacks occur, the Poisson packet for-warding probability of a certain interface toward the victim will increase. After all, the Poisson packet forwarding probability of the other interfaces except an interface toward victim is not changed.

After attacks occur, the victim generates an agent packet to find a real origin of at-tacker and sends it to the attacker. The source IP address of the agent packet is the IP address of the victim and the destination IP address is NULL value because we do not know the real IP address of the attacker.

The victim's edge router that receives the agent packet refers to its probabilistic packet forwarding table to forward this packet to next hop router. In this procedure, the edge router checks cumulative Poisson probability of the row of the interface number, which the agent packet comes from, in the probabilistic packet forwarding table. After this, the edge router chooses a column number of a field that has the highest Poisson probability among the row's Poisson probability value, which is the outgoing interface of the agent packet, to forward this agent packet to next hop router. And then, the edge router forwards this agent packet to next hop router through that interface by PRST algorithm not by the destination IP address. The intermediate router that receives the agent packet performs the same procedure. The agent packet finally reaches the attacker's edge so we can find the origins of attackers refer to this network traffic variation and the probabilistic packet forwarding table as mentioned above. If there are same Poisson probabilities more than one, which has the highest value, the router copies the agent packet and forwards the agent packet through several interfaces simultaneously. The operation of edge router of the attacker is described in subsection 3.3 in details.

Equation 2 represents the cumulative Poisson packet forwarding probability from ith incoming interface to oth outgoing interface. λ_{io} represents a mean of number of packets forwarded based on Poisson distribution from ith incoming interface to oth outgoing interface. k_{io} represents a number of packets that forwarded from ith incoming interface to oth outgoing interface. P_{io} represents the cumulative Poisson packet forwarding probability from ith interface to oth interface. For example, the cumulative Poisson packet forwarding probability from 1st incoming interface to 2nd outgoing interface is equal to P_{12}.

$$P_{io}(x = k_{io}) = \sum \frac{e^{-\lambda_{io}} \lambda_{io}^{k_{io}}}{k_{io}!} \quad ....(2)$$

In the equation 2, x means the random variable indicated that a number of packets that forwarded from ith incoming interface to oth outgoing interface.

Every router has its probabilistic packet forwarding table and the format of the table is as Figure 1.

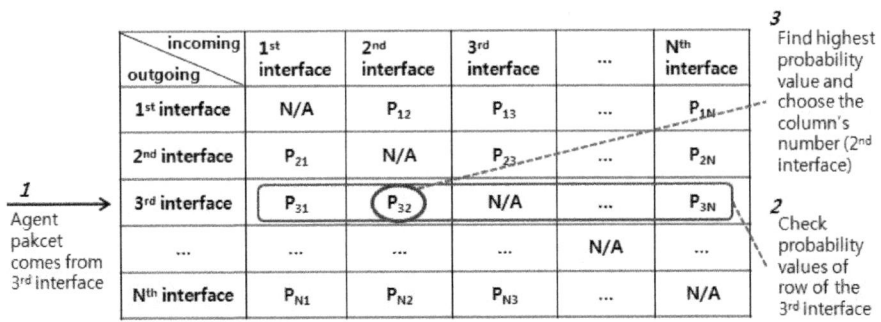

Fig. 1. Probabilistic Packet Forwarding Table

Fig 2 shows the example of probabilistic route selection traceback algorithm procedure.

An arrow indicates the attack path. A dotted arrow indicates the path of the agent packet to find attacker's real origin and a curved dotted arrow indicates the path of the reply agent packet.

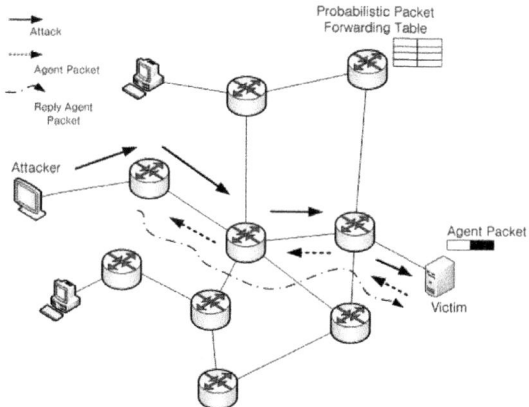

Fig. 2. An example of IP packet tracing using PRST algorithm

3.2 A Format of Agent Packet and Operation of Victim

PRST uses an agent packet that is modified the header of IP packet header to trace the real origin of the attacker. Nowadays, last 2 bits of ToS (Type of Service) field of Internet protocol header are not used because these 2 bits are reserved.

The victim generates an agent packet as set last 1 bit of TOS field to find the attack's real origin. The router that receives the agent packet checks the probabilistic packet forwarding table and then decides the backward attack path as choosing the interface that has the highest packet forwarding probability refer to PPFT. After this procedure, the router forwards the agent packet through that interface. The victim's edge router sends the agent packet periodically based on packet round trip time until receiving the reply agent packet. The reply agent packet is described next subsection in details.

3.3 Reply Agent Packet and Operation of the Edge Router of the Attacker

If edge router of the attacker receives the agent packet, the edge router generates the reply agent packet as set least second 1 bit of ToS field to 1. The destination IP address of reply agent packet is the IP address of the victim. The router that receives the reply agent packet forwards this packet to next hop router refers to a normal routing table, not the probabilistic packet forwarding table, because the victim's IP address is not spoofed. This reply agent packet can reach to the victim by a normal routing table.

If the victim receives the reply agent packet, the victim stops sending the agent packet to the edge router of attackers.

3.4 Pseudo Code of Probabilistic Route Selection Traceback Algorithm

Table 1. Pseudo code of PRST algorithm at the intermediate router

```
if(the last bit of ToS field == 1)
{
    check the interface id;
if(interface id == N)
{
    look up Nth row in the PPFT;
    find highest Poisson probability;
    float prob = highest Poisson probability;
    get column number of prob;
    outgoing interface = column number;
    send agent packet to outgoing interface;
}
else
{
    look up normal routing table;
    choose the next hop router;
    send this packet to next hop router;
}
```

Table 2. Pseudo code of PRST algorithm at the edge router

```
if(the last bit of ToS field == 1)
{
    check the source IP address;
    if(IP == my subnet)
{
    check the interface id;
    if(interface id == N)
    {
      look up Nth row in the PPFT;
      find highest Poisson probability;
      float prob = highest Poisson probability;
      get column number of prob;
      outgoing interface = column number;
      send agent packet to outgoing interface;
    }
    }
else
{
    make reply agent packet;
    least second bit of ToS = 1;
    Dest IP addr = Src IP addr;
    Src IP addr = my IP addr;
        look up normal routing table;
        choose the next hop router;
    send this packet to next hop router;
    }
}
```

4   Validation of PRST Algorithm

We use the cumulative Poisson packet forwarding probability based on Poisson distribution. We assume that a mean(λ_{io}) of number of packets forwarded based on Poisson distribution is calculated in the normal network condition by routers.

When attacks occur, the number of packets exceeding a mean of number of packets forwarded can be considered as attack packets. These packets are usually forwarded to the victim and the Poisson packet forwarding probability of the interface toward victim will increase.

Once, the router calculates its packet forwarding mean(λ_{io}) based on Poisson distribution, the number of packets forwarded k does not changed greatly in normal network condition. However, an attack occurs, the k changes its value more than λ_{io}, exactly $\lambda_{io} + d$. d means the number of attack packets.

Let the total number of incoming packets to a certain router be K in normal network condition. K packets forwarded through several j interfaces by routers. The number of packets forwarded through each interface except incoming interface is $k_{i1}, k_{i2}, k_{i3},...$ respectively and the total number of packets is $k_{i1} + k_{i2} + k_{i3} + ... + k_{ij} = K$.

If attacks occur, let the total number of packets be $K+d$. Here, d is the number of attack packets. Let the number of packets d exceeding K is all forwarded to interface number 3 toward victim.

In this case, the numbers of packets forwarded through interface number 3 increases from k_{i3} to $k_{i3} + d$ and the cumulative Poisson probability increases as much as P_{inc}. The equation for P_{inc} is as equation 3.

$$P_{inc} = \sum_{k_{i3}=0}^{k_{i3}+d} \frac{e^{-\lambda_{i3}} \lambda_{i3}^{k_{i3}}}{k_{i3}!} - \sum_{k_{i3}=0}^{k_{i3}} \frac{e^{-\lambda_{i3}} \lambda_{i3}^{k_{i3}}}{k_{i3}!} \quad \text{.......................................(3)}$$

The cumulative Poisson probability of interface 3 increases more than the other interfaces' cumulative Poisson probability. This probability is stored in the probabilistic packet forwarding table. If the victim sends the agent packet to its edge router, this agent packet comes into interface 3 and the router forwards this packet to next hop router referring to probabilistic packet forwarding table.

Generally, Poisson distribution has a characteristic that the probability $P(x = k)$ increases with k from 0 till $k \leq \lambda$ and falls off beyond λ.

In case of $k = \lambda$, cumulative Poisson probability is not changed greatly according to λ. If λ increases 20 times, the cumulated Poisson probability increases about 17%. However, if $k > \lambda$ then the cumulative Poisson probability has always high value than normal condition when k value is near λ. If $k \cong \lambda + \Delta$, Δ means the small traffic volume changes, the P_{io} has few difference but in case of $k \cong \lambda + d$, the cumulative Poisson probability from 0 till $k < \lambda + d$ has greater than normal condition(k value is near λ). This can be expressed as equation 4.

$$\sum_{k_{io}=0}^{\lambda_{io}+d} \frac{e^{-\lambda_{io}} \lambda_{io}^{k_{io}}}{k_{io}!} > \sum_{k_{io}=0}^{\lambda_{io}+\Delta} \frac{e^{-\lambda_{io}} \lambda_{io}^{k_{io}}}{k_{io}!} \dots\dots\dots(4)$$

To detect attacks, intrusion detection algorithm has the threshold of equation 5[8].

$$T_{io} = \lambda_{io} + n\sigma_{io} \dots\dots\dots(5)$$

In equation 5, T_{io} means the traffic volume threshold to detect attacks, λ_{io} means average traffic volume, n means integer number and σ_{io} means the standard deviation of traffic volume. If the measured traffic volume(k_{io}) is larger than T_{io}, intrusion detection system can regard that DoS based attack occurs. In this case, if n=3 and $k_{io} > T_{io}$, then cumulative Poisson probability has almost 1.

In this manner, the Poisson packet forwarding probability of the interface on the attack path is the highest value in the probabilistic packet forwarding table.

Therefore, the agent packet can be forwarded to the attacker's real origin refer to the probabilistic packet forwarding table.

5   Conclusion

We propose the probabilistic route selection traceback algorithm using an agent packet, a reply agent packet, probabilistic packet forwarding table and Poisson distribution in this paper. Using PRST algorithm, we can find the attacker's real origin by using a few packets, some agent packets and reply agent packet.

The PRST algorithm runs on the distributed routers refer to probabilistic packet forwarding table (PPFT). This table is stored and managed by routers. Moreover, we validate our PRST algorithm by using mathematical approach based on Poisson distribution which has characteristic that if k>λ then the cumulative Poisson probability has always higher value than normal cases such as k value is near λ. Therefore, the cumulative Poisson packet forwarding probability of the attacked interface has always higher value than the cumulative Poisson packet forwarding probability of the other interfaces after attack occurs.

Using this character, the agent packet can be forwarded to the attacker's edge router and that is the attacker's real origin.

The PRST algorithm has 3 major contributions as below.

The PRST algorithm is more efficient in terms of system modification, finding origin of attackers and the number of packets to find the origin of attacker. First of all, this algorithm can be implemented by S/W, not H/W, so this algorithm can be implemented on the intermediate routers without changing H/W. Second, there are many attack paths due to the characteristic of DDoS attack so attack path is less important than finding origin of attackers. Therefore, we focus on finding origin of attackers in this paper.

Third, PRST algorithm needs not many packets to find the origin of attackers as using an agent packet and a reply agent packet.

Acknowledgement

"This research was supported by the MKE(Ministry of Knowledge Economy), Korea, under the ITRC(Information Technology Research Center) support program supervised by the NIPA(National IT Industry Promotion Agency)" (NIPA-2010-(C1090-1031-0005)).

References

[1] Douligeri, C., Serpanos, D.N.: Network Security. IEEE Press, Los Alamitos (2007)
[2] Bellovin, S.: The ICMP traceback message, Network Working Group, Internet draft (March 2000)
[3] Burch, H., Cheswickk, H.: Tracing anonymous packets to their approximate source. In: Proceedings of USENIX LISA Conference, pp. 319–327 (2000)
[4] Savage, S., Wetherall, D., Karlin, A., Anderson, T.: Network Support for IP traceback. IEEE/ACM Transactions on Networking, 226–237 (2001)
[5] Snoeren, A.C., Partridge, C., Sanchez, L.A., Jones, C.E., Tchakountio, F., Kent, S.T., Strayer, W.T.: Hash-based IP Traceback. In: Proceedings of the ACM SIGCOMM 2001 Conference on Applications, Technologies, Architectures and Protocols for Computer Communication, pp. 3–14. ACM Press, New York (2001)
[6] Wang, X., Reeves, D.S., Wu, S.F., Yuill, J.: Sleepy watermark tracing: An active network-based intrusion response framework. In: Proceedings of the Sixteenth International Conference of Information Security (IFIP/SEC_ 2001), Paris (June 2001)
[7] Stone, R.: CenterTrack: An IP overlay network for tracking DoS floods. In: Proceedings of the Ninth USENIX security symposium, pp. 199–212 (2000)
[8] Lee, J., Yoon, M., Lee, H.: Monitoring and Investigation of DoS Attack. KNOM Reveiw 6(2), 33–40 (2004)

An Efficient Audio Watermarking Algorithm in Frequency Domain for Copyright Protection

Pranab Kumar Dhar[1], Mohammad Ibrahim Khan[1], Cheol-Hong Kim[2], and Jong-Myon Kim[3,*]

[1] Chittagong University of Engineering and Technology, Bangladesh
[2] Chonnam National University, Kwangju, Korea
[3] University of Ulsan, Usan, Korea
{pranab_cse,muhammad_ikhancuet}@yahoo.com,
{cheolhong,jongmyon.kim}@gmail.com

Abstract. Digital Watermarking plays an important role for copyright protection of multimedia data. This paper proposes a new watermarking system in frequency domain for copyright protection of digital audio. In our proposed watermarking system, the original audio is segmented into non-overlapping frames. Watermarks are then embedded into the selected prominent peaks in the magnitude spectrum of each frame. Watermarks are extracted by performing the inverse operation of watermark embedding process. Simulation results indicate that the proposed watermarking system is highly robust against various kinds of attacks such as noise addition, cropping, re-sampling, re-quantization, MP3 compression, and low-pass filtering. Our proposed watermarking system outperforms Cox's method in terms of imperceptibility, while keeping comparable robustness with the Cox's method. Our proposed system achieves SNR (signal-to-noise ratio) values ranging from 20 dB to 28 dB, in contrast to Cox's method which achieves SNR values ranging from only 14 dB to 23 dB.

Keywords: Copyright Protection, Digital Watermarking, Sound Contents, and Fast Fourier Transform.

1 Introduction

Digital watermarking has drawn extensive attention for copyright protection of multimedia data. A digital audio watermarking is a process of embedding watermarks into audio signal to show authenticity and ownership. Audio watermarking should meet the following requirements :(a) *Imperceptibility*: the digital watermark should not affect the quality of original audio signal after it is watermarked; (b) *Robustness*: the embedded watermark data should not be removed or eliminated by unauthorized distributors using common signal processing operations and attacks; (c) *Capacity*: capacity refers to the numbers of bits that can be embedded into the audio signal within a unit of time; (d) *Security*: security implies that the watermark should only be detectable by the authorized person. These requirements are often contradictory. Since robustness and imperceptibility are the most important requirements for digital audio watermarking, these should be satisfied first.

---

* Corresponding author.

T.-h. Kim et al. (Eds.): SecTech/DRBC 2010, CCIS 122, pp. 104–113, 2010.
© Springer-Verlag Berlin Heidelberg 2010

In this paper, we propose a new watermarking system in frequency domain for audio copyright protection. The watermarks are embedded into the selected prominent peaks of the magnitude spectrum of each non-overlapping frame. Experimental results indicate that the proposed watermarking system provides similar robustness as Cox's method [7] against several kinds of attacks such as noise addition, cropping, re-sampling, re-quantization, MP3 compression and low-pass filtering. However, our proposed watermarking system outperforms Cox's method in terms of imperceptibility. Our proposed system achieves SNR values ranging from 20 dB to 28 dB, in contrast to Cox's method which achieves SNR values ranging from only 14 dB to 23 dB.

The rest of this paper is organized as follows. Section 2 provides a brief description of related research including Cox's method. Section 3 introduces our proposed watermarking system including watermark embedding process and watermark detection process. Section 4 compares the performance of our proposed system with Cox's method in terms of imperceptibility as well as robustness. Section 5 concludes this paper.

2   Related Research

A significant number of techniques that create robust and imperceptible audio watermarks have been reported in recent years. *Lie et al.* [1] proposed a method of embedding watermarks into audio signals in the time domain that exploits differential average-of-absolute-amplitude relationships within each group of audio samples to represent single bit of information. It also utilizes a low-frequency amplitude modification technique to scale amplitudes in selected sections of samples so that the time domain waveform envelope can be well-preserved. In [3], the authors propose a blind audio watermarking system that embeds watermarks into the audio signal in the time domain. The strength of audio signal modifications is limited by the necessity to produce an output signal for watermark detection. The watermark signal is generated using a key, and watermark insertion depends on the amplitude and frequency of an audio signal that minimizes the audibility of the watermark signal. Ling *et al.* [4] introduce a watermarking scheme based on nonuniform discrete Fourier transform (NDFT), in which the frequency points of the embedding watermark are selected by a secret key. Zeng *et al.* [5] describe a blind watermarking system that embeds watermarks into discrete cosine transform (DCT) coefficients by utilizing a quantization index modulation technique. In [6], the authors propose a watermarking system that embeds synchronization signals in the time domain to resist several types of attack. Pooyan *et al.* [7] introduce an audio watermarking system that embeds watermarks in the wavelet domain. The watermarked data is then encrypted and combined with a synchronization code and embedded into low frequency coefficients of the sound in the wavelet domain. The magnitude of the quantization step and its embedding strength are adaptively determined according to the characteristics of the human auditory system.

In Cox's method [8] watermarks are embedded into the highest n DCT coefficients of a whole sound excluding the DC component according to the following equation:

$$v'_i = v_i(1 + \alpha x_i) \tag{1}$$

where v_i is a magnitude coefficient into which a watermark is embedded, x_i is a watermark to be inserted into v_i, α is a scaling factor, and v_i' is an adjusted magnitude coefficient. The watermark sequence is extracted by performing the inverse operation of (1) represented by the following equation:

$$x_i^* = (\frac{v_i^*}{v_i} - 1) / \alpha \qquad (2)$$

Cox's method provides good results in terms of robustness. However, this method cannot achieve good imperceptibility in terms of signal-to-noise ratio (SNR) because it embeds watermark into highest DCT components of the sound which sometimes affects the quality of the sound. To overcome this problem, we propose a new watermarking system which embeds watermarks into the selected prominent peaks of the magnitude spectrum of each non-overlapping frame. This provides better results than Cox's method in SNR aspect for watermarked audio signals, while keeping comparable robustness with Cox's method against several kinds of attacks.

3 Proposed Watermarking System

In this section, we present an overview of our basic watermarking system which consists of watermark embedded process and watermark detection process. In this study, a watermark consists of a sequence of real numbers $X= \{x_1, x_2, x_3,..., x_n\}$. We create a watermark where each value of x_i is chosen independently according to N(0,1) where $N(\mu, \sigma^2)$ denotes a normal distribution with mean μ and variance σ^2.

3.1 Watermark Embedding Process

The proposed watermark embedding process is shown in Fig. 1. The embedding process is implemented in the following seven steps:

1) The original audio is first segmented into non-overlapping frames.
2) Calculate the magnitude and phase spectrum of each frame using fast Fourier transform (FFT).
3) Find the n most prominent peaks $V= \{v_1, v_2, v_3,..., v_n\}$ from magnitude spectrum using a peak detection algorithm.
4) Place watermarks into the n prominent peaks of magnitude spectrum to obtain watermarked peaks $V'= \{v_1', v_2', v_3',..., v_n'\}$. This ensures that the watermark is located at the most significant perceptual components of the audio. When we insert the watermark X into V to obtain V', we specify a scaling parameter α, which determines the extent to which X alters V, shown in the equation (1) [8].
5) Insert back the n modified peaks into the magnitude spectrum of each non-overlapping frame.
6) Take an inverse FFT of the complex spectrum to calculate the watermarked frame.
7) Finally concatenates all watermarked frames to calculate the watermarked audio signal.

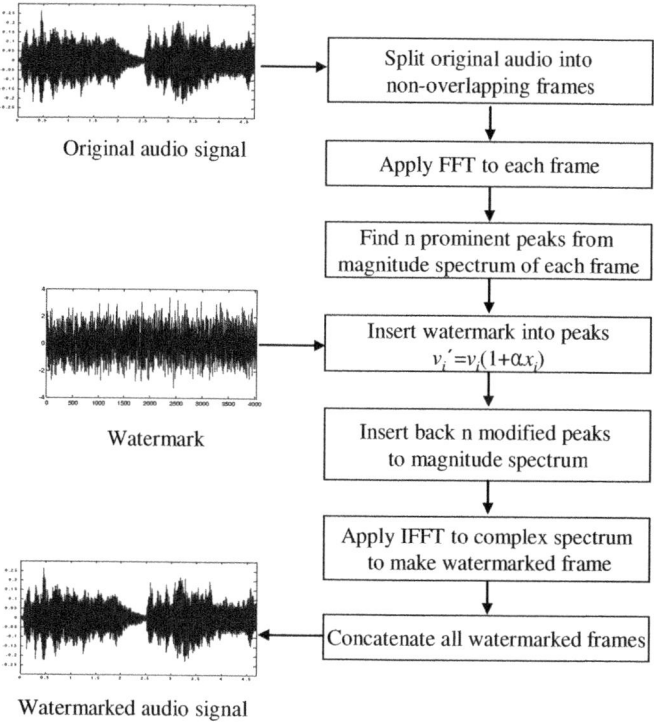

Fig. 1. Watermark embedding process

3.2 Watermark Detection Process

The proposed watermark detection process is shown in Fig. 2. The detection process is implemented in the following three steps:

1) Calculate the FFT of the attacked watermark audio frame.
2) Extract n peaks from the magnitude spectrum which are located at the same position in the embedding process above.
3) Extract the watermark sequence by performing the inverse operation of (1) represented by the equation (2).

4   Simulation Results and Discussion

In this section, we evaluate the performance of our watermarking system using four different types of 16 bit mono audio signals sampled at 44.1 kHz: (a) 'Let it be' written by Beatles; (b) 'the beginning of the Symphony No. 5 in c minor, Op. 67', written by Ludwig van Beethoven; (c) an instrumental song 'Hey Jude' played by a Korean traditional musical instrument called the gayageum; (d) a human voice providing TOEIC listening test instruction. Each audio file contains 206,336 samples (duration 4.679 sec).

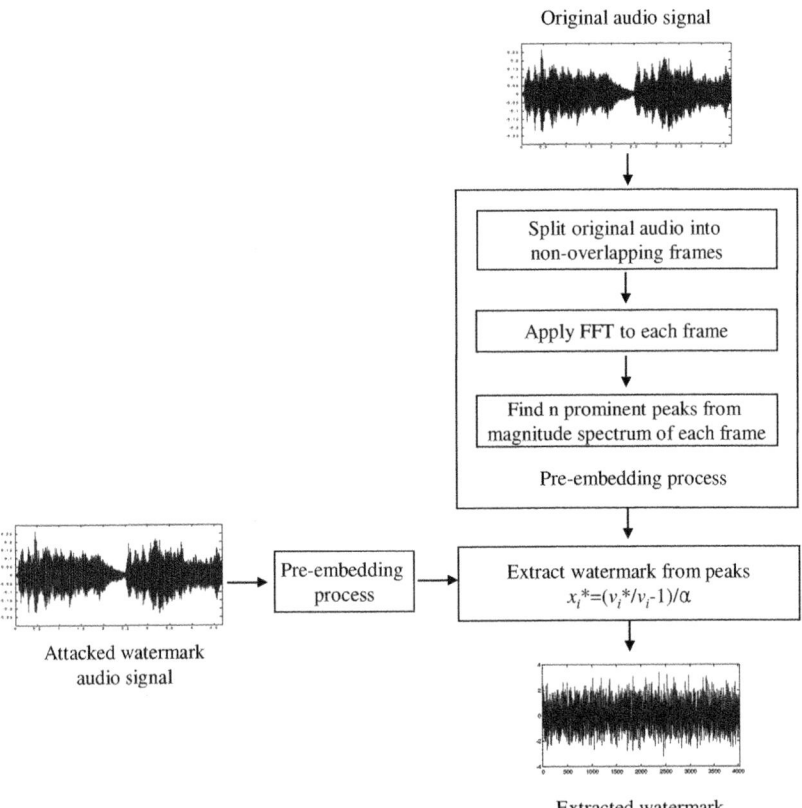

Fig. 2. Watermark detection process

By considering the frame size of 512 samples, we have 403 frames for each audio sample. From each frame we detect 10 peaks to embed watermark. Thus, the length of the watermark sequence is 10×403=4,030.

In order to evaluate the performance of the proposed watermarking system, the correlation coefficient between the original watermark X and the extracted watermark X^* is calculated by the following similarity $SIM(X, X^*)$ formula:

$$SIM(X, X^*) = \frac{X \cdot X^*}{\sqrt{X^* \cdot X^*}} \tag{3}$$

It is highly unlikely that X^* will be identical to X. To decide whether X and X^* match, we determine whether the $SIM(X, X^*) > T$, where T is a detection threshold. In this study, the selected detection threshold (T) value is 6 [8].

Figure 3 shows a qualitative evaluation of the original audio with a watermarked audio in which the watermarks are imperceptible using the proposed system.

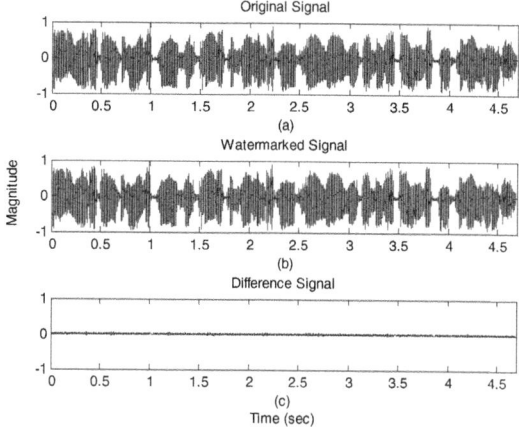

Fig. 3. Imperceptibility of the watermarked audio using the proposed method: (a) original human voice sound, (b) watermarked human voice sound (c) difference between original and watermarked human voice sound

In order to evaluate the quality of watermarked signal, the following signal-to-noise ratio (SNR) equation is used:

$$SNR = 10 \log_{10} \frac{\sum_{n=1}^{N} S^2(n)}{\sum_{n=1}^{N} \left[S(n) - S^*(n) \right]^2} \qquad (4)$$

where S(n) and S*(n) are original audio signal and watermarked audio signal respectively. After embedding watermark, the SNR of all selected audio signals using the proposed method are above 20 dB which ensures the imperceptibility of our proposed system.

Figure 4 shows the peak detection of first frame of human voice sound. In our proposed system, watermarks are embedded into the selected prominent peaks of the magnitude spectrum of each frame which provides high robustness against different kinds of attacks as well as good SNR values for watermarked audio signals.

In Cox's method, on the other hand, watermarks are embedded into the higher DCT coefficients of the whole sound excluding the DC component. Table 1 shows the SNR comparison between the proposed watermarking system and Cox's method for different values of α. Our proposed system achieves SNR values ranging from 20 dB to 28 dB for different watermarked sounds. This is in contrast to Cox's method which achieves SNR values ranging from only 14 to 23. In other words, our proposed watermarking system provides 6 dB higher SNR values than Cox's method for different watermarked sounds. Thus, our proposed watermarking system outperforms Cox's method in terms of imperceptibility.

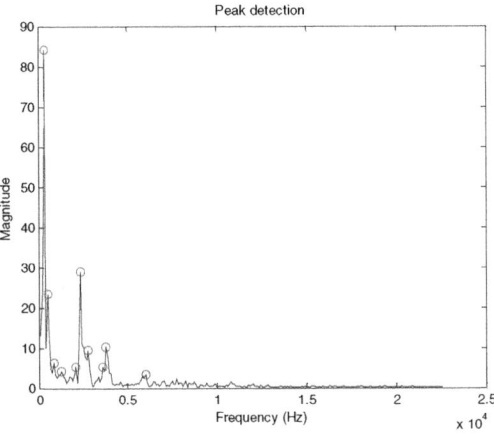

Fig. 4. Peak detection in frequency spectrum

Table 1. SNR comparison between proposed system and Cox's method

Types of Signal	Cox	Proposed	Cox	Proposed	Cox	Proposed
	α=0.1		α=0.2		α=0.3	
Let it be	23.561	25.654	17.586	23.176	14.067	20.202
Symphony No 5	23.772	27.395	17.611	23.652	14.089	20.649
Hey Jude	23.741	27.218	17.668	23.843	14.146	20.776
Human Voice	23.786	28.259	17.968	24.163	14.446	20.779

4.1 Imperceptibility Test

Informal listening using head set reveals that the watermark embedded into the original audio using the proposed watermarking system does not affect the quality of the
sound, which ensures imperceptibility of the embedded watermark.

4.2 Robustness Test

Table 2 shows the performance comparison in terms of similarity between the proposed system and Cox's method when no attack is applied to four different types of
watermarked audio signals for α=0.3. The proposed method is comparable with Cox's
method in terms of similarity.

In order to test the robustness of our proposed system, six different types of attacks, summarized in Table 3, were performed to the watermarked audio signal.

Table 2. Watermark detection result of the proposed system and Cox's method

Types of signal	SIM	
	Proposed	Cox
Let it be	64.6345	64.9933
Symphony No 5	64.4371	64.9933
Hey Jude	64.5267	64.9932
Human Voice	64.2483	64.9933

Table 3. Attacks used in this study for watermarked sound

Attacks	Description
Noise addition	Additive white Gaussian noise (AWGN) is added with the watermarked audio signal.
Cropping	We removed 10% samples from the beginning of the watermarked signal and then replaced these samples by the original signal.
Re-sampling	The watermarked signal originally sampled at 44.1 kHz is re-sampled at 22.050 kHz, and then restored by sampling again at 44.1 kHz.
Re-quantization	The 16 bit watermarked audio signal is quantized down to 8 bits/sample and again re-quantized back to 16 bits/sample.
MP3 Compression	MPEG-1 layer 3 compression with 128 kbps is applied to the watermarked signal.
Low-pass filtering	The low-pass filter used in this study is a second order Butterworth filter with cut-off frequency 10 kHz.

Figures 5 and 6 show the response of the watermark detector to 1000 randomly generated watermarks where correct watermark is at the 500th position against Gaussian noise attack for $\alpha=0.3$ using the proposed system and Cox method.

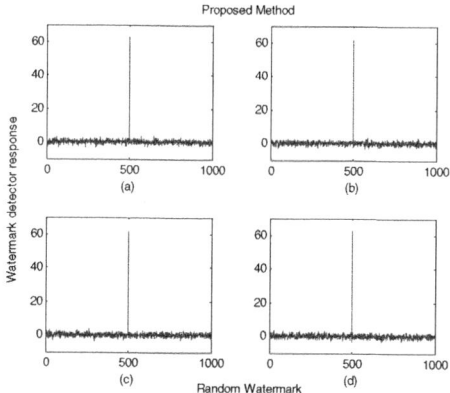

Fig. 5. Watermark detector response against Gaussian noise attack using the proposed method: (a) Let it be, (b) Symphony No. 5, (c) Hey Jude, (d) Human Voice

Table 4 shows the similarity results of the proposed scheme and Cox's method in terms of robustness against several kinds of attacks applied to four different types of watermarked audio signal 'Let it be', 'Symphony No 5', 'Hey Jude', and 'human voice' respectively for $\alpha=0.3$.

Overall, our proposed watermarking system outperforms Cox's method in terms of SNR values while keeping comparable robustness with Cox's method against several attacks such as noise addition, cropping, re-sampling, re-quantization, and MP3 compression.

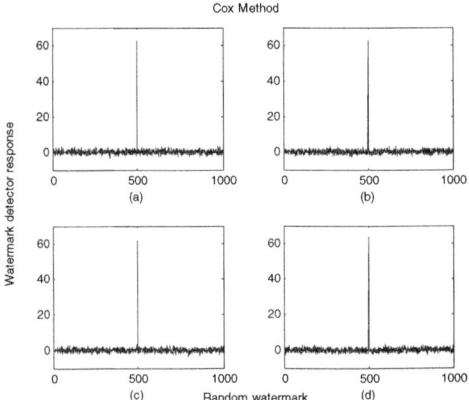

Fig. 6. Watermark detector response against Gaussian noise attack using the Cox method: (a) Let it be, (b) Symphony No. 5, (c) Hey Jude, (d) Human Voice

Table 4. Similarity results of the proposed system and Cox's method against different attacks

Types of Attack	Types of Signal	Cox	Proposed
			$\alpha = 0.3$
Noise addition	Let it be	62.937	62.538
	Symphony No 5	62.942	61.424
	Hey Jude	61.413	61.725
	Human Voice	63.923	62.735
Cropping	Let it Be	60.462	59.372
	Symphony No 5	59.266	61.478
	Hey Jude	59.269	60.348
	Human Voice	61.372	59.672
Re-sampling	Let it Be	64.992	63.846
	Symphony No 5	64.993	63.936
	Hey Jude	64.993	62.865
	Human Voice	62.893	61.784
Re-quantization	Let it Be	64.993	63.983
	Symphony No 5	62.876	60.795
	Hey Jude	62.876	60.795
	Human Voice	64.637	62.538
MP3 Compression	Let it Be	63.927	62.357
	Symphony No 5	62.268	60.674
	Hey Jude	63.945	62.213
	Human Voice	62.535	61.385
Low-pass filtering	Let it Be	61.826	61.436
	Symphony No 5	59.883	61.215
	Hey Jude	60.527	61.357
	Human Voice	59.927	61.727

5 Conclusion

In this paper, we have presented a new watermarking algorithm in frequency domain for audio copyright protection. Experimental results indicate that our proposed watermarking system shows better results than Cox's method in terms of imperceptibility while keeping comparable robustness with Cox's method against several kinds of attacks such as noise addition, cropping, re-sampling, re-quantization, and MP3 compression. Our proposed method achieves SNR values ranging from 20 dB to 28 dB for different watermarked sounds. This is in contrast to Cox's method which achieves SNR values ranging from only 14 dB to 23 dB. These results demonstrate that our proposed watermarking system can be a suitable candidate for audio copyright protection.

Acknowledgement

This work was supported by the National Research Foundation of Korea(NRF) grant funded by the Korea government(MEST) (No. R01-2008-000-20493-0 and No. 2010-0010863).

References

1. Lie, W.N., Chang, L.C.: Robust and High-Quality Time-Domain Audio Watermarking Based on Low-Frequency Amplitude Modification. IEEE Transaction on Multimedia 8(1), 46–59 (2006)
2. Xiang, S., Huang, Z.: Histogram-based audio watermarking against time-scale modification and cropping attacks. IEEE Transactions on Multimedia 9(7), 1357–1372 (2007)
3. Bassia, P., Pitas, I., Nikolaidis, N.: Robust Audio Watermarking in the Time domain. IEEE Transaction on Multimedia 3(2), 232–241 (2001)
4. Xie, L., Zhang, J., He, H.: Robust Audio Watermarking Scheme Based on Nonuniform Discrete Fourier Transform. In: IEEE International Conference on Engineering of Intelligent System, pp. 1–5 (2006)
5. Zeng, G., Qiu, Z.: Audio Watermarking in DCT: Embedding Strategy and Algorithm. In: 9th International Conference on Signal Processing (ICSP 2009), pp. 2193–2196 (2008)
6. Huang, J., Wang, Y., Shi, Y.Q.: A Blind Audio Watermarking Algorithm with Self-Synchronization. In: IEEE International Symposium on Circuits and Systems (ISCAS 2002), vol. 3, pp. 627–630 (2002)
7. Pooyan, M., Delforouzi, A.: Adaptive and Robust Audio watermarking in Wavelet Domain. In: International Conference on International Information Hiding and Multimedia Signal Processing (IIH-MSP 2007), vol. 2, pp. 287–290 (2007)
8. Cox, I., Killian, J., Leighton, F., Shamoon, T.: Secure Spread Spectrum Watermarking for Multimedia. IEEE Transactions on Image Processing 6(12), 1673–1687 (1997)

Robust Audio Watermarking Scheme Based on Deterministic Plus Stochastic Model

Pranab Kumar Dhar[1], Cheol Hong Kim[2], and Jong-Myon Kim[3,*]

[1] Chittagong University of Engineering and Technology, Bangladesh
[2] Chonnam National University, Gwangju, Korea
[3] University of Ulsan, Usan, Korea
pranab_cse@yahoo.com, chkim22@chonnam.ac.kr,
jongmyon.kim@gmail.com

Abstract. Digital watermarking has been widely used for protecting digital contents from unauthorized duplication. This paper proposes a new watermarking scheme based on spectral modeling synthesis (SMS) for copyright protection of digital contents. SMS defines a sound as a combination of deterministic events plus a stochastic component that makes it possible for a synthesized sound to attain all of the perceptual characteristics of the original sound. In our proposed scheme, watermarks are embedded into the highest prominent peak of the magnitude spectrum of each non-overlapping frame in peak trajectories. Simulation results indicate that the proposed watermarking scheme is highly robust against various kinds of attacks such as noise addition, cropping, re-sampling, re-quantization, and MP3 compression and achieves similarity values ranging from 17 to 22. In addition, our proposed scheme achieves signal-to-noise ratio (SNR) values ranging from 29 dB to 30 dB.

Keywords: Digital watermarking, copyright protection, spectral modeling synthesis, digital contents.

1 Introduction

Recent years have seen rapid growth in the availability of digital media. A major problem faced by content providers and owners is protection of their material. Digital audio watermarking, which is the process of embedding watermarks into an audio signal to demonstrate authenticity and ownership, has drawn extensive attention for copyright protection of audio data [1]. Audio watermarking schemes should meet the following requirements: (a) Imperceptibility: the digital watermark should not affect the quality of the original audio signal; (b) Robustness: unauthorized distributors should not be able to remove or eliminate the embedded watermark data using common signal processing operations; (c) Capacity: the numbers of bits that can be embedded into the audio signal within a unit of time should be sufficient; (d) Security: the watermark should only be detectable by an authorized person. These requirements are often

---

* Corresponding author.

T.-h. Kim et al. (Eds.): SecTech/DRBC 2010, CCIS 122, pp. 114–125, 2010.

contradictory. Since robustness and imperceptibility are the most important requirements for digital audio watermarking, these should be satisfied first.

In this paper, we propose a new watermarking scheme based on spectral modeling synthesis (SMS) [8-9] for audio copyright protection. SMS extracts synthesis parameters out of real sounds using analysis procedures to reproduce and modify the original sounds. This approach models sounds as stable sinusoids (partials) plus noise (residual components) to analyze sounds and generate new sounds. The analytic procedure detects partials by utilizing the time-varying spectral characteristics of a sound, and represents them as time-varying sinusoids [10]. These partials are then subtracted from the original sound, in which the remaining residual is represented as a time-varying filtered white noise component. The synthesis procedure is a combination of additive synthesis for the sinusoidal part and subtractive synthesis for the noise part [9]. In our proposed watermarking scheme, the original audio is segmented into non-overlapping frames and fast Fourier transform (FFT) is applied to each frame. Prominent spectral peaks of each frame are identified and removed to calculate the residual spectrum. The residual component is computed by transforming the spectrum back to the time domain using inverse FFT, and then adding the non-overlapping frames in time. In addition, a peak tracking unit links peaks across frames to form trajectories. Watermarks are then embedded into the most prominent peak of the magnitude spectrum of each non-overlapping frame in the peak trajectories. Each sinusoidal component is computed by sinusoidal synthesis. Finally, the watermarked signal is computed by adding the sinusoidal component to the residual component in the time domain. Watermarks are detected by the inverse operation of the watermark embedding process. Experimental results indicate that the proposed watermarking scheme shows strong robustness against several kinds of attacks including noise addition, cropping, re-sampling, re-quantization, and MP3 compression. In addition, our proposed scheme achieves signal-to-noise ratio (SNR) values ranging from 29 dB to 30 dB.

The rest of this paper is organized as follows. Section 2 provides a brief description of previous works related to audio watermarking. Section 3 introduces our proposed watermarking scheme, including the watermark embedding process and watermark detection process. Section 4 discusses the performance of our proposed scheme in terms of imperceptibility as well as robustness. Finally, section 5 concludes this paper.

2   Previous Works

A significant number of watermarking techniques have been reported in recent years in order to create robust and imperceptible audio watermarks. Some methods embed the watermark in the time domain of the audio signal [1-2]. Other watermarking techniques use transform methods, such as Discrete Fourier Transform (DFT) [3], Discrete Cosine Transform (DCT) [4-5], or Discrete Wavelet Transform (DWT) [6] to embed the watermark.

In Cox's method [7] watermarks are embedded into the highest n DCT coefficients of a whole sound excluding the DC component according to the following equation:

$$v_i' = v_i(1 + \alpha x_i) \qquad (1)$$

where v_i is a magnitude coefficient into which a watermark is embedded, x_i is a watermark to be inserted into v_i, α is a scaling factor, and v_i' is an adjusted magnitude coefficient. The watermark sequence is extracted by performing the inverse operation of (1) represented by the following equation:

$$x_i^* = (\frac{v_i^*}{v_i} - 1)/\alpha \qquad (2)$$

3   General Overview of the SMS Analysis and Synthesis Process

Figure 1 shows a block diagram for the SMS analysis process [8]. We analyzed the sound by multiplying it with an appropriate analysis window. Its spectrum is obtained by FFT and then the prominent spectral peaks are detected and incorporated into the existing partial trajectories by means of a peak continuation algorithm. It detects the magnitude, frequency, and phase of the partials presented in the original sound (the deterministic components). When the sound is pseudo harmonic, a pitch detection step can improve the analysis by utilizing the fundamental frequency information in the peak continuation algorithm as well as by selecting the size of the analysis window [8-9].

The stochastic component of the current frame is calculated by generating the deterministic signal with additive synthesis and then subtracting it from the original waveform in the time domain. The stochastic representation is then obtained by performing a spectral fitting of the residual signal.

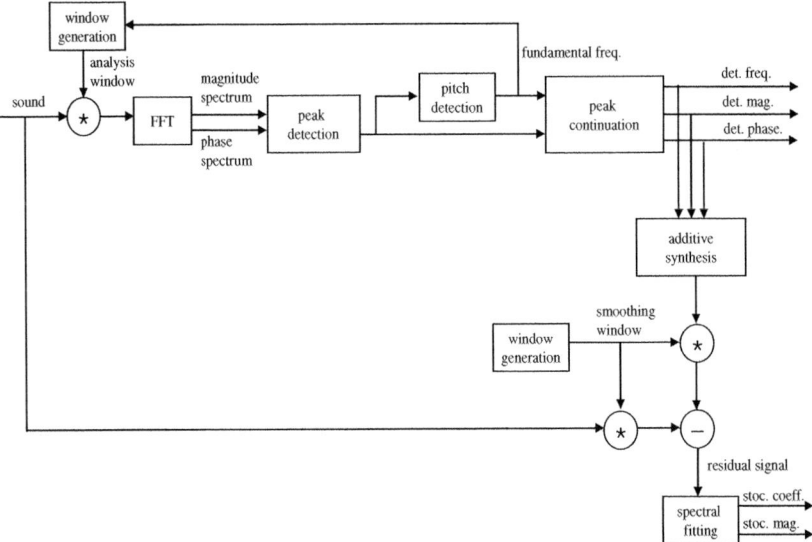

Fig. 1. Block diagram of the SMS analysis process

Figure 2 shows a block diagram of the SMS synthesis process. The deterministic component (sinusoidal component) is calculated from the frequency and magnitude trajectories. The result of the synthesized stochastic signal is a noise signal with a time varying spectral shape obtained in the analysis (i.e., subtractive synthesis). It can be implemented by a convolution in the time domain or by a complex spectrum for every spectral envelope of the residual and an inverse-FFT in frequency domain.

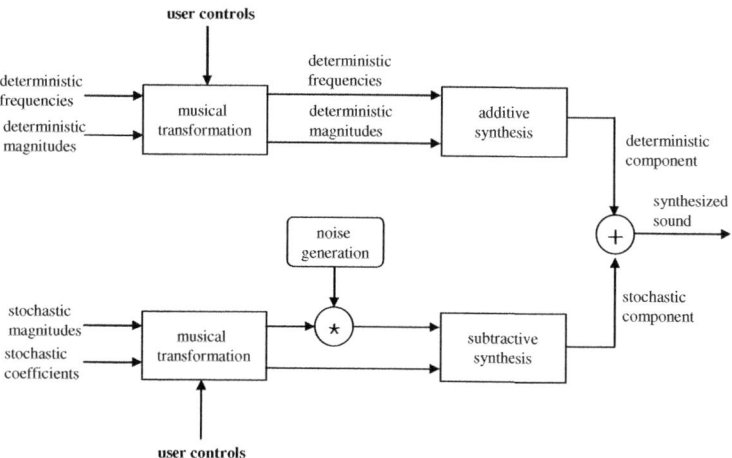

Fig. 2. Block diagram of the SMS synthesis process

4 Proposed Watermarking System

In this section, we present an overview of our basic watermarking scheme based on SMS which consists of watermark embedded process and watermark detection process. In this study, a watermark consists of a sequence of real numbers $X = \{x_1, x_2, x_3,..., x_n\}$. We create a watermark where each value of x_i is chosen independently according to $N(0,1)$ where $N(\mu, \sigma^2)$ denotes a normal distribution with mean μ and variance σ^2.

To embed a watermark into an audio signal, we first extract the sinusoidal component of the audio signal. This process is known as sinusoidal analysis. In sinusoidal analysis, the original signal is decomposed into a sinusoidal part and a frequency residual part. Watermarks are embedded into the sinusoidal part only; the residual part is kept unchanged.

4.1 Watermark Embedding Process

The proposed watermark embedding process is shown in Figure 3. The embedding process is implemented in the following seven steps:

Step 1: The original audio is segmented into non-overlapping frames and FFT is applied to each frame. The computation of the magnitude and phase spectra of the current frame is the first step in the analysis. The computation of the spectra is carried out by the FFT. Figure 4 shows the time domain representation of the original audio signal

118   P.K. Dhar, C.H. Kim, and J.-M. Kim

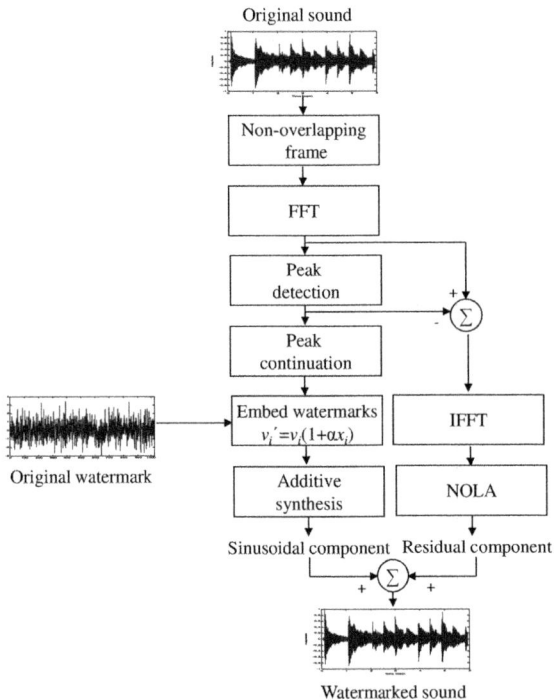

Fig. 3. Watermark embedding process

'Let it Be.' Figure 5 shows the magnitude and phase spectrum of the selected frame for the original audio signal.

Step 2: Prominent spectral peaks are detected from the frequency spectrum of each frame using a peak detection algorithm. Figure 6 shows the peak detection of the selected frame for the original audio signal 'Let it Be.'

Step 3: The peak tracking algorithm connects every peak in the ith frame to the $(i+1)^{th}$ frame to form trajectories. Figure 7 shows the peak tracking of the original audio signal 'Let it Be.'

Step 4: The residual component is computed by removing all the prominent peaks from the spectrum, transforming the spectrum back to the time domain by using inverse FFT (IFFT), and then nonoverlap-adding (NOLA) the frames in the time domain. Figure 8 shows the residual component of the audio signal 'Let it Be.'

Step 5: Watermarks are embedded into the most prominent peak of each frame as shown in Figure 6 to obtain watermarked peaks $V'= \{v_1', v_2', v_3',..., v_n'\}$ using the following equation:

$$v_i' = v_i(1 + \alpha x_i) \tag{6}$$

Step 6: A sinusoidal component is computed by using sinusoidal synthesis applied to watermarked and unwatermarked sinusoids, shown in the following equation:

$$D(t) = \sum_{r=1}^{R} A_r(t) \cos[\theta_r(t)] \tag{7}$$

where R is the number of sinusoids, $A_r(t)$ and $\theta_r(t)$ are the instantaneous amplitude and phase of the rth sinusoid, respectively. Figure 9 shows the time domain representation of the sinusoidal component for the audio signal 'Let it Be.'

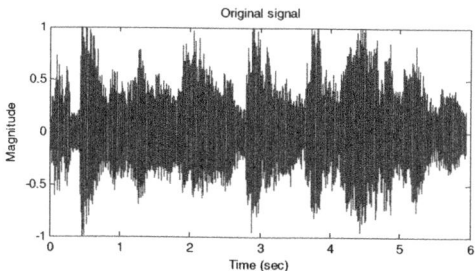

Fig. 4. Time domain representation of the original audio signal 'Let it Be'

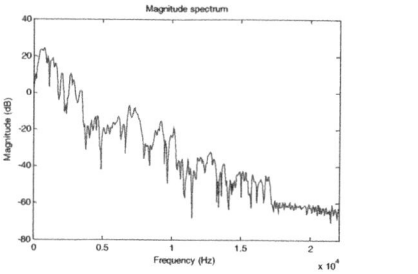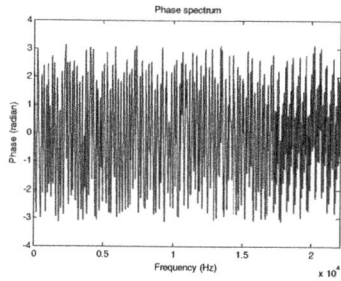

Fig. 5. Magnitude and phase spectrum of the selected frame of the original audio signal 'Let it Be'

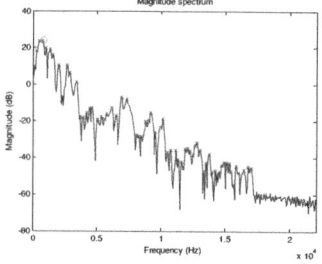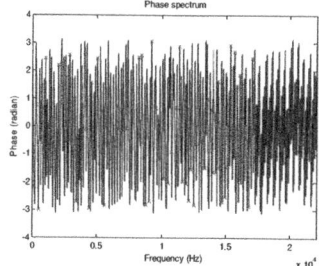

Fig. 6. Peak detection of the selected frame of the selected audio signal 'Let it Be'

Step 7: Finally, the watermarked signal is computed by adding the sinusoidal component and the residual component in the time domain. Figure 8 shows the time domain representation of the watermarked audio signal 'Let it Be.'

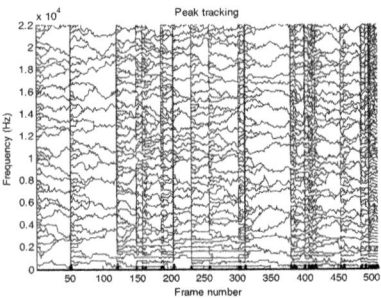

Fig. 7. Peak tracking of the selected audio signal 'Let it Be'

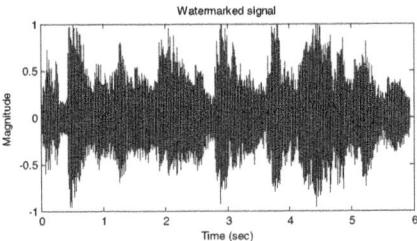

Fig. 8. Time domain representation of the watermarked audio signal 'Let it Be'

4.2 Watermark Detection Process

The proposed watermark detection process is shown in Figure 9. The detection process is implemented in the following three steps:

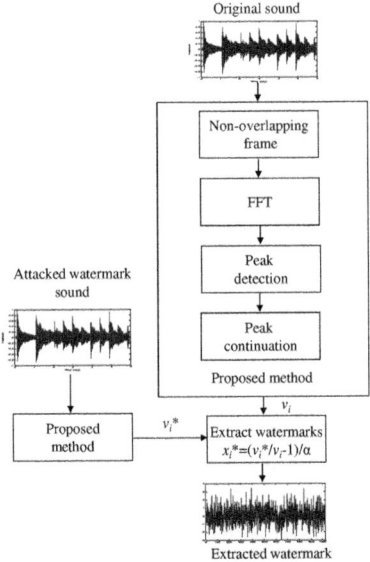

Fig. 9. Watermark detection process

Step 1: Calculate the FFT of the attacked watermark audio frame.

Step 2: Extract the most prominent peak from the magnitude spectrum of each non-overlapping frame in peak trajectories, which are located at the same position in the embedding process above.

Step 3: The watermark sequence $X^* = x_1^*, x_2^*, x_3^*, ..., x_n^*$ is then extracted by performing the inverse operation of (6) represented by the following equation:

$$x_i^* = (\frac{v_i^*}{v_i} - 1) / \alpha \qquad (8)$$

5   Simulation Results and Discussion

In this section, we evaluate the performance of our proposed watermarking scheme with 16-bit mono audio signals of four different types sampled at 44.1 kHz: (a) the song 'Let it Be,' by the Beatles; (b) the beginning of Symphony No. 5 in C Minor, Op. 67, by Ludwig van Beethoven; (c) an instrumental song, 'Hey Jude,' played by a Korean traditional musical instrument called the gayageum; (d) a human voice providing TOEIC (Test of English for International Communication) listening test instruction. Each audio file contains 262,000 samples (duration 5.94 sec). By considering a frame size of 512 samples, we have 512 non-overlapping frames for each audio sample. From each frame we detect the most prominent peaks to embed watermarks. Thus, the length of the watermark sequence is 512.

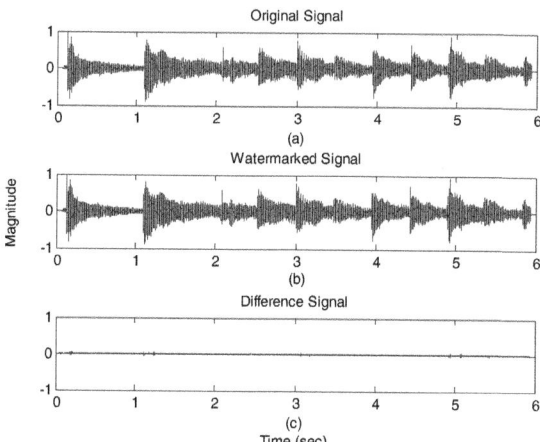

Fig. 10. Imperceptibility of watermarked audio using the proposed scheme: (a) Original audio signal 'Hey Jude' (b) watermarked audio signal 'Hey Jude' (c) difference between original and watermarked audio signal

In order to evaluate the performance of the proposed watermarking scheme in terms of watermark detection, the correlation coefficient between the original watermark X and the extracted watermark X^* is calculated by the following similarity SIM(X, X^*) formula:

$$SIM(X, X^*) = \frac{X \cdot X^*}{\sqrt{X^* \cdot X^*}} \qquad (9)$$

It is highly unlikely that X^* will be identical to X. To decide whether X and X^* match, we determine whether the $SIM(X, X^*) > T$, where T is a detection threshold. In this study, the selected detection threshold (T) value is 6 [7].

Figure 10 shows a qualitative evaluation of the original audio with a watermarked audio in which the watermarks are imperceptible using the proposed scheme.

5.1 Imperceptibility Test

Imperceptibility of the embedded watermark should be ensured. For the evaluation of imperceptibility for our proposed watermarking scheme, we used the following signal-to-noise (SNR) equation:

$$SNR = 10\log_{10} \frac{\sum_{n=1}^{N} S^2(n)}{\sum_{n=1}^{N} \left[S(n) - S^*(n) \right]^2} \qquad (10)$$

where S(n) and $S^*(n)$ are the original audio signal and watermarked audio signal, respectively. . In this study, the selected scaling factor value (α) value is 0.1 [7].

Table 1 shows the SNR result of the proposed scheme for the four selected different watermarked sounds. Our proposed scheme achieves SNR values ranging from 29 dB to 30 dB for different watermarked sounds.

Table 1. SNR results of Cox's method and proposed scheme for different watermarked sounds

Types of signal	SIM
'Let it Be'	29.4109
'Symphony No 5'	30.6853
'Hey Jude'	29.7108
'Human Voice'	30.1859

5.2 Robustness Test

Table 2 shows the similarity results of our proposed scheme when no attack is applied to four different types of watermarked audio signals.

Table 2. Watermark detection results of the proposed scheme without attack

Types of signal	SIM
'Let it Be'	22.2559
'Symphony No 5'	21.9061
'Hey Jude'	22.1179
'Human Voice'	20.0611

In order to test the robustness of our proposed scheme, different types of attacks, summarized in Table 3, were performed on the watermarked audio signals.

Table 3. Attacks used in this study to test the watermarked sound

Attacks	Description
Noise addition	Additive white Gaussian noise (AWGN) is added to the watermarked audio signal.
Cropping	10% of samples are removed from the beginning of the watermarked signal and then these samples were replaced with the original signal.
Resampling	The watermarked signal originally sampled at 44.1 kHz is resampled at 22.050 kHz, and then restored by sampling again at 44.1 kHz.
Re-quantization	The 16 bit watermarked audio signal is quantized down to 8 bits/sample and then re-quantized back to 16 bits/sample.
MP3 compression	MPEG-1 layer 3 compression with 128 kbps is applied to the watermarked signal.

Figures 11 shows the response of the watermark detector to 1000 randomly generated watermarks using the proposed scheme against cropping attack where the correct watermark is at the 500th position for different watermarked sounds.

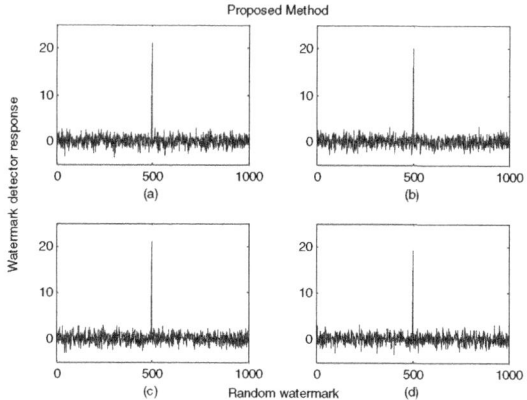

Fig. 11. Watermark detector response against cropping attack using the proposed method: (a) 'Let it Be', (b) 'Symphony No. 5', (c) 'Hey Jude', (d) 'Human Voice'

Table 4 shows the similarity results of the proposed scheme in terms of robustness against several kinds of attacks applied to four different types of watermarked audio signal 'Let it be', 'Symphony No 5', 'Hey Jude', and 'human voice' respectively for $\alpha=0.1$.

Table 4. Similarity results of proposed scheme against several attacks

Types of Attack	Types of Signal	SIM
Noise addition	Let it be	18.9603
	Symphony No 5	18.0536
	Hey Jude	13.3849
	Human Voice	17.9699
Cropping	Let it Be	21.0315
	Symphony No 5	20.1004
	Hey Jude	21.1396
	Human Voice	19.1142
Re-sampling	Let it Be	22.2551
	Symphony No 5	21.5139
	Hey Jude	19.3270
	Human Voice	20.0213
Re-quantization	Let it Be	22.2378
	Symphony No 5	21.2504
	Hey Jude	21.7355
	Human Voice	20.0142
MP3 Compression	Let it Be	22.1518
	Symphony No 5	21.4009
	Hey Jude	22.0136
	Human Voice	19.9082

6 Conclusion

In this paper, we have presented a new watermarking scheme based on SMS for audio copyright protection. Watermarks are embedded into the most prominent peaks of the magnitude spectrum of each non-overlapping frame in peak trajectories. Experimental results indicate that our proposed watermarking scheme shows strong robustness against several kinds of attacks such as noise addition, cropping, resampling, re-quantization, and MP3 compression and achieves similarity values ranging from 17 to 22. Moreover, our proposed scheme achieves SNR values ranging from 29 dB to 30 dB for different watermarked sounds. These results demonstrate that our proposed watermarking scheme can be a suitable candidate for audio copyright protection.

Acknowledgement

This work was supported by the National Research Foundation of Korea(NRF) grant funded by the Korea government(MEST) (No. R01-2008-000-20493-0 and No. 2010-0010863).

References

1. Lie, W.N., Chang, L.C.: Robust and High-Quality Time-Domain Audio Watermarking Based on Low-Frequency Amplitude Modification. IEEE Transaction on Multimedia 8(1), 46–59 (2006)

2. Bassia, P., Pitas, I., Nikolaidis, N.: Robust Audio Watermarking in the Time domain. IEEE Transaction on Multimedia 3(2), 232–241 (2001)
3. Xie, L., Zhang, J., He, H.: Robust Audio Watermarking Scheme Based on Nonuniform Discrete Fourier Transform. In: IEEE International Conference on Engineering of Intelligent System, pp. 1–5 (2006)
4. Zeng, G., Qiu, Z.: Audio Watermarking in DCT: Embedding Strategy and Algorithm. In: 9th International Conference on Signal Processing (ICSP 2009), pp. 2193–2196 (2008)
5. Huang, J., Wang, Y., Shi, Y.Q.: A Blind Audio Watermarking Algorithm with Self-Synchronization. In: IEEE International Symposium on Circuits and Systems (ISCAS 2002), vol. 3, pp. 627–630 (2002)
6. Pooyan, M., Delforouzi, A.: Adaptive and Robust Audio watermarking in Wavelet Domain. In: International Conference on International Information Hiding and Multimedia Signal Processing (IIH-MSP 2007), vol. 2, pp. 287–290 (2007)
7. Cox, I., Killian, J., Leighton, F., Shamoon, T.: Secure Spread Spectrum Watermarking for Multimedia. IEEE Transactions on Image Processing 6(12), 1673–1687 (1997)
8. Serra, X., Smith, J.: Spectral modeling synthesis: A sound analysis/synthesis system based on deterministic plus stochastic decomposition. Computer Music Journal 14(4), 12–24 (1990)
9. Serra, X.: Musical sound modeling with sinusoid plus noise. Musical Sound Processing, published in Roads, C., Pope, S., Picialli, A., De Poli, G. (eds.) by Sweets and Zeitlinger Publishers, pp. 91–122 (1997)
10. Depalle, P., Garcia, G., Rodet, X.: Tracking of Partials for Additive Sound Synthesis Using Hidden Markov Models. In: IEEE International Conference on Acoustics, Speech and Signal Processing, vol. 1, pp. 225–228 (1993)

Histogram-Based Reversible Data Hiding with Quadtree Concepts

Hsiang-Cheh Huang[1], Ting-Hsuan Wang[1], and Wai-Chi Fang[2]

[1] National University of Kaohsiung, Kaohsiung 811, Taiwan, R.O.C.
hchuang@nuk.edu.tw
[2] National Chiao-Tung University, Hsinchu 300, Taiwan, R.O.C.
Dr.Wfang@gmail.com

Abstract. Reversible data hiding has attracted much attention in researches during the past few years. With its characteristics of reversibility, the algorithm is required to fulfill the goals that at the encoder, the secret information needs to be embedded into the original image by some means, and at the decoder, both the secret information and the original image are required to be correctly extracted and recovered, and they should be identical to their embedding counterparts. Under the requirement of reversibility, for evaluating the performance of the algorithm, the output image quality, called imperceptibility, and the number of bits for embedding, called capacity, are the two important factors to access the effectiveness of the algorithm. Here we take the concepts of quadtree decomposition into consideration to watch the characteristics of the original content. And we propose a reversible data hiding algorithm that has the ability to reside more capacity than conventional algorithm, with similar output image quality after embedding, and comparable side information produced.

Keywords: Reversible data hiding, histogram, quadtree, imperceptibility, capacity.

1 Introduction

Reversible data hiding, also referred to as reversible watermarking, has been a newly developed branch and an interesting topic in watermarking researches [1, 2]. Suppose that the cover media for secret transmission of data are the digital images. With the term "reversibility", at the encoder, the user-defined data should be embedded into the original image by some means. And at the decoder, both the data and the original image should be recovered. This means that the extracted data and the recovered image should be identical to their counterparts at the encoder. Therefore, how to design an effective algorithm for reversible data hiding is an interesting task in both research and application.

There are requirements for designing a good reversible data hiding algorithm [3, 4, 5]. Three major requirements are: (a) the output image quality, called the imperceptibility, (b) the number of bits that can be hidden into the cover image, called the capacity, and (c) the overhead or side information that is necessary for performing data extraction at the decoder. And we can see that these requirements have some correlations or conflict with the others. For instance, embedding more capacity into the cover image would lead to the

T.-h. Kim et al. (Eds.): SecTech/DRBC 2010, CCIS 122, pp. 126–133, 2010.

more deterioration to the output image quality, and hence the degraded result in imperceptibility. From the viewpoint of practical applications, less overhead is much required. Therefore, how to develop a reversible data hiding algorithm that can hide more capacity, produce the output image quality with acceptable imperceptibility hat aims at utilizing the characteristics of its original counterpart, and generate as less overhead as possible is the major contribution of this paper.

This paper is organized as follows. In Sec. 2, we present fundamental descriptions of conventional histogram-based reversible data hiding algorithm. Then, in Sec. 3, we take the quadtree decomposition into consideration and look for the integration with the algorithm presented in Sec. 2. Simulation results are demonstrated in Sec. 4, which suggest the applicability of the algorithm and the integration proposed. Finally, we conclude this paper in Sec. 5.

2 Descriptions of Conventional Histogram-Based Reversible Data Hiding

The concept of data hiding is to embed information relating to the copyright owner into original multimedia content. For reversible data hiding, the information to be hidden is first embedded into the original image. Later on, by performing the reverse process of information embedding, both the embedded information and the exactly original image should be extracted. The main challenge of reversible data hiding is to develop an algorithm that is reversible, that is, all the inputs to the encoder, including the original image and hidden data, must be perfectly extracted at the decoder after delivery of the marked image. The outputs of the extractor must be identical to the inputs of encoder. Reversible data hiding can be categorized into two major branches, the first one is by modifying the histogram of original image for embedding the user-defined information, and the second one is called the difference expansion scheme, meaning that the difference value between two consecutive pixels is adjusted to embed the data [6]. In this paper, we concentrate on the former one because of its ease of implementation and little overhead generated.

2.1 Histogram-Modification for Reversible Data Embedding and Extraction

Histogram-modification scheme for data embedding is adopted from [5], which can be described as follows.

Step 1. *Generate the histogram of original image.* The luminance with the maximal occurrences in histogram is labeled as "max point," while that with no occurrence is labeled as "zero point." The luminance values of "max" and "zero" points, each is represented by 8 bits, are treated as overhead or side information. Hence, a total of 16 bits should be transmitted to the receiver for data extraction.

Step 2. *Select the range between max and zero points.* The range of luminance values between max and zero points is recorded in the histogram.

Step 3. *Modify of luminance values in selected range.* In the region between max and zero points recorded in Step 2, luminance values between the max and zero points are altered in advance. Luminance values in the selected range are all increased by 1.

Step 4. *Embed the data.* For the embedding of binary watermark, if the watermark bit is '1,' the luminance value is increased by 1; if the watermark bit is '0,' it is decreased by 1.

In extracting both the hidden data and the original image, the following steps should apply accordingly.

Step 1. *Locate selected range with side information.* Luminance values between the max and zero points are compared.

Step 2. *Extract the hidden data relating to the original.* Every pixel in the output image is scanned and examined sequentially to extract the data bits to compare to Step 3 of the embedding procedure.

Step 3. *Obtain the original image.* By moving the histogram into its original form, the original content is recovered. Only the max point is required.

We can see that performing data hiding is simply by shifting certain parts of the histogram of the image, and the luminance values of the max and zero points play an important role for making reversible data hiding possible.

2.2 Advantages and Drawbacks of the Conventional Scheme

The histogram-based reversible data hiding has the advantages of ease of implementation and little side information produced. On the contrary, the limited amount of embedding capacity is the major drawback for this algorithm. With the descriptions in Sec. 2.1, we observe the advantages of the histogram-based reversible data hiding, which are depicted as follows.

> ➢ Guaranteed imperceptibility: The mean squared error (MSE) between the original and output images would be at most 1.00 [5], meaning that the Peak Signal-to-Noise Ratio (PSNR) would be at least 48.13 dB.

> ➢ Little overhead: Only the luminance values of the max and zero points are required at the decoder for extracting the data and the original, meaning that 2 bytes of overhead is necessary, regardless of the size of original images.

On the contrary, the major drawback of the histogram-based reversible data hiding is described as follows.

> ➢ Limited amount of capacity: The embedding capacity is limited by the number of occurrences at the max point, and this value is directly affected by the characteristics of the original image. Suppose that the original image in grayscale has the size of $M \times N$ pixels, and each pixel is represented by 1 byte. Under the worst case when the occurrences of max points are the same for every luminance value, meaning that the histogram of the original image represents like the uniform distribution between 0 and 255, the capacity for embedding is only $M \times N \times \frac{1}{256} \times \frac{1}{8}$ bits. This implies that embedding capacity is only 0.049% of the filesize of original image.

From the observations above, we are able to take the characteristics of the original image into consideration, and try to increase the capacity at the expense of somewhat degraded quality of the output image. Side information should be comparable to that in the conventional scheme. Therefore, we employ the concept of quadtree decomposition for the implementation of histogram-based reversible data hiding algorithm.

3 Histogram-Based Reversible Data Hiding with Quadtree Decomposition

The quadtree decomposition analyzes the performance of the algorithm based on the block size and the characteristics of original image. It decomposes the original image into larger to small square blocks based on the smoothness of that region. We will regard each square block as a small image, and employ the histogram-based reversible data hiding to look for the increase in data capacity.

3.1 The Three-Round Embedding Process

In conjunction with the conventional histogram-based reversible data hiding described in Sec. 2, we propose the three-round embedding process with the characteristics of original image by using quadtree decomposition. The proposed scheme can be briefly outlined as follows.

Round 1.   Perform the quadtree decomposition to the original image, $\mathbf{X}$, and obtain different block sizes for the composition of original image. Find the luminance value of the zero point of the whole image. Save each block size and the luminance value of max point at the corresponding position as the block map (BM), $\mathbf{B}$.

Round 2.   Apply the histogram-based reversible data hiding for embedding information, $\mathbf{I}$, to each block in the original image $\mathbf{X}$. Output the image containing $\mathbf{I}$, and call it $\mathbf{X}'$.

Round 3.   Apply the histogram-based reversible data embedding again, and embed the block map $\mathbf{B}$ into $\mathbf{X}'$. Call the output image of this round as $\mathbf{X}''$. Transmit the side information $\mathbf{S}$ to the decoder.

Here we go into more details in each of the three rounds. At Round 1, we demonstrate the procedure in Fig. 1, with the original image "airplane" in Fig. 1(a). We can easily see that after quadtree decomposition, based on the characteristics of original image, it can be decomposed into square blocks with sizes among 16×16, 32×32, and 64×64, in Fig. 1(b). Homogeneity of each block of original image can be determined by a threshold T, which may be calculated by

$$\begin{cases} (\max(\text{block value}) - \min(\text{block value})) \geq T & \Rightarrow \quad \text{Keep decomposition;} \\ (\max(\text{block value}) - \min(\text{block value})) < T & \Rightarrow \quad \text{Stop.} \end{cases} \tag{1}$$

We set $T = \alpha \cdot 255$, $\alpha \in [0,1]$. The value of α can be adjusted by the users. Thus, for smaller threshold values, more blocks will be produced, and the size of the block map $\mathbf{B}$ will grow accordingly.

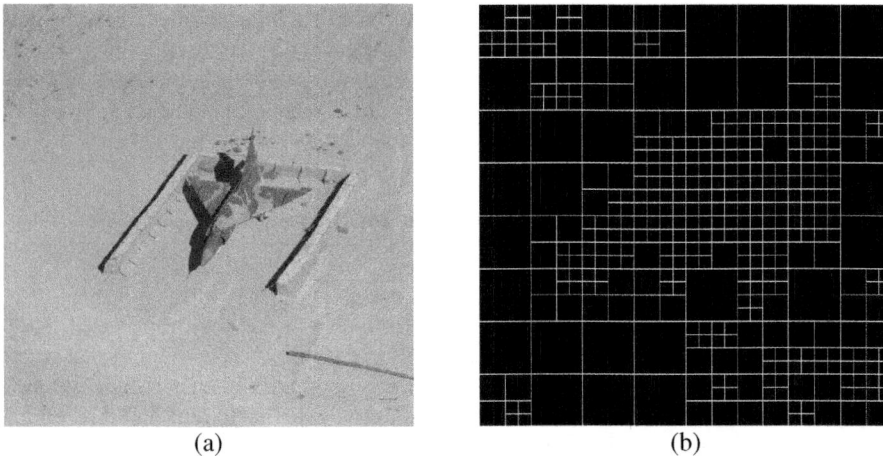

(a)   (b)

Fig. 1. Test materials in this paper. (a) The gray level image "airplane" with size 512×512. (b) The quadtree structure for "airplane", following the characteristics of the image.

Next, each square block in Fig. 1(b) can be regarded as a small image. From the descriptions in Sec. 2, we can see that after the embedding with histogram-based reversible data hiding, the two luminance values for max and zero points, namely, a_i for the max point and b_i for the zero point for the i-th block, respectively, and each can be represented by 8 bits, are served as the side information. Without loss of generality, we assume that $a_i < b_i, \forall i$. Under the extreme case that when the original image is highly active that implies that more blocks would be necessary for decomposing the original image, and each block in the image is represented by 16×16 block, there would be $\frac{512}{16} \times \frac{512}{16} = 1024$ blocks in total, and $1024 \times (8+8) = 16384$ bits of side information is produced.

Because only the value a_i is required for data extraction in each block, we set all the values of b_i to be the luminance value at zero point of the whole image, b, to reduce the overhead. By doing so, at most $1024 \times 8 + 8 = 8200$ bits of side information of the block map **B** is produced.

Finally, at the third round, after embedding the user-defined information **I** at the second round, histogram-based embedding should be performed on **X'**, and the max point in **X'**, a', should be at least 8200. If the max point in **X'** is incapable of embedding 8200 bits, we will search for luminance values $c' < a'$, such that the occurrences for both a' and c' are greater than 8200. After the embedding of the block map **B** is performed, the two-byte side information, containing a' and c', is transmitted to the decoder. That is, $\mathbf{S} = (a', c')$. Therefore, with our algorithm, very little overhead is needed for decoding. We can see that this amount of side information is comparable to those shown in literature.

3.2 The Three-Round Extraction Process

The goal for the extraction process is to recover both the original image $\mathbf{X}$ and the user-defined information $\mathbf{I}$ at the decoder, with the two-byte side information a' and c'. These are the reverse operations to the embedding process, and they can be outlined as follows.

Round 1. Perform the histogram-based reversible data extraction on $\mathbf{X}''$ with the side information $\mathbf{S}$. Reconstruct the block map $\mathbf{B}$ and obtain the luminance value of the max point for each block, a_i.

Round 2. Reconstruct the image $\mathbf{X}'$, which denote the original image $\mathbf{X}$ with the user-defined information $\mathbf{I}$.

Round 3. Generate the user-defined information $\mathbf{I}$ and the original image $\mathbf{X}$ with the conventional histogram-based reversible data extraction.

By following the descriptions above, we can effectively hide the user-defined information into the original image with high capacity and little overhead. At the decoder, after the reconstruction of the block map associated with quadtree decomposition, the both the user-defined information and the original image can be obtained. For verifying the correctness of out algorithm, both the inputs at the encoder and the outputs at the decoder are compared by calculating the MSE of images and the bit-error rate (BER) between embedded and extracted information. When both the MSE and the BER values are 0.0, the images and the information at the encoder and decoder are identical, and it implies that the correctness of the algorithm is verified.

4 Simulation Results

We perform the following simulations for the evaluation of our algorithm. All the three requirements are evaluated in comparison with conventional algorithm, including:

- ➢ the output image quality, represented by PSNR, after hiding the user-defined data;
- ➢ the capacity, represented by bits, of the user-defined data;
- ➢ the size of the overhead.

The first two requirements are easy for making comparisons. For the third one, we find that in Fig. 1(b), the block sizes after performing quadtree decomposition are different. Therefore, the different block sizes compose of the block map $\mathbf{B}$ for making data embedding and extraction possible. In order to make fair comparisons, we divide the original image into blocks with the same sizes of 512×512, 256×256, 128×128, 64×64, 32×32, and 16×16, respectively. In contrast with quatree decomposition, these configurations have regular patterns, and only one block size needs to be included into the block map. Hence, except for the block size, only the luminance of the max point in each block should be included in the block maps. On the contrary, with quadtree decomposition, we may expect the more overhead in the block map $\mathbf{B}$ because the side information of each block is composed of the block size and the luminance of max point. In order to make fair comparisons, even

Table 1. Comparisons of test image "airplane" with conventional scheme

Block size	512×512	256×256	128×128	64×64	32×32	16×16	Quadtree
Image quality (dB)	57.48	51.51	50.37	49.96	50.00	49.78	49.97
Capacity (bit)	30448	50844	75147	89979	97293	101475	95712

Table 2. Comparisons of image qualities and embedding capacities

Test image	airplane	F-16	Lena	pepper	tank	truck
Image size	512×512	512×512	512×512	512×512	512×512	512×512
Output image quality (dB)	49.97	51.34	51.13	51.03	51.80	51.81
Capacity	95712	25682	14303	12934	15254	15381
Increase in capacity over existing one (%)	214%	188%	384%	335%	61%	67%
MSE between original and recovered images	0.00	0.00	0.00	0.00	0.00	0.00
BER between embedded and extracted info	0.00%	0.00%	0.00%	0.00%	0.00%	0.00%

though the block map with quadtree decomposition is larger than the other cases, Round 3 of the embedding process comprise the block map even though somewhat degradation in output image quality can be expected. In order to embed the block map in Sec. 3.1, in the airplane image in Fig. 1, we choose $a' = 181$ and $c' = 172$ to serve as the side information, and the block map **B** can be embedded.

Table 1 depicts the comparisons between the image quality and embedding capacity under a variety of block sizes. For the block size of $512×512$, we see that the capacity is 30448 bits with the PSNR of 57.48 dB. These serve as a reference corresponding to existing scheme in [5]. We can see that when the block size gets smaller, more capacity can be embedded at the expense of degraded quality. Because the image qualities under all the block sizes are larger than 48.13 dB, we can claim that these qualities are acceptable. We can see that with quadtree decomposition, the performances accessed by quality and capacity lie between the block sizes of $32×32$ and $128×128$. If we set the PSNR the same, we can see that with quadtree decomposition, our algorithm can hide more capacity than the $64×64$ case.

Table 2 represents the simulation results with different test images. The image sizes are all $512×512$ for making fair comparisons. Regarding to the image qualities, they are all more than 48.13 dB. Corresponding capacities are also provided, and we can see that the capacities are highly correlated to the characteristics of original images, ranging from 12934 to 95712 bits. Next, the increases for the quadtree decomposition over existing method are provided. For instance, for the airplane image, the capacities for the quadtree and the conventional methods [5] are 95712 and

30448 bits, respectively. Therefore, we can easily calculate the increase in percentage by $\left(\frac{95712}{30448}-1\right)\times100\% = 214\%$.

At the decoder, after decoding with the 2-byte side information, the block map can be produced, and then both the original image and the user-defined information can be extracted. For verifying the reversibility of our algorithm, regarding to the image itself, we can see that all the mean square errors (MSE's) are 0.00, meaning that the recovered images are identical to their original counterpart. On the other hand, for the user-defined information, we can see that the bit error rates (BER's) between the embedded and extracted ones are all 0.00%, meaning that they are identical. Therefore, from the data shown in the bottom two rows in Table 2, we prove that our data hiding algorithm can reach the goal of reversibility.

5   Conclusions

In this paper, we proposed the three-round reversible data hiding algorithm with the characteristics of original image. Quadtree decomposition is taken into account in order to increase the embedding capacity with the acceptable quality of output image. With our simulation results, we have obtained the more embedding capacity, the acceptable output image quality, and the comparable amount of side information produced. Most important of all, we have verified that the proposed algorithm can reach the goal of reversibility.

We have conducted simulations based on the easily implemented algorithm by modifying the histogram of original image. The other branch for reversible data hiding, based on modifying the differences between consecutive pixels [6], can also be taken into account for further improvement of our algorithm in the future.

Acknowledgments. The authors would like to thank National Science Council (Taiwan, R.O.C) for supporting this paper under Grant No. NSC98-2221-E-390-017.

References

1. Pan, J.S., Huang, H.-C., Jain, L.C., Fang, W.C. (eds.): Intelligent Multimedia Data Hiding. Springer, Heidelberg (2007)
2. Huang, H.-C., Fang, W.C.: Metadata-Based Image Watermarking for Copyright Protection. Simulation Modelling Practice and Theory 18, 436–445 (2010)
3. Luo, L., Chen, Z., Chen, M., Zeng, X., Xiong, Z.: Reversible Image Watermarking Using Interpolation Technique. IEEE Trans. Inf. Forensics and Security 5, 187–193 (2010)
4. Sachnev, V., Kim, H.J., Nam, J., Suresh, S., Shi, Y.-Q.: Reversible Watermarking Algorithm Using Sorting and Prediction. IEEE Trans. Circuits Syst., Video Technol. 19, 989–999 (2009)
5. Ni, Z., Shi, Y.-Q., Ansari, N., Su, W.: Reversible Data Hiding. IEEE Trans. Circuits Syst., Video Technol. 16, 354–362 (2006)
6. Alattar, A.M.: Reversible Watermark Using the Difference Expansion of a Generalized Integer Transform. IEEE Trans. Image Process. 13, 1147–1156 (2004)

MAS: Malware Analysis System Based on Hardware-Assisted Virtualization Technology

Taehyoung Kim, Inhyuk Kim, Changwoo Min, and Young Ik Eom

School of Information and Communication Eng., Sungkyunkwan University,
300 Cheoncheon-dong, Jangan-gu, Suwon, Gyeonggi-do 440-746, Korea
{kim15m,kkojiband,multics69,yieom}@ece.skku.ac.kr

Abstract. There are many analysis techniques in order to analyze malicious codes. However, recently malicious codes often evade detection using stealthy obfuscation techniques, and attack computing systems. We propose an enhanced dynamic binary instrumentation using hardware-assisted virtualization technology. As a machine-level analyzer, our system can be isolated from almost the whole threats of malware, and provides single step analysis environment. Proposed system also supports rapid system call analysis environment. We implement our malware analysis system (referred as MAS) on the KVM hypervisor with Intel VT-x virtualization support. Our experiments with benchmarks show that the proposed system provides efficient analysis environment with low overhead.

Keywords: Malware, Dynamic Binary Instrumentation, Virtualization Technology, Intel VT, KVM.

1 Introduction

System security is the one of important issues to manage critical computing systems. Especially, malicious codes could leak confidential information of the individual and the enterprise, and infect hosts. Malware abuses incompleteness of system software and utilizes mistakes of system manager [1][2][3]. Thus, analyzing various malicious codes is essential to guarantee system security. However, complexity of obfuscation techniques has been increased continuously and newly modified malicious codes are generated exponentially. Therefore, more efficient and accurate analysis methods are required for secure system environments.

Recently, malware analysis methods which utilize virtualization technology are introduced such as Win32 API hooking, emulator, and full virtualization. Win32 API hooking shows excellent performance in the system call tracing, but can't trace instruction and memory access. Emulator, which realizes hardware function as software, can trace instruction and memory access, but it is too much slow and vulnerable to anti-debugging [4][5][6][7][8][9]. The full virtualization based on the binary translation is

T.-h. Kim et al. (Eds.): SecTech/DRBC 2010, CCIS 122, pp. 134–141, 2010.
© Springer-Verlag Berlin Heidelberg 2010

faster than emulator, but it is also vulnerable to anti-debugging. In case of full virtualization based on hardware-assisted VT, it shows better performance and escapes anti-debugging methods easily. Therefore, we propose the enhanced dynamic malware analysis system based on hardware-assisted VT.

2 Background

Dynamic code analysis method is utilized for various purposes such as observing behavior of process, developing applications, and so on. We design and implement dynamic code analysis system for analyzing malware. Therefore, in this section, we describe representative dynamic code analysis methods.

Because emulating environments is isolated from the real system, the emulator is utilized for various purposes. The emulator provides a virtual computing system through only software implementation without hardware support. Certainly, linux and other operating systems also can be executed on the emulator without code modification. Representative emulators are QEMU and Bochs. Also, representative dynamic code analyzers based on the emulator are BitBlaze [10], Renovo [11], VMScope [12], TTAnalyzer [13]. However, there is limitation to utilize emulator because of considerably slow executing speed.

In case of programs executing on general operating system, only general registers and user memory region are accessible. And another resource can be used through system call. On the other hand, the user-level dynamic code analyzer manage user context using shadow register, memory, and system call redirection. So, the user-level code analyzer can monitor all contexts without system call procedure in kernel context. Representative user-level code analyzers are Valgrind and Pin [14][15]. Even though user-level code analyzer is faster than emulator, it needs binary translation and can be easily exposed to anti-debugging.

Dinaburg proposed a machine-level dynamic code analyzer, Ether [16]. Ether is Xen based dynamic code analyzer using hardware-assisted function. Utilizing obfuscation break point of VAMPiRE, Ether supports memory trace, system call trace, and limited process trace. However, Ehter cannot analyze detail context such as DLL loading and API call information.

3 MAS

In this section, we introduce MAS: a transparent malware analysis system based on hardware-assisted virtualization technology. MAS provides two analysis phases: a single step phase, and a system call phase. Each analysis phase has special features. In the single step phase, MAS supplies detail analysis results of a whole process behavior. Especially, the single step phase is useful to analyze specific process. Simply observing behavior of process during user context, MAS provides an efficient analysis environment. Then, in the system call phase, MAS shows high performance close to a non-analysis phase.

3.1   Structure of MAS

Fig. 1 shows the structure of MAS. Using VT of Intel x86 processor, the full virtualization is implemented based on a KVM hypervisor. Memory virtualization is implemented as a shadow paging, and the device virtualization is implemented as the QEMU emulator.

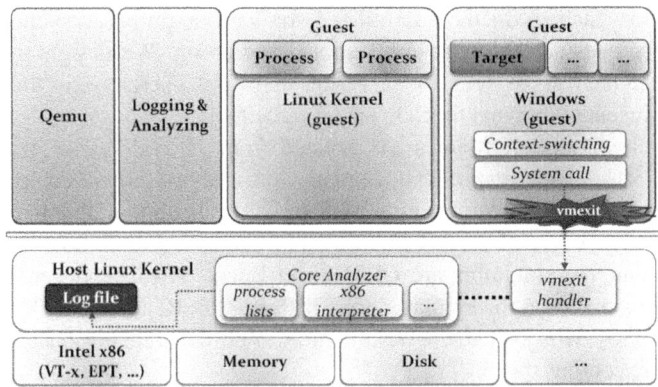

Fig. 1. Structure of MAS

We set a target process which runs on Windows guest OS. When the target process is switched by the scheduler, MAS begins analysis of target process. Invoking VMEXIT, MAS is able to analyze a whole context of guest depending on its purpose. Each VMEXIT handler carries out their duties such as page fault, general protection fault, and debug exception. A core analyzer component interprets instruction and manages process list which contains target process name. Also, the results of analyses are recorded whenever needed.

3.2   Single Step Phase

In the single step phase, the target process is observed by a unit of the instruction. For a complete single step analysis, MAS is designed to occur VMEXIT when guest OS access to cr register, or when debug exception is raised. The beginning of single step is to find a target process among all processes executing on guest OS. By the initialization setting, MAS invokes VMEXIT when the guest OS accesses to CR3 register for the context switching. In this case, the VMEXIT handler searches for a current process name in process lists to conform whether a current process is the target process or not. If the current process is the target process, MAS performs the single step analysis. Therefore, repeating the context switching check, we can select our concerned process. Fig. 2 shows the operation of the single step phase.

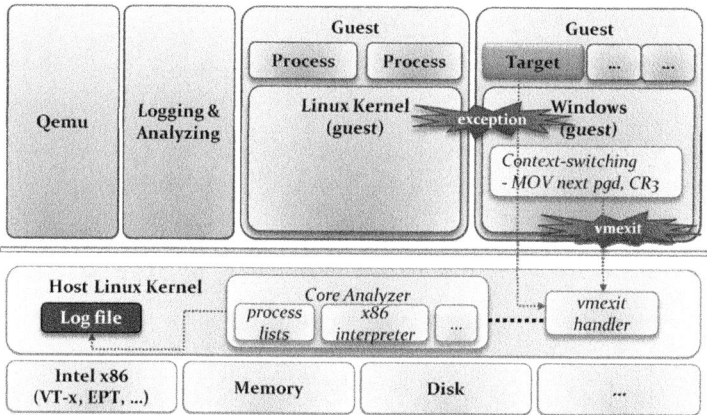

Fig. 2. Operation of single step phase

Once the target process is detected during context switching procedure, MAS sets up a trap flag of EFLAG register on x86 CPU. If the trap flag is turned on, guest OS will raise a debug exception immediately in the next instruction execution. According to the initialization setting of MAS, VMEXIT is occurred when the debug exception is raised. Then, the core analyzer interprets current context such as process id, instruction, register, stack, and memory. After logging necessary information, the trap flag is turned on once again. Therefore, the single step is continued until the not-target process is switched.

Furthermore, we can distinguish the current privileged level between the user level and the kernel level. Generally, it is required to monitor the user level context during the process execution for the malware analysis. Furthermore, malware frequently accesses disk and connects network. In many cases, these kinds of job require kernel services. And, malware which downloads new codes from the internet may require the procedure of network initialization. During the network connection, establishing connection is completed within a certain period of time. If the connection time is delayed by the process monitoring procedure, it is difficult to analyze the behavior of malware accurately. Therefore, our ring level detection scheme is powerful to monitor various malicious codes.

Ring level detection scheme is designed utilizing general protection fault. By setting guest machine to load a invalid descriptor during the context switching, we lead guest machine to invoke VMEXIT by the general protection fault. When the user mode is changed to kernel mode, and vice versa, VMEXIT is invoked. Then, we set the single step phase on/off state suitably. Thus, we can monitor only the user context.

Using single step, MAS supports several functions to meet requirements for dynamic malware analysis. Basically, instruction analysis is supported. When instruction accesses memory to read/write, corresponding related information are recorded in the logging file. Also, if instruction calls API, arguments and a return value of API call are recorded in the logging file. Fig 3 shows the algorithmic flow of single step.

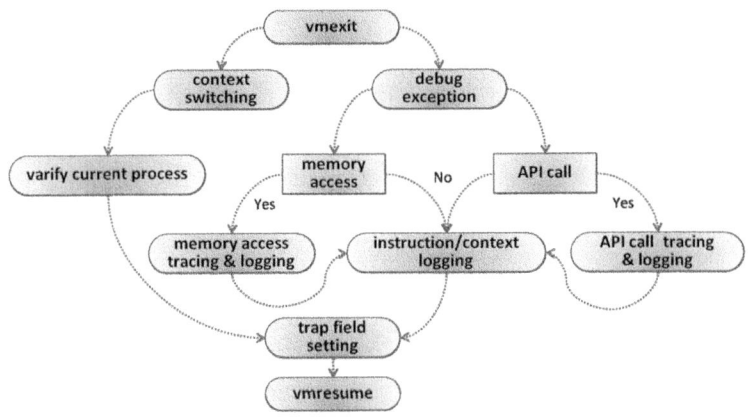

Fig. 3. Algorithmic flow of single step

3.3 System Call Phase

The system call tracing is possible in the single step phase. However, there is per-formance overhead in single step phase because the single step executes thousands of instruction to analyze one instruction. Therefore, MAS provides another analysis phase for tracing system call efficiently. Unlike the single step, the system call phase manages page fault by SYSENTER assembly instruction. As a fast system call, SYSENTER needs three MSR: SYSENTER_EIP_MSR, SYSENTER_CS_MSR, SYSENTER_ESP_MSR. MAS utilizes a feature of the SYSENTER operation. When the system call phase is set up, MAS injects invalid address to SYSENTER_EIP_MSR. Invalid address invokes page fault causing VMEXIT. Then, SYSENTER handler in hypervisor interprets system call information such as system call number and arguments. After logging related information, SYSENTER handler substitutes an invalid address of current EIP register by a valid address.

4 Implementation and Evaluation

Our proposed system, MAS, is implemented on the KVM hypervisor for the Intel x86 processor. KVM is a virtual machine monitor for Intel x86 architecture. KVM utilizes a modified version of QEMU for the device emulation. MAS is implemented as an extension version of KVM using Intel VT-x for the processor virtualization. In our implementation, we use Linux kernel 2.6.31. All the experiments are performed on a PC wih 2.8GHz Intel Core i7 processor and 4GB of physical memory. A guest OS is Windows XP with servicepack2.

In this section, we subscribe practical scenario by the single step phase of MAS and show experimental evaluation of MAS.

4.1 Practical Scenario of MAS

In this section, we verify that MAS provides powerful analysis environment by ana-lyzing the typical malicious code. Above all, we analyze packing malware. Malware utilizes packing methods in order to make analyzers to take a long time for analyzing the executing code. Using packing methods, malware can practice their object until packing is unpacked. Therefore, if packed malware is unpacked quickly, propagation of malware is minimized and the damage could be decreased.

Using MAS, we analyze the malicious packing code. We utilize the feature of the packing method. Fundamentally, packing codes copy some codes to specific address to restore original code. After unpacking the code, the corresponding code is executed on original entry point. Namely, the unpacking time is when the written code is executed. Therefore, we monitor the packing malware using a single step phase. We can analyze every instructions, memory accesses, and API calls. Especially, we trace a memory write operation. When there is the memory write operation, we record values of corresponding value of EIP, other registers, and instruction. Then, if the instruction on the logged address is executed, unpacked time is found finally. As above, MAS supports efficient malware analysis environment.

4.2   Performance Evaluation

The purposes of our experiments are to evaluate overhead of the system call phase and demonstrate effectiveness in the ring level detection scheme of the single step phase. In order to evaluate performance overhead, we utilize SPEC CPU 2006 benchmark. SPEC CPU 2006 is a CPU-intensive benchmark suite. We use 10 benchmarks among 29, which is composed of 12 integer benchmarks and 17 floating point benchmarks. Fig. 4 shows performance comparison of the system call phase in the proposed system. Baseline is the normalized running time when analysis phase is not applied. Total overhead of the whole benchmark is small, 1.33%. High overheads of some cases which need a lot of system call are lower than 6%.

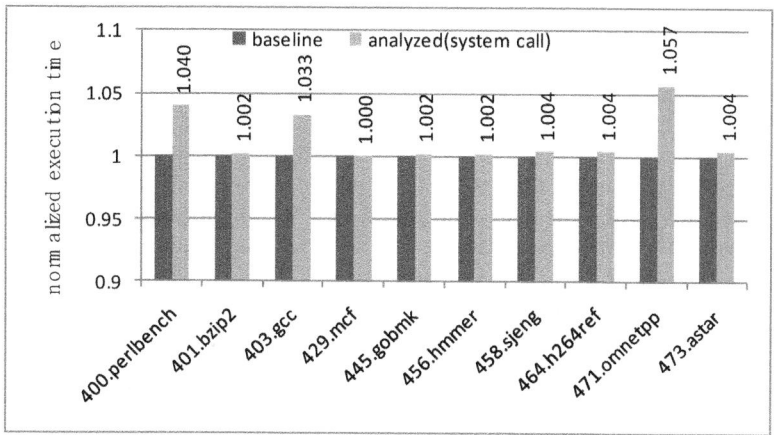

Fig. 4. Performance evaluation using SPEC 2006

In order to demonstrate effectiveness in the ring level detection scheme of the single step phase, we illustrate normalized execution time of representative GNU tools. Fig. 5 shows performance comparison of the single step phase in our system. Baseline is the general single step phase in which the overall execution context including both user context and kernel context are analyzed. User-only is the analysis mode which analyze only user context by the ring level detection scheme. Execution time of tar, md5sum, gzip, and wget are reduced significantly. Their performance gains over baseline are 48%, 32%, 14% and 42% respectively. In overall performance, the proposed system achieves 21% performance improvement.

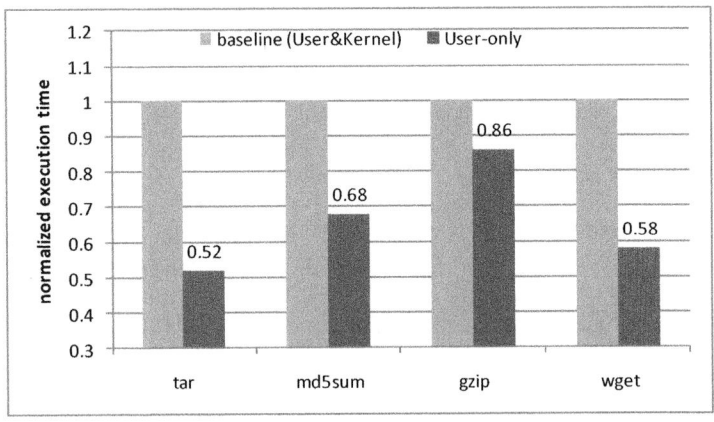

Fig. 5. Performance evaluation using representative GNU tools

5   Conclusion

In this paper, we introduced the enhanced malware analysis system based on hardware-assisted virtualization technology. Our system provided two analysis phases: single step phase and system call phase. In the single step phase, the detailed and various analyses are supported such as instruction tracing, memory tracing, and API call tracing. Especially, the ring level detection scheme strengthened efficiency of the single step phase. In case of the system call phase, it provides more efficient analysis environment. We implemented our system on KVM hypervisor using Intel VT-x. Throughout typical malware analyses, we show that our system provides the appropriate and efficient analysis environment. Our performance evaluations show that the system call phase of MAS has small performance overhead and the single step phase based on the ring level detection scheme significantly improves performance of analysis according to exclude analysis of kernel context.

Acknowledgement

This work is financially supported by the Ministry of Education, Science and Technology(MEST), the Ministry of Knowledge Economy(MKE) through the fostering project of HUNIC.

References

1. Idika, N., Mathur, A.P.: A Survey of Malware Detection Techniques. Research, Dept. of Computer Science, Purdue Univ. (2007)
2. Carvey, H.: Malware analysis for windows administrators. Digital Investigation 2, 19–22 (2005)
3. Pfleeger, C.P., Pfleeger, S.L.: Security in Computing. Prentice Hall, Englewood Cliffs (2003)
4. Garfinkel, T., Adams, K., Warfield, A., Franklin, J.: Compatibility is Not Transparency: VMM Detection Myths and Realities. In: Proc. of 11th Workshop on Hot Topics in Operating Systems (2007)
5. Ferrie, P.: Anti-unpacker tricks. In: CARO Workshop (2008)
6. Ferrie, P.: Attacks on Virtual Machines. In: AVAR Conf., pp. 128–143 (2006)
7. Listion, T., Skoudis, E.: On the Cutting Edge: Thwarting Virtual Machine Detection. SANS Internet Storm Center (2006)
8. Chen, X., Andersen, J., Mao, Z.M., Bailey, M., Nazario, J.: Towards an Understanding of Anti-virtualization and Anti-debugging Behavior in Morden Malware. In: DSN 2008, pp. 117–186 (2008)
9. Xu, M., Malyugin, V., Sheldon, J., Venkitachalam, G., Weissman, B.: ReTrace: Collecting Execution Trace with Virtual Machine Deterministic Replay. In: Proc. of 2007 Workshop on Modeling, Benchmarking and Simulation (2007)
10. BitBlaze Binary Analysis Platform, http://bitblaze.cs.berkeley.edu
11. Kang, M.G., Poosankam, P., Yin, H.: Renovo: A Hidden Code Extractor for Packed Executables. In: Proc. of WORM (2007)
12. Jiang, X., Wang, X., Xu, D.: Stealthy Malware Detection Through VMM-Based Out-of-the-Box Semantic View Reconstruction. In: Proc. of CCS, pp. 128–138 (2007)
13. Bayer, U., Kruegel, C., Kirda, E.: TTanalyze: A Tool for Analyzing Malware. In: Proc. of EICAR, pp.180–192 (2006)
14. Instrumentation Framework for building dynamic analysis tools, http://valgrind.org
15. A Dynamic Binary Instrumentation Tool, http://pintool.org
16. Dinaburg, A., Royal, P., Sharif, M., Lee, W.: Ether: Malware Analysis via Hardware Virtualization Extensions. In: Proc. of ACM CCS (2008)

Performance Analysis of Cyber Security Awareness Delivery Methods

Jemal Abawajy[1] and Tai-hoon Kim[2]

[1] School of Information Technology,
Deakin University, Melbourne, Australia
jemal@deakin.edu.au
[2] Department of Multimedia Engineering,
Hannam University, Daejeon, Korea
taihoonn@hannam.ac.kr

Abstract. In order to decrease information security threats caused by human-related vulnerabilities, an increased concentration on information security awareness and training is necessary. There are numerous information security awareness training delivery methods. The purpose of this study was to determine what delivery method is most successful in providing security awareness training. We conducted security awareness training using various delivery methods such as text based, game based and a short video presentation with the aim of determining user preference delivery methods. Our study suggests that a combined delvery methods are better than individual secrity awareness delivery method.

1 Introduction

As organisations of all sizes continue to depend on information technology to reduce costs and improve services, so have the likelihood of security risks that could damage or disable systems. Generally, organisations realise that information security is a critical facet to maintain profitability and a competitive edge. However, organisations tend to be more concerned about vulnerability to external threats. As a result, there has been increased spending on information security specialists and technology-based solutions. However, recent research suggests that a substantial proportion of security incidents originate from inside the organisation [1]. Many insider problems stem from ignorance rather than malicious motivation but this is equally dangerous because accidental failures can have large impacts. Thus, as organisations become more reliant on technology to achieve their business objectives, these mistakes become more critical and more costly.

The number of layers of technological defences can be as strong as possible, but information security is only as strong as its weakest link. Undeniably, technology-based information security solutions (e.g., firewalls, antivirus software, and intrusion detection system) are very important part of information security programs. Equally important though is the human factors such as user awareness and operator carelessness are as important as technical solutions [6]. It takes only a minor mishap from the people who access, use, administer, and maintain information resources to

T.-h. Kim et al. (Eds.): SecTech/DRBC 2010, CCIS 122, pp. 142–148, 2010.

undermine state-of-art technology-based security solutions. Thus, the success of information security program is ultimately relies on creating and maintaining security positive environments such that people understand and fully participate in the behaviours that are expected of them.

The need for user information security awareness is well documented [5, 6]. Although people constitute one of the most important assets of an organisation, they also represent one of the weakest loopholes in the security chain. If people fail to handle and protect organisation's assets in a secure manner, even stat-of-art technology-based solutions and security specialists alone can't provide the kind of overall security necessary to defend the wide variety of threats an organisation might face. Thus, the ultimate success of information security depends on appropriate information security practice behaviours by the end users.

The research question addressed in this paper is which security awareness training delivery method is most successful in providing information security awareness training. There is ample evidence that well designed user security awareness training can be effective to minimise information security risks [4]. It is important for a security awareness program to ensure that the appropriate topics are covered in the training. However, the critical success factor for an awareness program is the delivery methods [9]. Although there exist research on the efficiency of various information security delivery methods [4], the question of which delivery method is most successful in providing information security awareness training is yet to be answered.

The rest of the paper is organised as follows: In Section 2, we discuss social engineering attack in general and phishing in particular. In Section 3, we present various information security delivery methods. In Section 4, the methodology used in this paper is described. In Section 5, the result of the study is described. The conclusion is presented in Section 6.

2 Social Engineering Attacks

Information security awareness training program is about establishing, promoting and maintaining good security habits as a critical element of an effective information security management. The fundamental goal of information security awareness is to create "a change in attitudes which change the organisational culture. The cultural change is the realisation that information security is critical because a security failure has potentially adverse consequences for everyone. It aims to increase IT users understanding of how to follow responsible computing practices and why it is necessary. Increased staff awareness should also reduce the likelihood of accidental breaches and increase the probability of suspicious activities being recognised and reported.

In this paper, we focus on information security attacks that exploit user awareness vulnerabilities such as social engineering with particular emphases on phishing attacks. The reason for focusing on phishing attack is that it is a single topic that has a wealth of information for both technical and non technical users. Downs et al [7] found that some people may be aware of phishing, but they do not associate that awareness to their own vulnerability or to strategies for identifying phishing attacks.

There study also suggests that while people can protect themselves from familiar risks, they tend to have difficulties generalizing what they know to unfamiliar risks.

Phishing attacks exploit the fact that users tend to trust email messages and web sites based on cues that actually provide little or no meaningful trust information. They tend to target the most common activities (email and web) that the majority of users spend substantial times on. Also, phishers are increasingly setting their sights on such social networking sites as LinkedIn, Myspace, Facebook and Twitter. There is high level of user unfamiliarity with common phishing attacks suggesting educating users about online safety practices [2]. Lack of awareness of the dangers of reverse social engineering attacks can result in an unsuspecting employee disclosing company confidential information. Although automated systems can be used to identify some fraudulent email and web sites, these systems are not completely accurate in detecting phishing attacks [3].

3 Security Awareness Delivery Methods

One way to make people become security-conscious is through security awareness training. Thus, the mission of the information security awareness training is to create a security-conscious environment by removing vulnerabilities associated with human behaviours. As with any program, the success of a security awareness program will rely heavily on how the information is delivered. To this end, there are many information security awareness training delivery models.

The various delivery methods could be classified as informational awareness delivery methods, promotional delivery methods, online delivery methods, game-based delivery methods and simulation delivery methods. Examples of informational awareness delivery methods include leaflets, short articles, postings, e-mail warnings, tips-of-the-day, and newsletters. Examples of the promotional delivery methods include screen savers, banners, posters, pre-printed note pads/sticky notes, T-shirts, mugs and cups, mouse pads and stickers.

There are many different forms of online security awareness training delivery models. Web-based computer security awareness training (WBT) delivery methods offers user-friendly and flexible models that enable users to train at their own pace. It also provides the organization with the ability to train users to an enterprise-wide standard. The disadvantage of WBT-based delivery method includes [1]: (i) users attempt to complete the sessions with minimal time or thought; (ii) becomes monotonous; (iii) fails to challenge the user; (iv) and provides no dialogue for further elaboration. To address some of these shortcomings, the WBT-based delivery method designers may make the content engaging by including graphics, assessments, and animations to communicate regulatory requirements and company policies.

Games have become increasingly accepted as having enormous potential as powerful teaching tools that may result in an "instructional revolution" [8]. Several game-based security awareness and training delivery methods have been used currently. CyberCIEGE [1] is a game-based information security awareness training delivery methods. Another game-based awareness training system is Anti-Phishing Phil that aims to teach "users how to distinguish phishing URLs from legitimate once, where to look for cues in web browsers, and how to use search engines to find legitimate sites [3]. Game-based delivery methods are highly interactive and can be used to support organisational security training objectives while engaging typical users. It is believed that game-based awareness training delivery method offer an effective alternative to, or supplement for, more traditional modes of education [1].

Simulation-based information security awareness and training delivery methods have also been receiving some attentions. In simulation-based delivery model, users are sent simulated phishing emails by the experimenters to test users' vulnerability to phishing attacks. At the end of the study, users are given materials that inform them about phishing attacks. A study that compared simulation-based and pamphlet-based delivery models concluded that users who were sent the simulated phishing emails and follow-up notification were better able to avoid subsequent phishing attacks than those who were given a pamphlet containing information on how to combat phishing [11]. A similar approach, called embedded training that teaches users about phishing during their regular use of email is described in [4].

Information security awareness is an absolute necessity to ensure employees discharge their duties in the most secure way possible to prevent information security incidents. A major challenge with security awareness programs is the lack of a fully developed methodology to deliver them [10].

4 Methedology

The aim of the study was not to generalise, but to interpret some users' experiences of information security delivery methods. The design and analysis of this study draws on methodological experiences from those used in [3]. A total of 30 voluntary participants were involved in this study. The participants were chosen in such a way that we had a wide range of demographics. Each respondent completed pre-knowledge information questionnaires. All the participants are end users and 25% of them had received formal security training. Also 62% of the participants indicated that they enjoy playing games at least when playing for solely entertainment purposes. Furthermore, over 70% of the participants are reported as currently working either in a full time or a part time job.

We tested our participants' ability to identify phishing using a video-based, a game-based (i.e., Anti-Phishing Phil) and a text-based delivery models. The criteria we used for selecting appropriate awareness delivery method was that the materials should be easy to comprehend by non-technical users while at the same time not cause undue frustration with technical users. Most importantly, we were looking for materials that were short, to the point and easily accessible via a web browser, as we didn't want to consume too much of people's time by getting them to read lots of information to participate in this study.

We first asked the participants if they knew what phishing was. We then administrated the game-based awareness followed by the text-based delivery model, watch a short video and finally play the game again. After experiencing each different awareness training method, we collected data to see if the awareness training method improved the knowledge of the participants about phishing. At the end of the study, the participants were asked to complete an exit question that asked them what training method they felt informed them the most about the phishing attack.

5 Results and Discussion

Prior to undertaking the security awareness training, only half of the participants had an idea of what phishing is. However a definition does not equate to knowing the potential danger or the increasingly varied techniques used by those who wish to exploit users. As shown in Figure 1, after playing the game; awareness increased to 90% with about 30% of the participants changing their original answer. This is not surprising considering the game's focus on training the user to be able to spot illegitimate URLs. Even after playing the game, 8% of the participants still not knew what phishing was exactly.

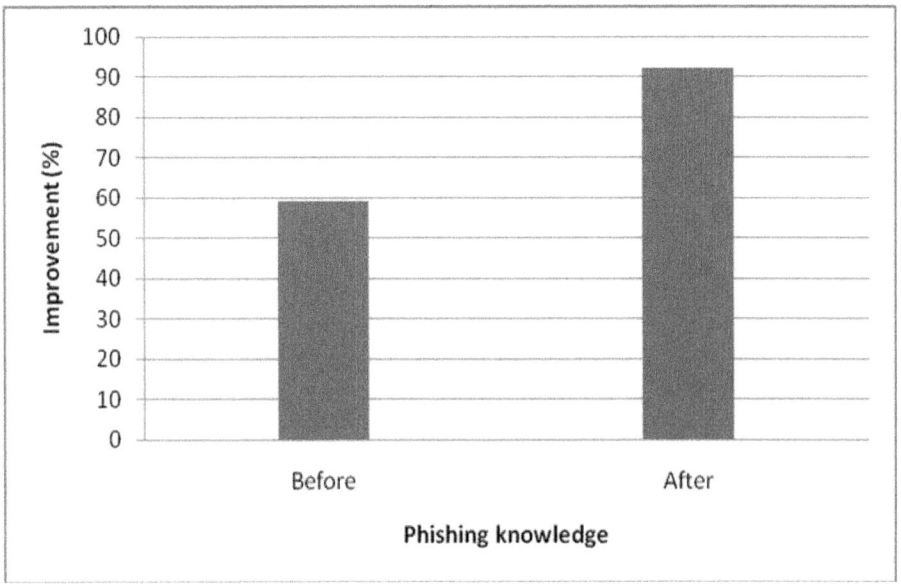

Fig. 1. Improvements in awareness about fishing

Note that the game-based delivery method consists of four rounds and each round focuses on a different class of phishing URLs. Also, each round is timed to limit how long one can take to consider the URLs. Ideally, an awareness program must influence behaviour changes that deliver measurable benefits. In order to see how much the text-based and the video-based awareness delivery methods increased the knowledge of the participants about phishing, we administrated the game-based awareness model one last time. This would also separate personal thought of those participants from what they had actually learnt.

Figure 2 shows the outcome of the experiment before and after the text-based and video-based awareness activities were administered to the participants. From the graph, it is clear that both the video-based and the text-based delivery methods improved the participants' knowledge about phishing attacks. The results for each round improved approximately by 50% on the second attempt of the game. Whilst

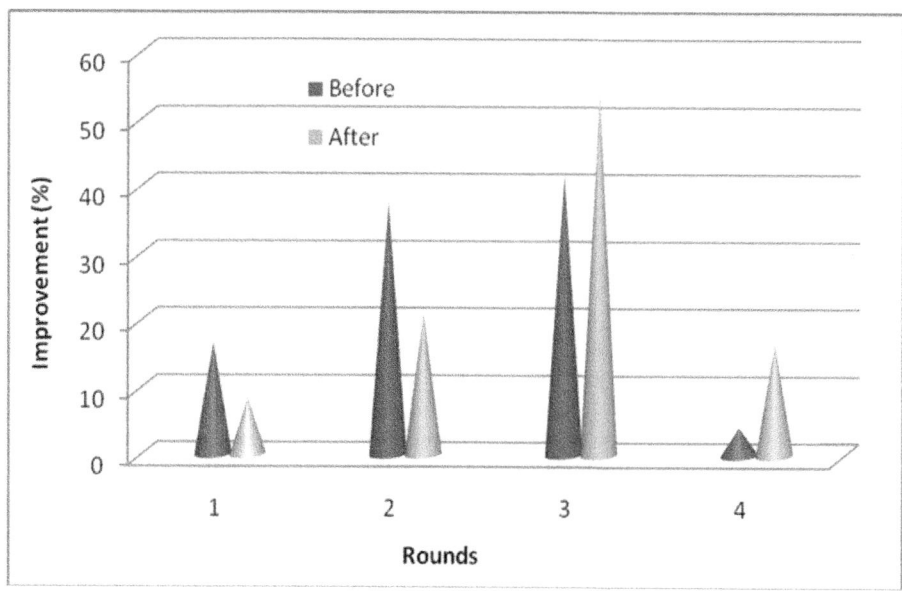

Fig. 2. Impact of conventional methods of security awareness training

these statistics present alarming support for video and text-based security awareness training, one cannot overlook the possibility that participants learnt by their mistakes after the first attempt and self-corrected their answers on the second attempt to suit. Also, A broadening in the knowledge of anti-phishing techniques was certainly evident through the text-based delivery model. The game-based delivery method was able to provide knowledge as to what to look for in the URL's, the text-based and the video-based awareness methods added the knowledge that emails are the main carrier of phishing attacks.

6   Conclusions

Despite the fact that people are the weakest link in the information security chain, organisations often focus on the technical solutions. In this paper, we looked at several information security awareness delivery methods in terms of their effectiveness in providing security awareness training. Our results suggest all information security awareness training delivery methods are powerful means of empowering people with knowledge on focused topics. Further, our investigation suggests that combining methods regularly improves the success of a security awareness campaign and helps keep the target audiences interested.

References

1. Cone, B.D., Thompson, M.F., Irvine, C.E., Nguyen, T.D.: Cyber Security Training and Awareness Through Game Play, Security and Privacy in Dynamic Environments. In: IFIP International Federation for Information Processing 2006, vol. 201, pp. 431–436 (2006)

2. Wu, M., Miller, R.C., Garfinkel, S.L.: Do Security Toolbars Actually Prevent Phishing Attacks? In: Grinter, R., Rodden, T., Aoki, P., Cutrell, E., Jeffries, R., Olson, G. (eds.) Proceedings of the SIGCHI Conference on Human Factors in Computing Systems, CHI, Montréal, Québec, Canada, April 22-27, pp. 601–610. ACM Press, New York (2006)
3. Sheng, S., Magnien, B., Kumaraguru, P., Acquisti, A., Cranor, L.F., Hong, J., et al.: Anti-Phishing Phil: The Design and Evaluation of a Game That Teaches People Not to Fall for Phish. In: Symposium On Usable Privacy and Security (SOUPS) 2007, Pittsburgh, PA, USA, July 18-20 (2007)
4. Kumaraguru, P., Rhee, Y., Acquisti, A., Cranor, L., Hong, J., Nunge, E.: Protecting People from Phishing: The Design and Evaluation of an Embedded Training Email System. In: Proceedings of the 2007 Computer Human Interaction, CHI (2007)
5. Albrechtsen, E.: A qualitative study of users' view on information security. Computers and Security 26(4), 276–289 (2007)
6. Abawajy, J.H., Thatcher, K., Kim, T.-h.: Investigation of Stakeholders Commitment to Information Security Awareness Programs. In: 2008 International Conference on Information Security and Assurance (ISA 2008), pp. 472–476 (2008)
7. Downs, J., Holbrook, M., Cranor, L.: Decision strategies and susceptibility to phishing. In: Proceedings of the Second Symposium on Usable Privacy and Security (SOUPS 2006), vol. 149 (2006)
8. Prenski M.: Digital game-based learning. McGraw-Hill, New York (2001); Gredler, M.E.: Games and simulations and their relationships to learning. In: Handbook of Research on Educational Communications and Technology, 2nd edn., pp. 571–581. Lawrence Erlbaum Associates, Mahwah (2004)
9. Shaw, R.S., Chen, C.C., Harris, A.L., Huang, H.-J.: The impact of information richness on information security awareness training effectiveness. Computers & Education 52, 92–100 (2009)
10. Valentine, J.A.: Enhancing the Employee Security Awareness Model. Computer Fraud & Security (6), 17–19 (2006)
11. New York State Office of Cyber Security & Critical Infrastructure Coordination. Gone Phishin, A Briefing on the Anti-Phishing Exercise Initiative for New York State Government. Aggregate Exercise Results for public release

Proxy Re-encryption with Keyword Search: New Definitions and Algorithms[*]

Wei-Chuen Yau[1], Raphael C.-W. Phan[2,**],
Swee-Huay Heng[3], and Bok-Min Goi[4]

[1] Faculty of Engineering, Multimedia University, Malaysia
`wcyau@mmu.edu.my`
[2] Electronic & Electrical Engineering, Loughborough University, United Kingdom
`r.phan@lboro.ac.uk`
[3] Faculty of Information Science & Technology, Multimedia University, Malaysia
`shheng@mmu.edu.my`
[4] Faculty of Engineering & Science, Tunku Abdul Rahman University, Malaysia
`goibm@utar.edu.my`

Abstract. We propose a new definition for searchable proxy re-encryption scheme (Re-PEKS), define the first known searchable proxy re-encryption scheme with a designated tester (Re-dPEKS), and then give concrete constructions of both Re-PEKS and Re-dPEKS schemes that are secure in the random oracle model.

Keywords: Searchable proxy re-encryption, public key encryption with keyword search, random oracle model.

1 Introduction

Public key encryption with keyword search (PEKS) schemes enable searching of keywords within encrypted messages. These schemes are desirable for mobile devices such as smartphones for selectively downloading encrypted messages from gateways, e.g. accessing to emails while on mobile internet. Consider an e-mail system that consists of three entities, namely, a sender (Bob), a receiver (Alice), and a server (email gateway). Bob sends an encrypted message M appended with some encrypted keywords $w_1, ..., w_n$ that are associated with the message to the email gateway in the following format:

$$\mathsf{PKE}(pk_A, M) || \mathsf{PEKS}(pk_A, w_1) || ... || \mathsf{PEKS}(pk_A, w_n),$$

where PKE is a standard public key encryption scheme and pk_A is the public key of Alice. Alice can give the email gateway a trapdoor associated with a searching keyword w. The PEKS scheme enables the gateway to test whether w is a keyword associated with the email but learns nothing else about the email.

The first PEKS scheme was proposed by Boneh et al. in 2004 [6]. Baek et al. [4] proposed a Secure Channel Free Public Key Encryption with Keyword Search

---

[*] Research supported by BGM Fund (MOSTI/BGM/R&D/500-2/8).
[**] Part of this work done while the author was visiting Multimedia University.

T.-h. Kim et al. (Eds.): SecTech/DRBC 2010, CCIS 122, pp. 149–160, 2010.
© Springer-Verlag Berlin Heidelberg 2010

(SCF-PEKS) scheme to remove the requirement of a secure channel for sending a trapdoor in PEKS of [6]. This scheme is also known as a PEKS scheme with a designated tester (dPEKS). A dPEKS scheme ensures that no one except the designated server is able to run the test function (dTest). Some other PEKS and dPEKS schemes in the literature include [1,3,4,9,10,11,12,13,14,15,18].

In some situations, Alice may need to delegate her decryption right to her assistant Carol. For such scenario, the email gateway needs to convert encrypted emails for Alice into ciphertexts which can be decrypted by Carol. This function can be achieved with proxy re-encryption (PRE) which was first introduced in [5]. More precisely, a proxy re-encryption scheme enables a semi-trusted proxy to convert a ciphertext encrypted under Alice's public key into a ciphertext of the same message for Carol with a given special information (i.e., a re-encryption key). However, the proxy should not learn secret keys of Alice or Carol and the plaintext during the conversion.

Since the original keyword ciphertext encrypted under Alice's public key cannot be tested with trapdoor generated by Carol, it is natural to ask how to enable searching of re-encrypted emails in the above-mentioned scenario. We need a way that enables Carol to instruct the gateway to search for those re-encrypted messages associated to certain keywords with her secret key. To do so, the gateway performs the re-encryption of message ciphertext with a standard proxy re-encryption (PRE) scheme, and re-encryption of keyword ciphertexts using a proxy re-encryption with keyword search (Re-PEKS) or searchable proxy re-encryption scheme. i.e.,

$$\mathsf{PRE}(rk, C) \| \mathsf{Re\text{-}PEKS}(rk, C_{w_1}) \| ... \| \mathsf{Re\text{-}PEKS}(rk, C_{w_n})$$

where rk is a re-encryption key to re-encrypt Alice's ciphertext into ciphertext for Carol, C is a message ciphertext encrypted with PKE, and $C_{w_1}, ..., C_{w_n}$ are keyword ciphertexts encrypted with PEKS. Shao et al. proposed a proxy re-encryption with keyword search (they called it as PRES) scheme [17] based on [7,8]. However, the formation of their scheme is different from the above formation of Re-PEKS scheme.

Contributions. In this paper, we propose a new definition for searchable proxy re-encryption scheme (Re-PEKS). Compared with the definition of proxy re-encryption with keyword search scheme (PRES) in [17], our definition has the following differences: Shao et al.'s PRES scheme encrypts the message and keyword in the same encryption algorithm. Our definition extends the original PEKS definition by including the algorithms of re-encryption key generation and re-encryption of keyword ciphertext. This approach keeps the encryption of message and encryption of keyword separate so that we can have the flexibility to select which standard PRE and Re-PEKS schemes to be used for satisfying the requirements of the actual applications . For example, we may combine a more efficient encryption function (Re-PEKS) used for keyword while encryption of the message uses standard PRE techniques.

A more substantial contribution of our work is that we define the first searchable proxy re-encryption scheme with a designated tester (Re-dPEKS). This scheme allows a proxy (e.g., an email gateway) with a re-encryption key to translate an keyword w encrypted under public key pk_A into the same keyword encrypted under a different public key pk_B. In addition, only a designated email gateway can test whether or not a given dPEKS ciphertext (encrypted keyword) is associated with an email upon receiving a trapdoor by using its private key, but learns nothing else about the email.

We give concrete constructions of both Re-PEKS and Re-dPEKS schemes and prove their security in the random oracle model under bilinear Diffie-Hellman (BDH) assumption.

We briefly describe some of the properties for re-encryption schemes [2] that are related to our proposed schemes:

- **Unidirectional:** Delegation from user X to user Y only allows re-encryption in one direction, i.e., $X \to Y$. If it allows re-encryption in both directions, i.e., from X to Y and vice versa ($X \leftrightarrow Y$), then the scheme is bidirectional. Our proposed scheme is bidirectional.
- **Multi-use:** A re-encryption ciphertext from user X to user Y can be re-encrypted again from user Y to user Z and so on, i.e., it can be re-encrypted multiple times. Our proposed scheme is multi-use.
- **Collusion safe:** Collusion of user X and proxy can recover user Y's secret key. Our scheme is not collusion safe, i.e., we assume no collusion between proxy and users.

2   Preliminaries

We briefly describe mathematical background and complexity assumptions that used throughout this paper.

Bilinear Maps. Let $\mathbb{G}$ and $\mathbb{G}_T$ denote two cyclic groups of prime order q. A bilinear map $e : \mathbb{G} \times \mathbb{G} \to \mathbb{G}_T$ satisfies the following properties:

- Bilinearity: For all $g \in \mathbb{G}$ and $a, b \in \mathbb{Z}_q$, $e(g^a, g^b) = e(g, g)^{ab}$.
- Non-degeneracy: There exists a $g \in \mathbb{G}$ such that $e(g, g) \neq 1$.
- Computability: There is an efficient algorithm to compute the map e.

Bilinear Diffie-Hellman (BDH) Problem. The BDH problem [7] is as follows: given $g, g^a, g^b, g^c \in \mathbb{G}$ as input, compute $e(g, g)^{abc} \in \mathbb{G}_T$. We say that BDH assumption holds if all polynomial time algorithms have a negligible advantage in solving the BDH problem.

Modified Bilinear Diffie-Hellman (mBDH) Problem. The mBDH problem [16] is as follows: given $g, g^a, g^b, g^c \in \mathbb{G}$ as input, compute $e(g, g)^{ab/c} \in \mathbb{G}_T$. We say that mBDH assumption holds if all polynomial time algorithms have a negligible advantage in solving the mBDH problem.

The mBDH problem is equivalent to the BDH problem, see the proof in [8] for the decisional variant of the assumption.

3   Bidirectional Re-PEKS Scheme

3.1   Definition

We define searchable proxy re-encryption scheme (Re-PEKS) and only consider bidirectional, multi-use Re-PEKS.

Definition 1. *(Bidirectional, Multi-use Re-PEKS) A bidirectional, multi-use, proxy re-encryption with keyword search (Re-PEKS) scheme consists of the following algorithms:*

- Setup(1^k): On input a security parameter 1^k, it returns a public parameter, $\mathcal{PP}$.
- KeyGen($\mathcal{PP}$): On input $\mathcal{PP}$, it returns a public-private key pair $[pk, sk]$.
- ReKeyGen($\mathcal{PP}, sk_i, sk_j$): On input $\mathcal{PP}$, a private key sk_i, and a private key sk_j, where $i \neq j$, it returns a re-encryption key $rk_{i \leftrightarrow j}$. [1]
- PEKS($\mathcal{PP}, pk_i, w$): On input $\mathcal{PP}$, pk_i, and a keyword $w \in$ keyword space $\mathcal{KW}$, it returns a PEKS ciphertext $C_{i,w}$ of w.
- RePEKS($\mathcal{PP}, rk_{i \leftrightarrow j}, C_{i,w}$): On input $\mathcal{PP}$, $rk_{i \leftrightarrow j}$, and an original PEKS ciphertext $C_{i,w}$, it returns a re-encryption PEKS ciphertext $C_{j,w}$ of w for receiver j.
- Trapdoor($\mathcal{PP}, sk_i, w$): On input $\mathcal{PP}$, sk_i, and a keyword w, it returns a trapdoor $T_{i,w}$.
- Test($\mathcal{PP}, C, T_w$): On input $\mathcal{PP}$, a PEKS ciphertext C=PEKS($\mathcal{PP}, pk, w'$), and a trapdoor T_w=Trapdoor($\mathcal{PP}, sk, w$), it returns 1 if $w = w'$ and 0 otherwise.

Correctness. Let key pairs $[pk_i, sk_i]$ and $[pk_j, sk_j] \leftarrow$ KeyGen($\mathcal{PP}$), $rk_{i \leftrightarrow j} \leftarrow$ ReKeyGen($\mathcal{PP}, sk_i, sk_j$), $C_{i,w'} \leftarrow$ PEKS($\mathcal{PP}, pk_i, w'$), $T_{i,w} \leftarrow$ Trapdoor($\mathcal{PP}, sk_i, w$), $T_{j,w} \leftarrow$ Trapdoor($\mathcal{PP}, sk_j, w$), $\forall w, w' \in$ keyword space $\mathcal{KW}$, it holds that

- Test($\mathcal{PP}, C_{i,w'}, T_{i,w}$) = 1 if $w = w'$, and 0 otherwise.
- Test($\mathcal{PP},$ RePEKS($\mathcal{PP}, rk_{i \leftrightarrow j}, C_{i,w'}$), $T_{j,w}$) = 1 if $w = w'$, and 0 otherwise.

We note that our searchable proxy re-encryption scheme (Re-PEKS) is an extended searchable public key encryption scheme (PEKS). In particular, we can add two algorithms, i.e., ReKeyGen and RePEKS, in a PEKS scheme to form a Re-PEKS scheme.

3.2   Security Model

The security of a Re-PEKS scheme requires that the adversary should not be able to distinguish which keyword corresponds to a given ciphertext without the trapdoor from the target receiver or a delegatee.

---

[1] This algorithm becomes noninteractive if the input of sk_j is replaced by public key pk_j, where the delegatee does not involve in the generation of re-encryption key.

Bidirectional, Multi-use Re-PEKS CKA-Security Game. We use the following game between a challenger and an active adversary $\mathcal{A}$ to define the security for the Re-PEKS scheme. The game consists of the following phases, which are executed in order. The oracles in each phase can be executed $\text{poly}(k)$ times in any order unless otherwise specified. We assume a static corruption model: i.e., adversary has to determine either corrupt a party or not at the time the key pair of each party is generated.

1. Game Setup:

   - **Public Parameter Generation**: The challenger runs $\text{Setup}(1^k)$ to generate the public parameter $\mathcal{PP}$ and gives it to the adversary $\mathcal{A}$. This oracle is executed first and only once.
   - **Uncorrupted Receiver Key Generation**: The challenger runs KeyGen$(\mathcal{PP})$ and returns a public-private key pair $[pk, sk]$. It gives pk to $\mathcal{A}$. Let $\mathcal{L}_H$ be the set of honest receiver indices.
   - **Corrupted Receiver Key Generation**: The challenger runs KeyGen$(\mathcal{PP})$ and returns a public-private key pair $[pk, sk]$. It gives $[pk, sk]$ to $\mathcal{A}$. Let $\mathcal{L}_C$ be the set of corrupt receiver indices.

2. Phase 1: $\mathcal{A}$ makes the following queries:

   - **Trapdoor Generation** $\mathcal{O}_{td}$: On input (i, w) by the adversary, where $i \in \mathcal{L}_H \cup \mathcal{L}_C$, $w \in$ keyword space $\mathcal{KW}$, the challenger runs Trapdoor$(\mathcal{PP}, sk_i, w)$ and returns a trapdoor $T_{i,w}$ associated with keyword w which generated by secret key of user i to $\mathcal{A}$.
   - **Re-encryption Key Generation** $\mathcal{O}_{rk}$: On input (i, j) by the adversary, where $i \neq j$, the challenger runs ReKeyGen$(\mathcal{PP}, sk_i, sk_j)$ and returns a re-encryption key $rk_{i \leftrightarrow j}$ to $\mathcal{A}$. We restrict that either both i and j are corrupted or both are uncorrupted, i.e., $i, j \in \mathcal{L}_H$ or $i, j \in \mathcal{L}_C$. In another words, re-encryption key queries between a corrupted and an uncorrupted party are not allowed.
   - **Re-encryption** $\mathcal{O}_{renc}$: On input (i, j) and an original PEKS ciphertext $C_{i,w}$ by the adversary, both either from $\mathcal{L}_H$ or $\mathcal{L}_C$, the challenger returns the re-encrypted PEKS ciphertext $C_{j,w} = \text{RePEKS}(\mathcal{PP}, \text{ReKeyGen}(\mathcal{PP}, sk_i, sk_j), C_{i,w})$. All re-encryption queries where $i = j$ or where $i \in \mathcal{L}_H$ and $j \in \mathcal{L}_C$ or where $i \in \mathcal{L}_C$ and $j \in \mathcal{L}_H$ are ignored, i.e., an output of $\bot$.

3. Challenge: On input (i^*, w_0, w_1) by the adversary, where $w_0, w_1 \in$ keyword space $\mathcal{KW}$, the challenger picks a random $b \in \{0, 1\}$ and returns the challenge ciphertext $C^* = \text{PEKS}(\mathcal{PP}, pk_{i^*}, w_b)$ to $\mathcal{A}$. The restriction is that $i^* \in \mathcal{L}_H$ and $\mathcal{A}$ did not previously ask for the trapdoors of $(i^*, w_0), (i^*, w_1)$ from $\mathcal{O}_{td}$. In addition, $\mathcal{A}$ did not previously ask for the re-encryption key of (i^*, j) or (j, i^*) from $\mathcal{O}_{rk}$ and the trapdoors of $(j, w_0), (j, w_1)$ from $\mathcal{O}_{td}$.

4. Phase 2: The adversary is allowed to ask the same types of queries as in Phase 1, except the following queries:

- $\mathcal{O}_{td}(i^*, w_b)$, where $b \in \{0, 1\}$.
- $\mathcal{O}_{rk}(i^*, j)$ and $\mathcal{O}_{td}(j, w_b)$, or $\mathcal{O}_{rk}(j, i^*)$ and $\mathcal{O}_{td}(j, w_b)$, where $b \in \{0, 1\}$.
- $\mathcal{O}_{renc}(i^*, j, C^*)$ and $\mathcal{O}_{td}(j, w_b)$, where $b \in \{0, 1\}$.

5. Guess: Finally, $\mathcal{A}$ outputs a guess $b' \in \{0, 1\}$ and wins the game if $b = b'$.

We define $\mathcal{A}$'s advantage in breaking the Re-PEKS scheme as:

$$\mathsf{Adv}_{\mathcal{A}}^{\mathsf{IND\text{-}CKA\ Re\text{-}PEKS}}(k) = |\Pr[b = b'] - 1/2|.$$

Definition 2. *We say that a Re-PEKS scheme is indistinguishability against an adaptive chosen keyword attack (IND-CKA) if for any polynomial time attacker $\mathcal{A}$ we have that $\mathsf{Adv}_{\mathcal{A}}^{\mathsf{IND\text{-}CKA\ Re\text{-}PEKS}}(k)$ is a negligible function.*

3.3   Construction

We construct a secure bidirectional, multi-use Re-PEKS scheme based on PEKS scheme in [6], except a slight modification in the structure of PEKS ciphertext and trapdoor. In addition, we use the re-encryption technique in [8,5]. These techniques are similar to the construction of PRES scheme in [17].

- Setup(1^k): Let $\mathbb{G}$ and $\mathbb{G}_T$ be bilinear groups of order q. Let $H_1 : \{0, 1\}^* \to \mathbb{G}$, and $H_2 : \mathbb{G}_T \to \{0, 1\}^k$ be independent hash functions. Given a security parameter k, the algorithm picks a random generator $g \in \mathbb{G}$. It returns a public parameter $\mathcal{PP} = (q, \mathbb{G}, \mathbb{G}_T, g, e, H_1, H_2)$.
- KeyGen($\mathcal{PP}$): On input $\mathcal{PP}$, select a random value $x \in \mathbb{Z}_q$. Set receiver's public key $pk = g^x$ and private key $sk = x$. Return $[pk, sk]$.
- ReKeyGen($\mathcal{PP}, sk_X, sk_Y$): On input $sk_X = x$ and $sk_Y = y$, output the bidirectional re-encryption key $rk_{X \leftrightarrow Y} = y/x \bmod q$.[2]
- PEKS($\mathcal{PP}, pk_X, w$): To encrypt a keyword $w \in$ keyword space $\mathcal{KW}$ under receiver's public key $pk_X = g^x$, select a random value $r \in \mathbb{Z}_q$ and compute the PEKS ciphertext $C_{X,w} = [A, B] = [g^{xr}, H_2(e(g^r, H_1(w)))]$.
- RePEKS($\mathcal{PP}, rk_{X \leftrightarrow Y}, C_{X,w}$): On input a re-encryption key $rk_{X \leftrightarrow Y}$, and a PEKS ciphertext $C_{X,w} = [A, B]$, compute $A' = A^{rk_{X \leftrightarrow Y}} = g^{(xr)(y/x)} = g^{yr}$. Output the re-encrypted PEKS ciphertext from receiver X to Y as $C_{Y,w} = [A', B]$.
- Trapdoor($\mathcal{PP}, sk_X, w$): On input a receiver's private key $sk_X = x$ and a keyword w, output the trapdoor as $T_{X,w} = H_1(w)^{1/x}$.
- Test($\mathcal{PP}, C, T_w$): On input a PEKS ciphertext $C = [A, B]$ and a trapdoor T_w, check if $B = H_2(e(A, T_w))$. It outputs 1 if the above equality holds, and 0 otherwise.

---

[2] User X with private key x can delegate to user Y with private key y by selecting a random $r \in \mathbb{Z}_q$ and sending $rx \bmod q$ to Y as well as r to proxy. Y sends $y/rx \bmod q$ to proxy. The proxy computes re-encryption key $rk_{X \leftrightarrow Y} = (r)(y/rx) \bmod q = y/x \bmod q$. We assume that communications among proxy and users are via a secure channel. In addition, the scheme makes no security guarantee if the proxy colludes with either party [8].

Correctness:
Assume the PEKS ciphertext of keyword w' is $[A, B] = [g^{xr}, H_2(e(g^r, H_1(w')))]$ and the trapdoor associated to keyword w is $T_{X,w} = H_1(w)^{\frac{1}{x}}$. If $w = w'$, $B = H_2(e(g^r, H_1(w'))) = H_2(e(g^{xr}, H_1(w')^{\frac{1}{x}})) = H_2(e(A, T_{X,w}))$. It is easy to verify that the correctness of the equation holds for multi-test as re-encrypted ciphertext has the same form as the original ciphertext.

3.4 Security Analysis

Theorem 1. *The Re-PEKS scheme is* IND-CKA *secure in the random oracle model assuming that the mBDH problem is intractable.*

Proof. Let $\mathcal{A}$ be a polynomial-time attack algorithm that has advantage ϵ in breaking the Re-PEKS scheme. Suppose $\mathcal{A}$ makes at most $q_{H_2} > 0$ queries to the random oracle H_2 and at most $q_{td} > 0$ trapdoor queries. We construct an algorithm $\mathcal{B}$ that has an advantage of $\epsilon/(e q_{td} q_{H_2})$ in solving the mBDH problem in $\mathbb{G}, \mathbb{G}_T$, where e is a base of the natural logarithm. On mBDH input $(g, u_1 = g^\alpha, u_2 = g^\beta, u_3 = g^\gamma \in \mathbb{G})$, $\mathcal{B}$'s goal is to compute $e(g, g)^{\alpha\beta/\gamma}$. $\mathcal{B}$ simulates the challenger and interacts with $\mathcal{A}$ as follows:

1. Game Setup:

   - **Public Parameter Generation**: $\mathcal{B}$ setups the public parameter $\mathcal{PP}$ and gives $\mathcal{PP} = (q, \mathbb{G}, \mathbb{G}_T, g, e, H_1, H_2)$ to $\mathcal{A}$.
   - **Uncorrupted Receiver Key Generation**: On input an index i, $\mathcal{B}$ selects a random $x_i \in \mathbb{Z}_q$, and outputs the public key $pk_i = u_3^{x_i} = (g^\gamma)^{x_i}$, where the private key is implicitly defined as $sk_i = \gamma x_i$. It adds the tuple $\langle i, pk_i, x_i \rangle$ in $\mathcal{L}_H$.
   - **Corrupted Receiver Key Generation**: On input an index i, $\mathcal{B}$ selects a random $x_i \in \mathbb{Z}_q$, and outputs $pk_i = g^{x_i}$ and $sk_i = x_i$. It adds the tuple $\langle i, pk_i, x_i \rangle$ in $\mathcal{L}_C$.

2. Hash Function Queries: $\mathcal{A}$ can query the random oracle H_1 or H_2 any time.

   - **H_1-query $\mathcal{O}_{H_1}$**: $\mathcal{B}$ maintains an H_1-list with tuples $\langle w_n, h_n, d_n, c_n \rangle$ which is initially empty. On input w_i, $\mathcal{B}$ responds as follows:
     - If the query w_i is found in the H_1-list with an entry $\langle w_i, h_i, d_i, c_i \rangle$, output $H_1(w_i) = h_i$.
     - Otherwise, $\mathcal{B}$ selects a random $d_i \in \mathbb{Z}_q$ and generates a random coin $c_i \in \{0, 1\}$ so that $\Pr[c_i = 0] = 1/(q_{td} + 1)$.
       - If $c_i = 1$, $\mathcal{B}$ computes $h_i = u_3^{d_i} = (g^\gamma)^{d_i}$.
       - If $c_i = 0$, $\mathcal{B}$ computes $h_i = u_1^{d_i} = (g^\alpha)^{d_i}$.
       $\mathcal{B}$ adds the tuple $\langle w_i, h_i, d_i, c_i \rangle$ to H_1-list and returns $H_1(w_i) = h_i$.
   - **H_2-query $\mathcal{O}_{H_2}$**: Similarly, $\mathcal{B}$ maintains an H_2-list with tuples $\langle t, M \rangle$ which is initially empty. On input $t \in \mathbb{G}_T$, $\mathcal{B}$ responds with $H_2(t) = M$. For each new t, $\mathcal{B}$ responds to the $H_2(t)$ query by selecting a new random value $M \in \{0, 1\}^k$ and setting $H_2(t) = M$. $\mathcal{B}$ then adds the tuple $\langle t, M \rangle$ to the H_2 list.

3. **Phase 1:** When $\mathcal{A}$ issues the following queries, $\mathcal{B}$ responds as follows:

- **Trapdoor Generation:** On input (i, w_i) to $\mathcal{O}_{td}$, do:
  - $\mathcal{B}$ gets the response from $\mathcal{O}_{H_1}$ to obtain an entry $\langle w_i, h_i, d_i, c_i \rangle$ in H_1-list. If $c_i = 0$, output $\perp$ and abort. Otherwise, we know $c_i = 1$ and we have $h_i = u_3^{d_i} = (g^\gamma)^{d_i} \in \mathbb{G}$ in the H_1-list.
  - If $i \in \mathcal{L}_C$, $\mathcal{B}$ selects a random $r' \in \mathbb{Z}_q$, and sets $U = g^{r'}$ and $V = h_i^{1/x_i} = (g^\gamma)^{d_i/x_i}$, where x_i is obtained from $\langle i, pk_i, x_i \rangle$ in $\mathcal{L}_C$
  - If $i \in \mathcal{L}_H$, $\mathcal{B}$ selects a random value $r' \in \mathbb{Z}_q$, and sets $U = g^{r'}$ and $V = g^{d_i/x_i}$, where x_i is obtained from the tuple $\langle i, pk_i, x_i \rangle$ in $\mathcal{L}_H$. Observe that $H_1(w_i)^{1/\gamma x_i} = (g^{\gamma \cdot d_i})^{1/\gamma x_i} = g^{d_i/x_i}$ and therefore V is the correct trapdoor component for the keyword w_i under the implicitly defined user's private key γx_i.
  - $\mathcal{B}$ gives $T_{i,w_i} = [U, V]$ to $\mathcal{A}$.

- **Re-encryption Key Generation:** On input (i, j) to $\mathcal{O}_{rk}$, do:
  - If (1) $i \in \mathcal{L}_H$ and $j \in \mathcal{L}_C$ or (2) $i \in \mathcal{L}_C$ and $j \in \mathcal{L}_H$ or (3) $i = j$ or (4) i or j not in $\mathcal{L}_H$ or $\mathcal{L}_C$, output $\perp$.
  - Otherwise, output $rk_{i\leftrightarrow j} = x_j/x_i$.

- **Re-encryption:** On input $(i, j, C_{i,w})$ to $\mathcal{O}_{renc}$ where $C_{i,w}$ is an original PEKS ciphertext, do:
  - If (1) $i \in \mathcal{L}_H$ and $j \in \mathcal{L}_C$ or (2) $i \in \mathcal{L}_C$ and $j \in \mathcal{L}_H$ or (3) $i = j$ or (4) i or j not in $\mathcal{L}_H$ or $\mathcal{L}_C$, output $\perp$.
  - If i and j are both from $\mathcal{L}_H$ or they are both from $\mathcal{L}_C$, $\mathcal{B}$ obtains the re-encryption key $rk_{i\leftrightarrow j} = x_j/x_i$ from $\mathcal{O}_{rk}$ and returns the re-encryption ciphertext $C_{j,w} = \mathsf{RePEKS}(\mathcal{PP}, x_j/x_i, C_{i,w})$ to $\mathcal{A}$.

4. **Challenge:** At some point, $\mathcal{A}$ gives the challenge tuple (i^*, w_0, w_1) to $\mathcal{B}$, where $w_0, w_1 \in$ keyword space $\mathcal{KW}$, do:

- If (1) i^* is not from $\mathcal{L}_H$ or (2) the trapdoors of $(i^*, w_0), (i^*, w_1)$ from $\mathcal{O}_{td}$ was asked by $\mathcal{A}$ in Phase 1, or (3) the re-encryption key of (i^*, j) from $\mathcal{O}_{rk}$ and the trapdoors of $(j, w_0), (j, w_1)$ from $\mathcal{O}_{td}$ were asked by $\mathcal{A}$ in Phase 1, $\mathcal{B}$ returns $\perp$.
- Otherwise, $\mathcal{B}$ asks $\mathcal{O}_{H_1}$ to obtain $h_0, h_1 \in \mathbb{G}$ such that $H_1(w_0) = h_0$ and $H_1(w_1) = h_1$. Let $\langle w_b, h_b, d_b, c_b \rangle$, where $i \in \{0, 1\}$, be the corresponding tuples in H_1-list. If both $c_0 = 1$ and $c_1 = 1$, $\mathcal{B}$ returns $\perp$ and aborts.
- Otherwise, at least one of c_0 or c_1 is equal to 0. $\mathcal{B}$ picks a random $b \in \{0, 1\}$ such that $c_b = 0$.
- $\mathcal{B}$ selects a random $M^* \in \{0, 1\}^k$ and sets $A^* = u_2^{x_{i^*}} = g^{\beta \cdot x_{i^*}}$ and $B^* = M^*$. Note that this challenge implicitly defines $A^* = (pk_{i^*})^{\beta/\gamma} = (g^{\gamma \cdot x_{i^*}})^{\beta/\gamma}$. Also, it defines $M^* = H_2(e(g^{\beta/\gamma}, H_1(w_b))) = H_2(e(g^{\beta/\gamma}, g^{\alpha d_b})) = H_2(e(g, g)^{(\alpha\beta/\gamma)(d_b)})$. Thus, $C^* = [A^*, B^*]$ is a valid PEKS ciphertext for w_b as required. $\mathcal{B}$ returns the challenge PEKS ciphertext C^* to $\mathcal{A}$.

5. Phase 2: $\mathcal{A}$ is allowed to ask the same query types as in Phase 1 and $\mathcal{B}$ responds identically in Phase 1, except the following queries where $\mathcal{B}$ returns $\perp$:

   – $\mathcal{O}_{td}(i^*, w_b)$, where $b \in \{0, 1\}$.
   – $\mathcal{O}_{rk}(i^*, j)$ and $\mathcal{O}_{td}(j, w_b)$, or $\mathcal{O}_{rk}(j, i^*)$ and $\mathcal{O}_{td}(j, w_b)$, where $b \in \{0, 1\}$.
   – $\mathcal{O}_{renc}(i^*, j, C^*)$ and $\mathcal{O}_{td}(j, w_b)$, where $b \in \{0, 1\}$.

6. Guess: Finally, $\mathcal{A}$ outputs a guess $b' \in \{0, 1\}$. $\mathcal{B}$ picks a random pair $\langle t, M \rangle$ from the H_2-list and outputs t^{1/d_b} as its guess for $e(g, g)^{\alpha\beta/\gamma}$, where d_b is the value used in the Challenge step. Since $\mathcal{A}$ must have asked a query of either $H_2(e(g^{\beta/\gamma}, H_1(w_0)))$ or $H_2(e(g^{\beta/\gamma}, H_1(w_1)))$, the H_2-list contains a tuple where $t = e(g^{\beta/\gamma}, H_1(w_b)) = e(g, g)^{(\alpha\beta/\gamma)(d_b)}$ with probability $1/2$. If $\mathcal{B}$ picks this tuple $\langle t, M \rangle$, then $t^{1/d_b} = e(g, g)^{\alpha\beta/\gamma}$ as required.

This completes the description of algorithm $\mathcal{B}$.

4 Bidirectional Re-dPEKS Scheme

4.1 Definition

We define searchable proxy re-encryption scheme with a designated tester (Re-dPEKS) and only consider bidirectional, multi-use Re-dPEKS.

Definition 3. *(**Bidirectional, Multi-use Re-dPEKS**) A bidirectional, multi-use, searchable proxy re-encryption with a designated tester (Re-dPEKS) scheme consists of the following algorithms:*

- GlobalSetup(1^k): On input a security parameter 1^k, it returns a global parameter, $\mathcal{GP}$.
- KeyGen$_S(\mathcal{GP})$: On input $\mathcal{GP}$, it returns a public-private key pair $[pk_S, sk_S]$ of the server S.
- KeyGen$_R(\mathcal{GP})$: On input $\mathcal{GP}$, it returns a public-private key pair $[pk_R, sk_R]$ of the receiver R.
- ReKeyGen($\mathcal{GP}, sk_{R_i}, sk_{R_j}$): On input $\mathcal{GP}$, a private key sk_{R_i}, and a private key sk_{R_j}, where $i \neq j$, it returns a re-encryption key $rk_{R_i \leftrightarrow R_j}$ for receiver R_j
- dPEKS($\mathcal{GP}, pk_{R_i}, pk_S, w$): On input $\mathcal{GP}$, pk_{R_i}, pk_S, and a keyword w, it returns a dPEKS ciphertext $C_{i,w}$ of w.
- RedPEKS($\mathcal{GP}, rk_{R_i \leftrightarrow R_j}, C_{i,w}$): On input $\mathcal{GP}$, $rk_{R_i \leftrightarrow R_j}$, pk_S, and an original dPEKS ciphertext $C_{i,w}$, it returns a re-encryption dPEKS ciphertext $C_{j,w}$ of w for receiver R_j.
- dTrapdoor($\mathcal{GP}, pk_S, sk_{R_i}, w$): On input $\mathcal{GP}$, pk_S, sk_{R_i}, and a keyword w, it returns a trapdoor $T_{i,w}$.
- dTest($\mathcal{GP}, sk_S, C, T_w$): On input $\mathcal{GP}$, sk_S, a dPEKS ciphertext C=dPEKS($\mathcal{GP}, pk_R, pk_S, w'$), and a trapdoor T_w=dTrapdoor($\mathcal{GP}, pk_S, sk_R, w$), it returns 1 if $w = w'$ and 0 otherwise.

Correctness. Let key pairs $[pk_{R_i}, sk_{R_i}]$ and $[pk_{R_j}, sk_{R_j}] \leftarrow$ KeyGen$_R(\mathcal{GP})$, $rk_{R_i \leftrightarrow R_j} \leftarrow$ ReKeyGen$(\mathcal{GP}, sk_{R_i}, sk_{R_j})$, $C_{i,w'} \leftarrow$ dPEKS$(\mathcal{GP}, pk_{R_i}, pk_S, w')$, $T_{i,w} \leftarrow$ dTrapdoor$(\mathcal{GP}, pk_S, sk_{R_i}, w)$, $T_{j,w} \leftarrow$ dTrapdoor$(\mathcal{GP}, pk_S, sk_{R_j}, w)$, $\forall w, w' \in$ keyword space $\mathcal{KW}$, it holds that

- dTest$(\mathcal{GP}, sk_S, C_{i,w'}, T_{i,w}) = 1$ if $w = w'$, and 0 otherwise.
- dTest$(\mathcal{GP}, sk_S, $RedPEKS$(\mathcal{GP}, rk_{R_i \leftrightarrow R_j}, C_{i,w'}), T_{j,w}) = 1$ if $w = w'$, and 0 otherwise.

We note that our searchable proxy re-encryption scheme with a designated tester (Re-dPEKS) is an extended searchable public key encryption scheme with a designated tester (dPEKS). In particular, we can add two algorithms, i.e., ReKeyGen and RedPEKS, in a dPEKS scheme to form a Re-dPEKS scheme.

4.2   Security Model

We need to consider the adversary is either a malicious server or a malicious user. A malicious server should not be able to distinguish which keyword corresponds to a given ciphertext without the trapdoor from the target receiver or a delegatee. A malicious user should not be able to distinguish which keyword corresponds to a target ciphertext without the server's secret key even s/he has the trapdoor of the keyword. We can model these two adversaries with two separate security games. Alternatively, we can use one game to simulate the capability of the adversaries by allowing them to call some restricted functions, such as dTrapdoor for malicious server and dTest for malicious user.

Re-dPEKS CKA-Security Game. Some parts of the security game are similar to those of Section 3.2, so for compactness this is left to the full version. Similarly, we define $\mathcal{A}$'s advantage in breaking the Re-dPEKS scheme as:

$$\mathsf{Adv}_{\mathcal{A}}^{\mathsf{IND\text{-}CKA\ Re\text{-}dPEKS}}(k) = |\Pr[b = b'] - 1/2|.$$

Definition 4. *We say that a Re-dPEKS scheme is indistinguishability against an adaptive chosen keyword attack (IND-CKA) if for any polynomial time attacker $\mathcal{A}$ we have that $\mathsf{Adv}_{\mathcal{A}}^{\mathsf{IND\text{-}CKA\ Re\text{-}dPEKS}}(k)$ is a negligible function.*

4.3   Construction

We construct a secure bidirectional, multi-use Re-dPEKS scheme based on dPEKS scheme in [15,14] and use the re-encryption technique in [8,5].

- GlobalSetup(1^k): Let $\mathbb{G}$ and $\mathbb{G}_T$ be bilinear groups of order q. Let $H_1 : \{0,1\}^* \to \mathbb{G}$, and $H_2 : \mathbb{G}_T \to \{0,1\}^k$ be independent hash functions. Given a security parameter k, the algorithm picks a random generator $g \in \mathbb{G}$. It returns a global parameter $\mathcal{GP} = (q, \mathbb{G}, \mathbb{G}_T, g, e, H_1, H_2)$.
- KeyGen$_S(\mathcal{GP})$: On input $\mathcal{GP}$, select a random value $a \in \mathbb{Z}_q$. Set server's public key $pk_S = g^a$ and private key $sk_S = a$. Return $[pk_S, sk_S]$.

- KeyGen$_R(\mathcal{GP})$: On input $\mathcal{GP}$, select a random value $x \in \mathbb{Z}_q$. Set receiver's public key $pk_R = g^x$ and private key $sk_R = x$. Return $[pk_R, sk_R]$.
- ReKeyGen$(\mathcal{GP}, sk_{R_X}, sk_{R_Y})$: On input $sk_{R_X} = x$ and $sk_{R_Y} = y$, output the bidirectional re-encryption key $rk_{R_X \leftrightarrow R_Y} = y/x \bmod q$.
- dPEKS$(\mathcal{GP}, pk_R, pk_S, w)$: To encrypt a keyword $w \in$ keyword space $\mathcal{KW}$ under receiver's public key $pk_R = g^x$ and designated server's public key $pk_S = g^a$, select a random value $r \in \mathbb{Z}_q$ and compute the ciphertext $C = [A, B] = [g^{xr}, H_2(e(g^a, H_1(w)^r))]$.
- RedPEKS$(\mathcal{GP}, rk_{R_X \leftrightarrow R_Y}, C_{X,w})$: On input a re-encryption key $rk_{R_X \leftrightarrow R_Y}$, and a dPEKS ciphertext $C = [A, B]$, compute $A' = A^{rk_{R_X \leftrightarrow R_Y}} = g^{(xr)(y/x)} = g^{yr}$. Output the re-encrypted ciphertext from user R_X to R_Y as $C' = [A', B]$.
- dTrapdoor$(\mathcal{GP}, pk_S, sk_{R_X}, w)$: On input a receiver's private key sk_{R_X} and a keyword w, select a random $r' \in \mathbb{Z}_q$ and output the trapdoor for a designated server S with public key $pk_S = g^a$ as $T_w = [U, V] = [g^{r'}, H_1(w)^{1/x} \cdot (g^a)^{r'}]$.
- dTest$(\mathcal{GP}, sk_S, C, T_w)$: On input a dPEKS ciphertext $C = [A, B]$ and a trapdoor $T_w = [U, V]$, the designated server with private key $sk_S = a$ first computes $\mathcal{T} = V/U^a$ and then checks if $B = H_2(e(A, \mathcal{T}^a))$. It outputs 1 if the above equality holds, and 0 otherwise.

Correctness:
Assume the dPEKS ciphertext of keyword w' is $[A, B] = [g^{xr}, H_2(e(g^a, H_1(w')^r))]$ and the trapdoor associated to keyword w is $[U, V] = [g^{r'}, H_1(w)^{\frac{1}{x}} \cdot (g^a)^{r'}]$, we have $\mathcal{T} = \frac{H_1(w)^{\frac{1}{x}} \cdot (g^a)^{r'}}{(g^{r'})^a} = H_1(w)^{\frac{1}{x}}$. If $w = w'$, $B = H_2(e(g^a, H_1(w')^r)) = H_2(e(g^{xr}, H_1(w')^{\frac{a}{x}})) = H_2(e(A, \mathcal{T}^a))$. It is easy to verify that the correctness of the equation holds for multi-test as re-encrypted ciphertext has the same form as the original ciphertext.

References

1. Abdalla, M., Bellare, M., Catalano, D., Kiltz, E., Kohno, T., Lange, T., Malone-Lee, J., Neven, G., Paillier, P., Shi, H.: Searchable encryption revisited: Consistency properties, relation to anonymous ibe, and extensions. In: Shoup, V. (ed.) CRYPTO 2005. LNCS, vol. 3621, pp. 205–222. Springer, Heidelberg (2005)
2. Ateniese, G., Fu, K., Green, M., Hohenberger, S.: Improved proxy re-encryption schemes with applications to secure distributed storage. ACM Trans. Inf. Syst. Secur. 9(1), 1–30 (2006)
3. Baek, J., Safavi-Naini, R., Susilo, W.: On the integration of public key data encryption and public key encryption with keyword search. In: Katsikas, S.K., López, J., Backes, M., Gritzalis, S., Preneel, B. (eds.) ISC 2006. LNCS, vol. 4176, pp. 217–232. Springer, Heidelberg (2006)
4. Baek, J., Safavi-Naini, R., Susilo, W.: Public key encryption with keyword search revisited. In: Gervasi, O., Murgante, B., Laganà, A., Taniar, D., Mun, Y., Gavrilova, M.L. (eds.) ICCSA 2008, Part I. LNCS, vol. 5072, pp. 1249–1259. Springer, Heidelberg (2008)
5. Blaze, M., Bleumer, G., Strauss, M.: Divertible protocols and atomic proxy cryptography. In: Nyberg, K. (ed.) EUROCRYPT 1998. LNCS, vol. 1403, pp. 127–144. Springer, Heidelberg (1998)

6. Boneh, D., Crescenzo, G.D., Ostrovsky, R., Persiano, G.: Public key encryption with keyword search. In: Cachin, C., Camenisch, J.L. (eds.) EUROCRYPT 2004. LNCS, vol. 3027, pp. 506–522. Springer, Heidelberg (2004)
7. Boneh, D., Franklin, M.K.: Identity-based encryption from the weil pairing. In: Kilian, J. (ed.) CRYPTO 2001. LNCS, vol. 2139, pp. 213–229. Springer, Heidelberg (2001)
8. Canetti, R., Hohenberger, S.: Chosen-ciphertext secure proxy re-encryption. In: Ning, P., di Vimercati, S.D.C., Syverson, P.F. (eds.) ACM Conference on Computer and Communications Security, pp. 185–194. ACM, New York (2007)
9. Crescenzo, G.D., Saraswat, V.: Public key encryption with searchable keywords based on jacobi symbols. In: Srinathan, K., Rangan, C.P., Yung, M. (eds.) IN-DOCRYPT 2007. LNCS, vol. 4859, pp. 282–296. Springer, Heidelberg (2007)
10. Gu, C., Zhu, Y., Pan, H.: Efficient public key encryption with keyword search schemes from pairings. In: Pei, D., Yung, M., Lin, D., Wu, C. (eds.) Inscrypt 2007. LNCS, vol. 4990, pp. 372–383. Springer, Heidelberg (2008)
11. Hwang, Y.H., Lee, P.J.: Public key encryption with conjunctive keyword search and its extension to a multi-user system. In: Takagi, T., Okamoto, T., Okamoto, E., Okamoto, T. (eds.) Pairing 2007. LNCS, vol. 4575, pp. 2–22. Springer, Heidelberg (2007)
12. Park, D.J., Kim, K., Lee, P.J.: Public key encryption with conjunctive field keyword search. In: Lim, C.H., Yung, M. (eds.) WISA 2004. LNCS, vol. 3325, pp. 73–86. Springer, Heidelberg (2005)
13. Rhee, H.S., Park, J.H., Susilo, W., Lee, D.H.: Improved searchable public key encryption with designated tester. In: Li, W., Susilo, W., Tupakula, U.K., Safavi-Naini, R., Varadharajan, V. (eds.) ASIACCS, pp. 376–379. ACM, New York (2009)
14. Rhee, H.S., Park, J.H., Susilo, W., Lee, D.H.: Trapdoor security in a searchable public-key encryption scheme with a designated tester. Journal of Systems and Software 83(5), 763–771 (2010)
15. Rhee, H.S., Susilo, W., Kim, H.J.: Secure searchable public key encryption scheme against keyword guessing attacks. IEICE Electronics Express 6(5), 237–243 (2009)
16. Sahai, A., Waters, B.: Fuzzy identity-based encryption. In: Cramer, R. (ed.) EU-ROCRYPT 2005. LNCS, vol. 3494, pp. 457–473. Springer, Heidelberg (2005)
17. Shao, J., Cao, Z., Liang, X., Lin, H.: Proxy re-encryption with keyword search. Inf. Sci. 180(13), 2576–2587 (2010)
18. Zhang, R., Imai, H.: Generic combination of public key encryption with keyword search and public key encryption. In: Bao, F., Ling, S., Okamoto, T., Wang, H., Xing, C. (eds.) CANS 2007. LNCS, vol. 4856, pp. 159–174. Springer, Heidelberg (2007)

One-Time Password System with Infinite Nested Hash Chains

Mohamed Hamdy Eldefrawy[1], Muhammad Khurram Khan[1], and Khaled Alghathbar[1,2]

[1] Center of Excellence in Information Assurance (CoEIA), King Saud University, Saudi Arabia
[2] Information Systems Department, College of Computer and Information Sciences,
King Saud University, Saudi Arabia
{meldefrawy,mkhurram,kalghathbar}@ksu.edu.sa

Abstract. Hash chains have been used as OTP generators. Lamport hashes have an intensive computation cost and a chain length restriction. A solution for signature chains addressed this by involving public key techniques, which increased the average computation cost. Although a later idea reduced the user computation by sharing it with the host, it couldn't overcome the length limitation. The scheme proposed by Chefranov to eliminate the length restriction had a deficiency in the communication cost overhead. We here present an algorithm that overcomes all of these shortcomings by involving two different nested hash chains: one dedicated to seed updating and the other used for OTP production. Our algorithm provides forward and non-restricted OTP generation. We propose a random challenge–response operation mode. We analyze our proposal from the viewpoint of security and performance compared with the other algorithms.

Keywords: One Time Password, Lamport Hashing, Nested Hash Chains, Authentication's Factors.

1 Introduction

Authentication is used by a system to determine whether or not a given *user* is who they claim to be. Authentication is the cornerstone of information security since a weak authentication mechanism will cause the rest of the security to be fragile. It is widely accepted that authentication uses one or more of the followings four factors [1]:

- The *user*'s knowledge, such as a password and/or PIN.
- The *user*'s possessions, such as a smart card and/or token.
- The *user*'s information, such as a fingerprint.
- The *user*'s behavior, such as a signature and/or voice.

Password based authentication is the most widely used of the above four methods because of its simplicity and low cost. A one-time password mechanism solves the password security problem that could result from reusing the same password multiple times.

The idea of one-way function chains or hash chains was first proposed by Lamport [2]. This method is also referred to as S/Key™ *OTP* [3]. It is computationally intensive

T.-h. Kim et al. (Eds.): SecTech/DRBC 2010, CCIS 122, pp. 161–170, 2010.
© Springer-Verlag Berlin Heidelberg 2010

on the *user* end; hence it uses backward and finite hash chains. The idea of using hash chains was proposed to enhance *OTP* production compared to algorithms that require time stamping with accurate time synchronization, e.g., RSA SecurID [4]. Since *OTP* has been employed in a wide range of applications [5], it would be very beneficial to overcome its insufficiencies. We propose a new algorithm that uses two different types of hash functions, which come with a nested chain. The resulting chain provides the forwardness and the infiniteness. Also we have reduced the number of exchanged messages between the *user* and *host*. The proposed protocol is compared with others in terms of its computational cost and security properties. The rest of this paper is organized as follows: Section 2 discusses the related work, Section 3 proposes our new algorithm, Section 4 analyzes the security attributes, and finally Section 5 concludes the paper.

2   Related Work

Hash functions $h(\cdot)$ are useful in the construction of *OTPs* and are defined straightforwardly as one-way hash functions (OWHFs) such that, given an input string, x, it is easy to compute $y = h(x)$ and, conversely, it is computationally infeasible to get $x = h^{-1}(y)$ given a randomly chosen y. The following subsection presents some of the published schemes for *OTPs* and their shortcomings.

2.1   Lamport's Scheme

The idea of hash chains was first proposed by Lamport [2]. Later, it was implemented to develop the S/Key™ *OTP* system [3]. It involves applying hash function $h(\cdot)$ for N times to a seed (s) to form a hash chain of length N:

$$h^1(s), h^2(s), \ldots, h^{N-1}(s), h^N(s) \tag{1}$$

The *t*-th authentication *host* sends a challenge to the *user*

$$Challenge(t) = N - t \tag{2}$$

then the *user* calculates the *t*-th *OTP* according to this challenge

$$OTP_t(s) = h^{N-t}(s) \tag{3}$$

and the *host* authenticates the *user* by checking that the following equality holds:

$$h\left(OTP_t(s)\right) = h^{N-t+1}(s) \tag{4}$$

where the value $h^{N-t+1}(s)$ is already saved in the *host* system's password file from the previous $(t-1)$-th authentication. After any successful authentication, the system password file is updated with the *OTP* that was saved before the *host* final hash execution as $h^{N-t}(s)$. In our case, the *host* then increments t by one and sends a new challenge to the user for the next authentication. This scheme has a limitation on the number of authentications, so that after reaching N authentications, a process restart is required. In addition, it has a vulnerability because an opponent, impersonating the host, can send a challenge with a small value to the user, who responds with the hash chain initial values, which allow the intruder to calculate further *OTPs* [6]. This attack can be referred to as a small challenge attack. In addition, the user computational requirements are high, which makes the system unsuitable for devices with limited resources.

2.2 Goyal et al.'s Scheme

In order to decrease the computational cost in [7]; Goyal *et al.* proposed a new idea of dividing this large N value into $\lfloor N/R \rfloor$ sub periods of length R to share this cost with the *host* itself. We will consider N to be a multiple of R to simplify the scheme's formula:

$$OTP_{N-t}(s) = OTP_{k+n}(s) = h^n\left(OTP_k(s) + \beta s\right) \tag{5}$$

where
$$\beta = \begin{cases} 1 & k \bmod R = 0 \\ 0 & Otherwise \end{cases}$$

Suppose the *user* wishes to authenticate himself to the *host* for the t-th time.

$$n = (N-t)\bmod R\big|_{n\neq0}, \text{ and } k = N-t-n \tag{6}$$

- *User* identifies himself to the *host* by logging.
- *Host* sends this pair of values to the *user* $\left(n, OTP_k(s)\right)$.
- *User* calculates $OTP_{k+n}(s)$ and sends it back to the *host* as an *OTP* that is equal to $h^n\left(OTP_k(s) + s\right)$.
- *Host* stores the last *OTP* to hash the received *OTP* and compare it with the stored one.
- The next time *user* wants to login, he will be prompted with values of $t+1$.

The *user* must have a knowledge of "s" during every login, which makes it essential to cipher the "s" seed. Re-initialization after N authentications is still necessary as in Lamport's scheme.

2.3 Bicakci et al.'s Scheme

The infinite length hash chains (ILHC) proposed by [8] use a public-key algorithm, A, to produce a forward and infinite one way function (OWF). This OWF is the *OTP* production core. Bicakci *et al.* proposed a protocol using RSA [9], where d is the private key and e is the public key. The *OTP* originating from initial input "s" using the RSA public-key algorithm for the t-th authentication is:

$$OTP_t(s) = A^t\left(s, d\right) \tag{7}$$

and the verification of the t-th *OTP* is done by decrypting $OTP_t(s)$ using e:

$$A\left(OTP_t(s), e\right) = OTP_{t-1}(s). \tag{8}$$

Increasing the number of cascaded exponentiations increases the computational complexity, making this algorithm very difficult to implement in limited computation devices, e.g., wireless sensor networks [10], etc.

2.4 Yeh et al.'s Scheme

Yeh *et al.*'s scheme [11] is divided into three phases: registration, login, and verification. In the registration phase, a *user* and a *host* set up a unique seed value " s " and the number of login times, N. After setting up s and N, the *user* computes an initial password $OTP_0 = h^N(K \oplus s)$, where $h(\cdot)$ is a hash function, K is a pass-phrase of the *user*, and $\oplus$ is a bitwise XOR function. The steady state authentication for the t-th login time is shown in Table 1.

Table 1. Yeh et al.'s scheme

Registration Phase	
$User \leftarrow Host$:	s
$User \leftarrow Host$:	$N, s \oplus D_0, h(D_0)$
$User \rightarrow Host$:	$OTP_0 \oplus D_0$
Login Phase	
$User \leftarrow Host$:	$(S_{t.1}, S_{t.2}, S_{t.3}) = (N - t, s \oplus D_t, h(D_t) \oplus OTP_{t-1})$
$User \rightarrow Host$:	$U_t = h^{N-t}(K \oplus s) \oplus D_t = OTP_t \oplus D_t$
Verification Phase	
$Host$:	$h((OTP_t \oplus D_t) \oplus D_t) \stackrel{?}{=} OTP_{t-1}$

For the t-th login, the *host* sends a challenge to the *user* with a random number, D_t, the D_t hashing value, $h(D_t)$, the shared secret, " s " and a stored value, OTP_{t-1}. After validating the challenge, the *user* responds with $OTP_t \oplus D_t$. Finally, the *host* checks this response and replaces the stored value OTP_{t-1} with OTP_t. This scheme is vulnerable to a pre-play attack [12] because of transferring password information in the both directions for the *host* and *user*. An attacker potentially has the ability to impersonate the *host* to the *user* (by sending the *user* a forged challenge). After that the attacker impersonates the *user* to the *host* using the new valid password-authenticator sent to him previously by the *user* [12]. In addition, [6] showed that Shen *et al.*'s scheme is practically the same as that in [2], but uses the closing of sensitive parts of transmitted messages with the help of the XOR operation, a hash function, and a random nonce. Finally, the calculation of the hash function numbers for the t-th login is equal to $N - t$, from the *user* side. This shows the algorithm's computational cost. Again, re-initialization after N authentications is still necessary.

2.5 Chefranov's Scheme

The scheme proposed in [6] is divided into two complicated phases: the registration phase and the login and authentication phase. In the following table, we show the procedure for the first run.

Table 2. Chefranov's scheme

Registration Phase

Host :	Set $n_H = 0$, generate random seed s_H
User :	Set $n_U = 0$, generate random seed s_U, generate random nonce D_{1U}
	K is the password phrase
User ← *Host* :	s_H
User → *Host* :	s_U
User Calculate:	$\pi = h(K \oplus s_H), \pi_1 = h(\pi)$
User → *Host* :	$p_1 = h(\pi_1)$

Login and Authentication Phase

User → *Host* :	$S_1 = (S_{1.1}, S_{1.2}, S_{1.3}, S_{1.4}) = \begin{pmatrix} \pi_1 \oplus h(D_{1U}), h(\pi \oplus p_1) \oplus h(D_{1U}), \\ h^2(\pi \oplus p_1) \oplus D_{1U}, s_U \oplus D_{1U} \end{pmatrix}$

Host Check :	$h(S_{1.1} \oplus h(s_U \oplus S_{1.4})) \overset{?}{=} p_1$	$h(S_{1.2} \oplus h(s_U \oplus S_{1.4})) \overset{?}{=} S_{1.3} \oplus D_{1U}$	
Host Calculate :	$D_{2U} = D_{1U} + 1$	$p_1 = S_{1.2} \oplus h(D_{1U})$	$n_H = n_H + 1$
User ← *Host* :	$(S_{2.1}, S_{2.2}) = (D_{2U} \oplus s_H, D_{2U} \oplus s_U)$		
User Check :	$S_{2.1} \oplus s_H \overset{?}{=} S_{2.2} \oplus s_U \overset{?}{=} D_{1U} + 1$		
User Update :	$\pi_2 = h(\pi_1) \oplus \pi, n_H = n_H + 1, p_2 = h(\pi_2)$		
User → *Host* :	p_2 to start the second session.		

The password generation procedure for the t-th authentication is $\pi_t = \pi \oplus h(\pi_{t-1})$ from the *user* side, and $p_t = h(\pi_t)$ from the *host* side. The author of this algorithm claimed that the *user* is occupied by only four hash function calculations, but actually he has to do more than this. Considering a steady state session, through the second phase, the S_t vector itself has three hash operations, $h(D_{tU}), h(\pi \oplus p_t)$, and $h^2(\pi \oplus p_t)$. Two additional hash operations are required for the *user* updating of *OTPs*, $\pi_{t+1} = \pi \oplus h(\pi_t)$ and $p_{t+1} = h(\pi_{t+1})$, which must be done by the *user* itself. After that, the *user* starts the $(t+1)$-th by sending p_{t+1} to the *host* in the registration phase.

3   Proposed Scheme

The idea behind our proposal is to expand Lamport's scheme with some modifications that produce the infiniteness and forwardness, avoiding the use of public key cryptography.

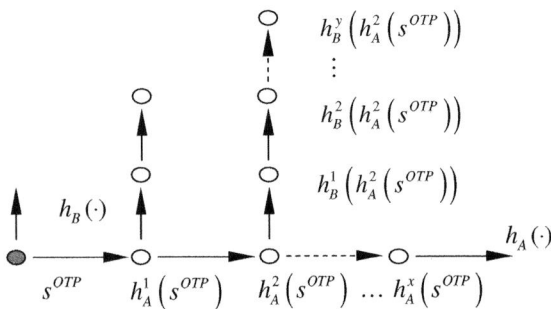

Fig. 1. One time password production considering a nested hash chain using two different hashes

The shortcoming of those two parameters, *infiniteness and forwardness*, causes the server vulnerabilities shown with respect to the previous work. Thus we need to integrate Lamport's scheme using two different one way hash functions, $h_A(\cdot)$ and $h_B(\cdot)$, one for the *seed chain* and the other for the *OTP*'s production, as shown in Fig. 1.

$$h_B^y\left(h_A^x(s)\right)\Big|_{x:1\to\infty,\, y:1\to\infty} \tag{9}$$

Our algorithm can operate in two modes, offline authentication and challenge response authentication. We consider the registration stage to be established manually between *user* and *host*. The establishment of the algorithms and seeds requires manual intervention, e.g., the *user* should go personally to the *host* administrator to establish the system.

Table 3. The Proposed Scheme Notation.

Notation	Description
$h_A(\cdot)$	Represents the first hash function.
$h_B(\cdot)$	Represents the second hash function.
s_{2t-1}^{Auth}	The authentication seed number $2t-1$ for the t-th authentication.
s_{2t}^{Auth}	The authentication seed number $2t$ for the t-th authentication.
s_t^{OTP}	The *OTP* seed number t for the t-th authentication.
OTP_t	The *OTP* number t for the t-th authentication.
$(v_{t.1}, v_{t.2})$	The challenge vector for the t-th authentication sent by *host* to *user*.
w_t	The response vector for the t-th authentication sent by *user* to *host*.
(x_t, y_t)	The nested hashing progress values for t-th authentication.
$h_B^{y_t}\left(h_A^{x_t}\left(s_t^{OTP}\right)\right)$	Hashing the *OTP* seed number t by $h_A(\cdot)$ for x_t times followed by $h_B(\cdot)$ hashing for y_t times.

3.1 Registration Phase

The *user* gets the two different hash functions established on his token plus two different seeds, one for the *OTP* production, s_1^{OTP}, and the other one for the authentication procedure, s_1^{Auth}, which are also installed on his token. To ensure that information is completely shared with the service provider, these two seeds are produced by the shared and unique parameters of the *host* and *user*.

3.2 Login and Authentication Phase

For the *first time* of the authentication process, the *host* sends a *challenge* to the *user* of

$$\left(v_{1.1}, v_{1.2} \right) = \left(\left(x_1, y_1 \right) \oplus h_B \left(h_A^2 \left(s_1^{Auth} \right) \right), s_1^{Auth} \oplus h_B \left(h_A \left(s_1^{Auth} \right) \right) \right) \tag{10}$$

The *user* calculates $h_B \left(h_A \left(s_1^{Auth} \right) \right)$ according to his knowledge of the hash functions, $h_A(\cdot)$ and $h_B(\cdot)$, and also the authentication seed, s_1^{Auth}. Upon the calculation of this value, the *user* can extract s_1^{Auth} from v_2 and compare it with his own. Unless positive results are obtained, the authentication process fails and the *user* terminates the procedure. Otherwise, the *user* calculates $h_B \left(h_A^2 \left(s_1^{Auth} \right) \right)$ to get $\left(x_1, y_1 \right)$ from the received vector v_1 to compute $OTP_1 = h_B^{x_1} \left(h_A^{y_1} \left(s_1^{OTP} \right) \right)$. The $\left(x_1, y_1 \right)$ values are the *challenge core*; these values determine the nested hashing progress. Normally they could be one by one stepping, but to increase the algorithm's robustness, they could be randomly selected by the *host*. In addition, the value of this current password OTP_1 is calculated by the *host* and *user* in parallel. After the *user* reaches the session OTP_1, the authentication seed is updated to $s_2^{Auth} = h_A^2 \left(s_1^{Auth} \right)$ in both the *user* and *host*.

Now, the *user* has to respond to this challenge with his OTP_1 in the following form:

$$\left(OTP_1 \oplus h_B \left(h_A \left(s_2^{Auth} \right) \right) \right) \tag{11}$$

The *host* calculates $h_B \left(h_A \left(s_2^{Auth} \right) \right)$ to extract the received OTP_1 and compares it with his own OTP_1, he has calculated by himself. Then, both the *user* and *host* update the *OTP* seed to get $s_2^{OTP} = h_A^{x_1} \left(s_1^{OTP} \right)$ and the next authentication seed is updated to $s_3^{Auth} = h_A \left(s_2^{Auth} \right)$. Those two values s_2^{OTP} and s_3^{Auth} are the next session initial seeds. This is the procedure for a complete session; the general steps are shown in Table 4.

Table 4. A Generalization of our Proposal

Registration Phase	

| *User & Host* : | $h_A(\cdot), h_B(\cdot), s^{Auth}$, and s^{OTP} |

Login and Authentication Phase	

| *User* ← *Host* : | $\left(v_{t.1}, v_{t.2}\right) = \left(\left(x_t, y_t\right) \oplus h_B\left(h_A^2\left(s_{2t-1}^{Auth}\right)\right), s_{2t-1}^{Auth} \oplus h_B\left(h_A\left(s_{2t-1}^{Auth}\right)\right)\right)$ |

| *User* : | *check* $v_{t.2} \oplus h_B\left(h_A\left(s_{2t-1}^{Auth}\right)\right) \overset{?}{=} s_{2t-1}^{Auth}$ *extract*$\left(x_t, y_t\right) = v_{t.1} \oplus h_B\left(h_A^2\left(s_{2t-1}^{Auth}\right)\right)$ |
| | *calculate* $OTP_t = h_B^{y_t}\left(h_A^{x_t}\left(s_t^{OTP}\right)\right)$ *update* $s_{2t}^{Auth} = h_A^2\left(s_{2t-1}^{Auth}\right)$ *user* and *host* |

| *User* → *Host* : | $w_t = OTP_t \oplus h_B\left(h_A\left(s_{2t}^{Auth}\right)\right)$ |

| *Host* : | *check* $OTP_t \overset{?}{=} w_t \oplus h_B\left(h_A\left(s_{2t}^{Auth}\right)\right)$ *check* $s_{t+1}^{OTP} = h_A^{x_t}\left(s_t^{OTP}\right)$ |
| | *update* $s_{2t+1}^{Auth} = h_A\left(s_{2t}^{Auth}\right)$ *host* and *user* |

4   Security Analysis

Naturally, the proposed scheme can resist an off-line guessing attack because it uses strong passwords of strong hash functions. Moreover, the gaining of unauthorized access by replaying reusable passwords is restricted by encoding passwords, which are used once. Also our proposal does not require time synchronization [13] for a certain reference between the user and host, which is not easy to apply in many applications, i.e., mobile phones that come with synchronization leaks considering roaming to different time zones. It is necessary to prevent having another token as the *OTP* generator for a certain account, if it already has an active generator [14]. A manual process should handle this situation. In this section, we will briefly give a security assessment of our proposed scheme [15], [16], [17].

4.1   Pre-play Attack

Unless the challenge is protected, a type of "suppress-replay attack" (known as a "pre-play attack") becomes possible [18]. Consider that an intruder E, who is able to predict the next challenge, wishes to impersonate A to B. E takes the B role, by impersonating it to A, and asks A to authenticate itself. E chooses the next challenge that will be chosen by B when authenticating A. The challenge's response sent by A is memorized by E. Then, at some future time, E can impersonate A to B, using this memorized response. Our proposal allows the *host* to challenge the *user* with unpredictable uniformly distributed values of x_t and y_t. If we suppose that x_t and y_t can take one value of forward m values, the probability of successfully guessing a challenge will be the joint probability of x_t and y_t, which is equal to $1/m^2$. We can refer to this property as the ability to *resist predictable attacks*. The restriction of transferring password information in just one direction, from *user* to *host*, also increases the robustness against this type of attack. The two exchanged vectors between *user* and *host* are transferred in a cipher format.

4.2 Insider Attack

If a *host* insider tries to impersonate the *user* to access other *host*s using the shared *OTPs* between them, s/he will not be able to do so because the cooperation of the *OTPs'* seed fabrication between this *user* and the different *hosts* is strong. Furthermore, as the *OTP* production, using two different types of strong hashes, $h_A(\cdot)$ and $h_B(\cdot)$, is strong, the *host* insider can't derive those *OTPs* by performing an off-line guessing attack on what he has received.

4.3 Small Challenge Attack

Attacks based on sending small challenges by intruders who impersonate the communication *host* only affect the backward hash chains' *OTPs*. Our scheme uses forward hashing techniques, which eliminates this type of attack completely.

5 Conclusions

A new one time password scheme based on forward hashing using two different nested hashes has been presented. These two hashes provide the authentication seed updating and the *OTP* production. This scheme achieves better characteristics than the other schemes discussed. Our proposal is not limited to a certain number of authentications, unlike the mentioned *OTP* hashing based schemes, and also does not involve computationally expensive techniques to provide the infiniteness. A security analysis was also performed that covered some types of attacks that could influence our scheme.

References

1. Kim, H., Lee, H., Lee, K., Jun, M.: A Design of One–Time Password Mechanism Using Public Key Infrastructure. In: Networked Computing and Advanced Information Management, vol. 1, pp. 18–24 (2008)
2. Lamport, L.: Password Authentication with Insecure Communication. Comm. ACM 24(11), 770–772 (1981)
3. Haller, N.: The S/KEY One–Time Password System. In: Proceedings of the ISOC Symposium on Network and Distributed System Security, pp. 151–157 (1994)
4. RSA SecurID, http://www.rsa.com/node.aspx?id=1156 (Accessed: May 04, 2010)
5. Rivest, R., Shamir, A.: Payword and micro–mint: Two simple micropayment schemes, pp. 7–11 (1996)
6. Chefranov, A.: One–Time Password Authentication with Infinite Hash Chains, Novel Algorithms and Techniques. In: Tele-Communications, Automation and Industrial Electronics, pp. 283–286 (2008)

7. Goyal, V., Abraham, A., Sanyal, S., Han, S.: The N/R one time password system. In: Proceedings of International Conference on Information Technology: Coding and Computing (ITCC 2005), vol. 1, pp. 733–738 (2005)
8. Bicakci, K., Baykal, N.: Infinite length hash chains and their applications. In: Proceedings of 1th IEEE Int. Workshops on Enabling Technologies: Infrastructure for Collaborating Enterprises (WETICE 2002), pp. 57–61 (2002)
9. Rivest, R., Shamir, A., Adleman, L.: A method for obtaining digital signatures and public–key cryptosystems. Communications of the ACM (1978)
10. Khan, M., Alghathbar, K.: Cryptanalysis and Security Improvements of Two–Factor User Authentication in Wireless Sensor Networks. In: Sensors, vol. 10(3), pp. 2450–2459 (2010)
11. Yeh, T., Shen, H., Hwang, J.: A secure one–time password authentication scheme using smart cards. IEICE Trans. in Commun. E85–B(11), 2515–2518 (2002)
12. Yum, D., Lee, P.: Cryptanalysis of Yeh–Shen–Hwang's one–time password authentication scheme. IEICE Trans. Commun. E88–B(4), 1647–1648 (2005)
13. Aloul, F., Zahidi, S., El–Hajj, W.: Two factor authentication using mobile phones. In: IEEE/ACS International Conference on Digital Object Identifier, pp. 641–644 (2009)
14. Raddum, H., Nestås, L., Hole, K.: Security Analysis of Mobile Phones Used as OTP Generators. In: IFIP International Federation for Information Processing, pp. 324–331 (2010)
15. Khan, M.K.: Fingerprint Biometric–based Self and Deniable Authentication Schemes for the Electronic World. IETE Technical Review 26(3), 191–195 (2009)
16. Khan, M.K., Zhang, J.: Improving the Security of A Flexible Biometrics Remote User Authentication Scheme. In: Computer Standards and Interfaces (CSI), vol. 29(1), pp. 84–87. Elsevier Science, UK (2007)
17. Eldefrawy, M.H., Khan, M.K., Alghathbar, K., Cho, E.-S.: Broadcast Authentication for Wireless Sensor Networks Using Nested Hashing and the Chinese Remainder Theorem. Sensors 10(9), 8683–8695 (2010)
18. Mitchell, C., Chen, L.: Comments on the S/KEY user authentication scheme. ACM Operating System Review 30(4), 12–16 (1996)

Optimal Intelligent Supervisory Control System in Cyber-Physical Intelligence

Hoon Ko and Zita Vale

GECAD / ISEP / IPP,
Rua Dr. Antonio Bernardino de Almeida, 431, 4200-072 Porto, Portugal
{hko,zav}@isep.ipp.pt

Abstract. This paper studies Optimal Intelligent Supervisory Control System (OISCS) model for the design of control systems which can work in the presence of cyber-physical elements with privacy protection. The development of such architecture has the possibility of providing new ways of integrated control into systems where large amounts of fast computation are not easily available, either due to limitations on power, physical size or choice of computing elements.

1 Introduction

A Cyber-Physical System (CPS) is the system of computer systems which is usually interacted with the physical world in real-time. These systems have to sense constraints imposed by dynamically changing environment and predictably react to these changes and it has physical world and logical world [1]. Optimal Intelligent Supervisory Control System (OISCS) that it studies offers location privacy by hash function when they use them in cyber-physical intelligence. OISCS has three layers. Smart Construction Environment (SCE) lies in bottom layer, IT layer (ITL) is put middle layer of between bottom layer and upper layer. The upper layer has User Devices (UD). SCE defines SCADA system; ModBUS protocol is going to use to exchange information of each device [2]. ITL helps interact of all devices in SCE, ModBUS also processes based on ITL. In UD layer, user monitors the flowing data in ITL. In this case, due to users remotely monitor out of home/office, they can be opened their location. Therefore, it has to study location privacy [3][4]. OISCS that it proposes provides location privacy by hash function when users use and supervisory control system to SCADA monitor and control. This paper is consists of, it explains the OISCS model in section 2; section 3 has the explanation about location privacy. Section 4 is for simulation of OISCS, and it describes the discussion into section 5. Finally, the conclusion for this paper put in section 6.

2 Optimal Intelligence Supervisory Control System

In this section, it defines OISCS. OISCS has monitor and control and it has four modules for privacy, ex. User logical location privacy, User physical location privacy, Function, and K-exchange. Also, it has three agents like Human Agent, ER (Energy Resource) Agent, and Control Agent.

T.-h. Kim et al. (Eds.): SecTech/DRBC 2010, CCIS 122, pp. 171–178, 2010.

2.1 Overview

Cyber-Physical System (CPS) is the system of computer systems which is usually interacted with the physical world in real-time. It has physical world and logical world, physical world means building, urban space, network devices etc, and logical world or cyber world means computational services in ITL [1]. Electronic information processed by SCADA which operates in physical world normally transmits to users through ITL, to data transmission between each device in SCADA; it uses ModBUS [2]. The Figure 1 shows internal structure of OISCS, the model is set by organic processing of all objects in service information.

Monitor: All energy flows which processed in home/office are exchanged by Mod-BUS, which usually gives and takes the information between electronic devices. It sends to Content Management (CM), and it regularly forwards UD through System Task Management (STM) which is in upper.

Control: Smart Object (SO) takes all intelligent processes; finally it can do active process according to user's information move or changes of networks or environment information around users. After users begin the monitoring, the signals are detected by Human Agent (HA), SO should recognize them, then it forwards to CM through Service Information (SI). This asking goes through CPS environment, and sends to Smart Energy System (SES).

2.2 Location Privacy

When users use remote OISCS, if users opened their current location, then all attackers absolutely attack the users. Therefore, it is necessary to use the location privacy [2][4]. At present, the users usually use mobile device and network which uses IP policy in OISCS. All devices of users usually has id, pd, k, ip, x, y, h, t, s. That is, the information that will be saved into UD is next,

$$Ud_1 = \{id,\ pd,\ sk,\ ip,\ x,\ y,\ h,\ t,\ s\} \leftarrow S\{|id|, |pd|, |k|, |ip|,\ t,\ s\}$$

However, if the user sends upper message without any protection process, some attacker can steal them and get Du_1. Therefore, it is necessary to send them with encryption.

$$Ud_1 \leftarrow S\ \{E_k(id,\ pd,\ sk,\ ip,\ t,\ s)\}$$
$$Ud_1 \colon Dk\ \{E_k(id,\ pd,\ sk,\ ip,\ t,\ s)\}$$

This encryption method provides us the data security. However, it sometimes offers location privacy also for the attackers don't know the exact owner of the captured information.

User logical location privacy: It means protection for user's devices, it provides that services by encrypting the *id, pd, ip*.

User physical location privacy: Physical location means users/devices real location by x, y, h. To protect of user physical location, it is forbid to send x, y, h in OISCS.

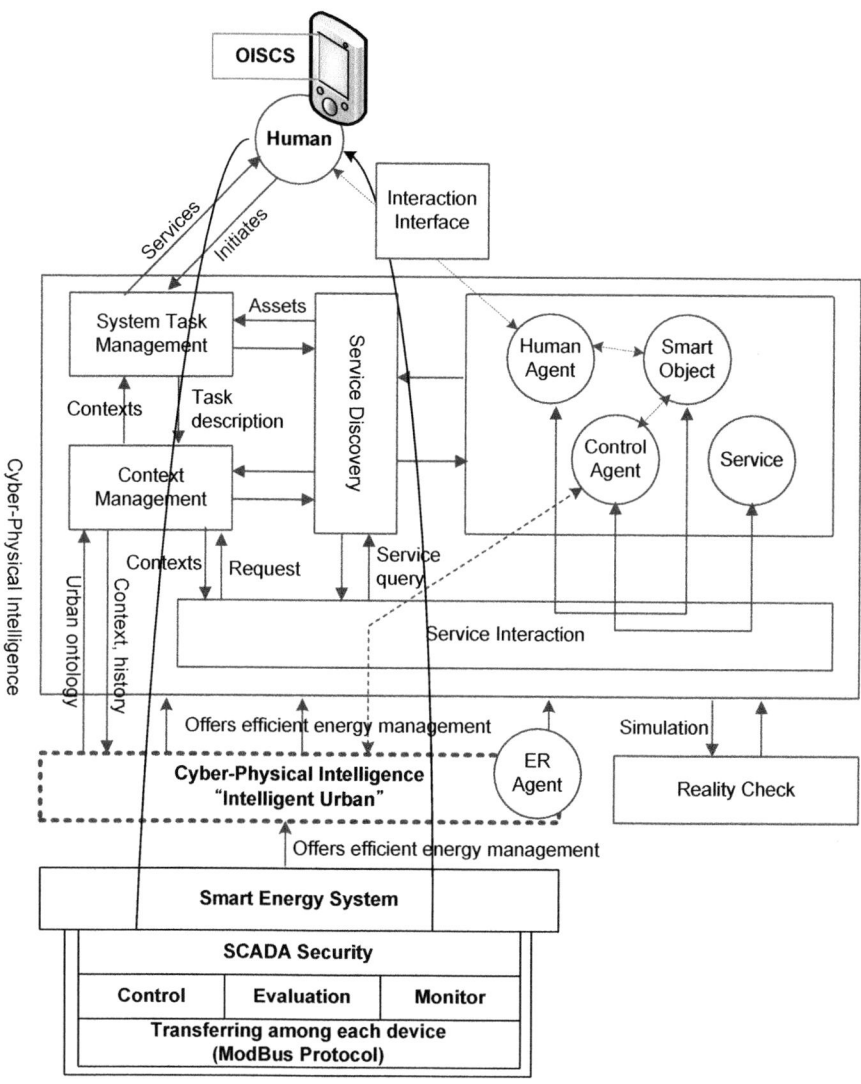

Fig. 1. Internal Structure (For one user)

Function: s_n is information which are generated by SCADA, it sends to users through ITL for OISCS. Also, it is protected by $S\{E_k(...)\}$ from attackers.

K-exchange: It references ref. [3] paper which used hash function for k-exchange in OISCS. Variable $t(time)$ offers unique value of hash values.

Table 1. Notation

Ud: Device of User(u)
S: Send
E/D: Encryption and Decryption
H: Hash function
id: User ID
pd: User Password
k: Session Key
ip: Internet Address
x: x-axis of user's location
y: y-axis of user's location
h: altitude of user's location
t: time of the last received data from status
s_n: each status of home or office in SCADA, n=1,....,n

2.3 Supervisory Control System

Fig. 2 shows OISCS. As it already explained in the fig. 1, users can know the energy flows through some steps in SI. Human Agent (HA) and Control Agent (CA) are in the fig. 1.

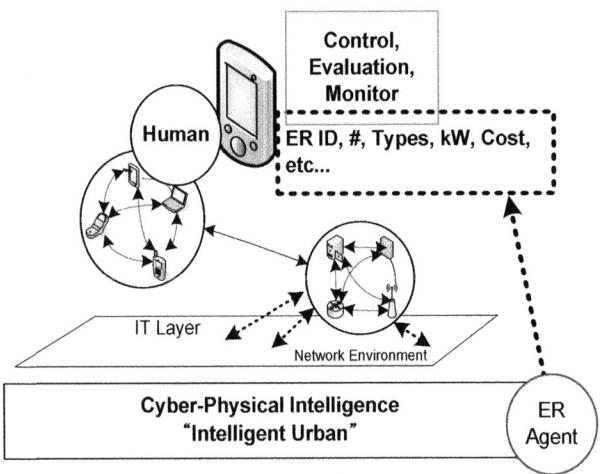

Fig. 2. OISCS flows

Human Agent: It takes a process as user gateway which makes user's profile in CPS; it defines real-time processes for user in system, the amount used of energy [6].

ER (Energy Resource) Agent: It defines information about ER, ex., ER ID.#, Energy Types (Solar cells, Micro Turbines, Fuel cells etc), Power Rate (kW), a region fuel availability, cost function, users agree to sell, ER availability (scheduled maintenance) as well as monitoring power level / control, connection / non-connection [6][7].

Control Agent: It processes to control and it defines electronic signal from main GRID including accidental situation, voltage / frequency monitoring system to detect the GRID failure (include $/k Wh, cost) [6].

3 Model Analysis and Discussion

It defines the SCADA system and security bottom of OISCS, and also the upper of this model has smart object, control agent based on human agent which usually processes user's request. Regarding user's requests, it gets interacting between system task management / context management and each agent with service discovery. Table 1 shows the model analysis by notation for user dynamic move which can apply OISCS.

Table 2. Model Analysis by Notation

Notation	Security mission in SSCSM
Ud	It defines each device or user unique ID.
E/D	It defines encrypt / decrypt of transferring data.
h	It defines the hash value; this value can be used E/D key in OISCS.
id	It defines user ID, it can use as factor in hash in future.
pd	It means user password, it can use as factor in hash in future.
k	It set a session key, it usually use in hash function to be stronger.
ip	It sets internet address, each device usually keep their unique IP. To be high level security, IP can use in hash function.
x	It defines x-axis of user; it can set various security or services items according to various services.
y	It defines y-axis of user; it can set various security or services items according to various services.
h	It defines h-axis (ex, what floor you are) of user; it can set various security or services items according to various services.
t	It defines user time; it can set various security items according to various user request and request time. For example, user can get different services following time flows.
sn	It defines each status of all devices in SCADA Home / SCADA Office.

Apart from Table 2 analyses, SCADA security system checks the area of control, evaluation and monitor.

3.1 Security

Key Exchange Module

Because session key (k) is static status, normally it feels dangerous to be opened by attacks. Therefore, it needs dynamic key modules; it shares with other user like below notation. First, hash function processes id, password and t which define request time. If it needs stronger hash value, it uses *ip* of devices to hash.

$HV = S \{H (id\|pd\|t\|(ip))\};$ *//Share between home/office and device*

Safe data transmission between devices

It is very important to evaluate the amount used energy of many electronic devices which are using by users. If the attackers give them the wrong data, each device which get these wrong information will make wrong decision. Those may make wrong results in monitor. By processing $E/D(sn)_{HV}$, each device keep dynamic key for encrypt/decrypt. If this system uses devices ID, shared password (*pd*) and user request Time (*t*) in hash function, they can have dynamic hash value at the same time, also, it can be used in data transmission as cipher key.

$E/D(sn)_{HV};$ *//Cipher of sn which are the status information of devices in Office or Home*

3.2 Modules Implement

Figure 3 shows OISCS module. To SCADA safety, before sending to user device, first it should process 'One-way Authentication', and then they encrypt all data with hash value, which generate from 'One-way Authentication'. That is, it sends control / evaluation information and control signal after encrypting which are in control, evaluation and monitor area.

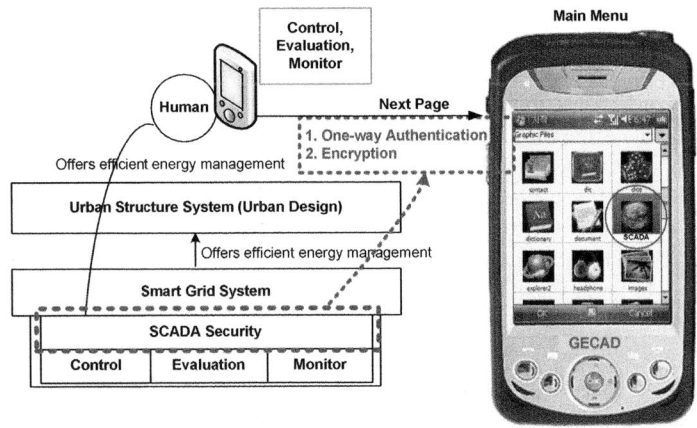

Fig. 3. Menu Module

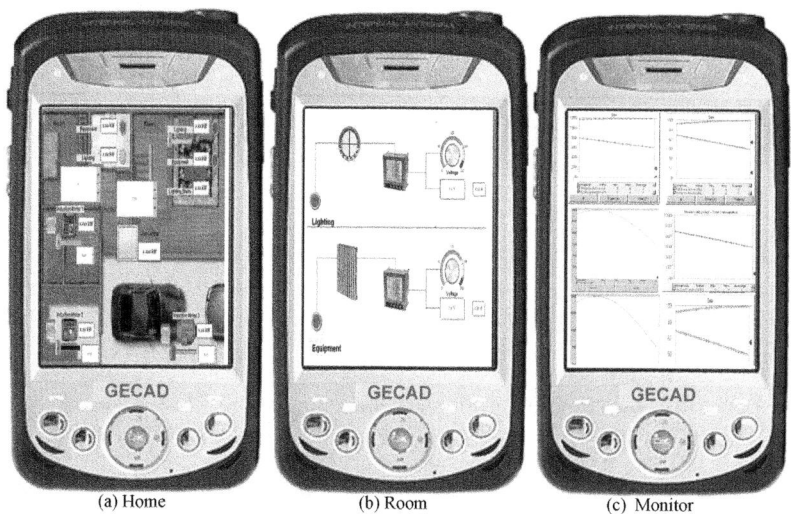

| (a) Home | (b) Room | (c) Monitor |

Fig. 4. Each Module

Figure 4 shows OISCS modules. '(a) Home' shows the whole area of home. If a user clicks (or touches) each area, the user can see the next steps (b). In '(b) Room', the user selected '(b) Room'. That room has some electronic devices. The user monitors all devices status of the room. According to each area, all users have to click or touches the area, then the device show the next steps to the user. '(c) Monitor' shows the energy flows. The users can know the amount used energy in real time through '(c) Monitor'.

4 Conclusion

OISCS is the system model which can detect, control and monitor all devices in SCADA home or SCADA office over user devices in remote area. To be secure user / devices, it added hash functions to generate dynamic encrypt key into OISCS, also, it suggested the encrypt/decrypt with dynamic generating hash value to transferring data. In future, it needs full implementation based on OISCS.

Acknowledgement

This work is partially supported under the support of the Portuguese Foundation for Science and Technology (FCT) in the aims of Ciência 2007 program for the hiring of Post-PhD researchers.

References

1. Lai, C.-F., Ma, Y.-W., Chang, S.-Y., Chao, H.-C., Huang, Y.-M.: OSGi-based services architecture for Cyber-Physical Home Control Systems. Computer Communications, 1–8, in Press, Corrected Proof, Available online April 2, 2010 (2010)

2. Cagalaban, G.A., So, Y., Kim, S.: SCADA Network Insecurity: Securing Critical Infrastructures through SCADA Security Exploitation. Journal of Security Engineering 6(6), 473–482 (2008)
3. Ko, H., Freitas, C., Goreti, M., Ramos, C.: A study on Users Authentication Methods for Safety Group Decision System in Dybanic Small Group. Journal of Convergence Information Technology 4(4), 68–76 (2009)
4. Krumm, J.: A survey of computational location privacy. Pervasive Ubiquitous Computing (13), 391–399 (2009)
5. Bradley, N.A., Dunlop, M.D.: Toward a Multidisciplinary Model of Context to Support Context-Aware Computing. Human-Computer Interaction 20, 403–446 (2005)
6. Pipattansaomporn, M., Feroze, H., Rahman, S.: Multi-Agent Systems in a Distributed Smart Grid: Design and Implementation. In: IEEE PES2009 Power Systems Conference and Exposition (PSCE 2009), Seattle, Washington, USA, pp. 1–7 (March 2009)
7. Mukherjee, T., Banerjee, A., Varsamopoulos, G., Gupta, S.K.S., Rungta, S.: Spatio-temporal thermal-aware job scheduling to minimize energy consumption in virtualized heterogeneous data centers. Computer Networks 53(17), 2888–2904 (2009)

Improved Hip-Based Individual Recognition Using Wearable Motion Recording Sensor

Davrondzhon Gafurov and Patrick Bours

Norwegian Information Security Lab
Gjøvik University College,
P.O. Box 191, 2802 Gjøvik, Norway
davrondzhon.gafurov@hig.no, patrick.bours@hig.no

Abstract. In todays society the demand for reliable verification of a user identity is increasing. Although biometric technologies based on fingerprint or iris can provide accurate and reliable recognition performance, they are inconvenient for periodic or frequent re-verification. In this paper we propose a hip-based user recognition method which can be suitable for implicit and periodic re-verification of the identity. In our approach we use a wearable accelerometer sensor attached to the hip of the person, and then the measured hip motion signal is analysed for identity verification purposes. The main analyses steps consists of detecting gait cycles in the signal and matching two sets of detected gait cycles. Evaluating the approach on a hip data set consisting of 400 gait sequences (samples) from 100 subjects, we obtained equal error rate (EER) of 7.5% and identification rate at rank 1 was 81.4%. These numbers are improvements by 37.5% and 11.2% respectively of the previous study using the same data set.

Keywords: biometric authentication, gait recognition, hip motion, accelerometer sensor, wearable sensor, motion recording sensor.

1 Introduction

Nowadays the demand for reliable verification of user identity is increasing. Although traditional knowledge-based authentication can be easy and cheap in implementation, it possesses usability limitations. For instance, it is difficult to remember long and random passwords/PIN codes, and manage multiple password. Moreover, password-based authentication is merely verifies that the claiming person knows the secret and it does not verify his/her identity per se. In the contrary, biometric authentication, which is based on physiological or behavioural characteristics of human being, establishes an explicit link to the identity. Thus it provides more reliable user authentication compared to password-based mechanisms. Conventional biometric modalities like fingerprint or iris can provide reliable and accurate user authentication. However, in some application scenarios they can be inconvenient. For instance, for periodic or frequent re-verification of the identity. We define identity *re-verification* as a process of assuring that user of the system is the same as who was previously authenticated. It is worth noting that the initial authentication mechanism can be different from the re-verification method. For example in a mobile phone user case, for the first time authentication the user can use a

T.-h. Kim et al. (Eds.): SecTech/DRBC 2010, CCIS 122, pp. 179–186, 2010.

fingerprint or PIN code but then for the subsequent re-verification implicit methods can be applied, e.g. speaker recognition (when talking on phone) or gait recognition (when walking).

Gait biometrics or gait recognition refers to verification and identification of the individuals based on their walking style. The advantage of gait biometrics is that it can provide an unobtrusive and implicit way of recognizing a person which can be very suitable in periodic re-verification. From a technological perspective (i.e. the way how gait is collected), gait recognition can be categorized into three approaches [1]:

- Video Sensor (VS) based,
- Floor Sensor (FS) based,
- Wearable Sensor (WS) based.

In the VS-based gait approach, gait is captured by using a video-camera and then image/video processing techniques are applied to extract gait features for recognition [2]. In the FS-based approach, a set of sensors are installed in the floor, and gait related features are measured when person walks on them [3,4,5]. In the WS-based approach, motion recording sensors (e.g. accelerometer, gyro sensors, etc.) are worn or attached to various locations on the body of the person such as shoe [6], waist [7], arm [8] etc. The motion signal recorded by the sensors is then utilized for person recognition purposes.

Most of the research in the area of gait recognition is focused on VS-based gait recognition [2]. Recently, WS-based approach is also gaining research focus [1,9,10]. Nevertheless, currently most of the WS-based studies are based on relatively small data sets. In this paper we present a WS-based gait recognition which is based on a relatively large data set (100 subjects in the experiment). In our approach we use an accelerometer sensor attached to the hip of the person, and the measured hip motion signal is analysed for identity verification purposes. The rest of the paper is organized as follow. Section 2 describes the experiments and data collection technology. Section 3 presents the gait recognition method. Section 4 contains the results of performance evaluation. Section 5 concludes the paper.

2   Hardware and Experiment

We used the so called Motion Recording Sensor (MRS), which has been developed at Gjøvik University College in Norway, for collecting gait of the subjects. The main components of the MRS include accelerometers, memory for storing acceleration data, USB and Bluetooth interfaces for data transfer, and a battery, see Figure 1(a). The sampling frequency of the MRS was about 100 observations per second. During the experiments it was attached to the hip of the person as shown in Figure 1(b). The reason for selecting hip for sensor placement was driven by an application point of view (e.g. people usually carry mobile phones in a similar location).

The number of subjects who participated in the experiment was 100, 30 female and 70 male in the age range 19-62. The experiment was conducted in an indoor location, and subjects were walking using their natural walking style on a level surface for a distance of about 20 meters. Data analysis was performed off-line, i.e. all collected gait samples were transferred to a PC for later processing. For each subject we collected 4 walking sequences (samples) and in total we had 400 gait sequences.

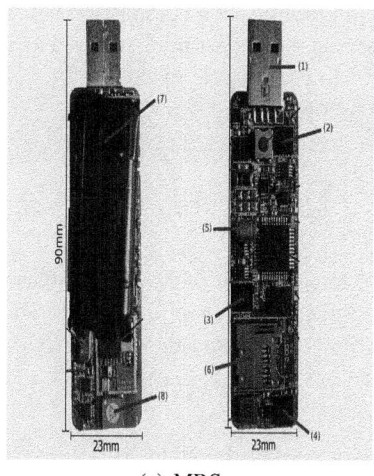   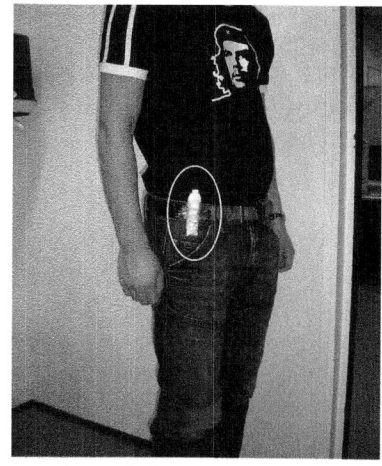

(a) MRS   (b) MRS attachment to the hip

Fig. 1. Motion recording sensor (MRS)

3   Recognition Method

Our gait recognition method consists of several steps which essentially include: a) pre-processing of the acceleration signal, b) detecting cycles in the signal and c) matching detected cycles.

Pre-processing and cycle detection: The MRS can output acceleration in three directions, namely up-down, forward-backward and sideways. From three acceleration we computed a resultant signal and use it for analyses. The resultant acceleration is calculated as follows:

$$r_i = \sqrt{x_i^2 + y_i^2 + z_i^2}, i = 1, ..., k \qquad (1)$$

where r_i, x_i, y_i and z_i are the magnitudes of resultant, up-down, forward-backward and sideway acceleration at observation point i, respectively, and k is the number of recorded observations in the signal. Then after some pre-processing of the signal (i.e. time normalization and noise reduction) we start to search for gait cycles in the signal. Figure 2 presents an example of acceleration signal with detected cycles. Few cycles in the beginning and ending of the signal are omitted since they may not represent the natural gait of the person [11]. More information on pre-processing and cycle detection steps can be found in [12].

Matching cycles: Once the gait cycles have been identified we conduct a cycle comparison process. In our previous study of the hip data set, we used an average cycle as a feature vector which was computed by combining normalized cycles into one [12]. In this paper instead of computing an average cycle we rather conduct cross comparison between two sets of cycles to find the best matching cycle pair. Assuming two sets of detected cycles are $C^E = \{C_1^E, ..., C_M^E\}$ and $C^F = \{C_1^F, ..., C_N^F\}$, where each cycle in the set consists of 100 acceleration value, e.g. $C_1^E = \{C_{1(1)}^E, C_{1(2)}^E, ..., C_{1(99)}^E, C_{1(100)}^E\}$.

If this two sets are from the same person's hip motion then comparison is referred as genuine matching otherwise (i.e. different persons) comparison is referred as impostor matching. We compare each cycle in set C^E to every cycle in set C^F by calculating their similarity using Euclidean distance, as follow.

$$SimScore(C_k^E, C_p^F) = \sqrt{\sum_{i=1}^{100}(C_{k(i)}^E - C_{p(i)}^F)^2} \qquad (2)$$

where $1 \leq k \leq M, 1 \leq p \leq N$. From the total number of $N \cdot M$ similarity scores we select a minimum one, i.e. $score_{min} = min\{SimScore(C_k^E, C_p^F)\}$. The pair of cycles which produced the minimum similarity score is considered as a best matching cycles. Then, this best (i.e. minimum) score, $score_{min}$, is considered as a similarity score between sets C^E and C^F.

Decision: Finally, a decision of either *accept* or *reject* is based on a specified threshold value. If the similarity score is equal or smaller than the threshold then *accept* otherwise *reject*.

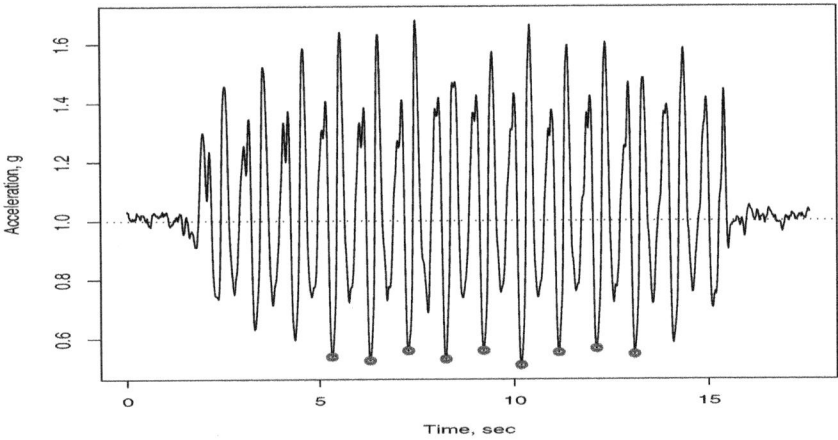

Fig. 2. An example of acceleration signal with detected cycles

4   Results and Discussion

We evaluate performance of the method both in verification (one to one comparison) and identification (one to many comparisons) modes. To evaluate performance in verification mode we use a DET (Decision Error Trade-off) curve, which is a plot of FAR (False Accept Rate) versus FRR (False Reject Rate). The DET curve shows the performance of a biometric system under different decision thresholds. To evaluate performance in identification mode we use Cumulative Match Characteristic (CMC) curve which is a plot of the rank vs. an identification rate [13]. The CMC curve indicates the cumulative probability of a match being within the top n closest matches.

The resulting DET and CMC curves using cycle matching (this paper) and the average cycle (described in [12]) method are shown in Figure 3. In addition, Table 1 presents the identification rates on ranks 1-5 and equal error rate (EER) of the methods, and the obtained improvements. The EER is a point in the DET curve where FAR=FRR.

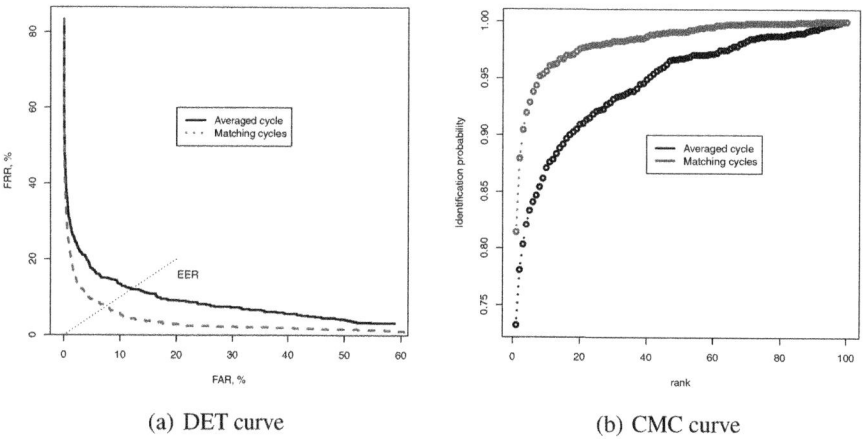

(a) DET curve   (b) CMC curve

Fig. 3. Recognition performances on verification (DET curve) and identification (CMC curve) modes

Table 1. Single value performance metrics for our previous method in [12] and proposed method in this paper. Numbers are given in %.

Performance metric	Method in [12]	This paper	Improvement
Identification rate at rank 1	73.2	81.4	11.2
Identification rate at rank 2	78.1	87.9	12.5
Identification rate at rank 3	80.3	90.4	12.6
Identification rate at rank 4	82.1	91.9	11.9
Identification rate at rank 5	83.3	92.8	11.4
Equal Error Rate (EER)	12	7.5	37.5

Table 2 presents a short summary of several WS-based gait recognition studies. In this table, in the third column performances are given in terms of recognition rate (Rr), equal error rate (EER) and identification rate at rank 1 (P_1). As it can be seen in this table, many studies are based on data sets from relatively small number of subjects (at most 60 subjects in the experiments) while in this paper our evaluation is based on data set from a (relatively) large number of subjects in the experiment. Another point one can notice from the table is that in general performance of WS-based gait recognition is not as accurate as other biometric modalities such as fingerprint or iris. This also holds for VS-based and FS-based gait recognition. The ways of further increasing performance

Table 2. Summary of the current WS-based gait recognitions

Study	MRS place-ment	Performance, %	#S
Morris [6]	shoe	$Rr = 97.4$	10
Huang et al. [15]	shoe	$Rr = 96.93$	9
Yamakawa et al. [16]	shoe	$FRR = 6.9$ at $FAR = 0.02$	10
Gafurov et al [17]	foot	$EER = \{ 5\text{-}18.3 \}$	30
Gafurov et al [18]	pocket	$EER = \{ 7.3\text{-}20 \}$	50
Gafurov and Snekkenes [8]	wrist	$EER = \{ 10\text{-}15 \}$	30
Ailisto et al. [7]	waist	$EER = 6.4$	36
Mäntyjärvi et al. [19]	waist	$EER = \{ 7\text{-}19 \}$	36
Rong et al. [20]	waist	$EER = 6.7$	35
Rong et al. [21]	waist	$EER = \{5.6, 21.1 \}$	21
Bours and Raju Shrestha [22]	hip	$EER = 1.6$	60
Sprager and Zazula [10]	hip	$Rr = 93.1$	6
This paper	hip	$EER = 7.5 \; P_1 = 81.4$	100

accuracies can be in combining WS-based gait recognition with other biometric modalities like in Vildjiounaite et al. [14], or combining motion information from different body location like in Pan et al. [9].

5   Conclusion

In this paper we presented a hip-based individual recognition method. Hip motion is collected by using an accelerometer attached to the belt of the subjects. The recorded hip motion is then analyzed for person recognition purposes. Using 400 hip motion samples from 100 subjects, we obtained an EER and identification rate at rank 1 of 7.5% and 81.4%, respectively. Such type of user authentication can be suitable for periodic or continous re-verification of the identity thanks to its unobtrisiveness and implicity. Although obtained results are promising, further work is required to improve recognition accuracy under the influence of challenging factors like walking on different surface, speed, shoe types etc. in gait recognition.

Acknowledgment

We would like to thank Professor Einar Snekkenes for providing motion recording sensor for our data collection.

References

1. Gafurov, D., Snekkenes, E.: Gait recognition using wearable motion recording sensors. EURASIP Journal on Advances in Signal Processing (2009); Special Issue on Recent Advances in Biometric Systems: A Signal Processing Perspective

2. Nixon, M.S., Tan, T.N., Chellappa, R.: Human Identification Based on Gait. Springer, Heidelberg (2006)
3. Middleton, L., Buss, A.A., Bazin, A., Nixon, M.S.: A floor sensor system for gait recognition. In: Fourth IEEE Workshop on Automatic Identification Advanced Technologies (AutoID 2005), pp. 171–176 (2005)
4. Suutala, J., Röning, J.: Towards the adaptive identification of walkers: Automated feature selection of footsteps using distinction sensitive LVQ. In: Int. Workshop on Processing Sensory Information for Proactive Systems (PSIPS 2004), June 14-15 (2004)
5. Jenkins, J., Ellis, C.S.: Using ground reaction forces from gait analysis: Body mass as a weak biometric. In: International Conference on Pervasive Computing (2007)
6. Morris, S.J.: A shoe-integrated sensor system for wireless gait analysis and real-time therapeutic feedback. PhD thesis, Harvard University–MIT Division of Health Sciences and Technology (2004), http://hdl.handle.net/1721.1/28601
7. Ailisto, H.J., Lindholm, M., Mäntyjärvi, J., Vildjiounaite, E., Mäkelä, S.-M.: Identifying people from gait pattern with accelerometers. In: Proceedings of SPIE. Biometric Technology for Human Identification II, vol. 5779, pp. 7–14 (2005)
8. Gafurov, D., Snekkenes, E.: Arm swing as a weak biometric for unobtrusive user authentication. In: IEEE International Conference on Intelligent Information Hiding and Multimedia Signal Processing (2008)
9. Pan, G., Zhang, Y., Wu, Z.: Accelerometer-based gait recognition via voting by signature points. Electronics Letters (2009)
10. Sprager, S., Zazula, D.: Gait identification using cumulants of accelerometer data. In: 2nd WSEAS International Conference on Sensors, and Signals and Visualization, Imaging and Simulation and Materials Science (2009)
11. Alvarez, D., Gonzalez, R.C., Lopez, A., Alvarez, J.C.: Comparison of step length estimators from weareable accelerometer devices. In: 28th Annual International Conference of the IEEE on Engineering in Medicine and Biology Society (EMBS), pp. 5964–5967 (August 2006)
12. Gafurov, D., Snekkenes, E., Bours, P.: Spoof attacks on gait authentication system. IEEE Transactions on Information Forensics and Security 2(3) (2007); Special Issue on Human Detection and Recognition
13. Jonathon Phillips, P., Moon, H., Rizvi, S.A., Rauss, P.J.: The FERET evaluation methodology for face-recognition algorithms. IEEE Transactions on Pattern Analysis and Machine Intelligence 22(10), 1090–1104 (2000)
14. Vildjiounaite, E., Mäkelä, S.-M., Lindholm, M., Riihimäki, R., Kyllönen, V., Mäntyjärvi, J., Ailisto, H.: Unobtrusive multimodal biometrics for ensuring privacy and information security with personal devices. In: Fishkin, K.P., Schiele, B., Nixon, P., Quigley, A. (eds.) PERVASIVE 2006. LNCS, vol. 3968, pp. 187–201. Springer, Heidelberg (2006)
15. Bufu, H., Chen, M., Huang, P., Xu, Y.: Gait modeling for human identification. In: IEEE International on Conference on Robotics and Automation (2007)
16. Yamakawa, T., Taniguchi, K., Asari, K., Kobashi, S., Hata, Y.: Biometric personal identification based on gait pattern using both feet pressure change. In: World Automation Congress (2008)
17. Gafurov, D., Snekkenes, E.: Towards understanding the uniqueness of gait biometric. In: IEEE International Conference Automatic Face and Gesture Recognition (2008)
18. Gafurov, D., Snekkenes, E., Bours, P.: Gait authentication and identification using wearable accelerometer sensor. In: 5th IEEE Workshop on Automatic Identification Advanced Technologies (AutoID), Alghero, Italy, June 7-8, pp. 220–225 (2007)
19. Mäntyjärvi, J., Lindholm, M., Vildjiounaite, E., Mäkelä, S.-M., Ailisto, H.J.: Identifying users of portable devices from gait pattern with accelerometers. In: IEEE International Conference on Acoustics, Speech, and Signal Processing (2005)

20. Rong, L., Zhiguo, D., Jianzhong, Z., Ming, L.: Identification of individual walking patterns using gait acceleration. In: 1st International Conference on Bioinformatics and Biomedical Engineering (2007)
21. Rong, L., Jianzhong, Z., Ming, L., Xiangfeng, H.: A wearable acceleration sensor system for gait recognition. In: 2nd IEEE Conference on Industrial Electronics and Applications (ICIEA) (2007)
22. Bours, P., Shrestha, R.: Eigenstep: A giant leap for gait recognition. In: 2nd International Workshop on Security and Communication Networks (2010)

Fusion of Moving and Static Facial Features for Robust Face Recognition

Dakshina Ranjan Kisku[1,*], Phalguni Gupta[2], and Jamuna Kanta Sing[3]

[1] Department of Computer Science and Engineering,
Asansol Engineering College,
Asansol – 713305, India
drkisku@ieee.org, drkisku@gmail.com
[2] Department of Computer Science and Engineering,
Indian Institute of Technology Kanpur,
Kanpur – 208016, India
pg@cse.iitk.ac.in
[3] Department of Computer Science and Engineering,
Jadavpur University,
Kolkata – 700032, India
jksing@ieee.org

Abstract. This paper presents a robust and efficient face recognition technique. It consists of six major steps. Initially the proposed techniques extract salient facial landmarks (eyes, mouth, and nose) automatically from each face image. SIFT descriptor is used to determine all facial keypoints from each landmark. These feature points are considered to obtain a relaxation graph. Given two relaxations graphs from a pair of faces, matching scores between two corresponding feature points has been determined with the help of iterative graph relaxation cycles. Dempster-Shafer decision theory is used to fuse all these matching scores for taking the final decision. The proposed technique has been tested against the three databases, namely, FERET, ORL and IITK face databases. The experimental results exhibit robustness of the proposed face recognition system.

Keywords: Face recognition, SIFT features, Graph relaxation, Dempster-Shafer theory.

1 Introduction

Face recognition can be considered as one of the most dynamic and complex research areas in machine vision and pattern recognition [1, 2] due to the variable appearance of face images. Changes in appearance may occur due to many factors, such as facial attributes compatibility complexity, the motion of face parts, facial expression, pose, illumination and partly occlusion. As a result face recognition problem become ill-posed.

There exist several techniques to similar faces with identical characteristics from a set of faces and to accelerate the face matching strategy. These techniques can broadly

---

[*] Corresponding author.

T.-h. Kim et al. (Eds.): SecTech/DRBC 2010, CCIS 122, pp. 187–196, 2010.
© Springer-Verlag Berlin Heidelberg 2010

classify into three categories: appearance-based, model-based and feature-based techniques. The appearance-based techniques are Principal Component Analysis (PCA) [1], Linear Discriminant Analysis (LDA) [1], Fisher Discriminant Analysis (FDA) [1], and Independent Component Analysis (ICA) [1]. Among the various model based techniques for face recognition AAM [21, 22], ASM [23], are worth to mention. Some local feature based techniques have been proposed in [3], [4], [5, 6]. One of the most well known feature based technique that is known as Elastic Bunch Graph Matching (EBGM) has been discussed in [3]. EBGM has been used to represent faces as graphs where vertices are the fiducial points (e.g., eyes, nose) and edges are the geometric distance between two fiducial points. Each vertex contains a set of 40 complex Gabor wavelet coefficients at different scales and orientations. They are called a Gabor Jet. A graph similarity function has been proposed in [3] and used for identification. The local feature based proposed in [6], is based on graph matching topology drawn on SIFT features [7, 16].

This paper proposes a new local feature based face recognition technique which makes use of dynamic (mouth) and static (eyes, nose) salient features of face obtained through SIFT operator [7, 16].

Differences in facial expression, head pose, illumination, and partly occlusion may result to variations of facial characteristics and attributes. To capture the face variations, face characteristics of dynamic (moving) and static parts are further represented by incorporating probabilistic graph relaxations drawn on SIFT features extracted from localized mouth, eyes and nose facial parts. The proposed technique has made an attempt to handle this problem. It first detects and extracts automatically the salient facial parts such as eyes, mouth and nose with the help of the algorithm proposed in [8, 9]. Invariant feature descriptor is used on each of these facial parts to determine SIFT features and finally a relaxation graph is drawn on the SIFT features for each facial part. For Matching between two faces is done by considering the pair of relaxation graphs of each salient facial part (i.e., nose, mouth, left eye and right eye) of two faces. For each point of a relaxation graph corresponding point having maximum score in another relaxation graph of the pair is obtained. These matching scores obtained from various facial parts are fused using Dempster-Shafer theory. The proposed techniques are evaluated against three face databases, namely, FERET [24, 25], ORL (formerly known as AT&T) [11] and IITK face databases.

The next section presents the overview of the invariant SIFT descriptor proposed in [7, 16]. Automatic detection of salient facial parts and the SIFT feature points of each parts have been discussed in Section 3. The method used to determine relaxation graph from each salient facial part has been discussed in the next Section. Section 5 deals with the fusion strategy used to obtain the matching scores for decision. Experimental results of the proposed system against four databases are analyzed in Section 6. Concluding remarks are given in last section.

2   Feature Extraction Using SIFT Descriptor

The SIFT descriptor, which is invariant to image rotation, scaling, partly illumination changes and the 3D camera view has been investigated for biometrics authentication in [6], [20].

It detects feature points efficiently through a staged filtering approach that identifies stable points in the scale-space of the image of pyramid obtained by convolving the image by a set of difference of Gaussian kernels. Each feature point is composed of four types of information – spatial location (x, y), scale (S), orientation (θ) and Keypoint descriptor (K). In this paper, only keypoint descriptor [6], [7], [16], [20] discussed in [6], has been used. The descriptor consists of a vector of 128 elements representing changes in neighborhood intensity of current points. More formally, local image gradients are measured at the selected scale in the region around each keypoint. The measured gradient information is then transformed into a vector of 128 elements. These keypoint descriptors represent local shape distortions and illumination changes. In Fig. 1, SIFT features are shown for a pair of face images.

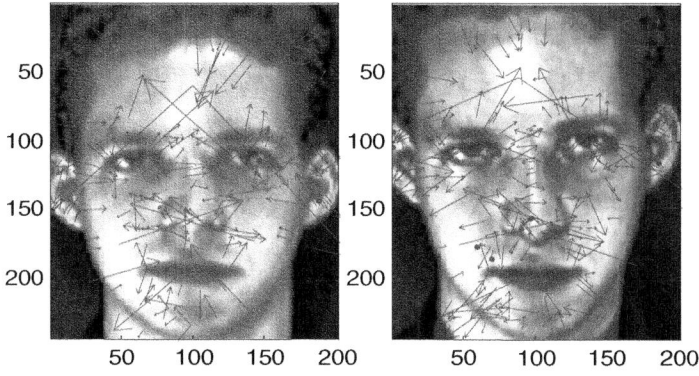

Fig. 1. SIFT features of a pair of faces

3   Salient Landmark Representation

Deformable objects are generally difficult to characterize with a rigid representation in feature spaces for recognition. With a large view of physiological characteristics in biometrics including iris, fingerprint, hand geometry, etc, faces are considered as highly deformable objects. Different facial regions, not only convey different relevant and redundant information on the subject's identity, but also suffer from different time variability either due to motion or illumination changes. A typical example is the case of a talking face where the mouth part can be considered as dynamic facial landmark part. But the eyes and nose can be considered as the static facial landmark parts which are almost still and invariant over time. As a consequence, the features extracted from the mouth area cannot be directly matched with the corresponding features from a static template. Moreover, single facial features may be occluded making the corresponding image area not usable for identification.

The eyes, mouth and nose positions are automatically located by applying the technique proposed in [8, 9]. A circular region of interest (ROI), centered at each extracted facial landmark location is considered to determine the SIFT features of the landmark.

4 Probabilistic Relaxation Graph Representation and Matching

In order to interpret the facial landmarks with invariant SIFT points and graph relaxation topology, each extracted feature can be thought as a node and the relationship between invariant points can be considered as edge between two nodes. At the level of feature extraction, invariant SIFT feature points are extracted and facial landmarks location with the landmark detection algorithms discussed in [10, 11, 12]. The final similarity measure can be obtained from the feature points extracted from facial landmarks only. Relaxation graphs are then drawn on the features extracted from landmarks. These relaxations are used for matching and verification.

Thus, the graph can be represented by $G=\{V, E, K, \zeta\}$, where V and E denote the set of nodes and set of edges, respectively, and K and ζ are the set of attributes associated with nodes and edges in the graph. K denotes the set of keypoint descriptors associated with various nodes and ζ denotes the relationship between two keypoint descriptors.

Suppose, $G_R = \{V_R, E_R, K_R, \zeta_R\}$ and $G_Q = \{V_Q, E_Q, K_Q, \zeta_Q\}$ are two graphs. These two graphs can be compared to determine whether they are identical or not. If it is found that $|V_R| = |V_Q|$ for the given two graphs, the problem is said to be exact graph matching problem. The problem is to find a one-to-one mapping $f: V_Q \rightarrow V_R$, such that $(u, v) \in E_Q$ iff $(f(u),f(v)) \in E_R$. This mapping f is called an isomorphism and G_Q is called isomorphic to G_R. In this case, isomorphism is not possible because identical SIFT feature points may not be present on two different landmarks. Hence, it is forced to apply inexact graph matching problem in the context of probabilistic graph matching where either $|V_R| < |V_Q|$ or $|V_R| > |V_Q|$. This may occur when the number of SIFT keypoints or vertices is different in both the graphs.

The similarity measure for vertex and edge attributes can be defined as the similarity measure for nodes $v_R^i \in V_R$ and $v_Q^j \in V_Q$ as $s_{ij}^v = s(v_R^i, v_Q^j)$ where $v_R^i \in K_R \in V_R$ and $v_Q^j \in K_Q \in V_Q$, and the similarity between edges $e_R^{ip} \in E_R$ and $e_Q^{jq} \in E_Q$ can be denoted as $s_{ipjq}^e = s(e_R^{ip}, e_Q^{jq})$, where $e_R^{ip} \in \zeta_R \in E_R$ and $e_Q^{jq} \in \zeta_Q \in E_Q$.

Now, v_Q^j would be best probable match for v_R^i, when v_Q^j maximizes the posteriori probability [10], [11], [12] of labeling. Thus for the vertex $v_R^i \in V_R$, we are searching the most probable label or vertex $v_R^i = v_Q^j \in V_Q$ in the graph. Hence, it can be stated as

$$\bar{v}_R^i = \arg \max_{j,v_Q \in V_Q} P(\psi_i^{v_Q^j} \mid K_R, \varsigma_R, K_Q, \varsigma_Q) \tag{1}$$

For efficient searching of matching probabilities from the query sample, we use relaxation technique that simplifies the solution of matching problem. Let $\bar{P}_{ij}^v$ denote the matching probability for vertices $v_R^i \in V_R$ and $v_Q^j \in V_Q$. Now, by reformulating Equation (1) one gets

$$\bar{v}_R^i = \arg \max_{j,v_{Q_j} \in V_Q} \bar{P}_{ij}^v \tag{2}$$

Equation (2) consider as an iterative relaxation algorithm for searching the best labels for v_R^i. This can be achieved by assigning prior probability $\bar{P}_{ij}^v$ proportional to $s_{ij}^v = s^v(k_R^i, k_Q^j)$. The following iterative relaxation rule can be used to define $\overline{P}_{ij}^v$;

$$\hat{P}_{ij}^v = \frac{\overline{P}_{ij}^v . Q_{ij}}{\sum\limits_{j, v_Q^j \in V_Q} \overline{P}_{ij}^v . Q_{ij}} \tag{3}$$

where, Q_{ij} is given by

$$Q_{ij} = \overline{P}_{ij}^v \prod_{v_i \in V_R} \sum_{v_j \in V_Q} s_{ij}^e . \overline{P}_{ij}^v \tag{4}$$

In Equation (4), Q_{ij} conveys the support of the neighboring vertices and $\hat{P}_{ij}^v$ represents the posteriori probability. The relaxation cycles are repeated until the difference between prior probability $\overline{P}_{ij}^v$ and posteriori probabilities $\hat{P}_{ij}^v$ becomes smaller than certain threshold Φ and when this would be reached only then it is assumed that the relaxation process is stable. When such a condition holds good, it is assume that relaxation process is stable.

Hence, the best match graph for query sample is established by using the posteriori probabilities in Equation (3).

5   Fusion of Facial Features

The Dempster-Shafer decision theory [17, 18, 19] is applied to combine the matching scores obtained from individual landmark. It is based on combining the evidences obtained from different sources to compute the probability of an event. This is obtained combining three elements: the basic probability assignment function (*bpa*), the belief function (*bf*) and the plausibility function (*pf*).

Let $\Gamma^{left-eye}$, $\Gamma^{right-eye}$, Γ^{nose} and Γ^{mouth} be the individual matching scores obtained from the four different matching of salient facial landmarks. Now, in order to obtain the combine matching score determined from the four salient landmarks pairs, Dempster combination rule has been applied. First, we combine the matching scores obtained from the pairs of left-eye and nose landmark features and in the next, we combine the matching scores obtained from the pairs of right-eye and mouth landmark features. Finally, we combine the matching scores determined from the first and second processes.   Also, let $m(\Gamma^{left-eye})$, $m(\Gamma^{right-eye})$, $m(\Gamma^{nose})$ and $m(\Gamma^{mouth})$ be the *bpa* functions for the Belief measures $Bel(\Gamma^{left-eye})$, $Bel(\Gamma^{right-eye})$, $Bel(\Gamma^{nose})$ and $Bel(\Gamma^{mouth})$ for the four classifiers, respectively. Then the Belief probability assignments *(bpa)* $m(\Gamma^{left-eye})$, $m(\Gamma^{right-eye})$, $m(\Gamma^{nose})$ and $m(\Gamma^{mouth})$ can be combined together to obtained a Belief committed to a matching score set $C \in \Theta$ according to the following combination rule or orthogonal sum rule

$$m(C_1) = m(\Gamma^{left-eye}) \oplus m(\Gamma^{nose}) = \frac{\sum\limits_{\Gamma^{left-eye} \cap \Gamma^{nose} = C_1} m(\Gamma^{left-eye})m(\Gamma^{nose})}{1 - \sum\limits_{\Gamma^{left-eye} \cap \Gamma^{nose} = \emptyset} m(\Gamma^{left-eye})m(\Gamma^{nose})}, \quad C_1 \neq \emptyset. \qquad (5)$$

$$m(C_2) = m(\Gamma^{right-eye}) \oplus m(\Gamma^{mouth}) = \frac{\sum\limits_{\Gamma^{right-eye} \cap \Gamma^{mouth} = C_2} m(\Gamma^{right-eye})m(\Gamma^{mouth})}{1 - \sum\limits_{\Gamma^{right-eye} \cap \Gamma^{mouth} = \emptyset} m(\Gamma^{right-eye})m(\Gamma^{mouth})}, \quad C_2 \neq \emptyset. \qquad (6)$$

$$m(C) = m(m(C_1)) \oplus m(m(C_2)) = \frac{\sum\limits_{m(C_1) \cap m(C_2) = C} m(m(C_1))m(m(C_2))}{1 - \sum\limits_{m(C_1) \cap m(C_2) = \emptyset} m(m(C_1))m(m(C_2))}, \quad C \neq \emptyset. \qquad (7)$$

The denominator in equations (5), (6) and (7) are the normalizing factors which denotes the art of Belief probability assignments $m(\Gamma^{left-eye})$, $m(\Gamma^{right-eye})$, $m(\Gamma^{nose})$ and $m(\Gamma^{mouth})$ are conflicting.

Let $m(m(C_1))$ and $m(m(C_2))$ are the two matching score sets obtained from the local and global matching strategies. They can be fused together recursively as:

$$m(FMS) = m(m(C_1)) \oplus m(m(C_2)) \qquad (8)$$

where $\oplus$ denotes the Dempster combination rule. The final decision of user acceptance and rejection can be established by the following equation and by applying the threshold Ψ to the final match $m(FMS)$

$$decision = \begin{cases} accept, & if \quad m(FMS) \geq \Psi \\ \\ reject, & otherwise \end{cases} \qquad (9)$$

6   Experimental Results

To investigate the effectiveness and robustness of the proposed graph-based face matching strategy, experiments have been carried out on the three face databases, namely FERET [24], ORL [11] and IITK face databases.

6.1   Evaluation with FERET Face Database

The FERET face recognition database [24] is a collection of face images acquired by NIST. For this evaluation, 1,396 face images are considered as training dataset out of which 200 images labeled as bk; that is 1396 face images in database. For query set we have considered 1195 images that are labeled as *fafb*. All these images have been downscaled to 140x100 from the original size of 150x130. For testing purpose, we take *fa* labeled dataset of 1,195 and the *duplicate 1* dataset of 722 face images as probe set. Prior to processing, the faces are well registered to each other and the background effects are eliminated. Moreover, only the frontal view face images are used, which have natural facial expressions (*fa*) and the face images which have taken under different lighting conditions.

The result obtained from the FERET dataset given in the Tab the recognition accuracy of the proposed system when tested on FERET dataset found to be 92.34%. Consequently, our proposed result proved to be an appropriate one for changing illumination and facial expression. In addition, use of invariant SIFT features along with the graph relaxation topology has made this system truly robust and efficient.

6.2 Evaluation with IIT Kanpur Database

The IITK face database consists of 1200 face images with four images per person (300X4). These images are captured under control environment with ±20 degree changes of head pose and with at most uniform lighting and illumination conditions, and with at most consistent facial expressions. For the face matching, all probe images are matched against all target images.

From the ROC curve in Fig. 2 it has been observed that the recognition accuracy is 93.63%, with the false accept rate (FAR) of 5.82%.

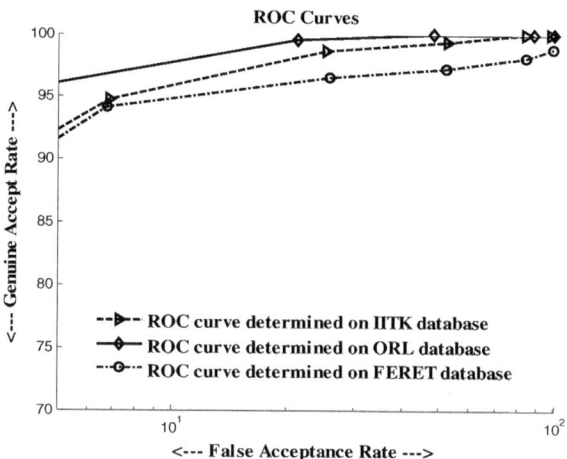

Fig. 2. ROC curves for Different Databases

6.3 Evaluation with ORL Database

The ORL face database [11] consists of 400 images taken from 40 subjects. Out of these 400 images 200 face images are considered for experiment. It has been observed that there exact changes in orientation in images which lying between -20^0 and 30^0. The face images are found to have the variations in pose and facial expression (smile/not smile, open/closed eyes). The original resolution of the images is 92 x 112 pixels. However, for the experiment the resolution is set to 120×160 pixels.

From the ROC curve in Fig. 2 it has been observed that the recognition accuracy for the ORL database is 97.33%, yielding FAR is about 2.14%. The relative accuracy of the proposed matching strategy for ORL database increases of about 3% and 5% over the IITK database and the FERET database respectively.

6.4 Comparison with Other Techniques

In order to verify the effectiveness of the proposed face matching algorithm for recognition and identification, we have compared it with the algorithms discussed in [6, 13, 14, 15]. It has been observed that the proposed algorithm is completely different from the algorithms discussed in [6, 13, 14, 15] in terms of performance and design issues. In [13], the PCA approach has been discussed for different view of face images without transformation and the algorithm has achieved 90% recognition accuracy for some specific views of faces. On the other hand, [14] and [15] have used gabor jets for face processing and recognition, where the algorithm in [14] makes use of the gabor jets without transformation and later one used the gabor jets with geometrical transformation. Both the techniques have been tested on Bochum and FERET databases [24]. These databases are characteristically different from IITK and ORL face databases [11] and the maximum achieved recognition rates are 94% and 96%, respectively. Further graph based face recognition techniques drawn on SIFT features have considered in [6] the whole face whereas the proposed face recognition algorithm has not only determined keypoints from the local landmarks, but also it combines the local features for robust performance.

7 Conclusion

In this paper, an efficient and robust face recognition technique by considering facial landmarks and using the probabilistic graph relaxation drawn on SIFT feature points has been proposed. During the face recognition process, the human faces are characterized on the basis of local salient landmark features. It has been determined that when the face matching accomplishes with the whole face region, the global features (whole face) are easy to capture and they are generally less discriminative than localized features. In the proposed face recognition method, local facial landmarks are considered for further processing. The optimal face representation using graph relaxation drawn on local landmarks then allows matching the localized facial features efficiently by searching the correspondence of keypoints using iterative relaxation.

References

1. Shakhnarovich, G., Moghaddam, B.: Face Recognition in Subspaces. In: Li, S., Jain, A. (eds.) Handbook of Face Recognition, pp. 141–168. Springer, Heidelberg (2004)
2. Shakhnarovich, G., Fisher, J.W., Darrell, T.: Face Recognition from Long-term Observations. In: Heyden, A., Sparr, G., Nielsen, M., Johansen, P. (eds.) ECCV 2002. LNCS, vol. 2352, pp. 851–865. Springer, Heidelberg (2002)

3. Wiskott, L., Fellous, J., Kruger, N., Malsburg, C.: Face Recognition by Elastic Bunch Graph Matching. IEEE Trans. on Pattern Analysis and Machine Intelligence 19, 775–779 (1997)
4. Zhang, G., Huang, X., Wang, S.L.Y., Wu, X.: Boosting Local Binary Pattern (lbp)-based Face Recognition. In: Li, S.Z., Lai, J.-H., Tan, T., Feng, G.-C., Wang, Y. (eds.) SINOBIOMETRICS 2004. LNCS, vol. 3338, pp. 179–186. Springer, Heidelberg (2004)
5. Heusch, G., Rodriguez, Y., Marcel, S.: Local Binary Patterns as An Image Preprocessing for Face Authentication. In: IDIAP-RR 76, IDIAP (2005)
6. Kisku, D.R., Rattani, A., Grosso, E., Tistarelli, M.: Face Identification by SIFT-based Complete Graph Topology. In: IEEE Workshop Automatic Identification Advanced Technologies, pp. 63–68 (2007)
7. Lowe, D.: Distinctive Image Features from Scale-invariant Keypoints. International Journal of Computer Vision 60(2), 91–110 (2004)
8. Smeraldi, F., Capdevielle, N., Bigün, J.: Facial Features Detection by Saccadic Exploration of the Gabor Decomposition and Support Vector Machines. In: 11th Scandinavian Conference on Image Analysis, pp. 39–44 (1999)
9. Gourier, N., James, D.H., Crowley, L.: Estimating Face Orientation from Robust Detection of Salient Facial Structures. In: FG Net Workshop on Visual Observation of Deictic Gestures (2004)
10. Bauer, M.: Approximation Algorithms and Decision-making in the Dempster-Shafer Theory of Evidence—An Empirical Study. International Journal of Approximate Reasoning 17, 217–237 (1997)
11. Samaria, F., Harter, A.: Parameterization of a Stochastic Model for Human Face Identification. In: IEEE Workshop on Applications of Computer Vision (1994)
12. Yaghi, H., Krim, H.: Probabilistic Graph Matching by Canonical Decomposition. In: IEEE International Conference on Image Processing, pp. 2368 – 2371 (2008)
13. Moghaddam, B., Pentland, A.: Face Recognition using View-based and Modular Eigenspaces. In: SPIE Conf. on Automatic Systems for the Identification and Inspection of Humans. SPIE, vol. 2277, p. 12 (1994)
14. Wiskott, L., Fellous, J.M., Kruger, N., von der Malsburg, C.: Face Recognition by Elastic Bunch Graph Matching. IEEE Transactions on Pattern Analysis and Machine Intelligence 19(7), 775–779 (1997)
15. Maurer, T., von der Malsburg, C.: Linear Feature Transformations to Recognize Faces Rotated in Depth. In: International Conference on Artificial Neural Networks, pp. 353–358 (1995)
16. Lowe, D.G.: Object Recognition from Local Scale-invariant Features. In: International Conference on Computer Vision, pp. 1150–1157 (1999)
17. Wilson, N.: Algorithms for Dempster-Shafer Theory. Oxford Brookes University (1999)
18. Barnett, J.A.: Computational Methods for a Mathematical Theory of Evidence. In: IJCAI, pp. 868–875 (1981)
19. Bauer, M.: Approximation Algorithms and Decision-making in the Dempster-Shafer Theory of Evidence—An Empirical Study. International Journal of Approximate Reasoning 17, 217–237 (1997)
20. Park, U., Pankanti, S., Jain, A.K.: Fingerprint Verification using SIFT Features. In: Vijaya Kumar, B.V.K., Prabhakar, S., Ross, A. (eds.) Biometric Technology for Human Identification V, SPIE, 6944:69440K-69440K-9 (2008)
21. Faggian, N., Paplinski, A., Chin, T.-J.: Face Recognition from Video using Active Appearance Model Segmentation. In: International Conference on Pattern Recognition, pp. 287–290 (2006)

22. Ivan, P.: Active Appearance Models for Face Recognition. Technical Report, Vrije
    Universiteit of Amsterdam (2007),
    http://www.few.vu.nl/~sbhulai/theses/werkstuk-ivan.pdf
23. Cootes, T.F., Taylor, C.J.: Active Shape Models. In: 3rd British Machine Vision
    Conference, pp. 266–275 (1992)
24. Phillips, P.J., Moon, H., Rauss, P.J., Rizvi, S.: The FERET Evaluation Methodology for
    Face Recognition Algorithms. IEEE Transactions on Pattern Analysis and Machine
    Intelligence 22(10), 1090–1104 (2000)

Human Authentication Based on ECG Waves Using Radon Transform

Chetana Hegde[1], H. Rahul Prabhu[2], D.S. Sagar[2], P. Deepa Shenoy[2], K.R. Venugopal[2], and L.M. Patnaik[3]

[1] Research Scholar, Bangalore University, Bangalore 560 001
[2] Department of CSE, UVCE, Bangalore University, Bangalore 560 001
[3] Vice Chancellor, DIAT, Pune, India
chetanahegde@yahoo.co.in

Abstract. Automated security is one of the major concerns of modern times. Secure and reliable authentication systems are in great demand. A biometric trait like electrocardiogram (ECG) of a person is unique and secure. In this paper, we propose a human authentication system based on ECG waves considering a plotted ECG wave signal as an image. The Radon Transform is applied on the preprocessed ECG image to get a radon image consisting of projections for θ varying from 0° to 180°. The pairwise distance between the columns of Radon image is computed to get a feature vector. Correlation Coefficient between feature vector stored in the database and that of input image is computed to check the authenticity of a person. Then the confusion matrix is generated to find False Acceptance Ratio (FAR) and False Rejection Ratio (FRR). This methodology of authentication is tested on ECG wave data set of 105 individuals taken from Physionet QT Database. The proposed authentication system is found to have FAR of about 3.19% and FRR of about 0.128%. The overall accuracy of the system is found to be 99.85%.

Keywords: FAR, FRR, Pairwise Distance, Pre-processing, Radon Transform.

1 Introduction

In the present times, security has become a critical issue in automated authentication systems. Biometrics is a science of identifying a person using their physiological or behavioral characteristics. Biometric traits are difficult to counterfeit and hence results in higher accuracy when compared to other methods such as using passwords and ID cards. Human physiological and/or behavioral characteristic can be used as a biometric characteristic when it satisfies the requirements like Universality, Distinctiveness, Permanence and Collectability. Moreover, one need to focus on some major issues like *Performance, Acceptability* and *Circumvention*[1]. Keeping all these requirements in mind, biometric traits like fingerprints, hand geometry, handwritten signatures[2], retinal patterns, facial images, ear pattern[3] etc., are used extensively in the areas which require security access.

T.-h. Kim et al. (Eds.): SecTech/DRBC 2010, CCIS 122, pp. 197–206, 2010.

Most of the biometric traits mentioned above, have certain disadvantages which threaten the level of security. Some of the traits can easily be forged to create false identities. Some may be altered to hide the identity of an individual. And few other traits can be used even in the absence of the person and even if he is dead. Certain biometric traits like hand-vein patterns may fail in case of hand-injury. Though it is possible to authenticate a person with a damaged hand-vein pattern[4], it is impossible to achieve 100% accuracy as there is a limitation of threshold. To overcome these problems, several researchers moved to multimodal biometric systems. But, it is possible to have a stronger authentication system using ECG of a person as a biometric trait[5].

The heartbeat of a person is collected in the form of an electrocardiogram recording. The ECG of a person varies from person to person due to change in size, position and anatomy of the heart, chest configuration and various other factors[6]. The heartbeat of a person cannot be copied to fake identity and it cannot be altered to hide identity. And hence, ECG is becoming a promising biometric trait. Since the proposed algorithm uses single-lead ECG signal image, even a palm-held ECG machine is suitable for the authentication purpose. This kind of machines will be more robust and useful for real-time applications.

This paper is organized as follows: Section 2 deals with the related work and Section 3 presents the architecture and model. Section 4 defines the problem. Section 5 describes the implementation of the proposed algorithm and the performance analysis. Section 6 contains the conclusions.

2   Related Work

A brief survey of the related work in the area of identification using ECG waves and the significance of Radon Transforms is presented in this section. Biel et al.[7] showed that it is possible to identify individuals based on an ECG signal. The initial work on heartbeat biometric recognition used a standard 12-lead electrocardiogram for recording the data. Later a single-lead ECG was being used. Biel et al.[7] used 30 features like $P-$wave onset, $P-$wave duration, $QRS-$wave onset etc. for each person. Then the method SIMCA (Soft Independent Modeling of Class Analogy)[8] was used to classify persons. The other approach proposed by Shen et al.[9] uses template matching and a Decision-Based Neural Network (DBNN). The next promising technique for human identification using ECG was from Singh et al.[10]. In their approach, the QRS complex delineator was implemented. All these works are for human identification but not authentication. Moreover, the previous works have used geometrical features which tend to be error-prone, as a minute change in the features like angle might have been ignored during approximation and/or normalization.

Considering a graph of ECG wave signals as an image is a new approach. Swamy et al.[11] presented that the ECG wave images are more adaptable. And image processing techniques can be applied on ECG wave image, instead of taking ECG signals.

Radon Transform holds a distinguishable place in the field of biometrics. It is well known for its wide range of imaging applications. Radon transform plays a key-role in the study of various biometric traits like thyroid tissue[12], face recognition[13], gait recognition[14], iris recognition[15] etc. The Radon transform fucntion is used to detect features within a two-dimensional image. This function can be used to return either the Radon transform, which transforms lines through an image to points in the Radon domain, or the Radon backprojection, where each point in the Radon domain is transformed to a straight line in the image. In this paper, we propose a technique for human authentication by implementing Radon transform on an ECG wave image. The obtained Radon backprojection image is then used to find feature vector through Standardized Euclidean pairwise distance. Then the authentication is done based on correlation coefficient between two feature vectors.

3   Architecture and Modeling

Every individual in the organization, which adopts the proposed system for authentication, will be given an identification number (ID). Having the database of ECG wave signals of all the people in an organization consumes more space and the complexity of the system will increase. So, we suggest to store only the calculated features of ECG against every ID. First, we will acquire ECG waves from a 10-second sample of every person. The conversion of ECG wave signal format into an image will improve the adaptability and also iterative image processing techniques can easily be applied[11]. So, the acquired ECG wave is converted as a gray-scale image. Pre-processing techniques are applied to remove the possible noise occured during image conversion. The pre-processed image will undergo Radon Transform to generate Radon feature-image. The pairwise distance between the columns of Radon image is computed and the feature vector is generated. This feature vector will be stored in the database against a particular ID. During authentication, the person has to provide his ID and his ECG is captured. The feature vector is generated for new ECG wave image. The correlation coefficient between the two feature vectors is used to decide the authenticity of that person.

The architectural diagram for the proposed algorithm is shown in Fig. 1. The steps involved in the proposed technique are explained hereunder.

3.1   Data Acquisition

The proposed algorithm uses one-lead ECG waves. The ECG signals for a specific time duration are captured from a person and are plotted as a graph. The plotted graph is then converted as an image for further processing. Fig. 2 shows the ECG wave sample for one of the subjects.

3.2   Pre-processing

The converted EGG image is in RGB format and is then converted into a gray-scale image. Morphological operations like erosion and dilation are applied on

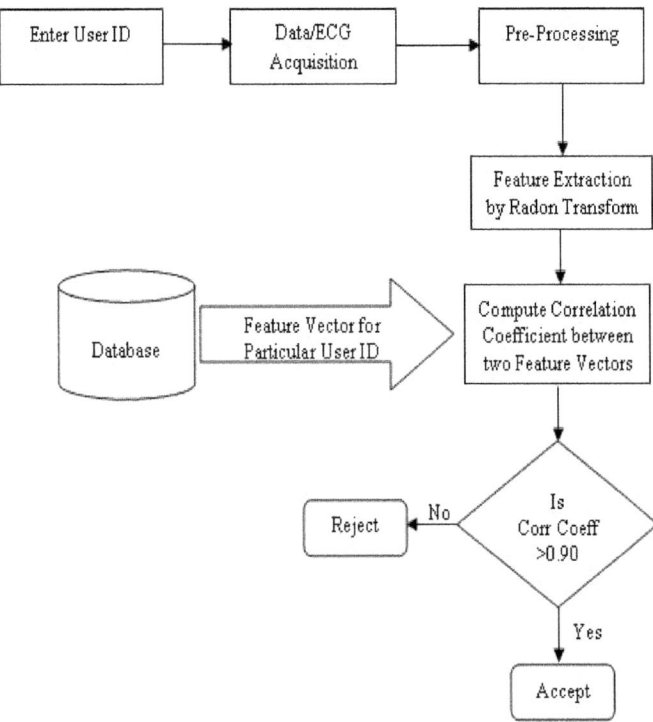

Fig. 1. Architectural Diagram

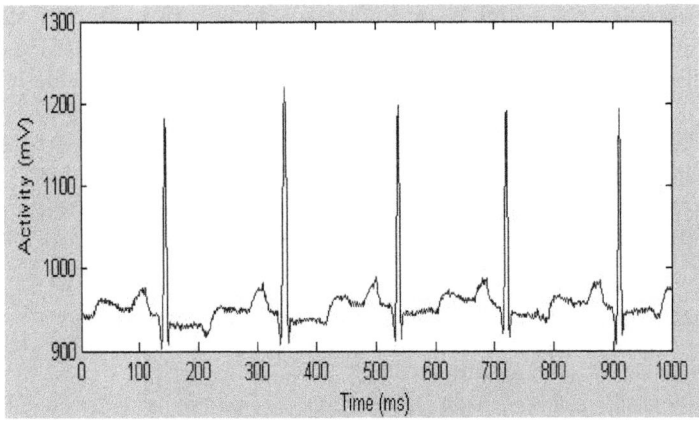

Fig. 2. ECG Wave Sample

the gray-scale image to improve its intensity. Then we apply median filter, a well-known order-statistic filter on the image. The image after pre-processing is shown in Fig. 3.

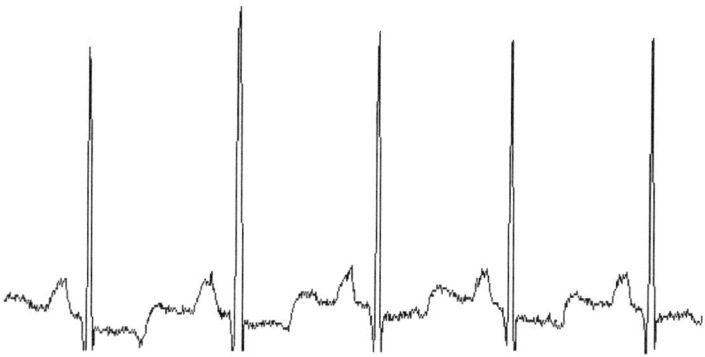

Fig. 3. Image after Pre-processing

3.3   Feature Extraction Using Radon Transform

The Radon Transform is the integral transform consisting of the integral of a function over straight lines. In other words, it is the projection of an image along specified direction[15]. Let (x, y) be the cartesian coordinates of a point in a 2D image and $u(x, y)$ be the image intensity. Then the 2D Radon transform denoted as $R_u(\rho, \theta)$ is given by -

$$R_u(\rho, \theta) = \int_{-\infty}^{+\infty} \int_{-\infty}^{+\infty} u(x, y)\, \delta(\rho - x\cos\theta - y\sin\theta)\, dx dy$$

Here ρ is the perpendicular distance of a line from the origin and θ is the angle formed by the distance vector. In the proposed technique we have taken θ to be varying from 0° to 180°. The Radon transform is applied on the pre-processed ECG image. The resulting Radon image is as shown in Fig. 4.

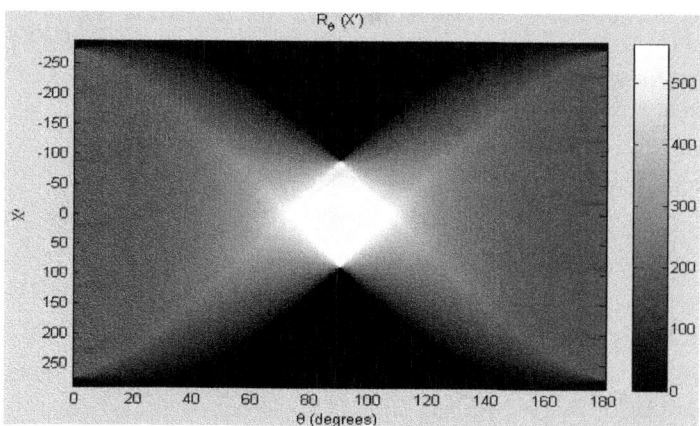

Fig. 4. Radon Image for Pre-processed ECG Image

On the obtained Radon image, we apply pairwise distance method. This method computes the distance between pairs of pixels in the image. In our algorithm, we use Standardized Euclidean distance for computing pairwise distance. Given an mxn data matrix X(in this case, image), which is treated as m $(1xn)$ row vectors $x_1, x_2 \ldots x_m$, the Standardized Euclidean distance between the vectors x_r and x_s is defined as -

$$d_{rs} = \sqrt{(x_r - x_s)D^{-1}(x_r - x_s)'}$$

Here D is the diagonal matrix with diagonal elements given by v_j^2, which denotes the variance of the variable X_j over the m objects.

The implementation of standardized Euclidean distance on ECG image will produce a feature vector. This feature vector is then used for authentication.

3.4   Feature Matching

For authentication purpose, we use Karl Pearson's Correlation Coefficient. Correlation is a method of identifying the degree of relationship between two sets of values. It reveals the dependency or independency between the variables. If X and Y are two vectors of size mxn, then the Karl Pearson's correlation coefficient between X and Y is computed using the formula -

$$\rho_{XY} = \frac{\sum_{i=1}^{m} \sum_{j=1}^{n} \left(X - \overline{X}\right)\left(Y - \overline{Y}\right)}{\sqrt{\left[\sum_{i=1}^{m} \sum_{j=1}^{n} \left(X - \overline{X}\right)^2\right]\left[\sum_{i=1}^{m} \sum_{j=1}^{n} \left(Y - \overline{Y}\right)^2\right]}}$$

Here, $\overline{X}$ and $\overline{Y}$ respectively denote the means of vectors X and Y. The value of correlation coefficient ρ_{XY} may range from -1 to $+1$. If the value of correlation coefficient is -1, the vectors X and Y are inversely related. If the value is 0, then the vectors are independent and if the value is $+1$, then the vectors are completely (or positively or directly) related. Thus, the high degree of positive correlation indicates that the values of vectors are very much close to each other. So, if the correlation coefficient between the feature vector of database image and that of new image is nearer to $+1$, the person can be authenticated. Otherwise, the person is rejected.

3.5   Authentication

The organization which adopts this authentication technique has to create a database of feature vectors against the ID number for every individual using the process as explained in Section 3.1 to Section 3.3. The authentication process involves a series of steps as listed hereunder.

1. The person who undergoes the authentication process should first enter his ID and his ECG is captured.
2. The captured ECG signals are plotted as a graph and it is converted to an image.

3. Now, the ECG image will undergo pre-processing to remove the possible noise and to increase the intensity.
4. Radon transform is applied on pre-processed ECG image to get a Radon image. Then pairwise distance is calculated for this image to get a feature vector.
5. The correlation coefficient between the feature vector retrieved from the database and newly created feature vector is computed as explained in Section 3.4.
6. If the computed correlation coefficient is greater than a threshold value 0.90, then the person can be authenticated. Otherwise he will be rejected.

4   Algorithm

4.1   Problem Definition

Given an ECG wave signal, the objectives are:

(1) To convert plotted ECG wave format as an image.
(2) To convert RGB image into gray-scale image and to apply pre-processing techniques.
(3) To apply Radon transform to get a Radon feature image and to apply pairwise distance to get a feature vector.
(4) To find correlation coefficient to check the authenticity of a person.

4.2   Algorithms

Four major functions are involved in the proposed technique. The first function is for pre-processing the ECG image. The next function is for applying Radon transform to get a Radon image. The third function is for computing standardized Euclidean distance for each pair of rows in the Radon image. The last function is for computing correlation coefficient to check the authenticity of a person. The algorithm for computing correlation coefficient is given in Table 1.

5   Implementation and Performance Analysis

The implementation of proposed technique is developed using MatLab 7.5. The proposed algorithm is tested on ECG wave formats taken from Physionet QT database[16]. The sampling tool provided by Physionet database reads signal files for the specified record and writes the samples as decimal numbers on the standard output. By default, each line of output contains the sample number and samples from each signal, beginning with channel 0, separated by tabs. The simulation of proposed technique is done on ECG signals of 105 individuals. Various research works based on ECG waves proposed earlier like[7] and[10] were focused on Human identification but not authentication. Also, the previous works on identification based on ECG uses geometrical features which are error-prone and increases computational complexity. In our algorithm, the problems

204   C. Hegde et al.

Table 1. Algorithm for Calculating Correlation Coefficient

//Input: The feature vectors X and Y.
//Output: The Correlation Coefficient between X and Y.

begin
  Intialize $SumX = 0$, $SumY = 0$, $SumSqX = 0$,
  $SumSqY = 0$ and $SumXY = 0$
  for $i = 1$ to $rows$
    for $j = 1$ to $columns$
      set $SumX = SumX + X\,(i,j)$
      set $SumY = SumY + Y\,(i,j)$
      set $SumSqX = SumSqX + X\,(i,j)^2$
      set $SumSqY = SumSqY + Y\,(i,j)^2$
      set $SumXY = SumXY + X\,(i,j) * Y\,(i,j)$
    end for
  end for

  $AvgX = SumX/(rows * cols)$
  $AvgY = SumY/(rows * cols)$
  $EXY = SumXY/(rows * cols)$
  $StdX = sqrt(SumSqX/(row * cols)AvgX^2)$
  $StdY = sqrt(SumSqY/(row * cols)AvgY^2)$
  $Corr = (EXY\,AvgX * AvgY)/(StdX * StdY)$
end

Table 2. Simulation Results

Database Image	Test Image	Corr Coeff	Expected Result	Actual Result
I1	I1	0.9983	Accept	Accept
I2	I1	0.1165	Reject	Reject
I3	I2	0.1204	Reject	Reject
I4	I3	0.9106	Reject	Accept
I5	I4	0.2317	Reject	Reject

in having mass storage of ECG data is overcome by storing the features of Radon image. Since the Radon transform is used with the angles varying from 0° to 180°, projection in all directions has been considered. This will improve the performance of the system.

The results obtained for some of the subjects from Physionet QT database is given in Table 2. The simulation results on ECG waves of 105 individuals resulted into a confusion matrix as shown in Table 3. With the help of confusion matrix, the false acceptance ratio is found to be 3.19% and false rejection ratio is 0.128%. And the overall performance of the system is found to be 99.85%.

Table 3. Confusion Matrix

		Actual	
		Genuine	Non-Genuine
Tested	Genuine	91	3
	Non-Genuine	14	10917

6   Conclusions

In this paper, we propose an efficient way for human authentication using ECG images. The proposed technique uses Radon transform and standardized Euclidean distance to find image features in an ECG image. The features are calculated for the ECG wave format of a specific time interval taken from a person who undergoes authentication process. To infer whether the newly extracted features matches with the features stored in the database for a particular ID, we compute Karl Pearson's correlation coefficient. The proposed technique is easily adoptable in real time situations as it is based on image processing techniques rather than signals. The computational complexity found in previous works for extracting geometrical features from wave signal is reduced by considering Radon image features. The proposed algorithm uses single-lead ECG signals for imaging and authentication. Even a palm-held ECG device is sufficient to acquire the data. Hence the proposed approach is suitable for real-time application in the organization. The proposed algorithm produced promising results with 3.19% of FAR and 0.128% of FRR. The overall performance of the system is found to be 99.85%.

References

1. Jain, A.K., Ross, A., Prabhakar, S.: An Introduction to Biometric Recognition. IEEE Trans. on Circuits Sys. 14(1), 4–20 (2004)
2. Hegde, C., Manu, S., Deepa Shenoy, P., Venugopal, K.R., Patnaik, L.M.: Secure Authentication using Image Processing and Visual Cryptography for Banking Applications. In: Proc. Int. Conf. on Advanced Computing (ADCOM-2008), pp. 65–72 (December 2008)
3. Hegde, C., Srinath, U.S., Aravind Kumar, R., Rashmi, D.R., Sathish, S., Deepa Shenoy, P., Venugopal, K.R., Patnaik, L.M.: Ear Pattern Recognition using Centroids and Cross-Points for Robust Authentication. In: Proc. Second Int. Conf. on Intelligent Human and Computer Interaction (IHCI 2010), pp. 378–384 (2010)

4. Hegde, C., Rahul Prabhu, H., Sagar, D.S., Vishnu Prasad, K., Deepa Shenoy, P., Venugopal, K.R., Patnaik, L.M.: Authentication of Damaged Hand Vein Patterns by Modularization. In: Proc. of IEEE Region Ten Conference, TENCON 2009 (2009)
5. Sufi, F., Khalil, I., Hu, J.: ECG-Based Authentication. In: Handbook of Information and Communcation Security, pp. 309–331. Springer, Heidelberg (2010)
6. Simon, B.P., Eswaran, C.: An ECG Classifier Designed using Modified Decision Based Neural Network. Computers and Biomedical Research 30, 257–272 (1997)
7. Biel, L., Pettersson, O., Philipson, L., Wide, P.: ECG Analysis: A New Approach in Human Identification. IEEE Trans. on Instrumentation and Measurement 50(3), 808–812 (2001)
8. Esbensen, K., Schonkopf, S., Midtgaard, T.: Multivarate Analysis in Practice, 1st edn., vol. 1 (1997)
9. Shen, T.W., Tompkins, W.J., Hu, Y.H.: One-Lead ECG for Identity Verification. In: Proc. of Second Joint Conf. of IEEE EMBS/BMES, pp. 62–63 (2002)
10. Singh, Y.N., Gupta, P.: Biometrics Method for Human Identification using Electrocardiogram. In: Tistarelli, M., Nixon, M.S. (eds.) ICB 2009. LNCS, vol. 5558, pp. 1270–1279. Springer, Heidelberg (2009)
11. Swamy, P., Jayaraman, S., Girish Chandra, M.: An Improved Method for Digital Time Series Signal Generation from Scanned ECG Records. In: Int. Conf. on Bioinformatics and Biomedical Technology (ICBBT), pp. 400–403 (2010)
12. Jose, C.R.S., Fred, A.L.N.: A Biometric Identification System based on Thyroid Tissue Echo-Morphology. In: Int. Joint Conf. on Biomedical Engineering Systems and Technologies, pp. 186–193 (2009)
13. Chen, B., Chandran, V.: Biometric Based Cryptographic Key Generation from Faces. In: Proc. of the 9th Biennial Conf. of the Australian Pattern Recognition Society on Digital Image Computing Techniques and Applications, pp. 394–401 (2007)
14. Boulgouris, N.V., Chi, Z.X.: Gait Recognition Using Radon Transform and Linear Discriminant Analysis. IEEE Trans. on Image Processing 16(3), 731–740 (2007)
15. Ariyapreechakul, P., Covavisaruch, N.: Personal Verification and Identification via Iris Pattern using Radon Transform. In: Proc. of First National Conf. on Computing and Information Technology, pp. 287–292 (2005)
16. Laguna, P., Mark, R.G., Goldberger, A.L., Moody, G.B.: A Database for Evaluation of Algorithms for Measurement of QT and Other Waveform Intervals in the ECG. Computers in Cardiology, 673–676 (1997)

Wireless Network Security Vulnerabilities and Concerns

Ahmad Mushtaq

Ghulam Ishaq Khan Institute, Topi
mushtaq_ahmad@hotmail.com

Abstract. The dilemma of cyber communications insecurity has existed all the times since the beginning of the network communications. The problems and concerns of unauthorized access and hacking has existed form the time of introduction of world wide web communication and Internet's expansion for popular use in 1990s, and has remained till present time as one of the most important issues. The wireless network security is no exception. Serious and continuous efforts of investigation, research and development has been going on for the last several decades to achieve the goal of provision of 100 percent or full proof security for all the protocols of networking architectures including the wireless networking. Some very reliable and robust strategies have been developed and deployed which has made network communications more and more secure. However, the most desired goal of complete security has yet to see the light of the day. The latest Cyber War scenario, reported in the media of intrusion and hacking of each other's defense and secret agencies between the two super powers USA and China has further aggravated the situation. This sort of intrusion by hackers between other countries such as India and Pakistan, Israel and Middle East countries has also been going on and reported in the media frequently. The paper reviews and critically examines the strategies already in place, for wired network. Wireless Network Security and also suggests some directions and strategies for more robust aspects to be researched and deployed.

Keywords: Internet, Network Security, Wireless Network Security, Intrusion, Hacking, Protocol.

1 Introduction

Wireless technology releases us from copper wires. These days a user can have a notebook computer, PDA, Pocket PC, Tablet PC, or just a cell phone and stay online anywhere a wireless signal is available. The basic theory behind wireless technology is that signals can be carried by electromagnetic waves that are then transmitted to a signal receiver. But to make two wireless devices understand each other, we need protocols for communication.

We will discuss the current security problems with wireless networks and the options for dealing with them. Then present methods that can be used to secure wireless networks. However, it is important to mention the ground reality that all the vulnerabilities that exist in a conventional wired network apply to wireless technologies [1].

T.-h. Kim et al. (Eds.): SecTech/DRBC 2010, CCIS 122, pp. 207–219, 2010.
© Springer-Verlag Berlin Heidelberg 2010

It will be appropriate to discuss some vital concepts about wireless networking [2]. It is easier to understand wireless infrastructures by categorizing them into three layers, as shown below. The three layers are device, physical and application and service (protocol).

Table 1. Different Layers of Wireless Technologies

Layer	Technologies
Application and service	Wireless applications: WAP, i-mode, messaging, Voice over Wireless network, VoIP, location-based services
Physical	Wireless standards: 802.11a, 802.11b, 802.11g, AX.25, 3G, CDPD, CDMA, GSM, GPRS, radio, microwave, laser, Bluetooth, 802.15, 802.16, IrDA
Device	Mobile devices: PDAs, notebooks, cellular phones, pagers, handheld PCs, wearable computers

In the device layer (mobile devices) are gadgets ranging from the smallest cell phone to PDAs and notebook computers. These devices use wireless technologies to communicate with each other. The physical layer contains different physical encoding mechanisms for wireless communications. Bluetooth, 802.11x, CDMA, GSM, and 3G are different standards that define different methods to physically encode the data for transmission across the airwaves. We will focus on networks built upon the 802.11x and Bluetooth standards. The application and service layer, also referred to as ISO layers 2 to 7, contains the protocols that enable wireless devices to process data in an end-to-end manner. Protocols like Wireless Application Protocol (WAP), Voice over IP (VoIP), and i-mode reside in this layer.

Many wireless networking security problems can be traced back to the end user in wired networks. Wireless networks are no exception, and it is typically the IT department's responsibility to protect the end user. Before an enterprise adopts the latest wireless network technologies, it will need to:

- Understand the capability of current products
- Understand its networking needs
- Understand the potential risk(s) it is facing

Then investigate and find the solution tailored to its environment.

2 Brief History of Wireless Communication

The world's first, wireless telephone conversation occurred in 1880 [3], when Alexander Graham Bell and Charles Sumner Tainter invented and patented the photo-phone, a telephone that conducted audio conversations wirelessly over modulated light beams (which are narrow projections of electromagnetic waves). In that distant era when utilities did not yet exist to provide electricity and lasers had not even been conceived of in science fiction, there were no practical applications for their invention, which was highly limited by the availability of both sunlight and good weather. Similar to free space optical communication, the photo-phone also required a clear line of sight between its transmitter and its receiver. It would be several decades before the photo-phone's principles found their first practical applications in military communications and later in fiber-optic communications.

3 Wireless Network Communication

Wireless network refers to any type of computer network that is wireless and is commonly associated with a telecommunications network whose interconnections between nodes are implemented without the use of wires. Wireless telecommunications networks [4] and [5] are generally implemented with some type of remote information transmission system that uses electromagnetic waves, such as radio waves, for the carrier and this implementation usually takes place at the physical level of the network.

Wireless networks have had a significant impact on the world as far back as World War II [6]. Through the use of wireless networks, information could be sent overseas or behind enemy lines easily, efficiently and more reliably. Since then, wireless networks have continued to develop and their uses have grown significantly. Mobile phones are part of huge wireless network systems. People use these phones daily to communicate with one another. Sending information overseas is possible through wireless network systems using satellites and other signals to communicate across the world. Emergency services such as the police department utilize wireless networks to communicate important information quickly. People and businesses use wireless networks to send and share data quickly whether it be in a small office building or across the world. Another important use for wireless networks is as an inexpensive and rapid way to be connected to the Internet in countries and regions where the telecom infrastructure is poor or there is a lack of resources, as in most developing countries.

Compatibility issues also arise when dealing with wireless networks. Different components not made by the same company may not work together, or might require extra work to fix these issues. Wireless networks are typically slower than those that are directly connected through an Ethernet cable.

A wireless network is more vulnerable, because anyone can try to break into a network broadcasting a signal. Many networks offer WEP - Wired Equivalent Privacy - security systems which have been found to be vulnerable to intrusion. Though WEP does block some intruders, the security problems have caused some businesses to stick with wired networks until security can be improved. Another type of security for wireless networks [7] is WPA - Wi-Fi Protected Access. WPA provides more security to wireless networks than a WEP security set up. The use of firewalls also helps with security breaches which can help to fix security problems in some wireless networks that are more vulnerable.

Wireless data communication can be via:

- Radio frequency communication,
- Microwave communication, for example long-range line-of-sight via highly directional antennas, or short-range communication, or
- Infrared (IR) short-range communication, for example from remote controls or via Infrared Data Association (IrDA).

210   A. Mushtaq

Applications may involve point-to-point communication, point-to-multipoint communication, broadcasting, cellular networks and other wireless networks. The data is communicated by means of frames [8], the frame information format includes; both the station and AP radiate and gather 802.11 frames as needed. The format of frames is illustrated below. Most of the frames contain IP packets. The other frames are for the management and control of the wireless connection.

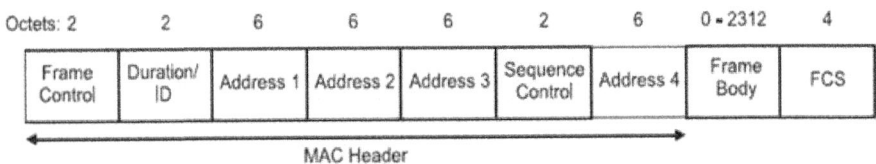

Fig. 1. An IEEE 802.11 Frame

There are three classes of frames.

1. The *management* frames establish and maintain communications. These are of Association request, Association response, Re-association request, Re-association response, Probe request, Probe response, Beacon, Announcement traffic indication message, Disassociation, Authentication, De-authentication types. The SSID-Security Set Identifier- is part of several of the management frames. Management messages are always sent in the clear, even when link encryption (WEP or WPA) is used, so the SSID is visible to anyone who can intercept these frames.
2. The *control* frames help in the delivery of data.
3. The *data* frames encapsulate the OSI Network Layer packets. These contain the source and destination MAC address, the BSSID, and the TCP/IP datagram. The payload part of the datagram is WEP-encrypted.
4. In the last fifty years, wireless communications industry experienced drastic changes driven by many technology innovations. There are two categories of wireless technology, distinguished by the distances they can cover: *wireless personal area network* (WPAN) and *wireless local area network* (WLAN), as discussed under:

WPAN: As the name "personal area network" suggests, such a network is small in the range of about 10 meters (30 feet). Infrared Data Association (IrDA) and Bluetooth are the main WPAN wireless technologies; they exist in the physical layer. The devices that take advantage of a WPAN include PDAs, printers, cameras, cell phones, and access points, to name a few. The support of IrDA enables a user to transfer data between a computer and another IrDA-enabled device for data synchronization, file transfer, or device control. The speed for IrDA is up to 4 Mbps per second and the distance is usually less than 30 feet in an unobstructed line of sight.

Bluetooth uses radio waves to transmit data and therefore doesn't have the line-of-sight restrictions of IrDA. Bluetooth also supports higher data transmission rates (11 Mbps) and uses the 2.4 GHz ISM bandwidth.

WLAN: The range of a wireless local area network (WLAN) is, of course, greater than that of a WPAN. For example, most 802.11b implementations will have a speed of 1 Mbps and a range of about 500 meters (1500 feet). With a closer proximity to the access point (AP), speeds of up to 11 Mbps can be reached. Many systems support the IEEE 802.11b standard; this standard uses Direct Sequence Spreading Spectrum (DSSS) to transmit the data in the bandwidth of 2.4 GHz—the *ISM band* (Industrial, Scientific and Medical band). Since this bandwidth is free for public use, other devices such as cordless phone can cause problems and interference.

3.1 Wireless Network Topology Concerns

The Wireless Network Topology has some shortcomings which are briefly outlined here. This will help understanding of the types of intrusions.

Current intrusion detection solutions tend to rely on the relatively static and contained nature of wired networks. Potential 'wired' intruders would need to gain physical access somehow, either through an accessible network jack or logically enter the network through well-defined pathways. Locating intrusion detection sensors was a matter of defining and inserting listeners in locations where all or most network traffic transited. These assumptions are no longer valid for wireless networks if both approved and rogue APs can be located anywhere on a network.

The IEEE 802.11 standard defines several types of wireless network topologies. The Independent Basic Service Set (IBSS, or "ad hoc") topology involves two or more wireless stations communicating peer-to-peer (Figure 2). The Basic Service Set (BSS, or "infrastructure") topology (Figure 3), adds an AP attached to a "distribution system" (usually a network, like Ethernet, through which all wireless communications pass before reaching their destination.

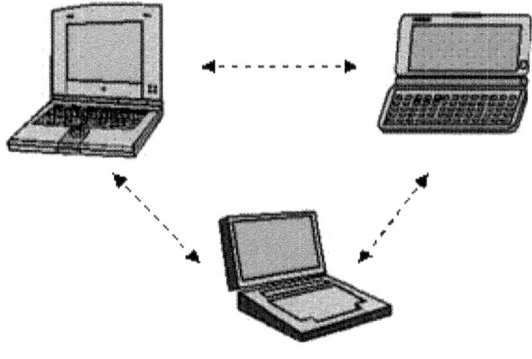

Fig. 2.

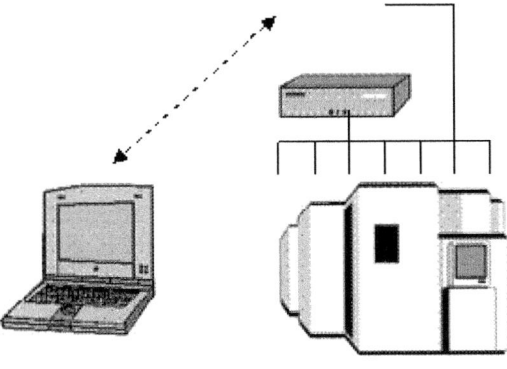

Fig. 3.

An ad-hoc network has some obvious disadvantages for intrusion detection. Yongguang Zhang and Wenke Lee have written an excellent paper [9] addressing this particular problem. They outline several fundamental issues with wireless ad-hoc networks:

- Wireless stations are all independent nodes. Each node must be responsible for its own protection from attack and compromise. Compromising only one node or introducing a malicious node may affect the viability of the entire network, and an affected node could be used as a launching point for subsequent attacks.
- No central point exists from which to monitor all network traffic, as the network is distributed.
- Differences between normal and anomalous traffic patterns may be practically indistinguishable. The mobile nature of the wireless stations can make legitimate network traffic appear suspect.

Zhang and Lee propose an architecture in which all nodes act as independent IDS sensor, able to act independently and cooperatively. Events are generated from a local detection engine. If analysis of the events are inconclusive or require more information, other networked 'local sensors'' can be utilized and consulted. Each independent sensor has six modules, three of which pertain to intrusion detection:

1. Data collection: the types of raw data used includes system and user activities, local communication activities, and "observable" communications activities
2. Local detection: since it is difficult to maintain and distribute an anomalous signature database, Zhang and Lee have proposed the definition of statistically "normal" activities specific to each node, which will therefore reside locally on each node.
3. Cooperative detection: if the local detection engine does not have enough evidence to alert on a suspected problem, it can ask other nodes for assistance. Information describing the event gets propagated to neighboring nodes. Evidence returned from neighboring nodes can then be used to create a new evaluation of the detected event.

4 Security Problems in Wireless

The most widely used and mature wireless network technology today is 802.11b. IEEE 802.11b, makes use of the 2.4 GHz ISM band and provides speeds from 1 Mbps up to 11 Mbps, with the range about 1500 feet. (Although in reality, you are hard-pressed to get this range out of products on the market today). This standard uses Direct Sequence Spread Spectrum (DSSS) to encode data before transferring it. IEEE 802.11, 802.11a, 802.11b, and 802.11g use Carrier Sense Multiple Access/Collision Avoidance (CSMA/CA) as the protocol in the data link layer. There are two names need to know in a wireless network:

- Station (STA)
- Access point (AP)

STA is a wireless network client—a desktop computer, laptop, or PDA. The AP is the central point (like a hub) that creates a basic service set to bridge a number of STAs from the wireless network to other existing networks. There are two different modes of wireless networking:

- Ad hoc mode, or independent basic service set (IBSS)
- Infrastructure mode, or basic service set (BSS)

Ad hoc and infrastructure modes are illustrated in the network blueprints. The ad hoc mode is equivalent to peer-to-peer networking. That means an ad hoc wireless network does not have an AP to bridge the STAs together. Every STA in an ad hoc wireless network can communicate with any other STA in the same network directly.

The infrastructure mode will have at least one AP to form a BSS. If there are multiple APs, they will form an extended service set (ESS). All traffic from or to an STA will go through the AP first. The AP in turn could be connected directly to another network, such as wired intranet.

Almost every protocol set has some mechanism to protect the data, and the same is true for IEEE 802.11b. An encryption mechanism called Wired Equivalent Privacy (WEP) protects the data as it travels through the airwaves. Security Alert after the WEP encryption mechanism was released, it was proved by Nikita Borisov, Ian Goldberg, and David Wagner, in 2001 [10], [11] and [12] to be vulnerable to multiple forms of attack. WEP [10] uses the symmetric cryptography system called RC4 with a user-specified key (64 bits and 128 bits) to protect the data. As a result, WEP alone is not enough to protect data.

5 Wireless Network Vulnerabilities

The possible scenarios which leave the Wireless Network open to hackers to try their craft and tools to play with it to serve their mission of hacking are briefly outlined. The information is not exhaustive, which is beyond the scope. However, it will provide an insight of the problems which are present in wireless communication.

The Trace
The passive way to identify an SSID is to sniff the network traffic [13] and look for three kinds of packets. The first one is called a *beacon*. An AP sends out a beacon periodically, usually once every 100 milliseconds. With this beacon, the STA will know there is an AP available. The beacon could contain the SSID as part of its information. The second packet is the *probe request and response*, and the third packet is the *association request and response*. All of these packets contain an SSID to identify a BSS or IBSS nearby. As long as the hacker is within the proper range, you basically cannot hide your wireless network. Some extreme methods do, of course, exist, such as surrounding the perimeter with metal or other substances that contain the wireless signals.

Passive Attack
This is the method of analyzing the intercepted network traffic and extracting useful information from the collected raw information. The common tool used for this is a sniffer such as AiroPeek. Due to the physical properties of a wireless network, one can perform traffic capture at any location as long as the signal reaches the system. It is known as a "parking lot attack" or "war driving", these methods illustrate that hackers can perform traffic analysis in a car by either parking the target building or just driving the surrounding streets.

Clear Text Traffic
Probably the best scenario for a hacker and the worst for the system administrator is *clear text traffic*. If there is no protection on the data being transmitted over wireless, then an attacker can easily sniff the traffic and perform protocol or data analysis later to crack into information gold mine: credit card information, passwords, and personal emails. If the data is not protected, then the odds are high that the rest of the network setup is also insecure.

5.1 Problems with WEP

If the wireless network has WEP enabled, the hacker's game is still not over. The following problems exist in the WEP algorithm [14], and can potentially be exploited.

Brute Force Attack
WEP makes use of a symmetric cryptography system called RC4. The user can use a shared secret key. The real key to encrypt the data with RC4 algorithm is generated by a pseudo random number generator (PRNG). But flaws in PRNG can cause the real key space to be less than 64 bits or 128 bits. The flaw actually reduces the key space of the 64-bit key to 22 bits. Therefore, it is possible for an attacker to collect enough information to try to discover the key offline.

Duplicate IV
Initiation vector (IV) is a 3-byte random number generated by the computer. It is combined with a key chosen by the user to generate the final key for WEP encryption/decryption. The IV is transmitted with the encrypted data in the packet without any protection so that the receiving end knows how to decrypt the traffic.

When a wireless network is using the same user-chosen key and duplicate IV on multiple packets, it might be in trouble. The hacker would know that all those packets with the same IV are being encrypted with the same key, and can then build a dictionary based on the packets collected. By knowing that the RC4 cryptography system uses the XOR algorithm to encrypt the plaintext (user data) with the key, the hacker can find the possible value of the packets. The hacker can do this because the XOR result of two different plaintext values is the same as the XOR result of two cipher-text-encrypted values with the same key. If the hacker can guess one of the plaintext packets, then they can decrypt the other packet encrypted with the same key.

Chosen/Known Plaintext

On the other hand, if a hacker knows the plaintext and cipher-text of a WEP-protected packet, he can determine the encryption key for that packet. There are several methods of determining the key, including sending an email or generating ICMP-Internet Control Message Protocol- echo request traffic (ping). A hacker who knows the corporate intranet pretty well could send in an email to the network. Knowing the contents of that email, the hacker could then capture the traffic on the wireless side, identify the packets related to the email, and find out the key, eventually building a dictionary for a real-time decryption attack.

Weakness in Key Generation

A weakness in the random key generator of the RC4 algorithm [15] used in WEP can permit a hacker to collect enough packets with IVs that match certain patterns to recover the user-chosen key from the IVs. Generally, a hacker would need to sniff for millions of packets to get enough "interesting" IVs to recover the key, so it could take days, if not weeks, to crack a moderately used wireless network. This is just a very basic attack, with several tools available to do the sniffing and decoding for hacker. Airsnort is the famous one: it runs on Linux and tries to break the key when enough useful packets are collected.

Bit-Manipulation Attack

WEP doesn't protect the integrity of the encrypted data. The RC4 cryptography system performs the XOR operation bit by bit, making WEP-protected packets vulnerable to bit-manipulation attack. This attack requires modification of any single bit of the traffic to disrupt the communication or cause other problems.

Authentication and Authorization

Once the hacker knows information such as the SSID of the network, MAC addresses on the network, and maybe even the WEP key, he can try to establish an association with the AP. There are currently three ways to authenticate users before they can establish an association with the wireless network.

Open Authentication

Open authentication usually means user only need to provide the SSID or use the correct WEP key for the AP. It can be used with other authentication methods, for example, using MAC address authentication. The problem with open authentication is that if a user doesn't have other protection or authentication mechanisms in place, then the wireless network is totally open, as the name indicates.

Shared Secret Authentication

The *shared secret authentication* mechanism is similar to a challenge-response authentication system. It is used when the STA shares the same WEP key with the AP. The STA sends the request to the AP, and the AP sends back the challenge. Then the STA replies with the challenge and encrypted response. The insecurity here is that the challenge is transmitted in clear text to the STA, so if a hacker captures both challenge and response, then he could figure out the key used to encrypt it.

5.2   Active Attacks and Denial of Service

Most of the security problems briefly described above related to passive attacks; however, there are also active attacks and denial of service [16]. One of the most interesting attacks is to set up a fake access point and let valid users establish associations, then collect information or perform a MITM (Man In The Middle) attack. In a corporate environment, if a malicious employee installs a rogue AP on the corporate intranet, then it's like creating a security hole—someone in the parking lot can easily hook on and surf the intranet. Another known hacking is to try and steal the key for WEP from a wireless network user's laptop. A tool called Lucent Orinoco Registry Encryption/Decryption [17] can break the encryption and extract the WEP key for Lucent Orinoco card users from the registry.

If an attacker tried all the above methods and failed, then the final choice might be denial of service attacks. Such attacks might bring down the wireless network and disrupt the service. We will describe the attacks from two different levels: physical level and protocol level.

Physical Level

There are two ways to disrupt the service of a wireless network physically]:

- Physical destruction: To physically destroy an AP, a hacker has first to locate the AP. Hacker can also try to find the antenna, since destroying the antenna probably has the similar effect as destroying the AP.
- Interference: Even if the hacker does not have an electromagnetic pulse gun, that doesn't mean you are safe from such attack. Remember we mentioned that 802.11b uses the 2.4 GHz ISM band, which is open and free for public use. So the signal of the 802.11b wireless network can be disrupted by the microwave in the kitchen or the new 2.4 GHz digital cordless phones.

Protocol Level

A hacker can disrupt service from the protocol level. If hacker can build an association, then there must be a way to disassociate. If one can authenticate, then there must be a way to unauthenticated. Unfortunately, in the IEEE 802.11b standard, both methods exist, and both methods do not require any authentication in the message. That means the hacker can send out a disassociated or unauthenticated message to an arbitrary wireless network user and disconnect them. This is a bad design from the protocol's perspective.

From the Wired Side
It should not be assumed that just because a hacker cannot get access to the wireless network that there is no other ways to attack it. Suppose one has a wireless network connected to the intranet and configured only for a few users. Another employee in the company discovers the AP from the internal network and accesses the management interfaces on the AP. He breaks in through a default SNMP community string and changes the configuration, so he is now part of the list of allowed users.

   This situation points out a problem: every AP has its own management interface(s). The most commonly used management interfaces are Telnet, FTP, web, and SNMP. If any of these management interfaces are not secured, there is always a chance that someone can take advantage of the default setup.

6   Current Countermeasures to Wireless Insecurity

Before a network administrator decides to convince his boss not to build a wireless network for company's intranet, think through how he can solve the problems already outlined. The problems may be scary, but they need to be resolved. Once he knows the methods a hacker can use to attack the wireless network, he can protect company network by closing those holes. According to: *The Art of War* by Sun Tzu [18], saying; "If you know the enemy and know yourself, you need not fear the result of a hundred battles."

6.1   Considerations for Wireless Network Security

The very sanguine advise and philosophy that one should never depend on a single mechanism to protect one's valuable assets. The historical old saying should be put into practice for protecting the wireless network. Some very vital aspects in this regard are briefly described here to make wireless network more safe and secure.

- **Change the SSID:** A wireless STA uses the SSID to identify the wireless network. There is currently no way to hide that from a potential hacker. The only thing one can do is change the SSID so it doesn't make immediate association to your company. For example, if you work for MIT, do not name the SSID "MIT_GM89." This technique is more obfuscation than protection.
- **Configure the AP correctly:** Make sure to change the default SSID, default password, and SNMP community string, and close down all the management interfaces properly.
- **Do not depend on WEP:** Use IPSec, VPN, SSH, or other substitutions for WEP. Do not use WEP alone to protect the data. It can be broken!
- **Adopt another authentication/authorization mechanism:** Use 802.1x, VPN, or certificates to authenticate and authorize wireless network users. Using client certificates can make it nearly impossible for an hacker to gain access.

- **Segment the wireless network:** The wireless network should be treated as a remote access network and separated from the corporate intranet. A firewall, packet filter, or similar device should be in between the AP and the corporate intranet. This can prevent the damage caused if the wireless network gets broken into.
- **Prevent physical access:** You can use directional antennas on your APs to restrict the directions of the signal. Shield your building or facility from electromagnetic interference as well. These methods can protect your wireless network and other electronic devices, but must often be weighed against the actual risk. MAC address filters can be implemented, but by sniffing the wireless traffic, the allowed list of MAC addresses can be easily.

7 Conclusion

The paper briefly describes foundations and vital aspects of wired Networking (Internet), in general, and Wireless Networking, in particular, to highlight the vulnerabilities and industry concerns of insecurity of Wireless Network. The paper briefly describes wireless communication modes, the wireless network security problems currently found in different infrastructures and wireless network insecurity features. It also suggests the ways and means which can be effectively applied to reduce the chances of hacking and make wireless network more safe and secure. However, the R&D industry experts of wireless communication, professional and academic researcher has not succeeded in finding out a 100 percent safe and secure strategy for adoption.

This does not mean that the human efforts and resources being spent to achieve the goal may be abandoned. The romance of R&D will continue like many other scientific and engineering fields. The end might not be insight yet, but the industry is approaching towards the goal.

References

1. Karygiannis, T., Owens, L.: Wireless Network Security: 802.11, Bluetooth and Handheld Devices, National Institute of Standards and Technology Gaithersburg, MD 20899-8930 (November 2002)
2. http://www.wirelesstutorials.info/wireless_networking.html
3. http://en.wikipedia.org/wiki/Photophone#World.27s_first_wireless_telephone_communication_E2.80.93_April_1880
4. Stallings, W.: Wireless Communications and Networks. Prentice Hall, Englewood Cliffs (August 2001)
5. Bidgoli, H.: The Handbook of Information Security. John Wiley & Sons, Inc., Chichester (2005)
6. Wireless networks have had a significant impact on the world as far back as World War II. Through the use of wireless networks, http://wikipedia.org/wiki/Wireless_network
7. Wi-Fi Protected Access (WPA and WPA2) is a certification program developed by the Wi-Fi Alliance to indicate compliance with the security protocol, http://wikipedia.org/wiki/Wi-Fi_Protected_Access

8. Brenner, P.: A Technical Tutorial on the IEEE 802-11 Protocol, Director of Engineering, BreezCom

9. Zhang, Y., Wenke, L.: Intrusion Detection in Wireless Ad-Hoc Networks. In: Proceedings of the Sixth Annual International Conference on Mobile Computing and Networking (2000); Arbaugh, W.A., Shankar, N., Justin Wan, Y.C.: Your 802.11 Wireless Network has No Clothes. Department of Computer Science, University of Maryland, March 31 (2001)

10. Borisov, N., Goldberg, I., Wagner, D.: Intercepting Mobile Communiccation Conference on Mobile Computing and Networking (2001),
http://www.springerlink.com/index/cjut5dxd8r9tvrpe.pdf

11. Borisov, N., Goldberg, I., Wagner, D., Berkeley, U.C., Cox, J.: LAN Services Set to Go Wireless, Network World, August 20 (2001); IEEE Working Group for WLAN Standards,
http://grouper.ieee.org/groups/802/11/index.html

12. Borisov, N.: Deploying Wireless LANs and Voice & Data. McGraw-Hill, New York (2001), http://doi.ieeecomputersociety.org/10.1109/6294.977772

13. Bradley, T.: CISSP-ISSAP, Introduction to Packet Sniffing, former About.com Guide

14. Borisov, N., Goldberg, I., Wagnert, D.: Security of the WEP algorithm, wep@isaac.cs.berkeley.edu

15. Paul, S., Preneel, B.: A new weakness in the RC4 keystream generator and an approach to improve the security of the cipher. In: Roy, B., Meier, W. (eds.) FSE 2004. LNCS, vol. 3017, pp. 245–259. Springer, Heidelberg (2004)

16. Khan, S., et al.: Denial of Service Attacks and Challenges in Broadband Wireless Networks. IJCSNS International Journal of Computer Science and Network Security 8(7) (July 2008)

17. Ingeborn, A., Ingeborn: Lucent Orinoco Registry Encryption/Decryption,
http://www.cqure.net/tools03.html

18. Tzu, S., Zi, S.: The Art of War. Dover Publications, New Paperback, 96 pages (2002) ISBN 0486425576

Figment Authentication Scheme in Wireless Sensor Network

N. Ambika[1] and G.T. Raju[2]

[1] Lecturer,
Dayananda Sagar College of Engg, Bangalore
Research Scholor, Bharathiar university, Coimbatore
ambika.nagaraj76@gmail.com
[2] Prof & Head, Dept of CS & Engg
RNSIT, Bangalore
drgtraju_rnsit@yahoo.com

Abstract. Sensor nodes are of low-cost and hence vulnerable to attacks. The adversaries need not endure hardship to control these nodes. Malicious nodes or compromised nodes are difficult to detect. These malicious nodes drain the energy available, give false readings, project itself to be as one of the routers hence attracting all the packets leading to denial of service attack.

This paper is trying to test the nodes for its fidelity by considering one of the normal procedures to initiate action among the normal nodes. The paper utilizes public key cryptographic methods and TDMA technology to accomplish the task.

Keywords: security, authentication, wireless sensor network, LEACH.

1 Introduction

Wireless sensor networks is one of the fields which has emerged during these years in spite of many hindrances. Self-organizing, rapid deployment and fault tolerance are some of its characteristics. Wireless sensor network is being utilized in many areas [1] like habitat monitoring, monitoring environmental conditions that affect the crops and livestock, irrigation, macro instruments for large-scale earth monitoring, planetary exploration, chemical/biological detection, battlefield surveillance, targeting, battle damage assessment and so on. These sensor network can be utilized to sense movement, pressure, humidity and so on. Sensor network is deployed in harsh environment, work under high pressure at the bottom of the ocean and so on.

Security is one of the critical issues in network. There are many types of security breaches found in these types of networks. Broadly classifying types of security breaches two major types are available namely internal attackers and external attackers. Internal attackers are the ones where in the nodes would have been compromised by the advertisers. This is a detective security solution that can make the network secure. This paper is proposing a better approach to identify the compromised nodes in the network.

T.-h. Kim et al. (Eds.): SecTech/DRBC 2010, CCIS 122, pp. 220–223, 2010.

2 Related Work

LEACH [2] is one of the algorithms that uses cluster based algorithms. After the deployment of nodes, they send HELLO messages to recognize their neighborhood nodes. The node that sends the message with higher signal strength is chosen as cluster head. The nodes within certain radius assemble to form the cluster. The nodes send the sensed data to their respective cluster head which is further aggregated and forwarded to the base station. The nodes rotate the cluster head position depending on the remaining energy in these nodes.

HEED [3] is a cluster based algorithm used in ad-hoc networks. The cluster head depending on many factors like residual energy in the nodes, their proximity to their neighbors, node degree.

SLEECH [4] utilizes leach concept with an additional feature to withstand the adversaries or the compromised nodes. The algorithm utilizes one-way hash chains and symmetric cryptographic operations to accomplish the purpose.

3 System Model

3.1 Deployment of Nodes and Distribution of Public Key

This paper utilizes public key cryptographic methods [5][6]. The private keys utilized to decrypt the message are embedded before the deployment of the nodes. The public key utilized to encrypt the message is broadcasted by the base station at random intervals.

3.2 Cluster Formation

After the deployment of the nodes, the clusters are formed choosing one of the nodes as its cluster head as in [2]. The cluster configuration time is estimated, a copy of it is sent to the base station and stored in the other nodes forming the cluster including the cluster head. Along with the configuration time it also sends the unique ID of all the nodes in the cluster. The time required to travel from the cluster head to the base station is estimated and entered in the database of the base station.

3.3 Setting Up TDMA for Transmission

TDMA is one of the channel access methods which can be utilized to avoid collision among the transmissions. This access method is utilized in all the rounds when the cluster head is chosen. All the cluster head are assigned a slot for its transmission. An additional slot to broadcast public key to the new nodes is also scheduled . This slot is scheduled randomly.

3.4 Report Generation

The broadcasting of the public key is chosen randomly and kept as a secret. When this is being broadcasted, the compromised node will have an assumption that the broadcast is being done for the newly deployed nodes. But those uncompromised nodes will get a hidden information to transmit additional information. The cluster head has to send the configuration time to the base station. This information is checked against the stored data. If it does not arrive in the estimated time or if it gives an improper information, the base station broadcasts the information to other nodes. The nodes then need to choose another cluster head. If the nodes do not get any such information it starts its own job of transmission.

The nodes send their sensed data along with configuration time. The cluster head has to cross check the information obtained by the nodes. If the configuration time sent by the nodes does not match what is being stored in itself, it has to send a report to the base station. This hence will help to identify the compromised node among the cluster.

4 Simulation Results

The LEACH scheme does not enclose any security methods. FAS is a modified LEACH scheme which not only provides confidentiality and integrity to the network but also makes a check on compromised nodes. Applying this scheme increases the energy consumption to 18.5% more than the LEACH scheme.

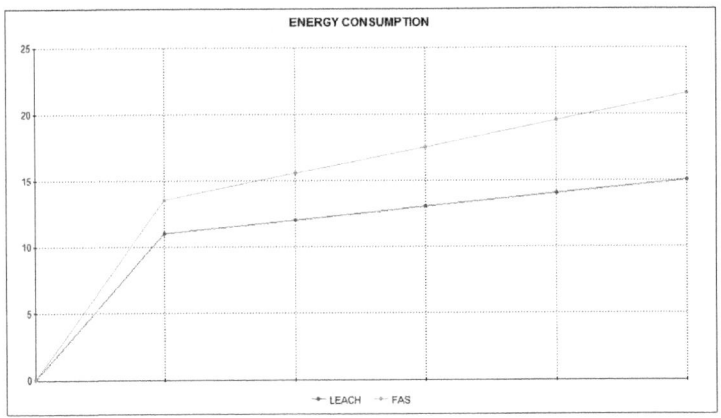

Fig. 1. Comparison of energy consumption in LEACH and FAS schemes

5 Conclusion

Utilizing a detective mechanism in a network, keeps a check on compromised nodes. This not only identifies the compromised nodes but also hinders the wastage of resources, will provide accurate information of the sensed data to the base station. This paper is an attempt to securely and accurately transfer the data.

References

1. Akyildiz, E., Su, W., Sanbrrsubrarnaoiam, Y., Cuyirci, E.: A survey OD SCOSUT network. IEEE Commmicariom Mngeirre 40(8), 102–114 (2002)
2. Heinzelman, W.R., Chandrakasan, A., Balakrishnan, H.: An application specific protocol architecture for wireless microsensor networks. IEEE Transactions on Wireless Communications 1(4), 660–667 (2002)
3. Younis, O., Fahmy, S.: Distributed clustering in ad-hoc sensor networks: A hybrid, energyefficient approach. In: Proc. 13th Joint Conf. on IEEE Computer and Communications Societies (March 2004)
4. Xiao-yun, W., Li-zhen, Y., Ke-fei, C.: SLEACH: Secure low energy adaptive clustering hierarchy protocol for WSNs. Wuhan University Journal of Natural Sciences 10(1), 127–131 (2005)
5. Damodaran, D., Singh, R., Le, P.D.: Group Key Management in Wireless Networks Using Session Keys. Presented at Third International Conference on Information Technology: New Generations, pp. 402–407 (2006)
6. Myles, A., Johnson, D.B., Perkins, C.: A Mobile Host Protocol Supporting Route Optimization and Authentication. IEEE Journal on Selected Areas in Communications 13(5) (June 1995)
7. Boyle, D., Newe, T.: The Impact of Java and Public Key Cryptography in Wireless Sensor Networking. In: The Fourth International Conference on Wireless and Mobile Communications (2008)

Issues of Security and Network Load
in Presence – A Survey

Zeeshan Shafi Khan[1,3], Khaled Alghathbar[1,2], Muhammad Sher[3], and Khalid Rashid[3]

[1] Center of Excellence in Information Assurance, King Saud University, KSA
[2] Information Systems Department, College of Computer and Information Sciences,
King Saud University, KSA
[3] International Islamic University, Islamabad, Pakistan

Abstract. Presence is a service that provides dynamic up-to-date status information of other users. Since presence is highly dynamic so it puts heavy load on
the core network as well as on air interface of the access network. Security is
another issue that needs to be address carefully because presence service is subject to various types of security threats. We, in this paper, conducted a detailed
survey on issues of security and network load in presence. At the end we discussed few open issues related to security of presence service.

Keywords: Presence, Flooding Attacks, Network Load.

1 Introduction

Presence allows the user to share their live and dynamic status with each other. The
status may contain information like current location of the user, the available devices,
preferred means of communication, currently supported applications etc. Presence
service contributes to change the current communication paradigm. You have information about a particular person before contacting him /her. The components of the
presence service include Personal User Agent or Publisher, Watcher and Presence
Server. The publisher provides the information to presence server who stores it and
provides it to the subscribed watchers. Subscription can be made to more then one
presentities at a time known as subscription to presentity list. Presentity can set different information for different watchers at different levels [1]. Figure 1 explains the
subscription of presence service while the figure 2 describes the publication of presence service.

2 Presence Service and Network Load

Pous et al. in 2002 presented evaluate the presence and instant messaging application
in UMTS network. According to authors since presence is dynamic live information
so it puts heavy load over the network. For instant messaging they found that average
delay is 16.6 seconds and 70% of total delay is due to the core network [2]. Miladinovic et al. in 2005 studied the presence event notification in UMTS. According to author subscription of presence information puts heavy load on air interface of user's

T.-h. Kim et al. (Eds.): SecTech/DRBC 2010, CCIS 122, pp. 224–230, 2010.
© Springer-Verlag Berlin Heidelberg 2010

network. Authors proposed that instead of subscribing presence information for short period of time, a watcher should subscribe the presence with an intermediate server for a very long period of time. The intermediate server is responsible for subscription of presence at presence server for short period of time. Since this intermediate server is proposed inside the core network so it reduces the load on the air interface [3].

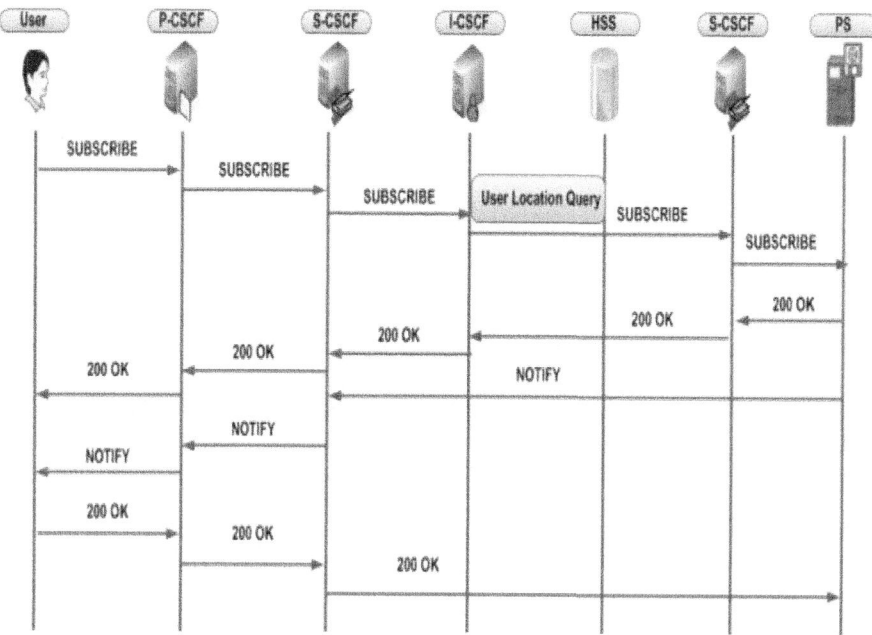

Fig. 1. Subscription to Presence

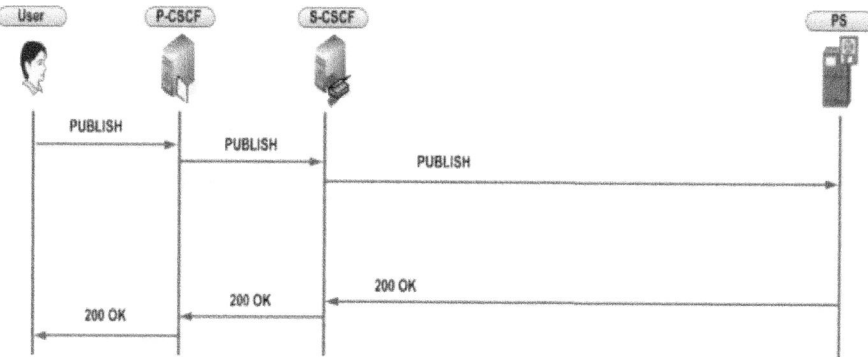

Fig. 2. Presence Information Publication

Rishi et al. in 2005 analyzed the effect of presence service over network. PULL and PUSH based communication mechanisms for presence service are discussed and compared. The authors pointed out that since the presence service is not point to point service so it adds a significant load of traffic over the network. Every change in the presence information of a presentity is communicated to all of its subscribers. Privacy issues are also discussed by the authors [4]. Alam et al. in 2005 analyzed the cost of presence service. According to them, it is essential to reduce the traffic load in order to make the presence service more attractive. In the paper they provided an analytical framework to measure the performance of the IMS presence service [5].

Yang in 2006 presented distributed presence service middleware architecture to cope with the problems like service provisioning, Quality of Service (QoS), bandwidth provisioning [6]. Florian et al. in 2006 described that instead of subscribing to presence service individually, subscription should be allowed to a Resource List Server (RLS). RLS collects the information and sends it in bundles. It reduced the number of messages thus results in efficient utilization of resources. Author also proposed that instead of providing information to subscriber after every change, the RLS should collect the information and provide it to the watcher only on demand [7]. Pailer et al. in 2006 proposed architecture for location service enablers in IMS. They proposed that trigger information and notification should be processed in the terminal. They argued that their solution is more efficient as compared to other solutions [8].

Nisha et al. in 2006 analyzed the IMS network by considering SIP delay as main parameter. Authors formulate a queuing model for IMS and studied work load on SIP server [9]. Alam et al. in 2007 proposed Weighted Class Based Queuing (WCBQ) in order to reduce the load at presence server. According to the authors a watcher who is subscribed for a list of 100 presentities will receive a notification message after every change in any of the 100 presentities. So it will result in consumption of resources at client side that is equipped with low processing devices. The WCBQ drop the low priority pre existing messages in order to reduce the load. The results showed that during the heavy traffic load this mechanism works well. The graphs showed that WCBQ only works well when there is a scenario of heavy traffic load [10].

Salinas in 2007 described the advantages and disadvantages of using presence service. Author described that on one side presence service facilitates many other services, makes the communication easy, reduces the unnecessary traffic etc. and on the other side it has privacy concerns. An intelligent user can guess the routine of other user by seeing the presence history. According to the author presence service also involves the end user so it requires that the end user must be aware that how to use presence service [11]. Sedlar et al. in 2007 proposed the use of presence information in an enterprise environment. According to authors if the presence information is collected from different sources and provided to the subscribers after aggregation then it can help the employees to organize themselves more efficiently [12]. Loreto et al. in 2008 uses the idea of presence network agent to improve the performance of the presence service by minimizing the load from radio access network. The author discussed few open issues those need to be resolved in order to improve the performance of the presence service [13].

Mckeon et al. in 2008 studies the effect of presence service over the latency and throughput of the network. The authors analyzed that the presence service can put a great load over the network by issuing too much traffic [14]. Beltern et al. in 2008 presented the fully distributed platform to deploy presence service. They proposed middleware architecture consists of two layers. First layers takes the intelligent decision to process and manage the presence information and the second layer is responsible for sending and receiving messages like subscribe and notify. The major emphasizes of the authors is on the management of the presence information in order to make it more efficient. RA rules defined by the authors restrict a user to communicate with other user [15].

Chen et al. in 2009 argued that presence notifications put an extra load on network as well as on watcher. Therefore to reduce the load of presence notifications they worked on introducing a new notification method called as weakly consistent scheme. In this scheme notifications are delayed up to a specific period of time and results in reducing network load [16]. Paolo et al. in 2009 worked on enhancing the location based services. Among the location based services authors focused on presence service. According to authors, implementation of presence service requires two main issues to be resolved. Firstly they focused on load balancing and secondly automatic activation and de-activation of presence service is considered [17]. Paolo et al. in 2009 argued that the major issue in success of presence service is the scalability. Since presence is a dynamic continuous service so due to heavy load a question on scalability arises. To solve this issue authors proposed three extensions to the presence service. First they optimized the inter-domain distribution of notify messages, secondly they proposed a framework for differentiated quality and thirdly client side buffering is proposed [18].

3   Security Issues in Presence Service

Magedanz et al. in 2005 proposed an "Open IMS Playground" a test bed for IMS. This testbed includes almost all the major components of IMS core. This open source can be used to test academic and industrial research on IMS. Open IMS Playground includes functionality of all call session control functions, home subscriber server, media or streaming server, application server, different types of SIP application servers etc. Application layer is designed with different types of applications like presence etc [19].

Vishal et al. in 2006 presented a survey on security issues in presence and proposed few solutions to solve these security issues. Authors emphasized on authentication of the watcher and presentity, authorization and access control over presence information and the integrity and confidentiality of the presence information. For authentication author proposed asserted identity, cryptographically verified identity and certificate based authentication. For data integrity and confidentiality of the presence information the authors proposed the use of private and public key [20]. M. Sher et. al. in 2006 proposed a Transport Layer security (TLS) along with the intrusion detection system to secure the IMS application server against various types of time dependent and time independent attacks [21]. M. Sher et.al in 2006 presents the trust domain relationship based inter domain security model for IMS. Keys are managed using public key infrastructure. For confidentiality and integrity IPSec is used [22]. Rosenberg in 2007 described that proper authorization should be implemented in presence service. For this purpose they developed the authorization rules. These authorization rules define that at what time what information should be delivered to how many watchers [23].

Sher et. al. in 2007 developed an Intrusion Detection and Prevention (IDP) system to secure the IMS application server. This IDP system compares all the incoming and outgoing requests and responses with the defined rules and decides whether to forward it or not. [24]. Sher et.al in 2007 describes a security model to secure the IMS application layer from time independent attacks like SQL injection. To attain this purpose author developed an intrusion detection and prevention system. Transport layer security is also provided in the paper [25]. Rebahi et.al in 2008 described that IMS is subject to various types of denial of service attack. In order to make the IMS successful author emphasize to secure it from these attacks. Solutions to mitigate the denial of service attack are presented in the paper [26].

4 Open Security Issues

Presence service is subject to various types of security threats those are described below:

4.1 Publish Flooding Attacks

A publish request is sent by a presentity to update her presence information at presence server. Multiple presentities can launch denial of service attack by sending enormous number of publish requests. A secure mechanism is required to handle this potential attack.

4.2 Notify Flooding Attacks

An attacker by spoofing the ID of presence server can send a large number of notification messages to launch denial of service attack on a particular user or on group of users.

4.3 Fake Publication

An attacker by spoofing the ID of a presentity can publish false presence information at presence server. This is a very alarming threat because information of one presentity can be distributed to a large number of watchers.

4.4 SQL Injection

SQL injection is another threat to presence server. An attacker can insert, delete, update the presence information by adding an SQL injection inside a legitimate request.

5 Conclusion and Future Work

Presence puts a heavy load on air interface of the access network and subject to various types of security threats. We present the latest work that has been done to reduce the network load of presence and to secure the presence information. We also discussed few open issues related to presence. In future we aimed to address the above mentioned open issues in order to secure the presence service.

References

[1] Poikselka, M., Mayer, G., Khartabil, H., Niemi, A.: IP multimedia concepts and services, 2nd edn. John Wiley & Sons Ltd., Chichester (2006)
[2] Pous, M., Pesch, D., Foster, G., Sesmun, A.: Performance Evaluation of a SIP Based Presence and Instant Messaging Service for UMTS. In: 4th International Conference on 3G Mobile Communication Technologies, 3G 2003 (2003)
[3] Miladinovic, I.: Presence and Event Notification in UMTS IP Multimedia Subsystem. In: Fifth IEE International Conference on 3G Mobile Communication Technologies (3G 2004), The Premier Technical Conference for 3G and Beyond (CP503) London, UK, October 18-20 (2004)
[4] Rishi, L., Kumar, S.: Presence and its effect on network. In: IEEE International Conference on Personal Wireless Communications (2005)
[5] Alam, M.T., da Wu, Z.: Cost Analysis of the IMS Presence Service. In: 1st Australian Confrence on Wireless Broadband and Ultra Wideband Communication (2006)
[6] Yang, S.B., Choi, S.G., Ban, S.Y., Kim, Y.-J., Choi, J.K.: Presence service middleware architecture for NGN. In: The 8th International Conference on Advanced Communication Technology (2006)
[7] Wegscheider, F.: Minimizing unnecessary notification traffic in the IMS presence system. In: 1st International Symposium on Wireless Pervasive Computing (2006)
[8] Pailer, R., Wegscheider, F., Bessler, S.: A Terminal-Based Location Service Enabler for the IP Multimedia Subsystem. In: Proceedings of WCNC (2006)
[9] Rajagopal, N., Devetsikiotis, M.: Modeling and Optimization for the Design of IMS Networks. In: Proceedings of the 39th Annual Simulation Symposium (2006)
[10] Alam, M.T., da Wu, Z.: Admission control approaches in the IMS presence service. International Journal of Computer Science 1(4) (2007)
[11] Salinas, A.: Advantages and Disadvantages of Using Presence Service, http://www.tml.tkk.fi/Publications/C/21/salinas_ready.pdf
[12] Sedlar, U., Bodnaruk, D., Zebec, L., Kos, A.: Using aggregated presence information in an enterprise environment, https://www.icin.biz/files/programmes/Poster-7.pdf
[13] Loreto, S., Eriksson, G.A.: Presence Network Agent: A Simple Way to Improve the Presence Service. IEEE Communications Magazine (2008)
[14] McKeon, F.: A study of SIP based instant messaging focusing on the effects of network traffic generated due to presence. In: IEEE International Symposium on Consumer Electronics (2008)
[15] Beltran, V., Paradells, J.: Middleware-Based Solution to Offer Mobile Presence Services. In: Mobilware 2008 (2008)
[16] Chen, W.-E., Lin, Y.-B., Liou, R.-H.: A weakly consistent scheme for IMS presence service. IEEE Transactions on Wireless Communications 8(7) (2009)
[17] Bellavista, P., Corradi, A., Foschini, L.: IMS-based presence service with enhanced scalability and guaranteed QoS for interdomain enterprise mobility. IEEE Wireless Communications 16(3) (2009)
[18] Bellavista, P., Corradi, A., Foschini, L.: Enhancing the Scalability of IMS-Based Presence Service for LBS Applications. In: Proceedings of the 2009 33rd Annual IEEE International Computer Software and Applications (2009)

[19] Magedanz, T., Witaszek, D., Knuettel, K.: The IMS Playground @ FOKUS – An Open Testbed for Next Generation Network Multimedia Services. In: Proceedings of the First International Conference on Testbeds and Research Infrastructures for the DEvelopment of NeTworks and COMmunities (TRIDENTCOM 2005) (2005)

[20] Singh, V.K., Schulzrinne, H.: A Survey of Security Issues and Solutions in Presence, http://www1.cs.columbia.edu/~vs2140/presence/presencesecurity.pdf

[21] Sher, M., Wu, S., Magedanz, T.: Security Threats and Solutions for Application Server of IP Multimedia Subsystem (IMS-AS). In: IEEE/IST Workshop on Monitoring, Attack Detection and Mitigation (2006)

[22] Sher, M., Magedanz, T., Penzhorn, W.T.: Inter-domains security management (IDSM) model for IP multimedia subsystem (IMS). In: The First International Conference on Availability, Reliability and Security (2006)

[23] Rosenberg, J.: A Presence Event Package for the Session Initiation Protocol (SIP). Request for Comments: 3856 (2004)

[24] Sher, M., Magedanz, T.: Developing Intrusion Detection and Prevention (IDP) System for IP Multimedia Subsystem (IMS) Application Servers (AS). Journal of Information Assurance and Security (2007)

[25] Sher, M., Magedanz, T.: Protecting IP Multimedia Subsystem (IMS) Service Delivery Platform from Time Independent Attacks. In: Third International Symposium on Information Assurance and Security (2007)

[26] Rebahi, Y., Sher, M., Magedanz, T.: Detecting flooding attacks against IP Multimedia Subsystem (IMS) networks. In: IEEE/ACS International Conference on Computer Systems and Applications (2008)

Discovering the Botnet Detection Techniques

Aneel Rahim[1] and Fahad T. bin Muhaya[1,2]

[1] Prince Muqrin Chair of IT Security,
[2] Management Information Systems Department, College of Business Administration,
King Saud University, Kingdom of Saudi Arabia
aneelrahim@ksu.edu.sa, fmuhaya@ksu.edu.sa

Abstract. Botnet is a network of compromised computers. It just fellow the master slave concept. Bots are comprised computers and do the tasks what ever their master orders them. Internet Relay Chat (IRC) is used for the communication between the master and bots. Information is also encrypted to avoid the effect of third party. In this paper we discuss the Botnets detection techniques and comparative analysis of these techniques on the basis of DNS query, History data and group activity.

Keywords: Botnet, detection, malicious.

1 Introduction

Botnet [1] [2] is a collection of compromised computers called bots. Bots just obey the instructions issued by the controller [3]. Botnet provides the disturbed platform for malicious activities (Denial of service attack [4], spam emails [5], phishing, steal information etc) [6]. They are three main areas of research in Botnet i.e. understand the concept of Botnet, detection and countermeasures [7]. This paper deals with detection of Botnet.

Mainly they are three ways for the detection of Botnet i.e. signature based, anomaly based and DNS based detections. Signature based detection can be used to detect only know Botnet where as anomaly based detection can be used detect known as well as unknown Botnets. DNS based detection is also helpful as bot used DNS to find the address of bot master, so DNS query can be used to find the malicious node[8].

We in this paper analyze the different Botnet detection techniques i.e. SlingBot, BotGAD, BotMiner, SBotMiner, BotSniffer, AutoRE etc. We also mention the characteristics, functionality and comparative analysis of Botnet detection techniques.

This paper is organized as follows: In section 2, we discuss the existing detection mechanism of Botnet and their functionality. In section 3, we describe the comparative analysis of existing techniques on the basis of DNS query, History data and group activity. Lastly in section 4 conclusions is given.

2 Detection Mechanisms

Botnet Detection is not an easy task. We can detect Botnet only when they communicate at large scale. Mainly two methods exist for Botnet detection i.e. active detection and passive detection. [9]

T.-h. Kim et al. (Eds.): SecTech/DRBC 2010, CCIS 122, pp. 231–235, 2010.
© Springer-Verlag Berlin Heidelberg 2010

2.1 SLINGbot

SLINGbot (System for live Investigation of Next Generation bots) [10] is a proactive approach to detect the current and future Botnets. Existing techniques focuses on current Botnets and ignore the future threats. So they are not suitable for Botnets detection because of the evolving nature of Botnets.

Python language is used to implement the SLINGbot as it support the platform independence. SLINGbot is composed of two fundamental parts i.e. Botnet Scenario Driver, which helps to manage the Botnet experiments and Composable Bot Framework provides the establishing and maintaining connectivity to Botnet and routing information.

2.2 BotGAD

BotGAD (Botnet Group Activity Detector) [11] detect know and unknown Botnets on the basis of group activity in large scale networks. DNS queries are useful to capture malicious nodes as bots in Botnet normally use DNS to search their master. [Criminology] BotGAD is implemented with help of DNS traffic and its performance is measured using real time network traces.

2.3 BotMiner

Gu et al proposed a framework [12] for Botnet detection that is independent of communication protocols, structure and history knowledge of Botnet. It captures identical communication and malicious traffic, and performs cross cluster correlation to determine the bots that distribute communication and malicious activity patterns. BotMiner is implemented in real scenario and produce low false rate.

2.4 SBotMiner

High rate traffic generated bots are easily detected through existing threshold techniques where as no method exists to capture low rate traffic generated bots.

Yu et al [13] proposed a system called SBotMiner to identify low rate traffic generated bots. SBotMiner focus on identifying group of bots rather than capturing individual bots. SBotMiner is mainly consisting of two fundamental steps i.e. to identify the group activity that is different from history and by using Matrix based scheme to differentiate between human traffic and Botnet generated traffic. Bots within the same Botnet perform the same malicious activities by running the script issued from the master where as human traffic contains diversity.

2.5 Bayesian Bot Detection

Botnet detection can be done by analyzing the communication between the controller and bots. Similar actions are performed by the bots within the same Botnet. Ricardo et al [14] proposed Bayesian approach for the detection of Botnet. So its approach just analyze the current DNS traffic with existing know bot traffic.

2.6 BotSniffer

Gu et al proposed system [15] to detect Botnet with the help of anomaly detection and require no history data of Botnet. It uses statistical methods to capture Botnet and identify the bots and controller communication and their malicious activities.

2.7 AutoRE

Yinglian et al [16] proposed AutoRE framework for the detection of spam emails and Botnet membership. AutoRE does not require history data and automatically generate URL signature to detect Botnet spam with low error rate. Current and future Botnet spam emails are detected with the help of these signatures.

2.8 Automatic Discovery

Lu et al proposed hierarchical framework for automatically detection of botnets at large-scale and categorize the network flow with the help of clustering algorithm and payload signature [17]. Core idea of this framework is to categorize the network traffic into network application and differentiate the malicious traffic from normal flow.

2.9 P2P Botnet Detection

Detection of centralized Botnet is some how easy as compare to P2P Botnet. Su et al proposed P2P Botnet detection [18] with help of behavior clustering and statistical test. Proposed scheme produce low false rate in simple and realistic scenarios.

2.10 Data Mining Approach

Muhammad et al proposed a technique to detect P2P Botnet [19] using data mining approach. Stream data classification can be used for the detection of Botnet but the proposed technique is more accurate than existing stream data classification schemes.

2.11 BotTracer

They are three main characteristics of botnet i.e. automatically startup (do not rely on user action), establish connection with bot controller and perform attack soon. Lei proposed BotTracer [20] to detect the above characteristics of botnet.

3 Comparative Study of Botnet Detection Techniques

In this section we mention the compare the main characteristics of Botnet detection. Most of the techniques use DNS queries to detect Botnet and some techniques use honey pots, history data and group activity to capture the spam traffic of Botnet.

Table 1. Characteristics of Botnet Detection Techniques

Techniques	Active	Proactive	DNS query	History Data	Group activity
SLINGbot	x	✓	✓	x	x
BotGAD	x	✓	✓	✓	✓
BotMiner	x	✓	x	x	✓
SBotMiner	✓	x	x	✓	✓
Bayesian	x	✓	✓	✓	x
BotSniffer	x	✓	✓	x	x
AutoRE	✓	x	✓	x	x
Auto Discovery	✓	x	x	✓	x
P2P Detection	x	✓	x	x	x
Data Mining	x	✓	x	✓	x
BotTracer	✓	x	✓	x	x

4 Conclusion

Botnet provides the distributed platform for malicious activities (Denial of service attack, spam emails, phishing, steal information etc). In this paper we discuss different approaches for Botnet detection. These approaches are mainly used DNS, History data and group activity for detection. So we present the comparative analysis of Botnet techniques on the basis of theses factors.

Acknowledgments

This research was supported by the Prince Muqrin Chair (PMC) for IT Security at King Saud University, Riyadh, Saudi Arabia.

References

1. Bailey, M., Cooke, B., Jahanian, F., Xu, Y.: A Survey of Botnet Technology and Defenses. In: Cybersecurity Applications & Technology Conference for Homeland Security. IEEE, Los Alamitos (2009)
2. Stone-Gross, B., Cova, M., Cavallaro, L., Gilbert, B., Szydlowski, M.: Your Botnet is My Botnet Analysis of a Botnet Takeover. ACM, New York (2009)
3. Leonard, J., Xu, S., Sandhu, R.: A Framework for Understanding Botnets. In: International Conference on Availability, Reliability and Security. IEEE, Los Alamitos (2009)
4. Collins, M.P., Shimeall, T.J., Kadane, J.B.: Using Uncleanliness to Predict Future Botnet Addresses. In: IMC 2007. ACM, New York (2007)
5. Pathak, A., Qian, F., Hu, C., Mao, M., Ranjan, S.: Botnet Spam Campaigns Can Be Long Lasting Evidence, Implications, and Analysis. ACM, New York (2009)
6. Zhu, Z., Lu, G.: Botnet Research Survey. In: Annual IEEE International Computer Software and Applications Conference. IEEE, Los Alamitos (2008)

7. Feily, M., Shahrestani, A.: A Survey of Botnet and Botnet Detection. In: Third International Conference on Emerging Security Information, Systems and Technologies. IEEE, Los Alamitos (2009)
8. Li, C., Jiang, W., Zou, X.: Botnet: Survey and Case Study. In: Fourth International Conference on Innovative Computing, Information and Control. IEEE, Los Alamitos (2009)
9. Govil, J., Govil, J.: Criminology of BotNets and their Detection and Defense Methods. IEEE, Los Alamitos (2007)
10. Jackson, A.W., Lapsley, D., Jones, C., Zatko, M., Golubitsky, C., Strayer, W.T.: SLING-bot A System for Live Investigation of Next Generation Botnets. In: Cybersecurity Applications & Technology Conference For Homeland Security. IEEE, Los Alamitos (2009)
11. Choi, H., Lee, H., Kim, H.: BotGAD: Detecting Botnets by Capturing Group Activities in Network Traffic. In: COMSWARE, Dublin, Ireland (2009)
12. Gu, G., Perdisci, R., Zhang, J., Lee, W.: BotMiner: Clustering Analysis of Network Traffic for Protocol- and Structure-Independent Botnet Detection. In: 17th USENIX Security Symposium (2008)
13. Yu, F., Xie, Y., Ke, Q.: SBotMiner: Large Scale Search Bot Detection. In: WSDM, February 4-6. ACM, USA (2010)
14. Villamarín-Salomón, R., Brustoloni, J.: Bayesian Bot Detection Based on DNS Traffic Similarity. In: SAC 2009, March 8-12 (2009)
15. Gu, G., Zhang, J., Lee, W.: BotSniffer: Detecting Botnet Command and Control Channels in Network Traffic. In: Proceedings of the 15th Annual Network and Distributed System Security Symposium (NDSS 2008) (2008)
16. Xie, Y., Yu, F., Achan, K., Panigrahy, R., Hulten, G., Osipkov, I.: Spamming Botnets: Signatures and Characteristics. In: SIGCOMM 2008, August 17-22 (2008)
17. Lu, W., Tavallaee, M., Ghorbani, A.: Automatic Discovery of Botnet Communities on Large-Scale Communication Networks. In: ASIACCS 2009, March 10-12 (2009)
18. Chang, S., Daniels, T.: P2P Botnet Detection using Behavior Clustering & Statistical Tests. In: AISec 2009, November 9. ACM, New York (2009)
19. Muhammad, M., Gao, J., Khan, L.: Peer to Peer Botnet Detection for Cyber-Security: A Data Mining Approach. In: CSIIRW 2008, Oak Ridge, Tennessee, USA (2008)
20. Liu, L., Chen, S., Yan, G., Zhang, Z.: BotTracer: Execution-based Bot-like Malware Detection. LNCS. Springer, Heidelberg (2008)

Contactless Biometrics in Wireless Sensor Network: A Survey

Muhammad Imran Razzak[1,3], Muhammad Khurram Khan[1], and Khaled Alghathbar[1,2]

[1] Center of Excellence in Information Assurance, King Saud University, Saudi Arabia
[2] Information Systems Department, College of Computer and Information Sciences,
King Saud University, KSA
[3] International Islamic University, Islamabad, Pakistan

Abstract. Security can be enhanced through wireless sensor network using contactless biometrics and it remains a challenging and demanding task due to several limitations of wireless sensor network. Network life time is very less if it involves image processing task due to heavy energy required for image processing and image communication. Contactless biometrics such as face recognition is most suitable and applicable for wireless sensor network. Distributed face recognition in WSN not only help to reduce the communication overload but it also increase the node life time by distributing the work load on the nodes. This paper presents state-of-art of biometrics in wireless sensor network.

Keywords: Biometrics, Face Recognition, Wireless Sensor Network, Contactless Biometrics.

1 Introduction

Contactless biometrics enhances the security through wireless sensor network and it remains a challenging task due to the limitations of wireless sensor network as compared to tradition system. Wireless sensor networks becomes the most important technology and used in wide range of security applications epically for espionage, target detection, habitat monitoring, military applications etc. [1-2]. Wireless sensor networks are showing more interest by both theoretical and practical problems after 9/11 due to high demand of security application. The flexibility of wireless sensor network for un-manned surveillance application make it more suitable for data transmission. The situation become more interesting when un-manned security application finds the suspicious and send the recognized identity.

Wireless sensor network consist of low power, battery equipped operated nodes used for remote monitoring. Generally, a wireless sensor node consists of low-power digital signal processor, radio frequency circuit, micro- electro mechanical system, and small battery. Wireless sensors are characterized by several constraints, such as poor processing power, less reliability, short transmission range, low transmission data rates, and very limited available battery power [3]. Wireless sensor network consists of multiple sensor nodes which are able to communicate with each other in order to perform the computation collaboratively by efficiently dividing the workload and avoiding the high communication within themselves. Thus, to overcome the limitations of

T.-h. Kim et al. (Eds.): SecTech/DRBC 2010, CCIS 122, pp. 236–243, 2010.

sensor network, sensor nodes collect the information from each other and perform the heavy task e.g. face recognition, object tracking by reducing the energy consumption [4]. Sensor node has not enough capability to process the heavy data locally such as image whereas image transmission is one of the most expensive task and it takes lot of energy due to the lot of communication overheads [5]. The network life time is when fist node died. Thus efficient distributed processing is required to overcome the issues in sensor networks.

2 Traditional Face Recognition System

Although, the computer is much faster and efficient in computation than human yet it fails in image processing and pattern recognition applications. The human is much more efficient than computer due to high contextual knowledge and extra ordinary viewing device such as eyes. Even a few year old child can perform better in pattern recognition than last algorithm exist today. Face recognition is to imitate the human face recognition power to the computer and it becomes the great demand after 9/11 for crimes and terrorism safety applications. Face recognition involved several challenges i.e. different types of face variabilities in different environments e.g. pose, illumination, expression. These challenges make face recognition much more difficult and less accurate. Face recognition is classified into face identification and verification. Face verification is the one-to-one match and it is suitable for mobile phones, login systems etc. Whereas face identification is one-to-many match, where a huge database is matched with probe face, shown in figure 1 and it is pure contactless biometrics. Face identification is the most suitable biometrics for face recognition.

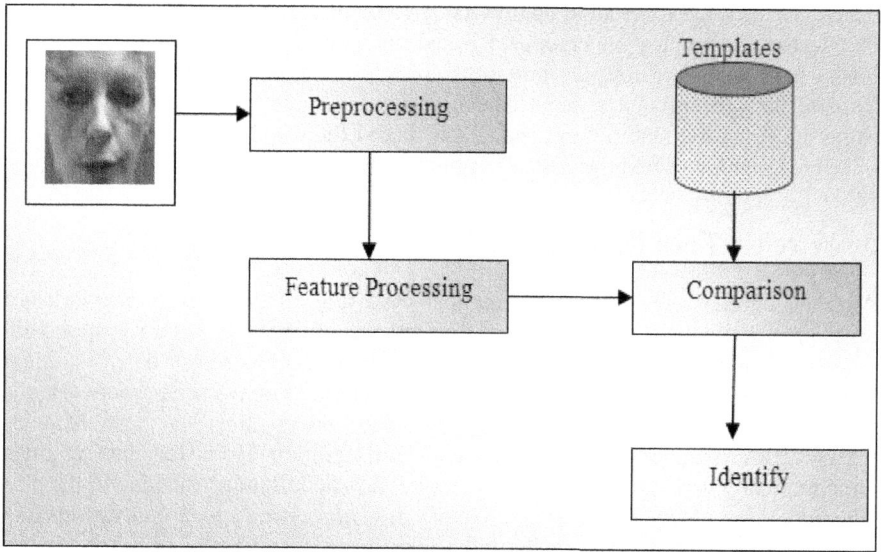

Fig. 1. Normal Face Recognition Process

During the last few decades, computer scientists, neuroscientists and psychologist's are working on face recognition algorithms. The psychologists and neuroscientists are modeling the visual perception for face recognition whereas the computer scientists are trying to develop methods based on the human brain modeling [6-8]. Face recognition includes face identification and face verification. Face identification shown in figure 1 is the one to many match in which a huge database is matched with probe image. It is more challenging as compared to face verification. Face verification includes one to one match and has been implemented in mobiles phone and personal login system by FaceCode, OMRON etc. [9]. The face identification is the contactless biometrics whereas face verification is partially contact biometrics. Face identification is the most popular biometrics used for security purposes due to its ease of end-user use, identification of an individual from distance. The contactless property of face identification make it more suitable for espionage applications by using wireless sensor networks.

PCA and LDA based methods are the most powerful methods for dimensionality reduction and have been successfully applied in many complex classification problems such as face recognition, speech recognition, etc [10]. LDA based methods perform better than PCA while LDA based methods are facing problems with SSS. The aim of LDA is to find the best representation of feature vector space. The conventional solution for small sample size problem and large data is the use of PCA into LDA. PCA is used for dimensionality reduction and LDA is performed on to the lower dimensional space obtained using PCA [11]. The use of LDA over PCA results in loss of significant discriminatory information. Direct linear discriminant analysis (D-LDA) is used to overcome this issue [12-13]. Fractional-step linear discriminant analysis (F-LDA) used weighting function by assigning the more weight to the relevant distance for dimensionality reduction to avoid misclassification [14]. Razzak et al. used layered discriminant analysis to overcome the issue of small sample set and large dataset [15]. Small dataset is extracted from large dataset using LDA instead of one single face. The further features templates are computed based on small new dataset. Finally the probe image is projected to fine the best separablity criteria. Razzak et al. presented bio-inspired face recognition system. The face dataset is reduced in layered process by using the structural features and appearance based futures [16]. The dataset is reduced in layered manner to find the best separablity.

3   Wireless Face Recognition System

After 9/11 trend towards security applications using wireless sensor network is increasing due to data acquisition and importance of WSN in security applications whereas it involves lot of issues. Face recognition in wireless sensor network recognition is a challenging task due to its several limitation. Wireless sensor network is energy, memory and processing power constrained network thus it is very difficult to perform pattern recognition tasks such as face recognition. Moreover, the face images are effected by various factors i.e. pose, expression and illumination, due to the physical structure of network. The limited battery, low processing power and various issues in face image normalization make unfeasible face recognition locally. The objective of wireless face is to increase the network life time and maintaining the accuracy by efficiently allocating the resources in distributed environment. The image communication takes lot of energy due to large image data and communication overhead, thus it is better to process the image either locally or in distributed environment by allocating the resources to neighbor nodes in efficient way rather than transmitting to the destination for recognition.

Muraleedharan et al. presented swarm intelligence based wireless face recognition and ant system is used for routing the wavelet coefficient. The swarm intelligence is used to optimize the routing in ant system in distributed time varying network by maintaining required bit error for various channel conditions [17]. The contourlet or wavelet coefficients are transmitted for central processing and assigned higher priority to ensure more accurate transmission and achieve 94% accuracy. Muraleedharan et al. presented face recognition for single or multi-hop ant based wireless sensor network using swarm intelligence [19]. They presented ant system for routing the wavelet or contourlet coefficients of faces to the sink node for processing with minimum energy consumption and reliable transmission. The swarm intelligence travel through the rout with less load and transmission error. The selected rout is evident to be more efficient and shorter. They evaluated three schemes raw format, compressed format by wavelet and compress format by contourlet on their performance. The transformed coefficient have different priority levels during image reconstruction.

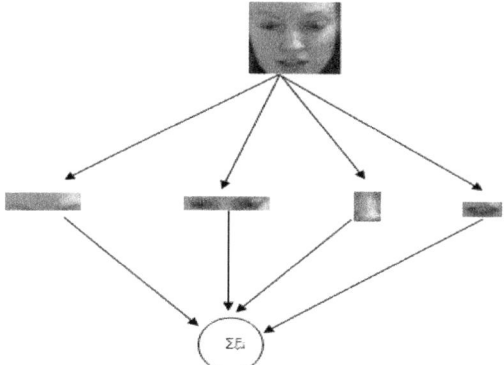

Fig. 2. Module based recognition process

Yan and Osadciw presented module (face, eye, nose, lips, forehead) based distributed wireless face recognition system [9]. They used five module (face and four sub modules) for wireless face recognition. The wireless sensor networks is divided into two groups i.e. feature nodes and database nodes. The feature nodes is responsible to calculate the features of probe image and transfer these features to the cluster node. The cluster node combines the features from all feature nodes and further transfers them to the database nodes. Database node compares with the stored templates and finally the score is transferred to the sink node. Although the workload is divided into sensor nodes, but the communication overload between feature nodes itself and database nodes is still an issue. It is more pressure on feature nodes and database nodes. Yan et al. presented contourlet based image compression for wireless communication in face recognition systems [18]. Yan et al. presented multistep static procedure to determine the confidence interval of features based on the Eigen decomposition of features and present a MIZM zone to present the interval [20].

Ikdong et al. presented face recognition system based on ZigBee transmission protocol and eigenface are computed with low power computation [24]. Yan et al presented discrete particle swarm optimization (DPSO) algorithm with a multiplicative likeliness enhancement rule for unordered feature selection and DPSO is applied on FERET face database [25]. The face recognition features pool are derived from DFLDA and each practical is associated with features subset. Features are selected based on assigned likeliness and the recognition performance is improved by both L1 and L2 norms distances metrics.

Razzak et al. present face recognition system in wireless sensor networks by efficiently reducing the dataset using layered process and presented three cases [22]. The image is divided into four sub modules i.e. forehead, eyes, nose and lips. The layered linear discriminant analysis is re-engineered to implement face recognition in wireless sensor network and instead of considering one cluster head in feature nodes and database nodes, four cluster heads are considered for each module in both feature and database net. The local cluster of each module is responsible for internal processing. Moreover instead of projecting the feature space onto the whole dataset, the result of one module is used to decrease the matching criteria for next module. It increased the computation overload on feature/database node while on the other hand communication load between the feature node to source node and database node to sink node is reduce.

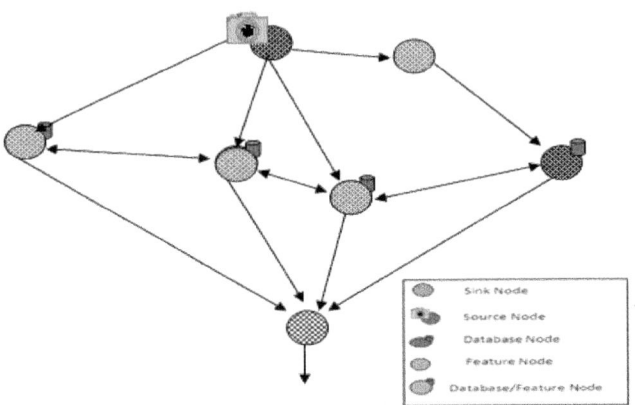

Fig. 3. Reduce dataset face recognition

Razzak et al. presented distributed face recognition system by dividing the load on the nodes and presented two different methods for training and recognition [23]. The previous face recognition system in wireless sensor network is only for recognition whereas the training is performed separately and feature matrix is stored on the feature nodes. They present efficient distributed wireless face recognition and discussed both training and recognition scenario by utilizing different algorithms. Instead of using one algorithm for training and recognition, they used two different methods for training and recognition. . Enrolment and identification of each sub modules is performed by separate cluster head. Each cluster head is responsible to process its sub module in distributed environment and each cluster head is responsible to communicate with sink cluster which perform the score level fusion. The net features of both methods are same, whereas both differentiate in computational complexity and consider separate cluster head for each module i.e. fore head, eye, lips and nose. Only the local cluster is responsible for internal module processing for both training and recognition and used the result of one module to reduce the matching dataset for other modes to find the best match and save the energy instead of projecting the feature space onto the whole dataset. The enrolment of faces is performed using linear discriminant analysis of principle component analysis and templates are stored in database nodes and the features and image templates of each sub module is stored on separate feature nodes and database nodes. For recognition, the probe modules of probe image are projected onto feature space to find the feature templates. These computed templates are compared with each templates stored in the database net to find the most similar identity. Figure 3 and figure 4 shows the distributed wireless sensor face recognition and enrolment system respectively.

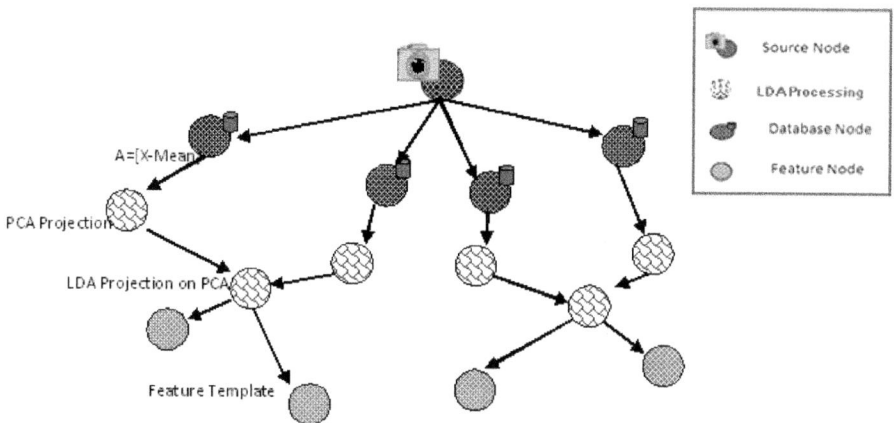

Fig. 4. Enrolment of Faces in Wireless Sensor Networks

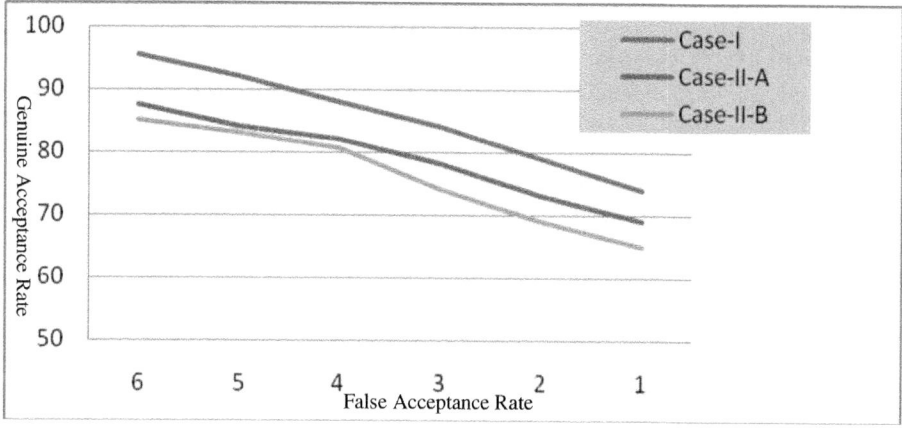

Fig. 5. Recognition rate of Face recognition system [22,23]

4   Open Issues in Face Recognition in WSN

Contactless biometrics in wireless sensor network is demanding task in security applications. It is challenging task and several open issues.

1. Distribute the face recognition algorithm and perform the task in distributed environment. Thus, distribution of face recognition according to sensor network capacity algorithm is required.
2. Instead of utilizing image based eigenface, face descriptor is better choice due to less processing power and communication overhead. Although the face descriptors provide less accuracy as compared to traditional system yet it can be a better choice to optimized the energy.
3. Categorization of face image into sub classes based on the external clue is required. This can help to reduce the processing cost by reducing the large dataset into very small dataset.

5   Conclusion and Future Work

Biometric based in wireless sensor network is very difficult due to energy, processing limitations. Image processing and image communication put heavy load on the network and reduces the life time of network whereas it is a demanding task. We present the latest work that has been done in face recognition in wireless sensor network. Moreover it also address few open issues related to biometrics security using wireless sensor networks. In future we aimed to address the above mentioned open issues in order to reduce the energy consumption and increasing the security by efficiently allocating the resources and using more robust face recognition algorithm.

References

[1] Estrin, D., Culler, D., Pister, K., Sukhatme, G.: Connecting the physical world with pervasive networks. IEEE Pervasive Computing 1(1), 59–69 (2002)
[2] Pottie, G.J., Kaiser, W.J.: Wireless integrated network sensors. Communications of the ACM 43(5), 51–58 (2000)
[3] Zhang, M., Lu, Y., Gonh, C., Feng, Y.: Energy-Efficient Maximum Lifetime Algorithm in Wireless Sensor Networks. In: 2008 International Conference on Intelligent Computation Technology and Automation (ICICTA) (October 2008)
[4] Razzak, M.I., Hussain, S.A., Minhas, A.A., Sher, M.: Collaborative Image Compression in Wireless Sensor Networks. International Journal of Computational Cognition 8(1) (March 2010)
[5] Hussain, S.A., Razzak, M.I., Minhas, A.A., Sher, M., Tahir, G.R.: Energy Efficient Image Compression in Wireless Sensor Networks. International Journal of Recent Trends in Engineering 2(1) (November 2009)
[6] Jain, A.K., Ross, A., Pankanti, S.: Biometrics: a tool for information security. IEEE Transactions on Information Forensics and Security 1(2), 125–143
[7] Prasad, S.M., Govindan, V.K., Sathidevi, P.S.: Bimodal personal recognition using hand images. In: Proceedings of the International Conference on Advances in Computing, Communication and Control, pp. 403–409. ACM, New York (2009)

 [8] Ross, A., Jain, A.K.: Multimodal Biometrics: An Overview. In: 12th European Signal Processing Conference (EUSIPCO), Vienna, Austria, pp. 1221–1224 (2004)
 [9] Yan, Y., Osadciw, L.A.: Distributed Wireless Face Recognition System. In: Proc. IS&T and SPIE Electronic Imaging 2008, San Jose, CA (January 2008)
[10] Ross, A., Jain, A.: Information Fusion in Biometrics. Pattern Recognition Letter 24, 2115–2125 (2003)
[11] Belhumeur, P.N., Hespanha, J.P., Kriegman, D.J.: Eigenfaces vs Fisherfaces: Recognition using Class Specific Linear Projection. IEEE Transaction Pattern Analysis Machine Intelligence 19 (1997)
[12] Yang, J., Yang, J.Y.: Why can LDA be Performed in PCA Transformed Space? Pattern Recognition 36 (2003)
[13] Yu, H., Yang, J.: A direct lda algorithm for high-dimensional data with application to face recognition. Pattern Recognit. 34, 2067–2070 (2001)
[14] Lotlikar, R., Kothari, R.: Fractional-step Dimensionality Data with Application to Face Recognition. IEEE Transaction Pattern Analysis Machine Intelligence 22 (2000)
[15] Razzak, M.I., Khan, M.K., Alghtabar, K., Yousaf, R.: Face Recognition using Layred Linear Discriminant Analysis and Small Subspace. In: International Conference on Computer and Information Technology, UK (2010)
[16] Razzak, M.I., Khan, M.K., Alghtabar, K.: Bio-Inspired Hybrid Face Recognition System for Small Sample Space and Large Data Set. In: 6th International Conference on Intelligent Information Hiding and Multimedia Signal Processing, Germany (2010)
[17] Muraleedharan, R., Yan, Y., Osadciw, L.A.: Constructing an Efficient Wireless Face Recognition by Swarm Intelligence. In: 2007 AGEP Academic Excellence Symposium, Syracuse, NY (June 2007)
[18] Yan, Y., Muraleedharan, R., Ye, X., Osadciw, L.A.: Contourlet Based Image Compression for Wireless Communication in Face Recognition System. In: Proc. IEEE-ICC 2008, IEEE International Conference on Communications (ICC 2008), Beijing, China (2008)
[19] Muraleedharan, R., Yan, Y., Osadciw, L.A.: Increased Efficiency of Face Recognition System using Wireless Sensor Network. Systemics, Cybernetics and Informatics 4(1), 38–46
[20] Yan, Y., Osadciw, L.A., Chen, P.: Confidence Interval of Feature Number Selection for Face Recognition. Journal of Electronic Imaging 17(1) (January 2008)
[21] Wu, H., Abouzeid, A.A.: Energy efficient distributed image compression in resource-constrained multihop wireless networks. Computer Communications 28 (2005)
[22] Razzak, M.I., Khan, M.K., Alghtabar, K.: Distributed Face Recognition in Wireless Sensor Network. In: The FTRA 2010 International Symposium on Advances in Cryptography, Security and Applications for Future Computing, Korea (2010)
[23] Razzak, M.I., Almogy, B.E., Khan, M.K., Alghtabar, K.: Energy Efficient Distributed Face Recognition in Wireless Sensor Network. Telecommunication System (accepted)
[24] Kim, I., Shim, J., Schlessman, J., Wolf, W.: Remote wireless face recognition employing zigbee. In: Workshop on Distributed Smart Cameras, ACM SenSys 2006, USA (2006)
[25] Yan, Y., Kamath, G., Osadciw, L.A.: Feature selection optimized by discrete particle swarm optimization for face recognition. In: Optics and Photonics in Global Homeland Security V and Biometric Technology for Human Identification SPIE, vol. 7306 (2009)

A Generic Approach to Security Assured Net-Centric Communications Network Architecture for C4I Systems

Abdullah S. Alghamdi, Syed Amanullah Quadri, Iftikhar Ahmad, and Khalid Al-Nafjan

Department of Software Engineering, College of Computer & Information Sciences, King Saud University, P.O. Box 51178, Riyadh 11543, Kingdom of Saudi Arabia
wattohu@gmail.com, syedshahaman@gmail.com, aghamdi@ksu.edu.sa

Abstract. The purpose of this paper is to suggest security assured data communications architecture in net-centric defense systems based on DoDAF 2.0. This architecture provides a finite security precision of network communication within the defense network like C4I System. In this proposed network communication architecture where security is being prioritized, we propose three security mechanism levels, the authentication level, the Business Rules Repository level & Security Rules Repository level and available techniques facilitating the functionality of the levels. Security can be coerced at every stage of the data transit. By utilization of various data security measures available, each level will substantiate the security of the data in the communication chain from end to end.

Keywords: Military Communications, C4I, Defense Communication Network, DODAF, Secured Communications.

1 Introduction

Networks and communications networking is one of the most crucial components of the military architecture systems like Command & Control (C2), Command, Control, Computers, Communication & Intelligence (C4I), C4I Surveillance, Target Acquisition and Reconnaissance (C4ISTAR), Department of Defense Architecture Framework (DoDAF), The Open Group Architecture Framework (TOGAF) and others [1]. The first line of operations designing of a given military architecture is doctrine of the communication heads and communicates (DoDAF OV4) [2]. This phase is actually the one that serves as the layout for comprehending the methodology, type, requirement of the technology (DoDAF SV2) [2] of the network architecture. Hence, properly designed, defined and secured net-centric communication network architecture equipped with fore-vision of approximate required changes in the future, change complaint and change tolerant technological measures can contribute invariably to a stable military system or system of systems like C4I and others, which bases in DoDAF [3]. The primary focus of this paper is to suggest a generic net-centric communication network model that can capture the ubiquitous participants of the military

T.-h. Kim et al. (Eds.): SecTech/DRBC 2010, CCIS 122, pp. 244–249, 2010.

communication system or system of systems like C4I, and to facilitate functionality of the complete communication system in a timely, reliable, secure and seamless manner. The description of the architecture has been organized into following sections: Background, Communication Network Architecture, Issues Threatening Communication Networks, Proposed Network Architecture, Conclusion and Future Works.

2 Research Background

The C4I systems are used in various departments such as defense, police, investigation, road, rail, airports, oil and gas where command and control scenarios exist. The main focus of these systems is in defense applications. C4I systems consist of people, procedures, technology, doctrine and authority and play a growing role in information management, data fusion and dissemination. The purpose of a C4I system is to help the commander accomplish his objective in any crucial situation. It consists of four words such as command, control, communications, computers and intelligence [11], [12].

Military data communications systems are, by their nature, shared systems. Host computers are shared by local and remote users; access lines are multiplexed; terminals are concentrated and interfaced to the network by terminal controllers; packet switches interface host computers to the network and handle data traveling to and from all users; and gateways handle data traveling among different networks. Then users, cleared to various security levels, generate, manipulate, send, and receive data at assorted levels of classification over a shared communications system, the potential exists for security violations and dangerous compromise [4].

3 Communication Network Architecture

The communication data in a defense system can come from various sources: sensor data gateways deployed in battlefield scenarios, various military applications, ground unit communication devices and air/ground mobile vehicles. In a way all these participants of the defense system, at a given point of time are either sending or receiving data via gateways. In defense communication architecture, these participants can also be referred to, as *communication nodes*. This data can be a blend of processed data via defense specific applications, signals from ground deployed sensors, and links from the vectors spanning the GPRS etc. This data is put across the transmission channel via gateways of the vertical to which the nodes belong to.

The participating nodes and communication process of the defense system are subjected to various threats. Given the threat severity, it is apparent that unprotected or loosely protected communications are at a higher stake of risk. The threats involve, unauthorized access to classified information, scrapping of critical data or muddling the correctness of the data eventually resulting in the potential loss of control over military forces [5]. Let's examine the participating types of nodes in a military system and, the under-laying security threats and issues at various levels of the data communication.

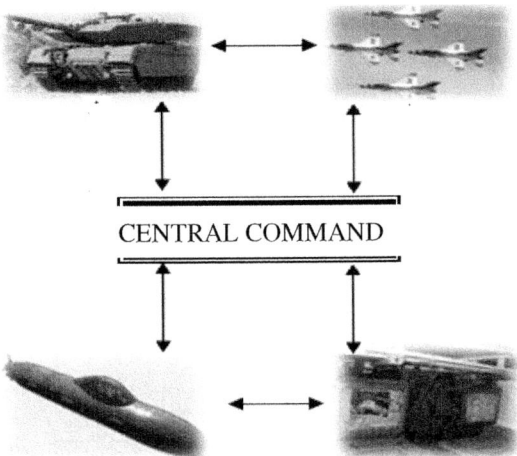

Fig. 1. Defense Network Participants

4 Issues Threatening Communication Networks

A network communication system as is being observed over the years is subjected to threats like Denial of Service (DoS) attack [14], Ping flooding, authenticity attacks, integrity attacks etc [13] to tackle these threats security measures applications have been elevated. However, the major concern of the Defense communication networks is that, the security is being considered as a sub system of the architecture instead of being considered as a system-wide concern. The current security policy in existence circles the security measures like physical security, encrypting bulk transmission lines using keyed crypto devices [5], implementing data packet encryption methodologies etc. However ensuring the implementation of the supra-mentioned measures simply doesn't ensure throughput security.

5 Proposed Network Architecture

The coverage of the Proposed Network Architecture spans the communication of nodes (N_1 to N_n). The fundamental policy of the architecture is to ensure that the nodes intending to communicate data over the network channel are not directly accessing the transmission lobe. The communication in the verticals will be initiated only when authentication server allows a node to communicate as depicted in figure 2, which is cleared via a Role Authentication. Secondly, Authentication server will confirm the data being transmitted is encrypted or digitally signed as it is the fundamental stone in the proposed network architecture.

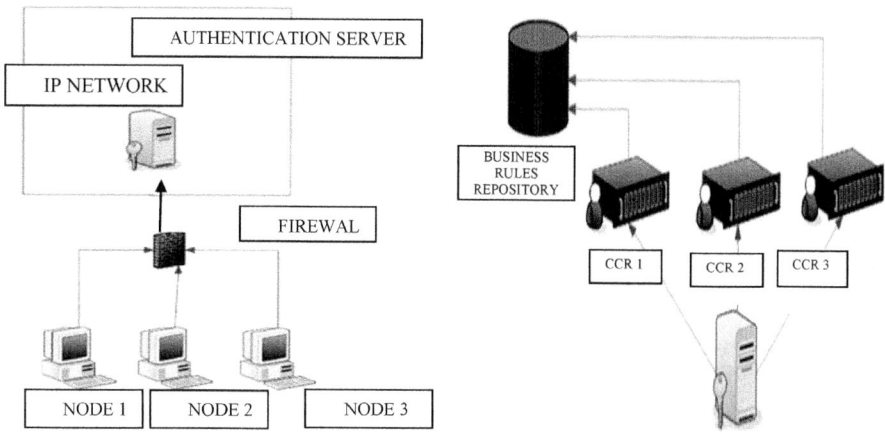

Fig. 2. Authentication Server   **Fig. 3.** Business Rules Repository

5.1 Level I

At this level, the concentration of the security aspect will be: role based authentic clearance and ensuring the security of the data in an encrypted form using crypto-graphic functionality. The cryptography [7] mechanism is considered to be the most suitable, when it comes to communicating classified information, high level security data among the roles of a military system. The different type of cryptography meth-odologies available are 1) Secret Key cryptography 2) Public Key Cryptography.

The symmetric cryptography can be mathematically represented as:

$$Encryption: C=Encrypt\ (K,\ M)$$
$$Decryption: M=Decrypt\ (K,\ C)$$
$$Message: M=Decrypt\ (K,\ Encrypt\ [K,\ M]) \qquad (1)$$

Asymmetric Cryptography uses two keys (public and private) to function

$$Encryption: C=E\ (K_{s\text{-}prv},\ M)$$
$$Decryption: M=D\ (K_{s\text{-}pub},\ C) \qquad (2)$$

Then the data is encrypted using a specific role's (R1) public key, it can be decrypted using R1's private key only (Restricted Access).

$$Encryption: C=E\ (K_{R1\text{-}pub},\ M)$$
$$Decryption: M=D\ (K_{R1\text{-}priv},\ C) \qquad (3)$$

Another way of securing the data before it is being initiated for transmission is to scrutinize the data with a *digital signature*. Firstly, the data is encrypted by senders private key $C=E\ (K_{s\text{-}priv},\ M)$, then this encrypted data is re-encrypted using the public key of the recipient $C2=E\ (K_{R\text{-}pub},\ C)$. The recipient using its private key there $M(C) =D\ (K_{R\text{-}priv},\ C2)$ and then using the senders public key $M=D\ (K_{S\text{-}pub},\ C)$ will decrypt the encrypted data.

5.2 Level II

Post receipt of the data packets, role authenticated and double encrypted the authentication server will forward the data packets the Communication Controllers (CCR) as depicted in figure 3. Generally, in shared system communications the security policy implemented is end-to-end encryption. In this proposed network architecture the requirement of the clear text headers is a mandate. The information will be utilized in order to ascertain the business rules for further securing the data at level 3. At this level, once the headers are read by the CCR's, the CCR's will communicate with the Business Rules Repository to request the communication security rules in accordance with the role of the communicates. *Business Rules for Communication* i.e., Designation of the Sender (Ds), Designation of the Receiver (Dr) and Severity of the Message being transmitted (Xn). Mathematically represented as:

Roles Designation: 1 =Low, 2= average and 3= high Data Severity: 1=Normal, 2=Essential, 3= Extremely Critical.

$$S_{r3} = D_{r3}(X_3, D_{s3}) \tag{4}$$

Once the severity of the data is identifies the BRR will stamp the data packets with S_{r3} (1), which implies Security rule 3. Similarly communication of the data between a sender and multiple receivers can also be denoted by

$$S_{r2} = D_{r1}(X_2, D_{s\,[2,\,3,\,1]}) \tag{5}$$

To facilitate the BRR functionality, whose emphasis is: 1) Identification of the participants. 2) Participants are authenticated users. 3) The role of the sender privileged enough to raise the given priority. Various models have been suggested to comply with the authentic communication under the banner of *RBAC (Role Based Access Control)* [8]. Three primary rules are defined for RBAC: (i) Role assignment, (ii) Role authorization: A subject's active role must be authorized for the subject. (iii) Transaction authorization: A subject can execute a transaction only if the transaction is authorized for the subject's active role. The RBAC can be customized into an application model [8].

5.3 Level III

Security Rules Repository: The Business Rules Repository application can be customized to add the Required Security details (RSD) for the data. On receipt of the data packets, Security Rules Repository (SRR) will Ensure: 1) Integrity of the data. 2) Confidentiality of the data. *Integrity service* [9]. Where, message hashing will concern the data with hashes and digital encryption will encrypt the hashes using the public and private keys, figure 3. This can be represented as:

$$Hash\ (H) = PS_{S-10},\ C_1 \tag{6}$$

Where PS= Packet Size, S=Sender and C_n=Check Sum. Once the data packet bundle has been hashed by the Message Hashing this has will be encrypted using the digital signature, via the public key of the recipient.

$$Encryption = C\ (H) = (K_{R-Pub},\ H) \tag{7}$$

6 Conclusion and Future Work

This layout of the defense architecture can contribute effectively towards a network system which is strong, reliable and affordable, secure data communication which is ready to meet challenges of intrusion detection and threats arising out of upgrading attack and data compromising techniques. Though, this architecture does not cover in detail security aspects of the communication architecture. The various aspects of the security levels will be answered through individual investigation of the security levels in the future works.

References

1. Bayne, J.S.: A Theory of Enterprise Command and Control. In: IEEE MILCOM, paper 10.1109/MILCOM, 302994, pp. 1–8 (2006)
2. DoD Architecture Framework, Version 2.0 – DoDAF Meta Model, vol. 3, Department of Defense, USA (2009)
3. Mahbub, H., Raj, J.: High Performance TCP/IP Networking concepts, Issues and Solutions. Prentice Hall of India (2004)
4. Anurag, D., Brain, H., Jhon, N.: Capacity planning strategies for net-centric applications. In: MILCOM IEEE, vol. 3, pp. 1686–1692 (October 2005)
5. Rona, S., Caser, D.: Computer Security and Networking protocols: Technical Issues in Military Data Communications Networks. IEEE Transactions on Communications 9, 1472–1477 (1980)
6. Abdullah, A.S., Tazar, H., Gulfaraz, K.: Enhancing C4I Security using Threat Modeling. In: Proc. IEEE, UKSIM, paper 10.1109 (2010)
7. Stallings, W. (ed.): Cryptography and Network Security, 4th edn. Prentice-Hall o f India
8. Wei, Z., Meinel, C.: Team and Task Based RBAC Access Control Model. In: Network Operations and Management Symposium, LANOMS 2007. Latin American, paper 10.1109, pp. 84–94 (2007)
9. Veselin, T., Dragomir, P.: Information Assurance in C4I Systems. ISN Information and Security 4, 43–59 (2000)
10. Alghamdi, A.S.: Evaluating Defense Architecture Frameworks for C4I System Using Analytic Hierarchy Process. J. Computer Sci. 5(12), 1078–1084 (2009)
11. Alghamdi, A., Shamim Hossain, M., Al Qurishi, M.: Selecting the best case tools for DoDAF-based C4I applications, inderscience Int. J. Advanced Media and Communication (2010) (in press)
12. Ahmad, I., Abdullah, A.B., Alghamdi, A.S.: Evaluating Intrusion Detection Approaches Using Multi-criteria Decision Making Technique. IJISCE 1(2), 60–67 (2010)
13. Ahmad, I., Abdullah, A.B., Alghamdi, A.S.: Towards the designing of robust IDS through an optimized advancement of neural networks. In: Kim, T.-h., Adeli, H. (eds.) AST/UCMA/ISA/ACN. LNCS, vol. 6059, pp. 597–602. Springer, Heidelberg (2010)
14. Ahmad, I., Abdullah, A.B., Alghamdi, A.S.: Application of Artificial Neural Network in Detection of DOS Attacks. ACM SIN, 229–234 (2009)

Collaborative Geospatial Data as Applied to Disaster Relief: Haiti 2010

A.J. Clark, Patton Holliday, Robyn Chau, Harris Eisenberg, and Melinda Chau

1400 North 14th Street, Arlington, Virginia 22209, USA
{ajclark,pholliday,rchau,heisenberg,mchau}@t-sciences.com

Abstract. The aftermath of Haiti's January 12 earthquake typified disaster relief in that efficiency and situational awareness were reduced by the chaotic, uncoordinated influx of relief and aid. The lack of an environment in which information could be shared was a major component of this chaos. The application of geographic information (GIS) technology was a significant contribution to the relief efforts due to the centrality of location to issues of danger, resources, safety, communications, and so on, and due to the universal understanding of information rendered geospatially using 3-D globes.

Concerned that existing solutions were restricting, U.S. Southern Command (SOUTHCOM) engaged Thermopylae to build a user-friendly GIS tool to reach a wide user base, fuse data from disparate sources, and immerse users in relevant content. The resulting SOUTHCOM 3D User-Defined Operational Picture (UDOP) united over 2,000 users to create, add, edit, update, and share data aggregated through GIS tools, existing databases, mobile applications and other resources, geospatially.

The UDOP was built on the enterprise geospatial framework, iSpatial™, which interacts with the Google Earth Plug-in™ browser application programming interface and provided SOUTHCOM's Joint Intelligence and Operations Center with interactive applications and an open platform for the integration of dynamic data for timely and publicly-accessible solutions. The application of the UDOP to relief efforts in Haiti optimized the gathering and management of data from government, military, non-government agency, and first responder resources, which consequently improved relief efforts simply by inviting a large user community to share data on an intuitive common platform. The experience in and lessons learned from Haiti promise great strides into the future of the geospatial technology.

Keywords: GIS, SDI, Google Earth, iSpatial, Haiti relief efforts, USSOUTHCOM, mobile applications, iPhone®, Android™.

1 Introduction

The January 12, 2010 earthquake completely compromised Haiti's already unstable infrastructure, rendering local communications useless for coordinating relief and aid. The ensuing chaos highlighted the lack of redundant information systems that were versatile and accessible by the Haitian people and relief community. Thermopylae

T.-h. Kim et al. (Eds.): SecTech/DRBC 2010, CCIS 122, pp. 250–258, 2010.
© Springer-Verlag Berlin Heidelberg 2010

teamed up with U.S. Southern Command (SOUTHCOM) to remedy this problem by developing geospatial software that engaged users and included them in the management of information being used to direct relief . The resulting development of the SOUTHCOM 3D User-Defined Operational Picture (UDOP) maximized the efficiency of the coordination of relief efforts of government, non-government, international, and local emergency response units by compiling spatial information from a variety of sources on a single platform for universal access. In conjunction with the Google Earth© browser plug-in and Thermopylae's iSpatial™ framework, the UDOP provides a three-dimensional Web portal where users can easily create and share spatial information.

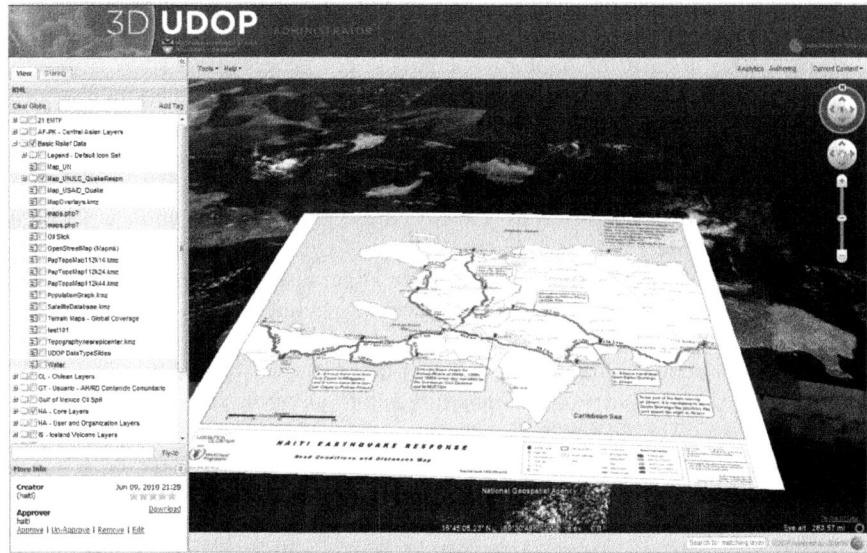

Fig. 1. The SOUTHCOM 3D UDOP Interface

2 Overview of Problem Set

The magnitude of the devastation in Haiti following the earthquake was defined by 220,000 dead and a dire shortage of food, water, medical care, and supplies for survivors, including approximately 300,000 injured and over 1 million displaced people. The initial crisis response was a flood of supplies and individuals to the already densely populated capital of Port-au-Prince from military units, federal agencies, state and local emergency response personnel, non-governmental relief organizations, and commercial industry members from across the globe. This massive response was overwhelming, but communication and logistical coordination was insufficient due to incorrect, scarce, or inaccessible data and tools for collaboration. Not having the necessary tools and modes of communication resulted in severe delays in the transport and delivery of much needed aid. Many of the contributing organizations possessed relevant data and implemented their own management practices, but their relief efforts, were hindered by the absence of an accessible and central environment for data and cooperation.

The SOUTHCOM 3D UDOP was initially an extension of SOUTHCOM's preexisting and non-geospatial collaboration portal, the All Partner Access Network which provided image, document and comment sharing capabilities crucial to information management within SOUTHCOM's disaster relief network, which integrated non-military participants. Although this network was widely used, users made more time for the UDOP when it was accessible on the Web outside of military networks, and eventually became a permanent fixture in the SOUTHCOM Crisis Action Center. Its first deployment was made just days after the earthquake leveraging Thermopylae's past experience as an enterprise partner with Google Earth and tracking vehicles and security assets, and rapidly spiraled updates installed frequent improvements. Their information management requirements, which the UDOP supported, were defined by a characteristic atypical of military operations, but necessary to address the crisis. Virtually all information available and pertinent to Haiti was unclassified according SOUTHCOM, meaning an inclusive environment was possible to engage the international community. While this opened the door to more information exchange, complications of language arose, Haiti being a multilingual nation itself, but geospatial display is intuitive and transcends some of these problems. Location is a common language to everyone.

Considering this, the UDOP was built for a large, disparate user community which came with the profound international response. A frequent limitation of GIS is that users are often dependent on a cadre of specialized geospatial technicians to collect, analyze, and disseminate data often only as printed maps. This practice can easily be overwhelmed so the greater user community is left out of the process and is passively involved at best. The UDOP allowed everyone to add information and visualize it without the need for a geospatial office to facilitate, making it impressively scalable. High user-volume is further enabled through the browser-based software, which is

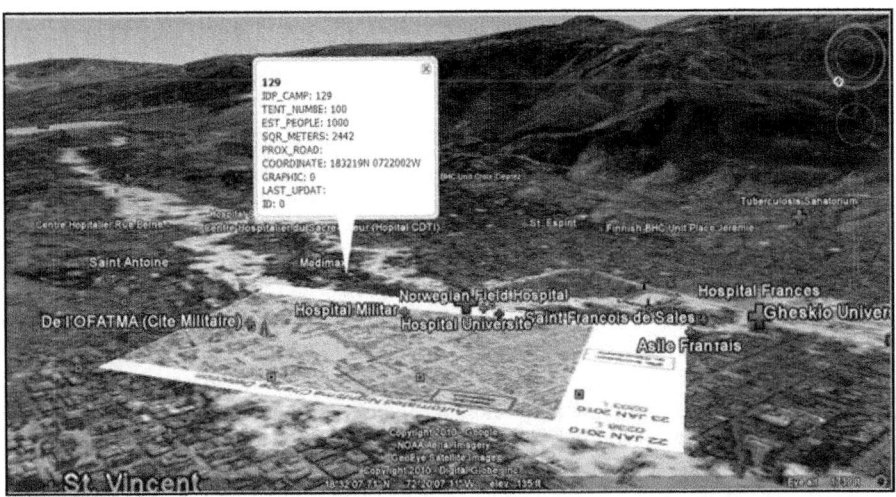

Fig. 2. Content Overlays

familiar from Google Earth's commercial use, and accessibility on multiple platforms, mobile and stationary. Crowd sourcing and social networking complement the content added from other sources and the effect of layering disparate information together in user-defined combinations opens up new ways of thinking through improved situational awareness. With this wide range of content, that can be analyzed through the UDOP's collaborative tools, data is now communicable in a geospatial sense without the need to print and can be used for strategic communications. No longer are users limited to just the information one managing organization thinks they want to see.

3 User-Created Content

The UDOP Haiti project addressed the challenge of creating a common picture of spatially-relevant data applicable to Haiti after the earthquake. The initial operating capability had three core features to support data collaboration. The first feature allowed a user to import any geospatial file and load it to the UDOP view. The second allowed users to link to a URL where users could send dynamic updates of their existing data stores to other spatial files and render them in the UDOP. The third feature, which was imperative to promoting an environment of sharing, was a spatial content export tool, which allowed users to use the UDOP as a "marketplace" of spatial data, even if users didn't ultimately use the tool for fusing the information into a single picture. This ensured that the UDOP served a dual purpose as both a repository within which content could be created or viewed, and as an index of available content, which was critical to its widespread use as an environment for data sharing. The system design team benefited tremendously by communicating with relief units in Miami, Fl. and Haiti, and the final system was heavily influenced by the individuals directly involved in coordinating logistics amongst all participating organizations.

The ability to link spatial data layers from sources outside of the UDOP is a key feature, giving the user the ability to define a custom view through their browser. An early concern was that the KML folder would easily become overloaded with disorganized layers of content, thus undermining the UDOP's purpose. As the volume of data increased, two additional tools, one allowing for the creation of lines, polygons, and points, along with a common labeling and icon scheme, rendered the content much more easily visualized on the UDOP globe which was a customized with almost daily updates of imagery in which the quality, origin, and time were defined by users.

Users could build video fly-through presentations or even construct a series of life views of current imagery, intelligence layers, and operations data that dynamically updated even after the presentation was compiled. The data was live, up-to-date and interactive, so when it was presented a user could stop at any point and drill down into a greater level of detail for facilities, mobile units, and landmarks as well as basic reporting and imagery. This supported an extremely adaptive environment for the intelligence personnel supporting the relief effort.

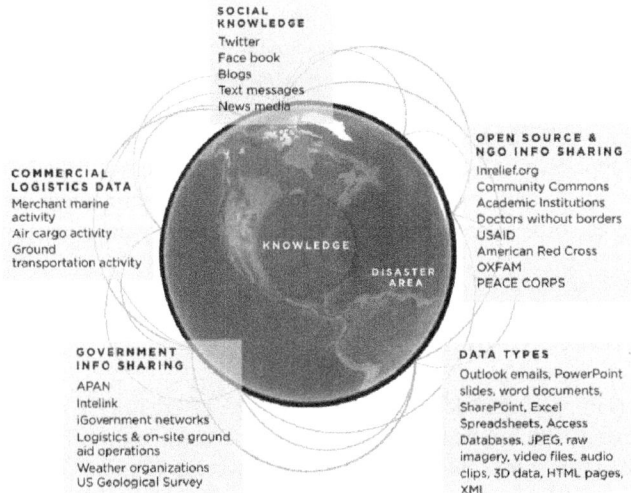

Fig. 3. Wide Range of Collaboration

Another challenge to usability was the limited access to high-speed communications, as many users interacting with the UDOP were on the ground in Haiti with compromised infrastructure. Due to preference settings in the Google Earth browser plug-in, users were able to cache and view imagery, content layers, and other data without having to necessarily be online. The damage assessments of key facilities by independent users were invaluable to the UDOP collaborative effort, as it contributed to the creation of 3D models in Google Sketch-Up, terrain features, and airborne LiDAR data. In addition, an inclusive environment for spatial collaboration was extremely valuable to users, as the 3D functionality, the up-to-date imagery, and a host of functions allowed the users not only to define, but also instantly update their view. The collection of these functions and abilities within a single place drove users to the UDOP, and increased the time users spent interacting with the site. Once the content creation tools were integrated and the overall volume of information in the UDOP increased, Thermopylae noticed major spikes in the time each user spent in their session. Within only one week of the earthquake, the average time a user spent interacting with the data was between two and three hours per session, which was up from little to no time spent in a spatial collaborative environment.

Collaboration and accessibility were also factored into the development components of the UDOP. Adherence to the KML/KMZ format of data throughout the UDOP was a logical choice as it was the language within the geospatial community based on robust, textual extensible markup, open standard format. A clearly-defined requirement for constructing an environment for inclusive spatial collaboration was crucial to avoiding proprietary formats. Other formats would have been more difficult to manage, and the resulting data would have been challenging to synthesize with other spatial data files across the user base. Finally, more tools were readily available for displaying and manipulating KML/KMZ files than those available for data in other geospatial formats. The decision to standardize using the KML/KMZ format ultimately proved beneficial, as information could be most easily and cohesively shared throughout the disaster response community.

4 Mobile Applications

One of the most effective methods for building knowledge within the system was to collect data directly from those individuals in the field during the crisis. Leveraging mobile applications is important because of their range of use and devices, importance to crowd sourcing, quick deployment, and their ability to become immediately omnipresent. To this end, SOUTHCOM officials took advantage of smart phone (i.e. iPhone® or Android™) technology and integrated customized software on various mobile platforms that complemented the UDOP, allowing relief workers to share and post data about their immediate surroundings in real-time. Integration of mobile applications leveraged the comprehensive 2D version of Google Maps™ for mobile phones and will soon include mobile Google Earth™. This included uploading geolocated text and descriptions, as well as photographs taken using the in-house developed mobile application Disaster Relief, and using GeoCam, jointly developed by NASA and Google. The UDOP also leveraged existing crowd source tools include Ushahidi-based services that generated layers from geolocated SMS messages sponsored by local telecoms immediately after the earthquake.

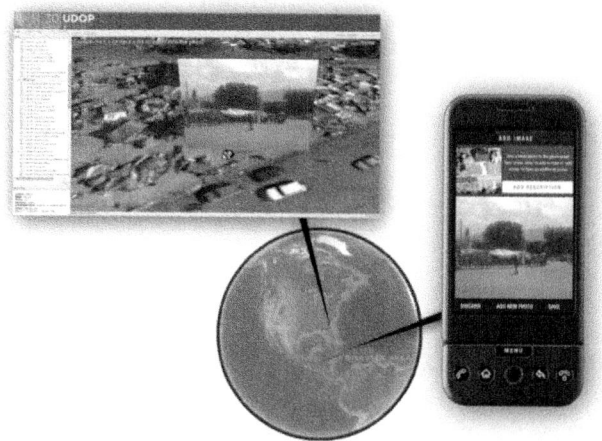

Fig. 4. GEOCAM App in UDOP

SOUTHCOM developers deployed Android G1 mobile phones in Haiti, loaded with a custom mobile application that allowed users to be "collectors." The phones were able to embed 3.2 megapixel photographs with a pinpoint-specific geolocation and the camera's heading at the time of the picture. This capability combined with Web connectivity and server space, military personnel in Haiti had the ability to provide all UDOP users with sharp, geospecific imagery that updated to a dynamic UDOP layer in near real-time. Within the UDOP, the image appears as an upright window with a zoom capability. Thus, phone carriers could effectively build a room where the walls make up a 360-degree view.

These applications provided quick and easy access to critical knowledge on an as-needed basis, such as locating the nearest medical facility or relief camp. An important additional feature of the application was an offline mode that allowed users to store data on their mobile device locally before finding a connectivity point, such as a Wi-Fi® hotspot or a working cell phone tower. Once connectivity was available, the mobile application prompted the user to submit the locally-stored data. The "Haiti Relief" application was created initially using the iPhone software development kit and was made freely available within Apple®'s "App Store," and allowed ad hoc distribution. The application was also ported to Android and other popular mobile platforms. By combining these resources, SOUTHCOM leaders were able to build a full-featured solution, supporting the sharing of information among relief supporters and coordinators, as well as enabling direct interaction with those on the ground in Haiti.

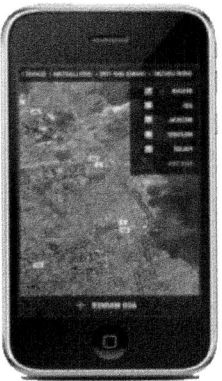

Fig. 5. iPhone UDOP App

5   Training, Best Practices and Notable Experiences

Thermopylae helped the spread of the SOUTHCOM 3D UDOP by deploying training and information where potential users were most likely to see them. Training was provided in a variety of formats to accommodate as many learning styles and operating resources as possible, as it was anticipated that resources, especially time and/or bandwidth, would be limited. A user manual was written which provided functional training by building interactive UDOP screens into the document: this simulated the UDOP's capabilities by jumping to relevant pages and graphics. The user, by referencing the manual, was able to build familiarity well before receiving an account or downloading the Google Earth plug-in. Training video podcasts were created to provide step-by-step lessons for all functions, and demonstrations of the range of content promoted the creation of more content while highlighting the contributions of others. Thermopylae trainers deployed to Haiti to familiarize their geospatial body Centre National de l'Information Géo Spatiale with the UDOP and how it could be applied to provide relief solutions to the approaching rainy season. The technical team was exposed to approximately 10-15 percent of the user base on the Web site, but even from this small cross-section, they were able to capture the group's prioritized needs, and then expand upon the capabilities the entire user community needed. Furthermore, once brief training videos were viewable directly from the UDOP splash page, requests for support dropped by 70 percent. The training material allowed users from a host of varied backgrounds to become familiarized with the UDOP's capabilities quickly and then pas that knowledge on to other users. The UDOP training program was created to track the standard operating procedures created by SOUTHCOM users. The program was structured to follow the expected evolution of content management, and the training schedule was coordinated with software update releases. The urgency and sudden commencement of relief efforts in Haiti entailed new incoming personnel daily, which necessitated continual training. Users could also operate with enhanced knowledge of Haiti before setting foot there, as Thermopylae's iHarvest profiled their UDOP use in the background and matched them with similar users and content as it was created, immersing users in the content base and improving collaboration. As SOUTHCOM's relief efforts geared up, the UDOP user base expanded with the addition of individuals from other Combatant Commands, primarily Joint Forces Command and Northern Command. Integrating disparate groups is important to both organizations because of the frequent need to include allied, federal, state, municipal, and NGO groups, a situation similar to the immediate nature of relief operations that teams groups with similar functions but unintegrated organization. The cumulative diversity and density of data that could be layered was testament to the demand for agility and innovation in content management. Through the UDOP a new GIS capability evolved in that software no longer just processing data, but fusing an ad hoc community of like-minded people and organizations in one place. Through the simplicity of linking dynamic content in, data custodians retained control of their own content and could reveal it on the UDOP as desired, but without having to conform their information systems to each other. Smoke stacks of information no longer

Fig. 6. 3D UDOP with Presentation Builder

emptied into the sky, by into one contained space equipped with tools to manage the diversity and variation. The relief community is heading towards a new expectation of continuity as the same groups which were gathered together on the UDOP, can immediately reconnect as they respond to future disasters in other locations.

6 Conclusion

The UDOP's ability to fill the former absence of the collaborative coordination of geospatial data for disaster relief efforts is one of the most notable and valuable aspects of the software. Thousands of users from partner nations, non-government organizations, and local and state first responders had a central location to access and share relevant intelligence. The UDOP allowed users to represent the human element of what was occurring on the ground in Haiti. From geo-tagged snapshots of infrastructure and floodplains on smart phones, to the creation of adaptive spot-reporting layers, the UDOP flexed to meet a variety of needs for relief workers and users can anticipate exciting developments in addressing these and future challenges.

During this project, much of the innovation was driven by the relief coordinators' immediate need for these tools. Due to the urgency for a timely response, SOUTH-COM officials broke from the implicit military norm and embraced an inclusive, collaborative, and open environment. The unanticipated synergy amongst users fostered profound innovation that quickly led to the first, second and third generations of improvement. The UDOP for Haiti demonstrated that if users are intellectually involved in improving the technical capability, they have a vested and therefore greater interest in the application. Also, having a committed, responsive design team capable of integrating features in a matter of days versus weeks is imperative to retain user buy-in. The humanitarian community at large benefits from this rapid development of tools as they are tailored to the most serious challenges. As the technical capabilities for sharing data increase over time, new ideas will be formed by users as they reset their understanding of the high-water mark of the inclusive sharing of spatial data.

Effects of Changes in Lugu Lake Water Quality on Schizothorax Yunnansis Ecological Habitat Based on HABITAT Model

Wei Huang [1] and Arthur Mynnet [2]

[1] College of Hydrology and Water Resources, Hohai University,
Nanjing, P.R. China
[2] Water Science and Engineering, UNESCO-IHE Institute for Water Education,
Delft, The Netherlands
wei.huang923@gmail.com

Abstract. Schizothorax Yunnansis is an unique fish species only existing in Lugu Lake, which is located in the southwestern China. The simulation and research on Schizothorax Yunnansis habitat environment have a vital significance to protect this rare fish. With the development of the tourism industry, there bring more pressure on the environmental protection. The living environment of Schizothorax Yunnansis is destroyed seriously because the water quality is suffering the sustaining pollution of domestic sewage from the peripheral villages. This paper analyzes the relationship between water quality change and Schizothorax Yunnansis ecological habitat and evalutes Schizothorax Yunnansis's ecological habitat impact based on HABITAT model. The results show that when the TP concentration in Lugu Lake does not exceed Schizothorax Yunnansis's survival threshold, Schizothorax Yunnansis can get more nutrients and the suitable habitat area for itself is increased. Conversely, it can lead to TP toxicity in the Schizothorax Yunnansis and even death. Therefore, unsuitable habitat area for Schizothorax Yunnansis is increased. It can be seen from the results that HABITAT model can assist in ecological impact assessment studies by translating results of hydrological, water quality models into effects on the natural environment and human society.

Keywords: Schizothorax Yunnansis, HABITAT Model, Water Quality, Ecological Habitat Assessment, Habitat Suitability Index.

1 Introduction

Habitat is the space and environment of biological survival and reproduction, and it is vital for the food chain and energy flow of biology that is the foundation of natural environment to keep healthy. Good habitats of ecological condition can nurture a good ecological quality. Because of human scale development of biological habitat, it will seriously affect the local ecological quality, and will further bring the ecological disaster [1-3]. The key to protecting habitat is to explore impact factors of the habitat, and build up a model to simulate and evaluate the habitat.

T.-h. Kim et al. (Eds.): SecTech/DRBC 2010, CCIS 122, pp. 259–268, 2010.
© Springer-Verlag Berlin Heidelberg 2010

Since 1970's, numbers of habitat evaluation studies were undertaken. Bovee was the first person to apply the Instream Flow Incremental Methodology (IFIM) into the habitat evaluation procedure [4, 5]. Zengchao Hao used a multi-objective assessment method based on physical habitat simulation for calculating ecological river flow demand in the mid-reach of the Erqisi River in Xinjiang Autonomous Region [6]. Hayes used the Logistic regression based on habitat preference models to predict the suitable habitat in the Three New Zearland River [7]. Binns developed a Habitat Quality Index model to predict trout standing crop in Wyoming streams [8].

All those methods mentioned above obtained fruitful results, but they also have some limitations as follows [9]. ① not considered to combine the water quality model; ② high requirements for parameter selection; ③ lack of wide adaptability.

In order to overcome the limitations, HABITAT model was developed by Deltares | Delft Hydraulics. HABITAT model is able to translate results of hydrological, hydraulics and water quality models into effects on the natural environmental and human society. It is also easy to setup and can be developed at different spatial scales for different predictive purposes. In this paper, a habitat assessment of Schizothorax Yunnansis was built up based on HABITAT.

2   Ecological Habitat Assessment Based on HABITAT Model

2.1 Knowledge Rules of HABITAT Model

HABITAT model can be easily built using different functions or so-called knowledge rules. The important environmental parameters of the evaluation species or species group and how these parameters affect the species must be defined in knowledge rules. These rules are the results of literature studies and in some cases combined with expert judgment. Within HABITAT, knowledge rules that describe cause-effect relations and were developed in specific studies can be stored in a database. They may consequently be re-used and adapted for other studies possibly in other areas.

In this paper, water depth, water temperature, flow velocity and water quality (TP) are taken into account. The relationship between the habitat suitability Z and these parameters is given by the follow equation [10]:

$$
\begin{aligned}
Z = \exp(a - b_1 \times x_1 - b_2 \times x_2 - b_3 \times x_3 + b_4 * x_4 \\
+ b_5 \times x_2 \times x_3 + b_6 \times x_3 \times x_4 + b_7 \times x_1 \times x_3 \\
+ b_8 \times x_2 \times x_3 \times x_4)
\end{aligned}
\tag{1}
$$

where Z is the habitat suitability of evaluation species; x_1 is water depth, the value between 0.2m to 3.5m; x_2 is river/lake temperature, the value between 0℃ to 40℃; x_3 is flow velocity, the value between 0m/s to 2m/s; x_4 is the concentration of TP; a is constant; b_1 L b_8 are regression coefficients;

The equation (1) is only valid the concentration of TP between 0 and 25μg/l. When the concentration of TP exceeds 25μg/l, the relationship between the suitability Z and these parameters is transformed to the follow equation:

$$Z = \exp(c - d_1 \times x_1 - d_2 \times x_2 - d_3 \times x_3 - d_4 \times x_4$$
$$+ d_5 \times x_2 \times x_4 + d_6 \times x_3 \times x_4 - d_7 \times x_2 \times x_3 \times x_4) \tag{2}$$

where x_4 is the concentration of TP, the value large than 25μg/l ; c is constant; d_1 L d_7 are regression coefficients;

All the regression coefficients can be get from HSI value using multiply regression. The probability of occurrence of evaluation species is presented as below.

$$P(Z) = Z / (1 + Z) \tag{3}$$

where P represents the probability of occurrence. It can be shown that the probability of occurrence for each location, each area, or each computational grid cell. The probability of occurrence can be converted to a habitat suitability index value.

2.2 Habitat Suitability Index

Habitat quality for selected evaluation species is documented with a Habitat Suitability Index (HSI) value. This value is derived from an evaluation of the ability of key habitat components to supply the life requisites of selected evaluation species. If the HSI value is equal to 1, this indicates that the suitability of the location is optimal for a certain habitat type. If the HSI value is lower than 1, this indicates that one or more of the parameters included in the model is limited. When the HSI value is 0, the location is not suitable[11].

HABITAT model allows users to analyses the ecological functioning of study areas in an integrated and flexible manner. The steps are described as follows: ① investigate the species information in study area from site visit; ② build up the HABITAT model; ③ prepare the relative GIS maps; ④ estimate the effect of water quality parameters on the habitats in study area; ⑤ run the model and get the result.

The schematic diagram of the HABITAT model is shown in Figure 1.

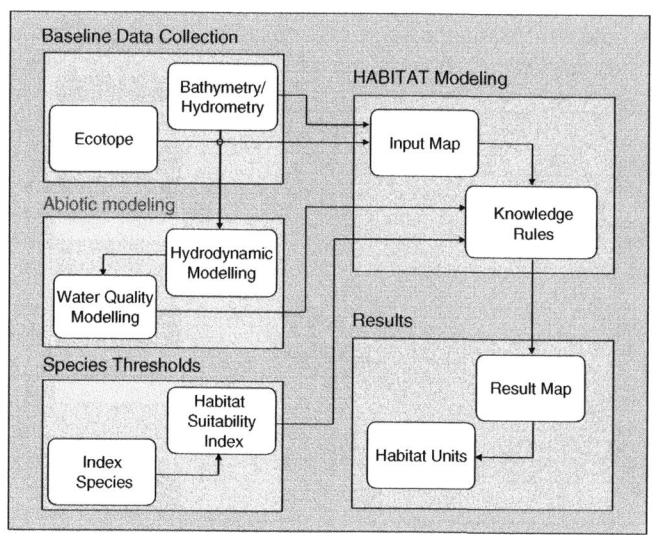

Fig. 1. Schematic Diagram of the HABITAT Model

3   Case Study

3.1   Study Area

Lugu Lake is situated in the southwestern china, connecting Yunnan with Sichuan province. The study area is shown in Figure 2. The mean depth of the lake is 40.3m, and the maximum depth is 93.5m. The Lugu Lake is about 9.4km in length and 5.2km in mean width. It is 48.45km^2 in surface area and 171.4km^2 in catchments area[12].

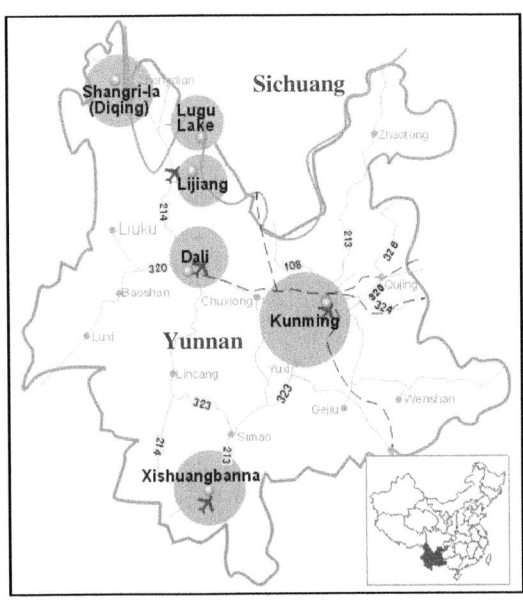

Fig. 2. Map of the Study Area

There are many villages scattered around the lake. The best-known two villages are Luoshui and Dazu, which are the main tourist centers of the area. The position of the two villages is shown in Figure 3. With the development of the tourism industry, Lugu Lake attracts numerous tourists come to the village to break down their past tranquility and destroy the environment. As a result, the water quality decreases and nutrient increases, which even lead to the eutrophication. There is a worsening tendency for the lake's ecology. The lake can no longer endure the disordered development and there are three special kinds of fish on the verge of extinction. To protect the those fish and to provide the criteria plans for the following wide of ranges lake management and eco-logical impact assessment, the relationship between environmental factors and habitat distribution should be known very clearly. In this paper, two villages were selected to analyze: Dazu village in Sichuan Province and Luoshui Village in Yunnan Province. The water quality was simulated by Delft-3D, and a habitat assessment model was built up based on HABITAT model.

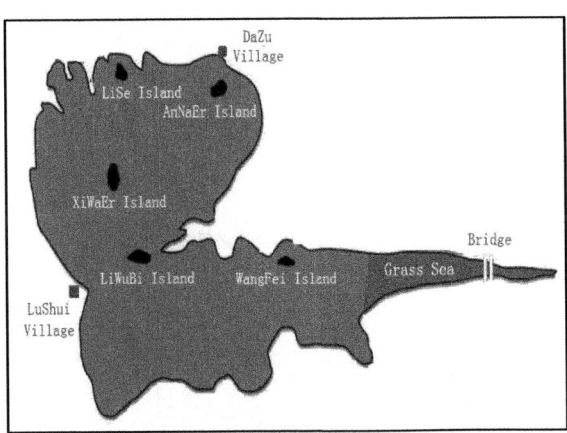

Fig. 3. Map of Lugu Lake

3.2 Selection of Evaluation Species

The criteria applied in the paper for selection of evaluation species are: ① sensitivity to environmental factors change; ② ecological importance in the local community and in the food chain; ③ perceived value to human society; and ④ availability for habitat suitability functions or information that could be translated into suitability functions. Based on the site visit and combined the criteria for selection of evaluation species, the evaluation species of this impact analysis focused on the special species of Yunnan Province: Schizothorax Yunnansis. Schizothorax Yunnansis is a unique fish species in Lugu Lake. Now, it is in endangering status. Sand, mud, and rock- habitat were not considered in this impact assessment. All the habitat suitability functions of the Schizothorax Yunnansis were found in the literature.

3.3 HSI of Evaluation Species

The HSI value of temperature for Schizothorax Yunnansis in this study is received from literature review. The HSI Graph of Schizothorax Yunnansis is shown in Figure 4. From the Figure 4, it can be seen very clearly that the temperature at a certain location is less than 26°C, but above 18°C, the suitable value for Schizothorax Yunnansis is 1. When temperatures are above 39°C or less than 3°C, no Schizothorax Yunnansis will survive at that location. The tolerance limits of Schizothorax Yunnansis for TP is in the range from 10µg/l to 100µg/l. When the concentration of TP in the range from 12µg/l to 25µg/l, the HSI value equals to 1; when the TP concentration increases all the way, the HSI value will decrease to 0. When the TP concentration exceeds 100µg/l, this concentration is considered lethal[13-15].

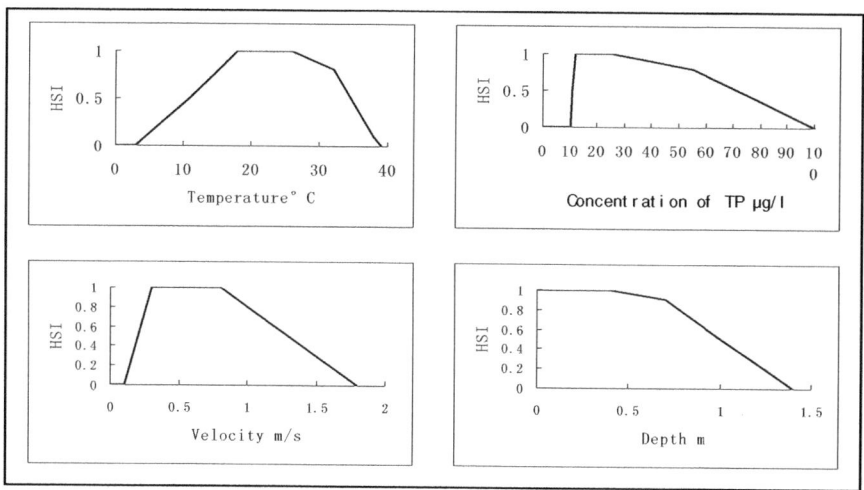

Fig. 4. HSI Graph of Schizothorax Yunnansis

3.4 Water Quality Modeling

The study area was meshed and the meshing figure of its water depth and temperature were created according to the actual investigation. Water pollution is mainly due to the Lugu Lake tourist and local residents living source, considering the Lugu Lake tourist is in Dazu village and Luoshui village compared with developed area, therefore the two villages are regarded as the source of pollution. The Delft-3D water quality model was built up and forecast results in 2010 and 2060 can be obtained, which can be used as input data in the HABITAT model.

3.5 Different Scenarios

At the beginning of simulation, the original situation of the evaluation species' habitat distributions in the Lugu Lake should be considered. Because Lugu Lake belongs to two provinces, there are four assumptions presented here: (a) there is no pollution falling into the Lugu Lake; (b) the pollution only falls into Yunnan Province part; (c) the pollution only falls into Sichuan Province part; (d) the pollution falls into the two provinces.

The habitat changes in the year 2010 and 2060 are presented for the four assumptions respectively. The concentration of total phosphate (TP) is assumed to be increased by 4% per year from 2010 to 2060, and the water quality results maps are provided by the Delft3D-WAQ model results. Based on the four assumptions, the different Scenarios in Lugu Lake are shown in Table 1.

Table 1. Description of the Different Scenarios in Lugu Lake Case

Scenarios	Evaluation Species	Decision rules	Pollution	Years
Scenario 1	Schizothorax Yunnansis	Temperature/Depth/Velocity	NA	2010 2060
Scenario 2	Schizothorax Yunnansis	Temperature/Depth/Velocity/TP	Luoshui Village	2010 2060
Scenario 3	Schizothorax Yunnansis	Temperature/Depth/Velocity/TP	Dazu Village	2010 2060
Scenario 4	Schizothorax Yunnansis	Temperature/Depth/Velocity/TP	Both	2010 2060

3.6 Simulation Results

The model results are presented in terms of changes in the water quality parameters of the four scenarios. The water temperature is considered to be 18 °C and the results are discussed below.

① No pollution falls into the Lugu Lake

The habitat distributions for Schizothorax Yunnansis in Scenario 1 are shown in Figure 5. The high value means the high habitat suitability, and the low value means the low habitat suitability. The Figure 5-(a) and Figure 5-(b) are shown the habitat suitability of Schizothorax Yunnansis in the year 2010 and 2060 respectively. Compared with the Figures 5-(a) and (b), it can be seen that the deep color area of Figure 5-(b) increase that means few Schizothorax Yunnansis can live in that location.

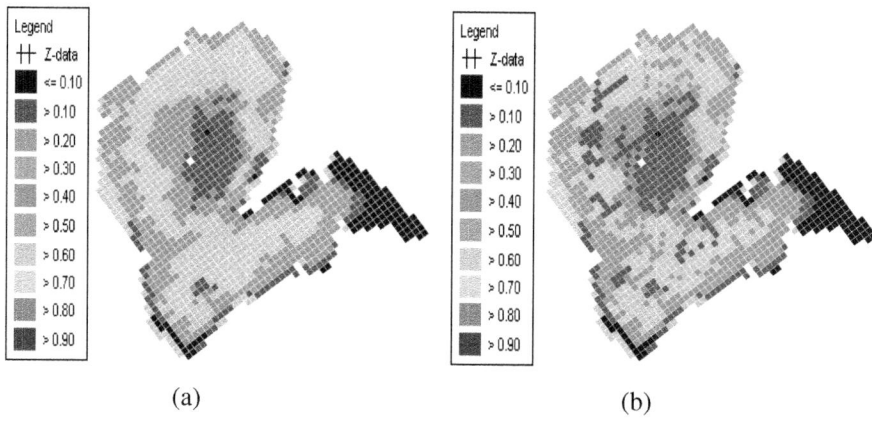

(a)   (b)

Fig. 5. Habitat Distributions for Schizothorax Yunnansis (Scenario 1)

② The pollution only falls into Lugu Lake from Luoshui village

The habitat distributions for Schizothorax Yunnansis in Scenario 2 are shown in Figure 6. Compared with the Figure 5, the habitat suitability area of Schizothorax Yunnansis near the Luoshui village increased, which means more appropriate Schizothorax Yunnansis survival. The reason is that the emissions of phosphate in a certain range can be as nutrients of Schizothorax Yunnansis, thus to facilitate its growth. But to 2060 years, along with the TP concentration increasing, toxic is produced in the body of Schizothorax Yunnansis and cause Schizothorax Yunnansis to be death. Therefore, the water near the Luoshui village has completely unsuited for Schizothorax Yunnansis survival.

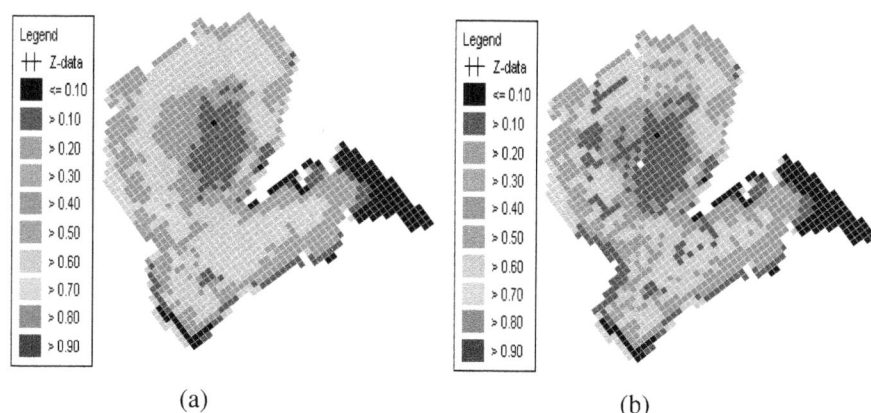

(a)   (b)

Fig. 6. Habitat Distribution for Schizothorax Yunnansis (Scenario 2)

③ The pollution only falls into Lugu Lake from Dazu village

The habitat distributions for Schizothorax Yunnansis in Scenario 3 are illustrated in Figure 7. It can be seen the habitat suitability area near Dazu village was increasing due to the same reason of scenario 2. However, the water quality near Dazu village is unsuitable for the survival of Schizothorax Yunnansis in 2060.

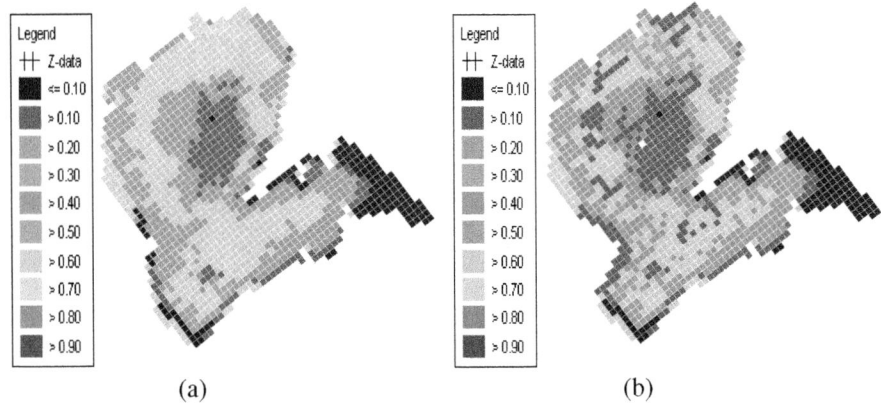

(a)   (b)

Fig. 7. Habitat Distributions for Schizothorax Yunnansis (Scenario 3)

④ The pollution falls into Lugu Lake from Luoshui village and Dazu village

The habitat distributions for Schizothorax Yunnansis in Scenario 4 are shown in Figure 8. When the lake received the TP pollution from the two villages, which arrive at 12μg/l (Dazu village) and 15μg/l (Luoshui village), respectively, the result maps show that the evaluation species' area increased. That is because the TP concentration increased from 2μg/l to 12μg/l and 15μg/l, the HSI value also increased to 0.8 and 1.0.

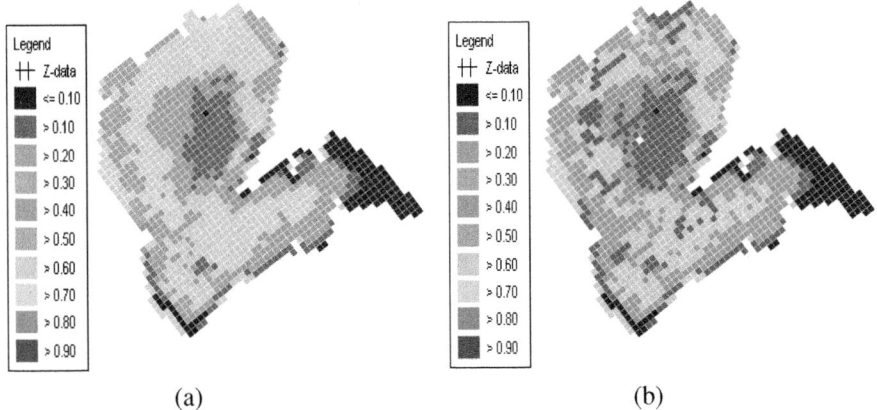

(a)   (b)

Fig. 8. Habitat Distribution for Schizothorax Yunnansis (Scenario 4)

Therefore, more Schizothorax Yunnansis can live in that location and habitat suitability area increases. But 50 years later, the TP concentration grows to 85.3µg/l and 106.6µg/l, and the HSI decreases to 0.2 and 0, respectively. Then, the habitat suitability area for Schizothorax Yunnansis decreases significantly in 50 years.

From all the figures, it can be seen very clearly when the water pollutants concentration does not exceed Schizothorax Yunnansis existent threshold, the suitable habitat area for Schizothorax Yunnansis increases, otherwise the unsuitable habitat area increases.

4 Conclusions

This paper built an assessment model of the water quality and the Schizothorax Yunnansis's habitat using habitat evaluation method based on HABITAT model. The results show that when the Lugu Lake water pollutants' concentration does not exceed Schizothorax Yunnansis' survival threshold, Schizothorax Yunnansis gets more nutrients and suitable habitat area increased. Conversely, when the Lugu Lake water pollutants' concentration exceeds Schizothorax Yunnansis' survival threshold, it may even cause Schizothorax Yunnansis's death and unsuitable habitat area increased.

The results presented in this paper is shown that HABITAT model can assist in ecological impact assessment studies by translating results of hydrological, water quality models into effects on the natural environment and human society. It also can provide the basis of watershed comprehensive research and scientific management for the southwestern region of China.

Due to the lack of much monitoring data, the results biased to the actual situation in this work. In addition, only four factors are considered: the temperature, the depth of water, the flow velocity and the TP concentration. The four factors providing existent environment for species are considered to be independent, but they have some intertwined relationship. Therefore, in the future works, bias analysis of computing results and synthetically affecting species' survival environment by four factors should be reinforced.

References

1. Mynett, A.: Science-Technology and Management Panel, Hydroinformatics in ecosystem restauration and management. In: 3rd World Water Forum, Japan (2003)
2. Mynett, A.: Hydroinformatics Tools for Ecohydraulics Modeling. In: International Conference on Hydroinformatics, Singapore (2004)
3. Knudby, A., Brenning, A., LeDrew, E.: New approaches to modelling fish-habitat relationships. J. Ecological Modelling 221, 503–511 (2009)
4. Bovee, K.: Guide to stream habitat analysis using the instream flow incremental methodology. Western Energy and Land Use Team, Office of Biological Services, Fish and Wildlife Service, vol. 248, U.S. Dept. of the Interior (1982)
5. Bovee, K., Lamb, B., Bartholow, J., Stalnaker, C., Taylor, J., Henriksen, J.: Stream habitat analysis using the instream flow incremental methodology. Biological Resources Division Information and Technology Report USGS (1998)

6. Hao, Z., Shang, S.: Multi-objective assessment method based on physical habitat simulation for calculating ecological river flow demand. J. Journal of Hydraulic Engineering 39, 557–561 (2008)

7. Hayes, J., Jowett, I.: Microhabitat models of large drift-feeding brown trout in three New Zealand rivers. J. North American Journal of Fisheries Management 14, 710–725 (1994)

8. Binns, N., Eiserman, F.: Quantification of fluvial trout habitat in Wyoming. J. Transactions of the American Fisheries Society 108, 215–228 (1979)

9. Haasnoot, M., Verkade, J., Bruijn, K.: HABITAT, A Spatial Analysis Tool for Environmental Impact and Damage Assessment. In: 8th Hydroinformatics Conference, Chile (2009)

10. Haasnoot, M., Kranenbarg, J., Van Buren, J.: Seizoensgebonden peilen in het IJsselmeergebied, Verkenning naar optimalisatie van het peil voor natuur binnen de randvoorwaarden van veiligheid, scheepvaart en watervoorziening (2005) (in Dutch)

11. User's manual and exercise of Physical Habitat Simulation Software: USGS

12. Jin, J., Yang, F.: Preliminary analysis on the hydrological Characteristics of Lake Lugu. J. Chinese Academy of Sciences 3, 214–225 (1983)

13. Chen, Y., Zhang, W., Huang, S.: Speciation in Schinzothoracid Fishes of Lugu Lake (in Chinese). J. Acta Zoologica Sinica 28, 217–225 (1982)

14. Chen, Y.: The Fishes of the Hendduan Mountains Region (in Chinese). Science Press, Beijing (1998)

15. Jýrgensen, S., Costanza, R., Xu, F.: Handbook of ecological indicators for assessment of ecosystem health. CRC Press, Florida (2005)

Internet SCADA Utilizing API's as Data Source

Rosslin John Robles[1], Haeng-kon Kim[2], and Tai-hoon Kim[1,*]

[1] Multimedia Engineering Department, Hannam University,
Daejeon, Korea
[2] Dept. of Computer and Communication, Catholic Univ. of DaeGu, Korea
rosslin_john@yahoo.com, taihoonn@hnu.kr

Abstract. An Application programming interface or API is an interface implemented by a software program that enables it to interact with other software. Many companies provide free API services which can be utilized in Control Systems. SCADA is an example of a control system and it is a system that collects data from various sensors at a factory, plant or in other remote locations and then sends this data to a central computer which then manages and controls the data. In this paper, we designed a scheme for Weather Condition in Internet SCADA Environment utilizing data from external API services. The scheme was designed to double check the weather information in SCADA.

Keywords: SCADA, Control Systems, API, Control Systems.

1 Introduction

SCADA stands for Supervisory Control and Data Acquisition. SCADA refers to a system that collects data from various sensors at a factory, plant or in other remote locations and then sends this data to a central computer which then manages and controls the data. Data acquisition is the process of retrieving control information from the equipment which is out of order or may lead to some problem or when decisions are need to be taken according to the situation in the equipment. So this acquisition is done by continuous monitoring of the equipment to which it is employed. The data accessed are then forwarded onto a telemetry system ready for transfer to the different sites. To improve the accuracy of data and to improve the performance of SCADA systems, we design a double checking scheme for Weather. This scheme uses data from weather API Providers. Many API Provider such as Google, Yahoo, etc have Weather API's. Weather API's can give weather condition and forecast about a specific place.

2 SCADA and API

2.1 SCADA Systems

Supervisory Control and Data Acquisition software can be divided into proprietary type or open type. Proprietary software are developed and designed for the specific

---

* Corresponding author.

T.-h. Kim et al. (Eds.): SecTech/DRBC 2010, CCIS 122, pp. 269–275, 2010.
© Springer-Verlag Berlin Heidelberg 2010

hardware and are usually sold together. The main problem with these systems is the overwhelming reliance on the supplier of the system. Open software systems are designed to communicate and control different types of hardware. It is popular because of the interoperability they bring to the system. [1] WonderWare and Citect are just two of the open software packages available in the market for SCADA systems. Some packages are now including asset management integrated within the SCADA system.

Typically SCADA systems include the following components: [2]

1. Operating equipment such as pumps, valves, conveyors and substation breakers that can be controlled by energizing actuators or relays.
2. Local processors that communicate with the site's instruments and operating equipment.
3. Instruments in the field or in a facility that sense conditions such as pH, temperature, pressure, power level and flow rate.
4. Short range communications between the local processors and the instruments and operating equipment.
5. Long range communications between the local processors and host computers.
6. Host computers that act as the central point of monitoring and control.

The measurement and control system of SCADA has one master terminal unit (MTU) which could be called the brain of the system and one or more remote terminal units (RTU). The RTUs gather the data locally and send them to the MTU which then issues suitable commands to be executed on site. A system of either standard or customized software is used to collate, interpret and manage the data.

Supervisory Control and Data Acquisition (SCADA) is conventionally set upped in a private network not connected to the internet. This is done for the purpose of isolating the confidential information as well as the control to the system itself. Because of the distance, processing of reports and the emerging technologies, SCADA can now be connected to the internet. This can bring a lot of advantages and disadvantages which will be discussed in the sections.

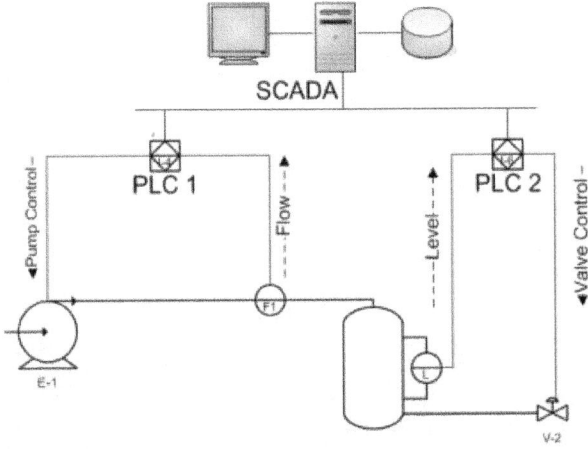

Fig. 1. Typical SCADA System

Conventionally, relay logic was used to control production and plant systems. With the discovery of the CPU and other electronic devices, manufacturers incorporated digital electronics into relay logic equipment. Programmable logic controllers or PLC's are still the most widely used control systems in industry. As need to monitor and control more devices in the plant grew, the PLCs were distributed and the systems became more intelligent and smaller in size. PLCs (Programmable logic controllers) and DCS (distributed control systems) are used as shown in Figure 1.

2.1.1 Hardware and Software
SCADA systems are an extremely advantageous way to run and monitor processes. They are great for small applications such as climate control or can be effectively used in large applications such as monitoring and controlling a nuclear power plant or mass transit system.

SCADA can come in open and non proprietary protocols. Smaller systems are extremely affordable and can either be purchased as a complete system or can be mixed and matched with specific components. Large systems can also be created with off the shelf components. SCADA system software can also be easily configured for almost any application, removing the need for custom made or intensive software development.

2.1.2 Human Machine Interface
SCADA system includes a user interface which is usually called Human Machine Interface (HMI). The HMI of a SCADA system is where data is processed and

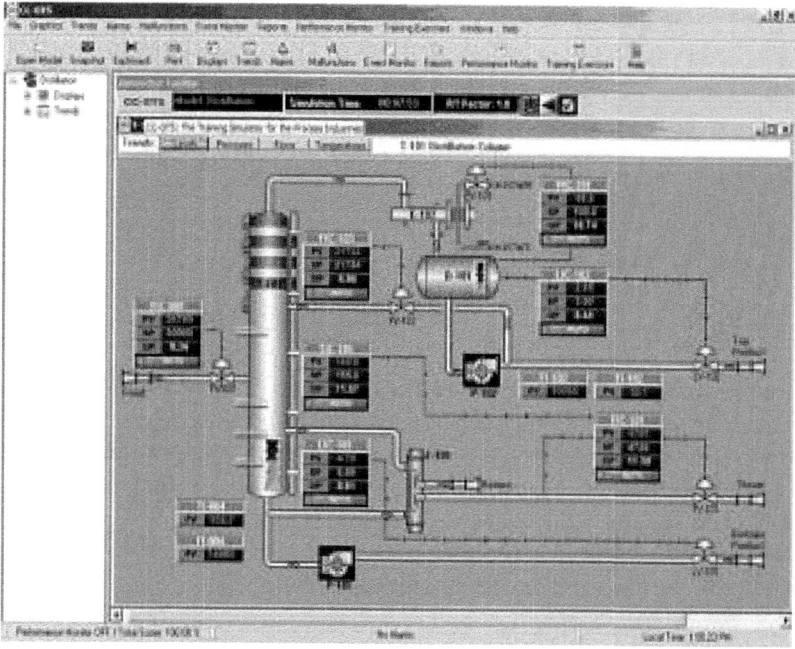

Fig. 2. Human Machine Interface of SCADA

presented to be viewed and monitored by a human operator. This interface usually includes controls where the individual can interface with the SCADA system. HMI's are an easy way to standardize the facilitation of monitoring multiple RTU's or PLC's (programmable logic controllers). Usually RTU's or PLC's will run a pre programmed process, but monitoring each of them individually can be difficult, usually because they are spread out over the system. Because RTU's and PLC's historically had no standardized method to display or present data to an operator, the SCADA system communicates with PLC's throughout the system network and processes information that is easily disseminated by the HMI. HMI's can also be linked to a database, which can use data gathered from PLC's or RTU's to provide graphs on trends, logistic info, schematics for a specific sensor or machine or even make troubleshooting guides accessible. In the last decade, practically all SCADA systems include an integrated HMI and PLC device making it extremely easy to run and monitor a SCADA system.

2.2 Application Program Interface

API's or application program interface, are set of routines, protocols, and tools for building software applications. A good API makes it easier to develop a program by providing all the building blocks. A programmer then puts the blocks together. [5]

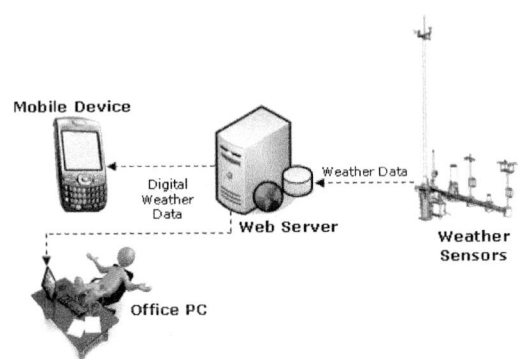

Fig. 3. Data transmission of Weather API's

   Most operating environments, such as MS-Windows, provide an API so that programmers can write applications consistent with the operating environment. Although APIs are designed for programmers, they are ultimately good for users because they guarantee that all programs using a common API will have similar interfaces. This makes it easier for users to learn new programs. [5]

   Many API Provider such as Google, Yahoo, etc have Weather API's. Weather API's can give weather condition and forecast about a specific place.

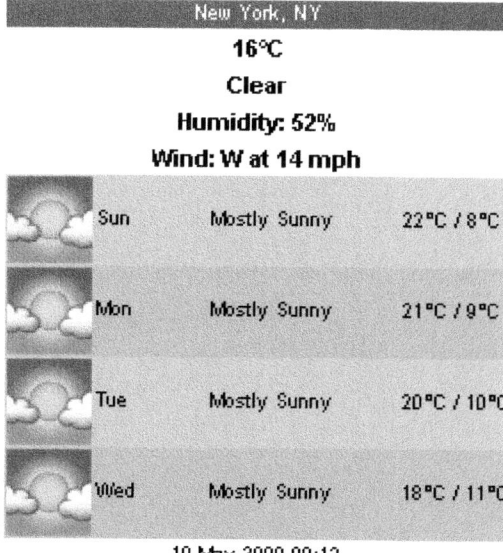

Fig. 4. An Example of Weather API

3 Proposed Solution

Weather API's can be integration to SCADA systems to double check the weather condition. Weather sensors of SCADA systems may not gather correct data. This is very crucial and integration of API's can improve the data gathered.

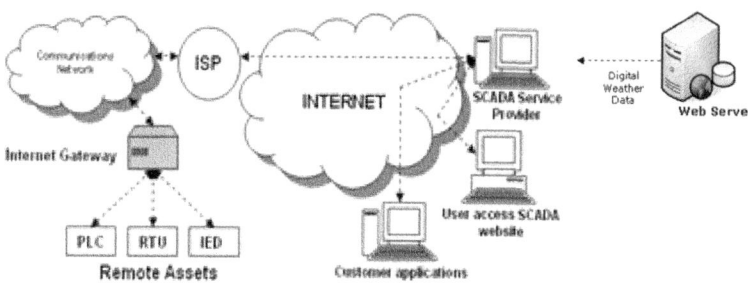

Fig. 5. SCADA Service Provider getting information from API service server

SCADA controller or SCADA master station can get both data from the sensor (x) and the data from the Weather API (γ). Usually, the controller only bases the commands on the sensor data. Since we integrate the Weather API to the system, we can also gather its data and we propose to get the average between the Sensor data and the API's data to get the base data (λ) in which the commands will be based.

$$\lambda = (x + \gamma) / 2 \qquad (1)$$

Formula (1) will be the bases of the SCADA Controller in executing commands to the remote terminals. In Figure 6, we can see the comparison between the gathered Sensor data, API data and the average data. We will notice that there's sometimes a difference between the Sensor data and API data.

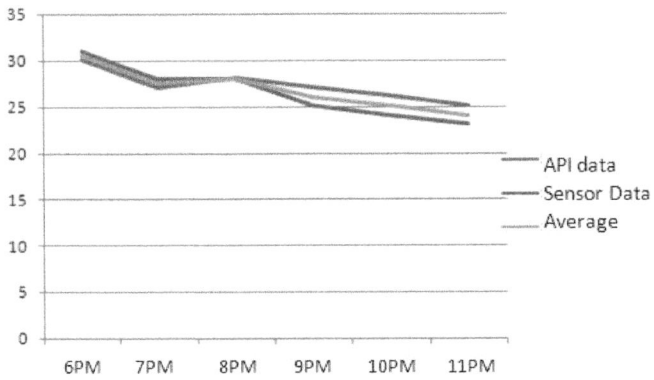

Fig. 6. Comparisons of Gathered Sensor Data, API Data and the Average

4 Conclusion

SCADA systems are used to monitor and control a plant or equipment in industries such as telecommunications, water and waste control, energy, oil and gas refining and transportation. A SCADA system gathers information, such as where a leak on a pipeline has occurred, transfers the information back to a central site, alerting the home station that the leak has occurred, carrying out necessary analysis and control, such as determining if the leak is critical, and displaying the information in a logical and organized fashion. SCADA systems can be relatively simple, such as one that monitors environmental conditions of a small office building, or incredibly complex, such as a system that monitors all the activity in a nuclear power plant or the activity of a municipal water system.The data that is gathered by the system is very important. The system reacts to the data it gets. Imagine what will happen if the data is not accurate. It can damage the society. To improve the accuracy of data and to improve the performance of SCADA systems, we design a double checking scheme for Weather Condition in Internet SCADA Environment. This scheme uses data from weather API Providers. Many API Provider such as Google, Yahoo, etc have Weather API services.

Acknowledgement. This work was supported by the Security Engineering Research Center, granted by the Korean Ministry of Knowledge Economy.

References

1. Bailey, D., Wright, E.: Practical SCADA for Industry (2003)
2. Hildick-Smith, A.: Security for Critical Infrastructure SCADA Systems (2005)
3. Wallace, D.: Control Engineering. How to put SCADA on the Internet (2003),
   http://www.controleng.com/article/CA321065.html
   (accessed: January 2009)
4. Internet and Web-based SCADA,
   http://www.scadalink.com/technotesIP.htm (accessed January 2009)
5. What is API? A word definition from the Webopedia Computer Dictionary,
   http://www.webopedia.com/TERM/A/API.html (accessed April 2010)

Insecure Information System's Solution Using Isolation Method

Maricel Balitanas and Tai-hoon Kim[*]

Multimedia Engineering Department, Hannam University,
133 Ojeong-dong, Daeduk-gu, Daejeon, Korea
jhe-c1756@yahoo.com, taihoonn@hnu.kr

Abstract. In this paper, we define Intrusion Confinement through isolation to address such security issue, its importance and finally present an isolation protocol. Security has emerged as the biggest threat to information systems. System protection mechanisms such as access controls can be fooled by authorized but malicious users, masqueraders, and trespassers. As a result, serious damage can be caused either because many intrusions are never detected or because the average detection latency is too long.

Keywords: Intrusion detection, Isolation, Information Systems.

1 Introduction

The methodology of intrusion can be roughly classed as being either based on statistical profile or known patterns of attacks, called signatures or another classification, the anomaly-based. In Anomaly-based, system detects computer intrusion and misuse by monitoring system activity and classifying it as either normal or anomalous. Intrusion detection is a type of security management system for computer and networks. An ID gathers and analyzes information from various areas within a computer or a network to identify possible security breaches, which includes both intrusion (attack from outside the organization) and misuse (attack from within the organization)[1].The latter case includes seemingly authorized users, such as masqueraders operating under another user's identification (ID) and password, or outside attackers who successfully gained systems access but eluded detection of the method of entry. In this paper we solely concentrate in the Statistical profile-based system. In the following section we define further the Statistical profile-based system, Intrusion confinement thru isolation and the importance. We also present an isolation protocol in the file system.

Importance of intrusion confinement Statistical profile-based system compare relevant data by statistical or other methods to representative profiles of normal, expected activity on the system or network [2]. Deviations indicate suspicious behavior. In these systems, there are stringent requirements on not only reporting an intrusion accurately (this is necessary because abnormal behavior is not always an intrusion) but also detecting as many intrusions as possible (usually, not all intrusions can be

---

[*] Corresponding author.

T.-h. Kim et al. (Eds.): SecTech/DRBC 2010, CCIS 122, pp. 276–281, 2010.
© Springer-Verlag Berlin Heidelberg 2010

detected. Based on the assumption the more significant the deviation, the larger the possibility that the behavior of a user is an intrusion, in order to ensure a high degree of intrusion reporting, significant anomaly is required to raise a warning. Moreover, when the anomaly of an intrusion is accumulated, detecting it can still cause a long latency even if it is characterized by significant anomaly. As a result, substantial damage can be caused by an intruder within the latency.

2 Suspicious Behaviors

Suspicious behavior is the behavior that may have already caused some damage, or may cause some damage later on, but was not reported as an intrusion when it happened. Suspicious behavior emerges in several situations:

In statistical profile-based detection:

(a) In order to get a high degree of soundness of intrusion reporting, some intrusions characterized by gradual deviations may stay undetected. The corresponding behaviors can be reported as suspicious.
(b) For a detection with a long latency, the corresponding behavior can be reported as suspicious in the middle of the latency.
(c) Legitimate behavior can be reported as suspicious if it is sufficiently unlike the corresponding profile.

(2) In signature-based detection, partial matching of a signature can trigger a report of suspicious behavior.

3 Profile-Based Detection

A statistical profile-based detection system, a user Ui accesses the system through sessions. A session of Ui begins when Ui logs in and ends when Ui logs out. A behavior of Ui is a sequence of actions that can last across the boundaries of sessions. A short term behavior of Ui is a behavior that is composed of a sequence of Ui's most recent actions. In contrast, a long term behavior of Ui is also a sequence of Ui's most recent actions but it is much longer than the short term behavior. We assume the intrusion detector is triggered in every m actions (or m audit records), that is, after m new actions are executed, both the current short term behavior and long term behavior of Ui will be upgraded and the deviation of the new short term behavior from the new long term behavior will be computed. When a short term behavior is upgraded, its oldest m actions will be discarded and the newest m actions will be added.

3.1 Signature-Based Detection

A sequence of signature-based events leading from an initial to a final compromised state are specify [3].

Each event causes a state transition from one state to another state. We identify a signature with length n, denoted sig(n), as $sig(n) = s0E1s1...En$, where Ei is an event and si is a state, and Ei causes the state transition from si-1 to si. For simplicity, intra-event conditions are not explicitly shown in sig(n), although they are usually part of a signature.

A partial matching of a signature sig(n) is a sequence of events that matches a prefix of sig(n), A partial matching is not an intrusion, however, it can predict that an intrusion specified by sig(n) may occur. The accuracy of the prediction of a partial matching, denoted s0E1s1...Emsm, can be measured by the following parameter: Pm, the probability that the partial matching can lead to an intrusion later. Assume the number of the behaviors that match the prefix is Np and the number of the intrusions that match the prefix is Ni, then Pm = Ni / Np.

In signature-based detection, the set of actions that should be isolated is defined as follows. Isolating suspicious behavior can surely confine damage in signature-based detection because the behavior that is actually an intrusion will, with a high probability, be prevented from doing harm to the system.

In signature-based detection, a behavior is suspicious if it matches the prefix of a signature but not the whole signature, and Pm of the prefix is greater than or equal to a threshold that is determined by the SSO.

3.2   Application of Intrusion Confinement Support

In signature-based detection, the decision of whether to enforce intrusion confinement on a known attack that is specified by a signature is dependent on the seriousness of the damage that will be caused by the attack and the value of Pm for each prefix of the signature.

In statistical profile-based detection, however, it can be tricky to make the decision since degrading the requirement on Re usually can improve Rd, the SSO may want to find a tradeoff between Rd and Re; thus, the cost of isolation would be avoided. However, a satisfactory tradeoff may not be achievable in some systems since the relationship between Rd and Re can dramatically differ from one system to another.

3.2.1   Architecture Support
The Policy Enforcement Manager enforces the access controls in accordance with the system security policy on every access request [4]. We assume no data access can bypass it. We further assume that users' accesses will be audited in the audit trail.

The Intrusion Detection and Confinement Manager applies either statistical profile-based detection techniques or signature-based detection techniques, or both to identify suspicious behavior as well as intrusions. The detection is typically processed based on the information provided by the audit trail.

Architecture of an intrusion confinement system in information welfare perspective is showed in Figure 1.

When a suspicious behavior is detected, the corresponding user is marked suspicious. At this point, first we need to deal with the effects that the user has already made on the Main Data Version because these effects may have already caused some damage. In signature-based detection systems, we can accept these effects because a partial matching is not an intrusion. In statistical profile-based detection systems, if the SSO does not think these effects can cause any serious damage, we can accept these effects; if the SSO thinks these effects can cause intolerable damage, we can isolate and move these effects from the main data version to a separate Suspicious Data Version, which is created to isolate the user. The process of isolation may need to roll back some trustworthy actions that are dependent on the suspicious actions. At

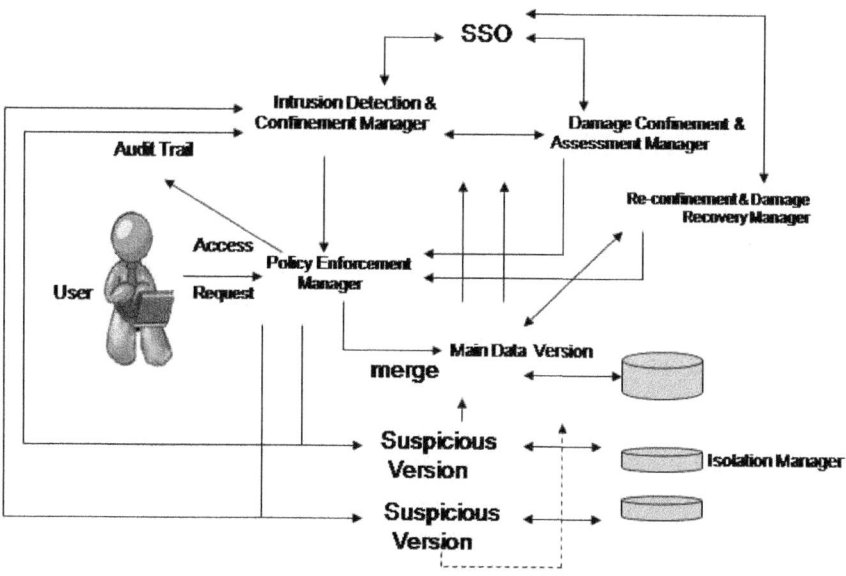

Fig. 1. Architecture of the Intrusion Confinement System

this point, we can apply another strategy that moves the effects of these suspicious actions as well as the affected trustworthy actions to the suspicious data version.

Second, the Intrusion Detection and Confinement Manager notify the Policy Enforcement Manager to direct the subsequent suspicious actions of the user to the separate data version. Since we focus on the isolation itself, we can simply assume that when a suspicious behavior starts to be isolated, no damage has been caused by the behavior. Note that there can be several different suspicious users, e.g., S1,...., Sn, being isolated at the same time. Therefore, multiple suspicious data versions can exist at the same time.

When a suspicious user turns out to be malicious, that is, his/her behavior has led to an intrusion; the corresponding suspicious data version can be discarded to protect the main data version from harm. On the other hand, when the user turns out to be innocent, the corresponding suspicious data version is merged into the main data version.

A suspicious behavior can be malicious in several ways:

(1) In signature-based detection, a complete matching can change a suspicious behavior to malicious.
(2) Some statistics of gradual anomaly, such as frequency and total number, can make the SSO believe that a suspicious behavior is malicious.
(3) The SSO can find that a suspicious behavior is malicious based on some nontechnical evidences.

A suspicious behavior can be innocent in several ways:

(1) In signature-based detection, when no signatures can be matched, the behavior proves innocent.

(2) The SSO can prove it to be innocent by some nontechnical evidence. For example, the SSO can investigate the user directly.
(3) Some statistics of gradual anomaly can also make the SSO believe that a behavior is innocent.

After the damage is assessed, the Reconfiguration Manager reconfigures the system to allow access to continue in a degraded mode while repair is being done by the Damage Recovery Manager. In many situations damage assessment and recovery are coupled with each other closely. For example, recovery from damage can occur during the process of identifying and assessing damage. Also, the system can be continuously reconfigured to reject accesses to newly identified, damaged data objects and to allow access to newly recovered data objects. Interested readers can refer to [5] for more details on damage confinement, damage assessment, system reconfiguration, and damage recovery mechanisms in the database context.

4 The Isolation Protocol

The isolation protocol which is specified as follows is adapted from [6], where a protocol is proposed to detect and resolve mutual inconsistency in distributed file systems. In this protocol, the isolation is processed in terms of each file. When a file fi is modified by a suspicious user Si, the modification and the possible following modifications of Si on fi will be isolated until Si proves to be malicious or innocent. To identify the conflicts between the modifications of Si on fi and the modifications of trustworthy users on fi we associate a version vector with the main version and every isolated version of fi.

To identify and resolve the conflicts between these two versions, we need to first pad the suspicious version vector such that the two vectors have the same set of dimensions. The padding is done by inserting each missed dimension with the value 0 into the suspicious version vector.

5 Conclusion

In this paper we have shown that a second level in addition to access control intrusion confinement can dramatically enhance the security especially integrity and availability of a system in many situation. It showed that intrusion confinement can effectively resolve the conflicting design goals of an intrusion detection system by achieving both a high rate of detection and a low rate of errors. Developing a more concrete isolation protocols will further be studied in our future research.

Acknowledgment

This work was supported by the Security Engineering Research Center, granted by the Korean Ministry of Knowledge Economy.

References

[1] Graubart, R., Schlipper, L., McCollum, C.: Defending database management systems against information warfare attacks. Technical report, The MITRE Corporation (1996)

[2] Ammann, P., Jajodia, S., Liu, P.: Recovery from malicious transactions. Technical report, George Mason University, Fairfax, VA,
`http://www.isse.gmu.edu/~pliu/papers/dynamic.ps`

[3] Jajodia, S., Liu, P., McCollum, C.: Applicationlevel isolation to cope with malicious database users. In: Proceedings of the 14th Annual Computer Security Application Conference, Phoenix, AZ, pp. 73–82 (1998)

[4] Northcutt, S.: Network Intrusion Detection. New Riders, Indianapolis (1999)

[5] Ilgun, K., Kemmerer, R., Porras, P.: State transition analysis: A rulebased intrusion detection approach. IEEE Transactions on Software Engineering 21(3), 181–199 (1995)

Communication Security for Control Systems in Smart Grid

Rosslin John Robles and Tai-hoon Kim[*]

[1] Multimedia Engineering Department, Hannam University,
Daejeon, Korea
rosslin_john@yahoo.com, taihoonn@hnu.kr

Abstract. As an example of Control System, Supervisory Control and Data Acquisition systems can be relatively simple, such as one that monitors environmental conditions of a small office building, or incredibly complex, such as a system that monitors all the activity in a nuclear power plant or the activity of a municipal water system. SCADA systems are basically Process Control Systems, designed to automate systems such as traffic control, power grid management, waste processing etc. Connecting SCADA to the Internet can provide a lot of advantages in terms of control, data viewing and generation. SCADA infrastructures like electricity can also be a part of a Smart Grid. Connecting SCADA to a public network can bring a lot of security issues. To answer the security issues, a SCADA communication security solution is proposed.

Keywords: SCADA, Security Issues, Encryption, Crossed Crypto-scheme, Smart Gird.

1 Introduction

Smart Grid refers to an improved electricity supply chain that runs from a major power plant all the way inside your home. In short, there are thousands of power plants throughout the United States that generate electricity using wind energy, nuclear energy, coal, hydro, natural gas, and a variety of other resources. These generating stations produce electricity at a certain electrical voltage. Smart Grid was built when energy was relatively inexpensive. While minor upgrades have been made to meet increasing demand, the grid still operates the way it did almost 100 years ago—energy flows over the grid from central power plants to consumers, and reliability is ensured by maintaining excess capacity. Infrastructures like electricity which is controlled by SCADA can play a big role on Smart Grids.

SCADA systems are used to monitor and control a plant or equipment in industries such as telecommunications, water and waste control, energy, oil and gas refining and transportation. A SCADA system gathers information, such as where a leak on a pipeline has occurred, transfers the information back to a central site, alerting the home station that the leak has occurred, carrying out necessary analysis and control, such as

---

[*] Corresponding author.

T.-h. Kim et al. (Eds.): SecTech/DRBC 2010, CCIS 122, pp. 282–289, 2010.
© Springer-Verlag Berlin Heidelberg 2010

determining if the leak is critical, and displaying the information in a logical and organized fashion. SCADA systems can be relatively simple, such as one that monitors
environmental conditions of a small office building, or incredibly complex, such as a
system that monitors all the activity in a nuclear power plant or the activity of a municipal water system.

On the Next parts of this paper, we discuss SCADA, the conventional setup and the
Smart Grid. Advantages which can be attained using the Smart Grid are also covered.
Security issues are being pointed out. We also suggest a security solution for a Web
based SCADA using symmetric key encryption.

2   SCADA Control Systems

SCADA systems are primarily control systems. A typical control system consists of
one or more remote terminal units (RTU) connected to a variety of sensors and actuators, and relaying information to a master station.

For the most part, the brains of a SCADA system are performed by the Remote
Terminal Units (sometimes referred to as the RTU). The Remote Terminal Units
consists of a programmable logic converter. The RTU are usually set to specific requirements, however, most RTU allow human intervention, for instance, in a factory
setting, the RTU might control the setting of a conveyer belt, and the speed can be
changed or overridden at any time by human intervention. In addition, any changes or
errors are usually automatically logged for and/or displayed. Most often, a SCADA
system will monitor and make slight changes to function optimally; SCADA systems
are considered closed loop systems and run with relatively little human intervention.

One of key processes of SCADA is the ability to monitor an entire system in real
time. This is facilitated by data acquisitions including meter reading, checking
statuses of sensors, etc that are communicated at regular intervals depending on
the system. Besides the data being used by the RTU, it is also displayed to a human
that is able to interface with the system to override settings or make changes when
necessary.

2.1   Hardware and Software

Supervisory Control and Data Acquisition software can be divided into proprietary
type or open type. Proprietary software are developed and designed for the specific
hardware and are usually sold together. The main problem with these systems is the
overwhelming reliance on the supplier of the system. Open software systems are designed to communicate and control different types of hardware. It is popular because
of the interoperability they bring to the system. [2] WonderWare and Citect are just
two of the open software packages available in the market for SCADA systems. Some
packages are now including asset management integrated within the SCADA system.

Supervisory Control and Data Acquisition Systems usually have Distributed Control System components. PLCs or RTUs are also commonly used; they are capable of
autonomously executing simple logic processes without a master computer controlling it. A functional block programming language, IEC 61131-3, is frequently used to
create programs which run on these PLCs and RTUs. This allows SCADA system

engineers to perform both the design and implementation of a program to be executed on an RTU or PLC. From 1998, major PLC manufacturers have offered integrated HMI/SCADA systems, many use open and non-proprietary communications protocols. Many third-party HMI/SCADA packages, offering built-in compatibility with most major PLCs, have also entered the market, allowing mechanical engineers, electrical engineers and technicians to configure HMIs themselves. [1]

2.2 Human Machine Interface

SCADA system includes a user interface which is usually called Human Machine Interface (HMI). The HMI of a SCADA system is where data is processed and presented to be viewed and monitored by a human operator. This interface usually includes controls where the individual can interface with the SCADA system. HMI's are an easy way to standardize the facilitation of monitoring multiple RTU's or PLC's (programmable logic controllers). Usually RTU's or PLC's will run a pre programmed process, but monitoring each of them individually can be difficult, usually because they are spread out over the system. Because RTU's and PLC's historically had no standardized method to display or present data to an operator, the SCADA system communicates with PLC's throughout the system network and processes information that is easily disseminated by the HMI. HMI's can also be linked to a database, which can use data gathered from PLC's or RTU's to provide graphs on trends, logistic info, schematics for a specific sensor or machine or even make troubleshooting guides accessible. In the last decade, practically all SCADA systems include an integrated HMI and PLC device making it extremely easy to run and monitor a SCADA system.

3   Installation of SCADA Systems

SCADA systems are highly distributed systems used to control geographically dispersed assets, often scattered over thousands of square kilometers, where centralized data acquisition and control are critical to system operation. They are used in distribution systems such as water distribution and wastewater collection systems, oil and gas pipelines, electrical power grids, and railway transportation systems. A SCADA control center performs centralized monitoring and control for field sites over long-distance communications networks, including monitoring alarms and processing status data. Based on information received from remote stations, automated or operator-driven supervisory commands can be pushed to remote station control devices, which are often referred to as field devices. Field devices control local operations such as opening and closing valves and breakers, collecting data from sensor systems, and monitoring the local environment for alarm conditions.[3][4]

3.1 Conventional Supervisory Control and Data Acquisition

The function of SCADA is collecting of the information, transferring it back to the central site, carrying out any necessary analysis and control and then displaying that information on a number of operator screens. Systems automatically control the actions and control the process of automation.

Conventionally, relay logic was used to control production and plant systems. With the discovery of the CPU and other electronic devices, manufacturers incorporated digital electronics into relay logic equipment. Programmable logic controllers or PLC's are still the most widely used control systems in industry. As need to monitor and control more devices in the plant grew, the PLCs were distributed and the systems became more intelligent and smaller in size. PLCs (Programmable logic controllers) and DCS (distributed control systems) are used as shown in Figure 1.

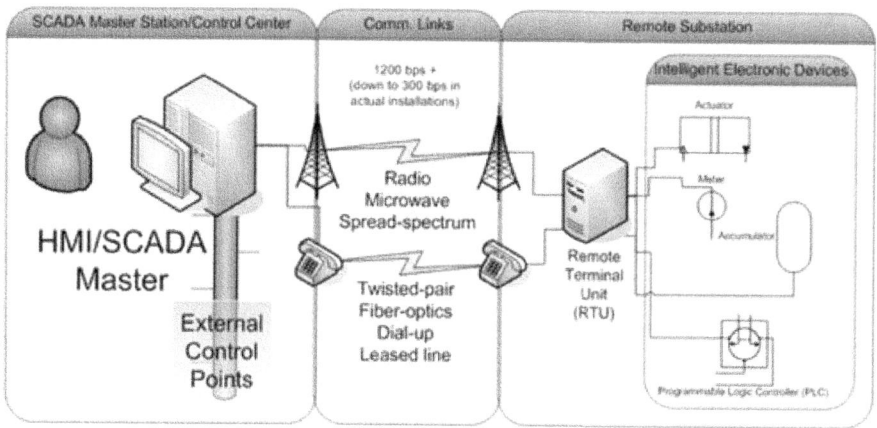

Fig. 1. Common SCADA Installation utilizing Remote Terminals (PLC/DCS, Sensors) and Master Station connected using a fieldbus

4 Smart Grid

A smart grid includes an intelligent monitoring system that keeps track of all electricity flowing in the system. It also incorporates the use of superconductive transmission lines for less power loss, as well as the capability of integrating alternative sources of electricity such as solar and wind. When power is least expensive a smart grid could turn on selected home appliances such as washing machines or factory processes that can run at arbitrary hours. At peak times it could turn off selected appliances to reduce demand. Similar proposals include smart electric grid, smart power grid, intelligent grid (or intelligrid), FutureGrid, and the more modern intergrid and intragrid. In principle, the smart grid is a simple upgrade of 20th century power grids which generally "broadcast" power from a few central power generators to a large number of users, to instead be capable of routing power in more optimal ways to respond to a very wide range of conditions, and to charge a premium to those that use energy at peak hour.

The conditions, to which a smart grid, broadly stated, could respond, occur anywhere in the power generation, distribution and demand chain. Events may occur generally in the environment (clouds blocking the sun and reducing the amount of solar power, a very hot day), commercially in the power supply market (prices to meet a high peak demand), locally on the distribution grid (MV transformer failure requiring a temporary shutdown of one distribution line) or in the home (someone leaving for work, putting various devices into hibernation, data ceasing to flow to an IPTV), which motivate a change to power flow.

Latency of the data flow is a major concern, with some early smart meter architectures allowing actually as long as 24 hours delay in receiving the data, preventing any possible reaction by either supplying or demanding devices. [3]

The Smart Grid is the application of modern information, communication, and electronics technology to the electricity delivery infrastructure as shown in figure 2.

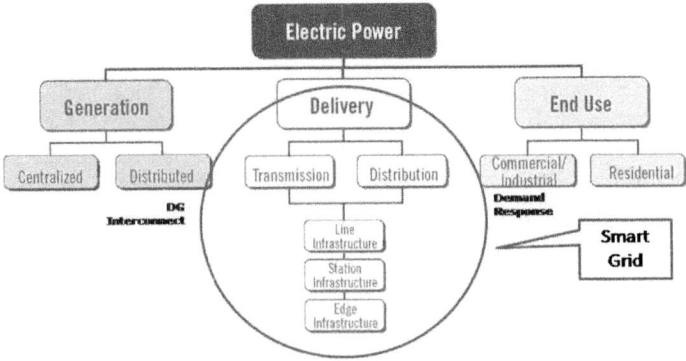

Fig. 2. Smart Grid

The earliest, and still largest, example of a smart grid is the Italian system installed by Enel S.p.A. of Italy. Completed in 2005, the Telegestore project was highly unusual in the utility world because the company designed and manufactured their own meters, acted as their own system integrator, and developed their own system software. The Telegestore project is widely regarded as the first commercial scale use of smart grid technology to the home, and delivers annual savings of 500 million euro at a project cost of 2.1 billion euro. [5]

5   SCADA and Smart Grid

SCADA can be integrated to Smart Grid easily. Central & distributed generation Virtual aggregation of generators and loads for system management Grid components connected by both electrical and data networks.

Bi-directional power flows. The following figure shows how Smart Grid will look like.

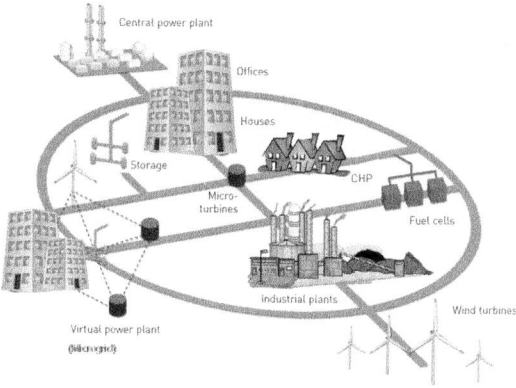

Fig. 3. Vision of Smart Grid

5.1 Advantages of SCADA in Smart Grid Environment

- Accommodates a wide variety of generation options – central and distributed, intermittent and dispatchable.
- Empowers the consumer – interconnects with energy management systems in smart buildings to enable customers to manage their energy use and reduce their energy costs.
- Self-healing – anticipates and instantly responds to system problems in order to avoid or mitigate power outages and power quality problems.
- Tolerant of attack – mitigates and stands resilient to physical and cyber attacks
- Provides power quality needed by 21st century users
- Fully enables competitive energy markets – real-time information, lower transaction costs, available to everyone
- Optimizes assets – uses IT and monitoring to continually optimize its capital assets while minimizing operations and maintenance costs – more throughput per $ invested.

6   Crossed-Crypto Scheme for SCADA in Smart Grid

In cryptography, there are major types of encryptions: the symmetric encryption and the asymmetric encryption. From the two major types of encryptions we can say that Asymmetric encryption provides more functionality than symmetric encryption, at the expense of speed and hardware cost. On the other hand symmetric encryption provides cost-effective and efficient methods of securing data without compromising security and should be considered as the correct and most appropriate security solution for many applications. [6] In some instances, the best possible solution may be the complementary use of both symmetric and asymmetric encryption. Diagram of a crossed crypto-scheme is shown in Figure 4.

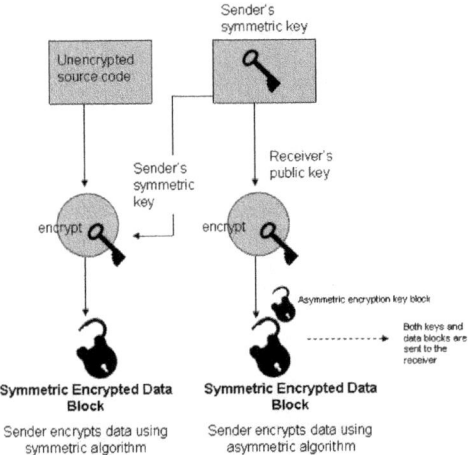

Fig. 4. Crossed crypto-scheme

6.1 System Integration

The crossed crypto-scheme can be integrated in the communication of the SCADA master and SCADA assets. The algorithm presented here combines the best features of both the symmetric and asymmetric encryption techniques. The plain text data is to be transmitted in encrypted using the AES algorithm. Further details on AES can be taken from [7].

The AES key which is used to encrypt the data is encrypted using ECC. The cipher text of the message and the cipher text of the key are then sent to the SCADA assets. The message digest by this process would also be encrypted using ECC techniques.

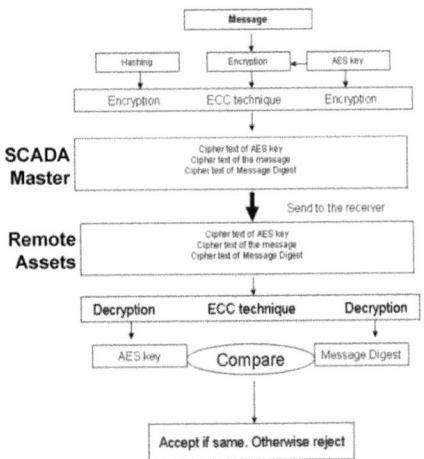

Fig. 5. Chain of operation

The cipher text of the message digest is decrypted using ECC technique to obtain the message digest sent by the SCADA Master. This value is compared with the computed message digest. If both of them are equal, the message is accepted otherwise it is rejected. You can see this scenario in figure 5.

7 Conclusion

Smart Grid builds on many of the technologies already used by electric utilities but adds communication and control capabilities that will optimize the operation of the entire electrical grid. Smart Grid is also positioned to take advantage of new technologies, such as plug-in hybrid electric vehicles, various forms of distributed generation, solar energy, smart metering, lighting management systems, distribution automation, and many more.It is easy to observe that SCADA technology holds a lot of promise for the future.

The economic and performance advantages of this type of system are definitely attractive. The security of any future Smart Grid is dependent on successfully addressing the cyber security issues associated with the nation's current power grid. The implementation of Smart Grid will include the deployment of many new technologies and multiple communication infrastructures. In this paper, we propose the integration of the Crossed crypto-scheme to the SCADA system in Smart Grid.

Acknowledgement. This work was supported by the Security Engineering Research Center, granted by the Korean Ministry of Knowledge Economy.

References

1. Hildick-Smith, A.: Security for Critical Infrastructure SCADA Systems (2005)
2. Bailey, D., Wright, E.: Practical SCADA for Industry (2003)
3. http://earth2tech.com/2008/05/01/silver-springs-the-cisco-of-smart-grid/ (accessed May 2010)
4. http://earth2tech.com/2009/05/20/utility-perspective-why-partner-with-google-powermeter/ (accessed May 2010)
5. National Energy Technology Laboratory (2007-08) (pdf). NETL Modern Grid Initiative — Powering Our 21st-Century Economy. United States Department of Energy Office of Electricity Delivery and Energy Reliability. p. 17, http://www.netl.doe.gov/smartgrid/referenceshelf/whitepapers/Modern%20Grid%20Benefits_Final_v1_0.pdf (accessed May 2010)
6. Balitanas, M., Robles, R.J., Kim, N., Kim, T.: Crossed Crypto-scheme in WPA PSK Mode. In: Proceedings of BLISS 2009, Edinburgh, GB, IEEE CS, Los Alamitos (August 2009)
7. Federal Information Processing Standards Publication 197, Announcing the Advanced Encryption Standard (AES) (2001), http://csrc.nist.gov/publications/fips/fips197/fips-197.pdf (accessed January 2009)

NMACA Approach Used to Build a Secure Message Authentication Code

Raed Alosaimy[1], Khaled Alghathbar[1,2], Alaaeldin M. Hafez[1,2],
and Mohamed H. Eldefrawy[1]

[1] Center of Excellence in Information Assurance (CoEIA), King Saud University,
Saudi Arabia
[2] Information Systems Department, College of Computer and Information Sciences,
King Saud University, Saudi Arabia
rosaimi@nic.gov.sa, kalghathbar@ksu.edu.sa,
ahafez@ksu.edu.sa, meldefrawy@ksu.edu.sa

Abstract. Secure storage systems should consider the integrity and authentication of long-term stored information. When information is transferred through communication channels, different types of digital information can be represented, such as documents, images, and database tables. The authenticity of such information must be verified, especially when it is transferred through communication channels. Authentication verification techniques are used to verify that the information in an archive is authentic and has not been intentionally or maliciously altered. In addition to detecting malicious attacks, verifying the integrity also identifies data corruption. The purpose of Message Authentication Code (MAC) is to authenticate messages, where MAC algorithms are keyed hash functions. In most cases, MAC techniques use iterated hash functions, and these techniques are called iterated MACs. Such techniques usually use a MAC key as an input to the compression function, and this key is involved in the compression function, f, at every stage. Modification detection codes (MDCs) are un-keyed hash functions, and are widely used by authentication techniques such as MD4, MD5, SHA-1, and RIPEMD-160. There have been new attacks on hash functions such as MD5 and SHA-1, which requires the introduction of more secure hash functions. In this paper, we introduce a new MAC methodology that uses an input MAC key in the compression function, to change the order of the message words and shifting operation in the compression function. The new methodology can be used in conjunction with a wide range of modification detection code techniques. Using the SHA-1 algorithm as a model, a new (SHA-1)-MAC algorithm is presented. The (SHA-1)-MAC algorithm uses the MAC key to build the hash functions by defining the order for accessing source words and defining the number of bit positions for circular left shifts.

Keywords: Secure Hash Algorithm, Hash-Based Message Authentication Codes.

1 Introduction

The fast growth of open systems and the adoption of the Internet in daily business life have opened up many opportunities. A new set of challenges has also arisen and

T.-h. Kim et al. (Eds.): SecTech/DRBC 2010, CCIS 122, pp. 290–298, 2010.
© Springer-Verlag Berlin Heidelberg 2010

continues to tax this new way of computing. These include the ability of the open systems to provide security and data integrity [1]. Computer systems typically require authentication. At the same time, attackers try to penetrate information systems, and their goal is often to compromise the authentication mechanism protecting the system from unauthorized access [2]. Usually, integrity comes in conjunction with the authentication algorithm. Integrity refers to assuring that the receiver receives what the sender has transmitted, with no accidental or intentional unauthorized modification having affected the transmitted data [3], [5], [6]. Many modification detection code algorithms (MDC) [3], [7], [8] are block-cipher based. Those with relatively short MAC bit lengths (e.g., 32-bits for MAA [8]) or short keys (e.g., 56 bits for MACs based on DES-CBC [3]) may still offer adequate security. Many iterated MACs can be described as iterated hash functions. In this case, the MAC key is generally part of the output transformation; it may also be an input to the compression function in the first iteration, and be fed to the compression function at every stage. An upper bound on the security of MACs should be considered, based on an iterated compression function, which has an internal chaining variable with n-bits, and is deterministic (i.e., the m-bit result is fully determined by the message). Most of the commonly used MAC algorithms are based on block ciphers that make use of cipher-block-chaining (CBC) [1], [4], [7], [6]. A common suggestion is to construct a MAC algorithm from a modification detection code (MDC) algorithm, by simply including a secret key, k, as part of the MDC input [3], [9], [10], [6]. A more conservative approach for building a MAC from an MDC is to make the MAC compression function depend on k, implying that the secret key be involved in all of the intervening iterations. This provides additional protection in a case where a weakness in the underlying hash function becomes known. Such a technique is employed using MD5. It provides performance slightly slower to that of MD5. Alternatively, a MAC technique can be based on cyclic redundancy codes [8], [11]. There have been new attacks on hash functions such as MD5 and SHA-1, which require the introduction of more secure hash functions. In [10], an attack on MD5 was introduced that finds collisions of MD5 in about 15 minutes to an hour of computation time. The attack is a differential attack, where XORs are not used as a measure of difference. Instead, it uses modular integer subtraction as the measure. The same attack could find collisions of MD4 in less than a second. In [12], the attack was applied to SHA-0 and all variants of SHA-1. The attack could find real collisions of SHA-0 in less than 2^{39} hash operations. The attack was implemented on SHA-1, and collisions could be found in less than 2^{33} hash operations. In this paper, we adopt the NMACA technique that was introduced in [4]. NMACA uses an input MAC key in the compression function, to change the order of the message words and shifting operation in the compression function. The new methodology can be used in conjunction with a wide range of modification detection code techniques. Using the SHA-1 algorithm as a model, a new NMACA (SHA-1) algorithm is presented. The (SHA-1) NMACA algorithm uses the MAC key in building the hash functions by defining the order for accessing source words and defining the number of bit positions for circular left shifts. The rest of this paper is organized as follows: Section 2 provides a review of the literature in the area of message authentication coding, Section 3 describes the new methodology, Section 4 presents the experimental results, and finally our paper is concluded in Section 5.

2 Literature Review

There are two major approaches to implementing authentication/integrity mechanisms, the use of a digital signature and the use of a Message Authentication Code [13], [14], [6]. The digital signature approach uses two keys, a public and private key. A sender signs a message digitally by computing a hash function (or checksum) over the data, and then encrypts the hash function value using the private key. The encrypted hashing value is sent to the receiver accompanied by the data. The receiver verifies the authenticity of the received data by recalculating the hash value and decrypting the transmitted hashing value using the public key. The two hash values are then compared. If they match, the message is authentic and came from the claimed sender. In a Message Authentication Code (MAC), a shared secret key is used instead of the private key. There are several ways to provide authentication/integrity by using the secret key [15, 16]. The main two are Hash-Based Message Authentication Codes (HMAC) and Encryption-Based Message Authentication Codes. In HMAC, a strong hash function algorithm such as MD5 or SHA1 is used to create a hashing value over the data and the embedded secret key. The sender concatenates a symmetric key with the message using any of the different embedding strategies. A hashing algorithm generates a MAC value, and the MAC value is appended to the message. The sender sends the message with the attached MAC value to the receiver. At the receiver side, the same hash function is applied to the concatenated data and key to again generate the MAC value. The receiver compares the two MAC values. If they are the same, the message has not been modified [17]. The structure of the HMAC algorithm is illustrated in Fig. 1.

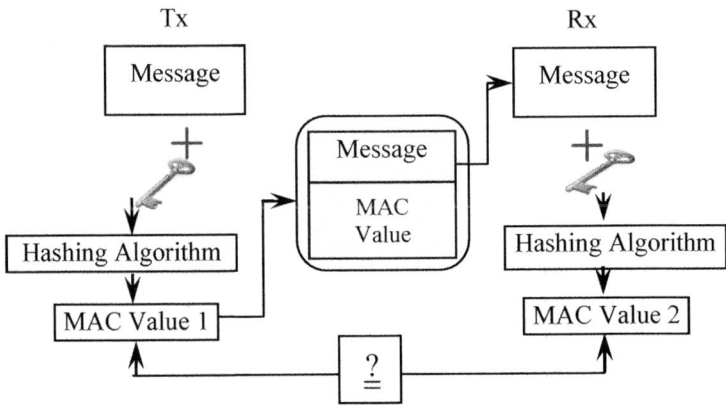

Fig. 1. Hash-Based Message Authentication Code Structure

Many algorithms have been proposed as mechanisms to provide integrity checks based on a secret key [3], [7], [15], [18]. These mechanisms are known as Message Authentication Code (MAC) mechanisms. Message Authentication Codes are used with a secret key in order to authenticate transmitted or stored information. Typically, these mechanisms use a cryptographic hash function in conjunction with the secret key to guarantee the authenticity of the information.

3 The NMACA Approach

This section discusses a NMACA approach based on the Secure Hash Standard, which specifies a secure hashing algorithm SHA-1 technique. The new technique is called the NMACA-(SHA-1) Message Authentication Code algorithm. When a message of any length $n < 2^{64}$ bits is input, along with a 160-bit secret key, the NMACA-(SHA-1) produces a 160-bit output called a Message Authentication Code MAC. It is computationally impossible to find a message that corresponds to a given MAC, or to find two different messages that produce the same MAC. Any change to a message in transit will result in a different MAC. The NMACA-(SHA-1) algorithm does not require any large substitution tables; the algorithm can be coded quite compactly. NMACA-(SHA-1) is more conservative in design than previous well-known algorithms. The structure of the proposed algorithm is illustrated in Fig. 2.

3.1 The NMACA-(SHA-1) Message Authentication Code Algorithm

The new NMACA-(SHA-1) involves the key, K, in the different steps of the SHA-1 algorithm. K is used to determine the access order for message words and to determine the shift amounts in the distinct rounds. In the proposed algorithm, only two changes are done to the SHA-1 algorithm. Both algorithms use the same initial chaining values (IVs), apply the same hash functions, and use the same padding process to adjust the length of the transmitted message. The two differences between the SHA-1 and the NMACA-(SHA-1) techniques are the order of the message words, and the order of the values that are used in circular left shifts on the four auxiliary functions. The 160-bit secret key, K, is divided into two parts, each of 80 bits. The first 80 bits are used to rearrange the order of the message words. These 80-bits of K are divided into four divisions, each with 20 bits. Each of these 20-bit divisions of K is used to rearrange a block of 20 words (32-bit words) of the input message. Starting from a vector of a predefined order of accessing each of 20 words, the order of such a vector

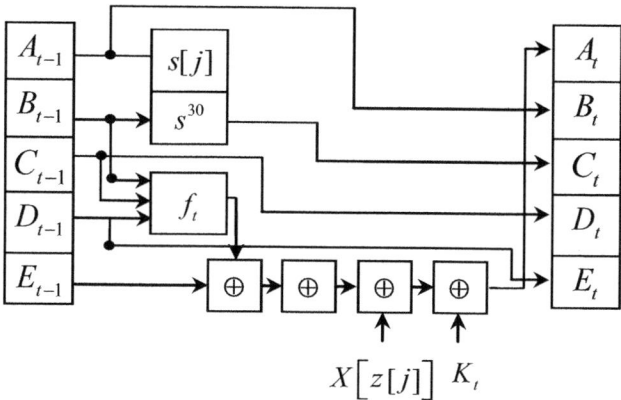

Fig. 2. One NMACA-(SHA-1) Operation (single round)

is changed according to the related part in K. The other 80 bits of K are used to define the numbers of circular left shifts used in the four auxiliary functions. Using the same key related permutations, the order of the circular shifts in each of the four auxiliary functions is defined by using one of the 20-bit divisions of K.

The proposed algorithm is as fast and as robust as SHA-1. The algorithm is depicted below.

INPUT: bit string x of arbitrary bit length $b \geq 0$ and 160-bit key K.

OUTPUT: 160-bit hash-code of x.

Define five 32-bit initial chaining values (IVs):

$$h_1 = 0x67452301 \qquad h_2 = 0xefcdab89 \qquad h_3 = 0x98badcfe$$

$$h_4 = 0x98badcfe \qquad h_5 = 0xc3d2e1f0$$

Four auxiliary functions are defined:

Each takes as input three 32-bit words and produces, as an output, a 32-bit word. They apply the logical operators *and*, *or*, *not*, and *xor* on the input bits.

$$f(B,C,D) = (B \vee C) \wedge (\neg B \vee D) \quad g(B,C,D) = (B \oplus C \oplus D)$$

$$h(B,C,D) = (B \vee C) \wedge (B \vee D) \wedge (C \vee D) \quad i(B,C,D) = (B \oplus C \oplus D)$$

Define per-round integer 32-bit additive constants:

$$y_1 = 0x5a827999 \quad y_2 = 0x6ed9eba1 \quad y_3 = 0x8f1bbcdc \quad y_4 = 0xca62c1d6$$

Use secret key:

- Define order for accessing source words by using the secret key K:

$$z[0::19] = \text{Permutation } P_0 \text{ of the 1}^{st}\text{ 20 bits of } K, \ P_0 : \{0,1,\text{K},19\} \rightarrow \{O_i|_{0 \leq O_i \leq 19}\}$$

$$z[20::39] = \text{Permutation } P_1 \text{ of the 2}^{nd}\text{ 20 bits of } K, \ P_1 : \{20,21,\text{K},39\} \rightarrow \{O_i|_{20 \leq O_i \leq 39}\}$$

$$z[40::59] = \text{Permutation } P_2 \text{ of the 3}^{rd}\text{ 20 bits of } K, \ P_2 : \{40,21,\text{K},59\} \rightarrow \{O_i|_{40 \leq O_i \leq 59}\}$$

$$z[60::79] = \text{Permutation } P_3 \text{ of the 4}^{th}\text{ 20 bits of } K, \ P_3 : \{60,21,\text{K},79\} \rightarrow \{O_i|_{60 \leq O_i \leq 79}\}$$

- Define the number of bit positions for left shifts (rotates) by using the secret key K:

$$z[0::79] = \text{Permutation } P_s \text{ of the last 80 bits of } K, \ P_s : \{0,1,\text{K},79\} \rightarrow \{O_i|_{0 \leq O_i \leq 79}\}$$

3.2 Preprocessing

The message padding is provided to make a final padded message a multiple of 512 bits, as follows. First append a "1" followed by as many "0"s as necessary to make it 64 bits short of a multiple of 512-bits. Finally, a 64-bit integer is appended to the end of the zero appended messages to produce a final padded message of length $n \times 512$ - bits. The 64-bit integer "l" represents the length of the original message. The padded message is then processed by the NMACA-(SHA-1) as $n \times 512$ -bit blocks. The formatted input consists of 16 m 32-bit words: $x_0, x_1, \text{K } x_{16m-1}$.

Initialize: $(h_1, h_2, h_3, h_4, h_5) \rightarrow (H_1, H_2, H_3, H_4, H_5)$.

Processing

For each $i_{0 \rightarrow m-1}$ copy the ith block of the sixteen 32-bit words into temporary storage: $X[j] = x_{16i+j}\big|_{0 \le j \le 15}$, then process them as below in four 20-step rounds before updating the chaining variables:

- Expand 16-word block into 80-word block; let X_j denotes $X[j]$, for $i_{16 \rightarrow 79}$,
$$X_j\left(\left(X_{j-3} \otimes X_{j-8} \otimes X_{j-14} \otimes X_{j-16}\right) \leftarrow 1\right)$$
- Initialize working variables
$$(A, B, C, D, E) \leftarrow (H_1, H_2, H_3, H_4, H_5).$$

Round 1

For j from 0 to 19 do the following:
$$t \leftarrow \left((A \leftarrow s[j]) + f(B, C, D) + E + X[z[j]] + y_1\right), \ (A, B, C, D, E)(t, A, B \leftarrow 30, C, D).$$

Round 2

For j from 19 to 39 do the following:
$$t \leftarrow \left((A \leftarrow s[j]) + g(B, C, D) + E + X[z[j]] + y_2\right), \ (A, B, C, D, E)(t, A, B \leftarrow 30, C, D).$$

Round 3

For j from 40 to 59 do the following:
$$t \leftarrow \left((A \leftarrow s[j]) + h(B, C, D) + E + X[z[j]] + y_3\right), \ (A, B, C, D, E)(t, A, B \leftarrow 30, C, D).$$

Round 4

For j from 60 to 79 do the following:
$$t \leftarrow \left((A \leftarrow s[j]) + i(B, C, D) + E + X[z[j]] + y_4\right), \ (A, B, C, D, E)(t, A, B \leftarrow 30, C, D).$$

- Update *chaining values*
$$(H_1, H_2, H_3, H_4, H_5) \leftarrow \begin{pmatrix} H_1 + A, H_2 + B, H_3 + C, \\ H_4 + D, H_5 + E \end{pmatrix}$$

Completion

The final MAC value is the concatenation: $H_1 \, PH_2 \, PH_3 \, PH_4$ (with the first and last bytes the high- and low-order bytes of H_1, H_5, respectively).

4   Security of NMACA-(SHA-1)

- Four rounds are being excited with different orders of values.
- A different message word is provided.

- Each step has a unique additive constant.
- Each step adds in the result of the previous step.
- The left circular shift amounts are optimized, to yield an accepted avalanche effect. The four shifts used in each round are different from the ones used in other rounds.

5   Experimental Results

In this section, experimental results are used to show the performance of SHA-1 and NMACA-(SHA-1) in terms of their speed and avalanche effect. We performed our experiments on a 2.6-GHz machine, with 4 GB of RAM and running Microsoft Windows XP professional. Messages of up to 1-Mbytes were used. From the results obtained when comparing the speed performance of the NMACA-(SHA-1) algorithm

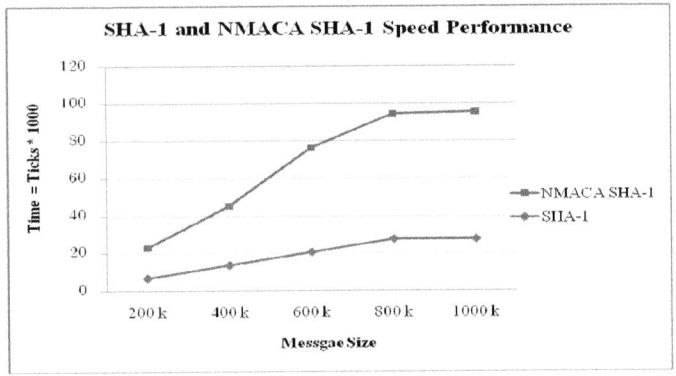

Fig. 3. Speed performance of SHA-1 and NMACA-(SHA-1)

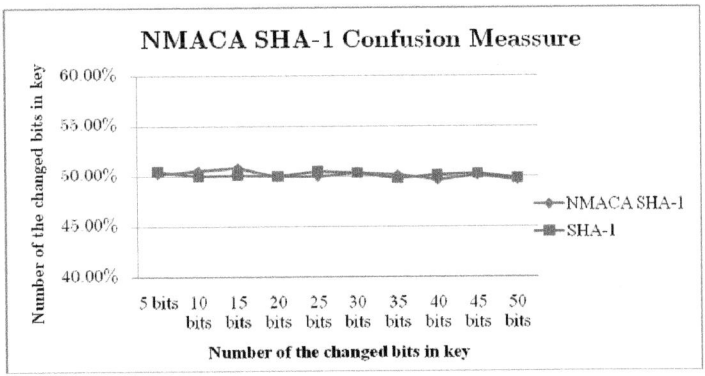

Fig. 4. Confusion Measure or Avalanche Effect of key

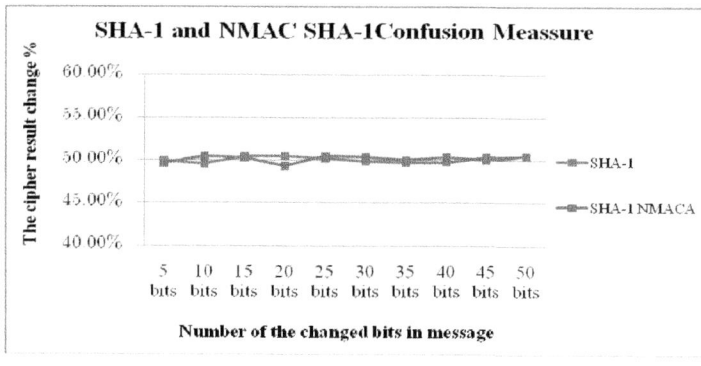

Fig. 5. Diffusion Measure or Avalanche Effect of Message X

and SHA-1, we found that SHA-1 is faster but the NMACA-(SHA-1) algorithm provides greater security, making it harder to crack. Actually, such a performance was
predictable since the only difference between SHA-1 and NMACA-(SHA-1) is the
part where the word order and circular left shifts are defined in the initial phase of
NMACA-(SHA-1). In addition, the experimental results showed that by using different bit changes in the MAC key, K, the confusion effect of the proposed approach was
almost 50%, which is considered an indicator of the quality of the hash function used.
These results were the same as the SHA-1 approach, which means the use of
NMACA with SHA-1 did not degrade the quality of the SHA-1 approach. The same
applies to the diffusion effect.

6   Conclusions

We have proposed a new technique that is based on the Message Authentication Code
approach NMACA. In NMACA, a 160-bit secret key, K, is used to determine the access order for message words and the shift amounts in distinct steps in each round. In
this paper, we adopted the SHA-1 technique to demonstrate the proposed NMACA
approach. The new technique is called the NMACA-(SHA-1) algorithm. In the experiments performed, the proposed algorithm, NMACA-(SHA-1), was compared to
SHA-1. The results showed that the speed performances were comparable. This was
because the only extra overhead needed for NMACA-(SHA-1) is the processing time
for defining the reordering of the message words and circular left shifts. The diffusion
and confusion effects were studied by studying the effect of changes in the message
bits (diffusion) and MAC key bits (confusion). These two measures illustrate the avalanche effect of the underlying hash function. The experimental results showed that,
by using different bit changes in the input message and MAC key K, the confusion
and diffusion effects of the proposed approach were almost 50%, which is considered
an indicator of the quality of the hash function used. This proposed technique could
be useful in applications presented in [19].

References

1. Little, D., Skip, B., Elhilali, O.: Digital Data Integrity The Evolution from Passive Protection to Active Management. John Wiley & Sons Ltd., England (2007)
2. Todorov, D.: Mechanics of User Identification and Authentication Fundamentals of Identity Management
3. Coskun, B., Memon, N.: Confusion/Diffusion Capabilities of Some Robust Hash Functions. In: Conference on Information Sciences and Systems, pp. 22–24 (2006)
4. Alghathbar, K., Hafez, A., Muhaya, F.B., Abdalla, H.M.: NMACA: A Novel Methodology for Message Authentication Code Algorithms. In: 8th WSEAS Int. Conf. on Telecommunications and Informatics (TELE-INFO 2009), Turkey (2009)
5. Wright, C., Spillane, R., Sivathanu, G., Zadok, E.: Extending ACID Semantics to the File System. ACM Transactions on Storage (2007)
6. The Keyed-Hash Message Authentication Code (HMAC). In: The Federal Information Processing Standards Publication 198 (2002)
7. Haber, S., Kamat, P.: A Content Integrity Service For Long-Term Digital Archives. In: The IS&T Archiving 2006 Conference, Canada (2006)
8. Malone, D., Sullivan, W.: Guesswork is not a substitute for entropy. In: Proceedings of the Information Technology and Telecommunications Conference (2005)
9. Fridrich, J.: Robust bit extraction from images. In: ICMCS 1999, Italy (1999)
10. Wang, X., Yin, Y., Yu, L.H.: Finding collisions in the full SHA-1. In: Shoup, V. (ed.) CRYPTO 2005. LNCS, vol. 3621, pp. 17–36. Springer, Heidelberg (2005)
11. Zahur, Y., Yang, T.A.: Wireless LAN Security and Laboratory Designs. Journal of Computing Sciences in Colleges 19, 44–60 (2004)
12. Por, L.Y., Lim, X.T., Su, M.T., Kianoush, F.: The Design and Implementation of Background Pass-Go Scheme Towards Security Threats. Wseas Transactions on Information Science and Applications 5(6), 943–952 (2008)
13. Preneel, B., Oorschot, P.: MDx-MAC and building fast MACs from hash functions. In: Coppersmith, D. (ed.) CRYPTO 1995. LNCS, vol. 963, pp. 1–14. Springer, Heidelberg (1995)
14. Venkatesan, R., Koon, S., Jakubowski, M., Moulin, P.: Robust image hashing. In: Proc. IEEE Int. Conf. Image Processing (2000)
15. Shannon, C.E.: Communication theory of secrecy systems. Bell System Technical Journal 28, 656–715 (1949)
16. Stevens, M., Lenstra, A., de Weger, B.: Chosen-prefix collisions for MD5 and colliding X.509 certificates for different identities. In: Naor, M. (ed.) EUROCRYPT 2007. LNCS, vol. 4515, pp. 1–22. Springer, Heidelberg (2007)
17. Certified Information Systems Security Professional (CISSP) Book
18. Wang, X., Yu, H.: How to break MD5 and other hash functions. In: Cramer, R. (ed.) EUROCRYPT 2005. LNCS, vol. 3494, pp. 19–35. Springer, Heidelberg (2005)
19. Eldefrawy, M.H., Khan, M.K., Alghathbar, K., Cho, E.-S.: Broadcast Authentication for Wireless Sensor Networks Using Nested Hashing and the Chinese Remainder Theorem. Sensors 10(9), 8683–8695 (2010)

Author Index